THE LAST SIEGE

THE LAST SIEGE

The Mobile Campaign, Alabama 1865

PAUL BRUESKE

CASEMATE

Philadelphia & Oxford

Published in the United States of America and Great Britain in 2018 by
CASEMATE PUBLISHERS
1950 Lawrence Road, Havertown, PA 19083, USA
and
The Old Music Hall, 106–108 Cowley Road, Oxford OX4 1JE, UK

Hardback Edition: ISBN 978-1-61200-631-4
Digital Edition: ISBN 978-1-61200-632-1

A CIP record for this book is available from the British Library

Printed and bound in the United States of America

For a complete list of Casemate titles, please contact:

CASEMATE PUBLISHERS (US)
Telephone (610) 853-9131
Fax (610) 853-9146
Email: casemate@casematepublishers.com
www.casematepublishers.com

CASEMATE PUBLISHERS (UK)
Telephone (01865) 241249
Email: casemate-uk@casematepublishers.co.uk
www.casematepublishers.co.uk

For my parents, Ken and Rae Beth Brueske.

Contents

Acknowledgments

Many wonderful people assisted me with this work. I would like to first thank Slade Watson for insisting I write this book, for prodding me to dig deeper, and giving me a head start on my research. Pamela Hovell provided tremendous support, technical expertise, and editing assistance; without her I would have been lost. Dr. Philip Theodore and Paula Webb of the University of South Alabama both gave me critical feedback and writing assistance. Special thanks to Dr. Richard J. Sommers of the Army Heritage and Education Center for his encouragement, guidance, and expertise, and to Mike Bunn, Brian DesRochers, and Richard Sheely of Historic Blakeley State Park for their knowledge and for putting up with my endless barrage of questions. I received generous help from Michael D. Shipler of Bay Minette, Alabama and Mike Randall of Mobile, Alabama in locating rare photographs and maps. They also readily shared their vast knowledge of the campaign. Special thanks to Kirk Barrett, Donnie Barrett, Dave Brasell, and Roger Hansen for taking the time to share their insight of lesser-known battle facts and locations. I greatly appreciate my father, Ken Brueske, for taking the time to review early drafts of the book and offer suggestions. I am also indebted to the following individuals for their assistance:

Franklin Ard, University of South Alabama; Ken Barr, Alabama Department of Archives and History; David Barnett, Auburn, Alabama; Donnie Barrett, Director, Fairhope Historical Museum, Fairhope, Alabama; Kirk Barrett, Spanish Fort, Alabama; Nick Beeson, History Museum of Mobile, Mobile, Alabama; Bert Blackmon, Baldwin County, Alabama; David Brasell, Loxley, Alabama; Ken Brueske, Gulf Breeze, Florida; Mike Bunn, Director, Historic Blakeley Park; Tim Bode, Belleville, Michigan; Randy Butler, Mobile, Alabama; Keith Davis, Lucedale, Mississippi; Brian DesRochers, Interpretative Ranger, Blakeley State Park; Donald E. Dixon, Fairfax, Virginia; Scott Donaldson, Mobile, Alabama; A. J. Dupree, Mobile, Alabama; Valerie Ellis, Mobile Local History Library, Mobile, Alabama; JoAnne Flirt, Historic Blakeley Park; Pat Galle, Mobile, Alabama; Stacey Gardner, Baldwin County, Alabama; Ben Gessner, Minnesota Historical Society, St. Paul, Minnesota; Ashley Gordon, Mobile, Alabama; Art Greene, Mobile, Alabama; Pat Greenwood, Mobile, Alabama; Roger Hansen, Mobile, Alabama; Dr. Krista Harrell, University of South Alabama; Dr. Robert Houston, University of South Alabama; Ronnie Hyer, Mobile, Alabama; Shawn-Patrick Hynes, Spring Hill College Archives, Mobile,

Alabama; Josh Jones, University of South Alabama; Seth Kinard, History Museum of Mobile; Sandra Ladd, Mobile, Alabama; Lance Lane, Shinto, Arizona; Ron Manzow, Plainview Minnesota Historical Center, Plainview, Minnesota; Meredith McDonough, Digital Assets Coordinator, Alabama Department of Archives and History; Tom McGehee, Museum Director, Bellingrath Gardens, Mobile, Alabama; Dr. Henry McKiven, University of South Alabama; Rachel Melum, Minneapolis, Minnesota; Hesper Montford, Mobile Local History Library; Mobile Historical Museum; Dennis Northcott, Associate Archivist for Reference, Missouri History Museum Library and Research Center, St. Louis, Missouri; David Ogden, Historian, Gulf Islands National Seashore, National Parks Service, Fort Pickens; Dr. Jim Parker, University of South Alabama; Mickey Parker, Pensacola, Florida; Bob Peck, Minnie Mitchell Archives, Mobile Historic Preservation Society; Ann Pond, Mobile, Alabama; David Preston, Daphne, Alabama; Mike Randall, Mobile, Alabama; Lt. Colonel Timothy Rey, University of South Alabama ROTC; Joe Ringhoffer, Mobile, Alabama; Richard Sheely, Interpretative Ranger, Historic Blakeley Park; Michael D. Shipler, Bay Minette; Wayne Sirmon, Mobile, Alabama; David Smithweck, Mobile, Alabama; Dr. Richard J. Sommers, Senior Historian of the U. S. Army Heritage and Education Center, Pennsylvania; Kevin Stoots, Mobile, Alabama; Dr. Philip Theodore, University of South Alabama, Mobile, Alabama; Elizabeth Theris, Mobile Local History Library, Mobile, Alabama; Chuck Torrey, History Museum of Mobile, Mobile, Alabama; Sarah Towey, Mobile, Alabama; Dr. Steven Trout, University of South Alabama; Jason Wilson, Summerdale, Alabama.

In addition, I am grateful for the assistance of the staffs of the Beauvoir Jefferson Davis Presidential Library, Butler Center for Arkansas Studies, the Mobile Local History Library, Minnesota Historical Society, Minnie Mitchell Archives, History Museum of Mobile, Fairhope Museum of History, Plainview History Center, and the Tulane University Archives.

Preface

My interest in the American Civil War started when I was an adventurous boy growing up in northwest Florida. Fort Pickens and Fort Barrancas were practically in my backyard, a constant exposure to Civil War battle sites. I remember fondly my friends and I, armed with our toy guns, playing war at Fort Pickens during the summer months. In between these mock battles, I often visited the fort's small museum where the Civil War era photographs and artifacts captivated my childhood curiosity.

When it was time to attend college, I moved a short distance west on the Gulf Coast to Mobile, Alabama, to attend the University of South Alabama. For most of the last twenty years, I have continued to live in the history-rich Port City area. During this time, my interest in studying the Civil War on the Gulf Coast has grown into a near obsession. I became particularly fascinated with the 1865 land campaign for Mobile. Surprisingly, I found that historians rarely mention this campaign even though it was reported in newspapers all over the country. Most of the literature on the War Between the States tends to focus on the principal armies and battles in the eastern theater. Nevertheless, I endeavored to learn as much as possible about the Mobile campaign.

What I discovered through years of research is that the campaign for Mobile was more significant than has been generally acknowledged. Shortly after the fall of Mobile, one Iowa newspaper reporter aptly wrote: "It may safely be said, [the capture of Mobile] has not received that share of public attention which its importance merited."[1] Despite holding out nine days longer than Richmond (the Confederate capital), the siege and capture of the city was overshadowed by events that transpired further east in Virginia and North Carolina. Nonetheless, the siege of Mobile was an important part of the overall war effort and deserves more attention. It is true that the excessive amount of time it took the Federals to capture the city rendered some of their objectives obsolete. Although the Unionists were slow, it does not diminish the strategic significance that U.S. General-in-Chief Ulysses S. Grant saw in taking Mobile when he issued his orders.[2]

Through my research, I have grown to admire the bravery and resiliency displayed by the soldiers who fought in the Mobile campaign, both Federal and Confederate.

Not knowing the war would soon be over, soldiers on both sides were still trying to win by utilizing evolved military tactics and advanced innovations and operations.

Many acts of heroism were shown by both armies during the last siege of the war and deserve attention.[3] My goal, in writing this book, is to shed further light on the brave men who fought for their respective causes and to examine the events that occurred in this seemingly forgotten but important campaign.

Key Military Officers
Referenced in the Book

Confederates

Lieutenant General Richard S. Taylor, Commander, Department of Alabama, Mississippi, and East Louisiana

Major General Dabney H. Maury, Commander, District of the Gulf

Commodore Ebenezer Farrand, Commander of Mobile's naval squadron

Brigadier General John R. St. Liddell, Commander, Eastern Division of the District of the Gulf, Commanding Officer of Fort Blakeley

Brigadier General Randall L. Gibson, Commander of Spanish Fort

Brigadier General James T. Holtzclaw, Second-in-Command of Spanish Fort

Brigadier General Francis Cockrell, Second-in-Command of Fort Blakeley

Brigadier General Bryan M. Thomas, Commander, Alabama Volunteer Corps, Fort Blakeley

Lieutenant Colonel Philip B. Spence, Commander, 12th Regiment Mississippi Cavalry

Federals

Major General Edward Richard Sprigg Canby, Commander, Military Division of West Mississippi

Admiral Henry K. Thatcher, Commander, West Gulf Blockading Squadron

Major General Gordon Granger, Commander, XIII Army Corps

Major General A. J. Smith, Commander, XVI Army Corps

Brigadier General Thomas K. Smith, Commander, District of South Alabama

Brigadier General C. C. Andrews, Commander, Second Division, XVI Army Corps

Major General Frederick Steele, Commander, Steele's Column from Fort Barrancas

Brigadier General James R. Slack, Commander, First Brigade, First Division, XIII Army Corps

Brigadier General Thomas J. Lucas, Commander, District of West Florida's Cavalry Division

Lieutenant Colonel Andrew B. Spurling, Second Maine Cavalry, Commander, Second Brigade, West Cavalry Division

Summary of Principal Events

March 11, 1865	Union General Frederick Steele's Column starts from Fort Barrancas to Pensacola, Florida, where they encamped from March 12 to 20, 1865.
March 17	The advance of the Union forces under General E. R. S Canby moves forward from Mobile Point and Dauphin Island, Alabama.
March 18–22	Expedition from Dauphin Island to Fowl River, Alabama, and skirmishes.
March 19	Brigadier General Thomas K. Smith, Union army, assumes command of the District of South Alabama.
March 20	The advance of the Union forces under General Frederick Steele departs from Pensacola, Florida.
March 23–24	Skirmishes near Dannelly's Mill, Alabama.
March 24	Affair near Dannelly's Mill, Alabama. Affair near Evergreen, Alabama.
March 25	Skirmishes on the Deer Park Road, Alabama. Skirmish at Cotton Creek, Florida. Skirmish at Mitchell's Creek, Florida. Action at Canoe Creek or Bluff Springs, Florida. Skirmish at Escambia River, Florida.
March 26	Skirmish near Spanish Fort, Alabama. Skirmish at Muddy Creek, Alabama. Union forces enter Pollard, Alabama.
March 27	Steele's Column reaches Canoe Station, Alabama.
March 27–April 8	Siege and capture of Spanish Fort, Alabama.
March 29	Steele's Column reaches Weatherford, Alabama.
March 31	Steele's Column reaches Stockton, Alabama.
April 1	Skirmish near Blakeley, Alabama.
April 2–9	Siege and capture of Fort Blakeley, Alabama.
April 7	Scout from near Blakeley toward Stockton, Alabama.
April 9–11	Bombardment and capture of Batteries Huger and Tracy, Alabama.
April 9–17	Expedition from Fort Blakeley to Claiborne, Alabama.
April 11	Confederate forces evacuate Mobile, Alabama.

	Cavalry skirmish at Little River Bridge (North Baldwin County, Alabama) and Eliska, Alabama (Monroe County, Alabama).
April 12	Union forces occupy Mobile, Alabama.
April 13	Skirmish at Whistler or Eight Mile Creek Bridge, Alabama.
April 17–30	Expedition from Blakeley, Alabama to Georgetown, Georgia, and Union Springs, Alabama.
April 29	Armistice agreement at McGhee Farm at Kushla, Alabama.
May 4	Surrender of the Confederate forces of the Department of Alabama, Mississippi, and East Louisiana, at Citronelle, Alabama.[1]

Prologue

With Alabama's secession in early 1861, the Confederacy gained Mobile's fine harbor and commercial seaport. "It was, before the war, next to New Orleans, the most extensive cotton port in the Union—more than 600,000 bales having been exported in a single year," declared the *New York Times*.[1] Once New Orleans fell in 1862, it became the most important Confederate port city on the Gulf Coast. Despite the U.S. naval blockade, Mobile managed to remain an open port during the first three years of the war. Mobile Bay was a port of entry and refuge for swift vessels called blockade runners that made their way through the Union blockade.[2]

The adventurous blockade runners, motivated by enormous profits, risked their lives bringing in a steady stream of war supplies, including weapons, munitions, and medicines. They also smuggled in luxuries, such as liquor, fabrics, clothing, and cigars. Many citizens of Mobile continued to suffer through food shortages and other hardships during the war.[3] Still, valuable cargoes smuggled in by the blockade runners allowed some of the population to continue a relatively "gay existence."[4]

Mobile was described as the "Paris of the Confederacy," and several of its inhabitants tried to continue an aristocratic lifestyle during the conflict.[5] Food shortages within the city and terrible battles raging elsewhere in the Confederacy did not stop some residents from hosting balls and receptions. "Some shook their heads in disapproval of our levity, as they considered it, and wondered how, with so many dear ones away and in danger, and our country in such peril, we could sing and dance and make merry," remembered Mobile resident Mary E. Brooks. She believed that as they worked and prayed for the Confederate soldiers, it was only right to make bright the lives of the soldiers in Mobile. During the summer of 1864, Admiral Franklin Buchanan, commander of the Confederate naval squadron at Mobile Bay, hosted a ball with several prominent generals, including Joseph E. Johnston, in attendance. "Mrs. Augusta Evans Wilson told me that as Gen. Johnston looked upon that scene of festivity," wrote Brooks, "she heard him make a remark of disapproval, but it did not reach our ears, and would probably have been unheeded if it had."[6]

Located at the entrance of the Alabama River and the Mobile & Ohio railroad terminus, Mobile was considered a relatively safe place of refuge.[7] Southern soldiers, sometimes referred to as graycoats, often visited the city on their way to and from the battle front. "We once more enjoy comfortable rooms and beds, bells, servants, and all the conveniences of civilized life, to which we have been strangers for several months while in Virginia," wrote Lieutenant William M. Owen of the Confederacy's Washington Artillery of his January 1863 visit. Shortly after arriving in Mobile, Owen was invited to a grand ball, hosted by Admiral Franklin Buchanan of the Southern navy, where he met charming and beautiful women. "But for the uniforms of the officers present one could scarcely realize that these were war times," recalled Owen.[8] By August 1864 conditions in Mobile would begin to worsen considerably.

The Importance of Mobile

The Federal fleet had been struggling unsuccessfully to stop blockade running into Mobile Bay. So, on the morning of August 5, 1864, they launched an attack that finally succeeded in preventing all ship access from the Gulf of Mexico.[9] Although the Union victory at the battle of Mobile Bay was a significant achievement, it fell short of gaining control of Mobile and attaining access to the interior of Alabama.[10]

Mobile, the second largest city still lingering under Confederate control, the largest being Richmond, was a politically alluring target.[11] In addition to its political significance, the city remained a key Confederate logistical center with access to two navigable rivers and two principal railroads. These rivers and railroads linked the Alabama-Mississippi theater to the Georgia-Carolinas theater.[12]

The Mobile & Ohio and the Mobile & Great Northern railroads were essential to moving Confederate forces and supplies throughout Mississippi, Alabama, and even much of Georgia. The terminus of the Mobile & Great Northern railroad was located opposite Mobile on the eastern shore of Mobile Bay. This rail line connected to the Alabama & Florida at Pollard, Alabama, providing Mobile with rail access to Montgomery and beyond.[13] The Mobile & Ohio railroad—a primary supply line for General Hood's Tennessee campaign—was key to the Confederate war effort throughout the conflict. Despite being damaged by General Benjamin H. Grierson's Union Cavalry raid in late December 1864, the Confederates repaired it in time to send the Mobile garrison reinforcements and supplies.[14] Mobile's railroad access continued to allow the uninterrupted transportation of much needed reinforcements and ordnance stores in early 1865.[15]

In addition to railroads, no other state in the Confederacy possessed such a superb internal water system as Alabama. The city's location at the outlet of some of the most considerable rivers in the South made its possession of the greatest importance.[16] "The Tombigbee and the Alabama were important to the Confederacy," observed Union Major Charles J. Allen, "the latter especially, as it was navigated by large steamers to Montgomery."[17] The Federals still considered the capture of Mobile, with its year-round railroad and river access into the interior, one of the keys to the state of Alabama and the Confederacy.[18] "In our possession, the entire territory of Middle and Northern Alabama and Middle and Northern Mississippi

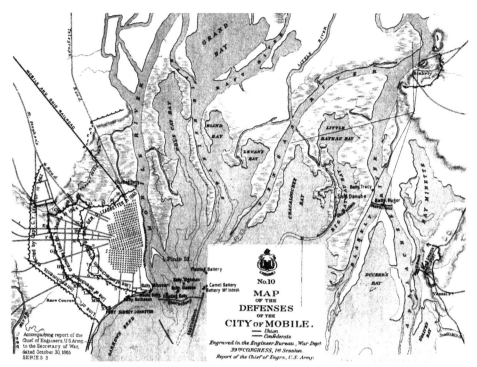

Map of the Defenses of the City of Mobile (*Courtesy of* Michael D. Shipler)

is at our mercy," wrote a *New York Times* reporter.[19] Ever since the fall of Vicksburg in the summer of 1863, General Grant had wanted to capture Mobile to prevent its benefit to the Confederacy as a blockade-running port; by the following year he also sought access to Mobile's rail lines and rivers to supply General William T. Sherman's invasion of Georgia.[20]

During the eight months that followed the battle of Mobile Bay, the Confederacy suffered a series of military reverses. General John B. Hood's Army of Tennessee abandoned Atlanta in September 1864 and then suffered devastating losses at the battles of Franklin and Nashville in November and December of that year. On January 15, 1865, North Carolina's Fort Fisher, on the Atlantic coast, was captured. The fall of Fort Fisher led to the capture of the port town of Wilmington a month later. On February 18, the port city of Charleston, where the first battle of the Civil War began, also fell. At the same time as the Confederacy was crumbling around it, Mobile remained one of the last significant Gulf Coast cities east of the Mississippi River still held by the Southerners.[21]

In late 1864, the Federals identified the capture of Mobile as one of the keys to ending the war. After the defeat of the Army of Tennessee at Nashville and the fall of the eastern port cities, the Union focused their military might on two points, Richmond and Mobile. On Christmas day, 1864, Lieutenant General Richard S.

Taylor, commander of the Department of Alabama, Mississippi, and East Louisiana, informed General Dabney H. Maury, his District of the Gulf commander, of the "severe reverse" at Nashville and his belief that Mobile would soon face a serious threat. He urged Maury to make active preparations for the expected movement, and to plan every way possible that his cavalry could harass the Northerners.[22]

Five days later, Union Major General Henry W. Halleck suggested in a letter to General Grant that elements of the Army of the Cumberland be sent to the Gulf Coast to "assist (General E. R. S.) Canby in taking Mobile." Halleck proposed using Mobile as a base to operate against Selma and Montgomery, where the Southerners maintained a large stockpile of supplies. He believed they could hasten the end of the war by destroying the railroads in the region and capturing Selma, which would deny the Confederates much-needed ordnance stores and ammunition. Halleck reasoned an invasion of south Alabama "would prevent any of Hood's force from being sent against [General William T.] Sherman, and the capture of Selma would be as disastrous to the enemy as that of Atlanta." He advocated invading Alabama from the south because "Mobile was less swampy, and, moreover, the operating army could be supplied by steamers on the Alabama River."[23]

Ironically, in the summer of 1863, it was Grant who had unsuccessfully petitioned then General-in-Chief Halleck for a campaign against Mobile.[24] Now that their roles were reversed, he did not need much convincing. Grant had long ago identified Alabama as a major source of munitions, supplies, and food for the Confederacy. On January 18, 1865, as General Taylor predicted, he ordered two major invasions into Alabama—General James H. Wilson's cavalry from the north and General Edward Richard Sprigg Canby's forces from the south, moving against Mobile, Montgomery, and Selma. Grant also wanted them to capture and destroy all the military infrastructure in the region, especially Selma's Ordnance and Naval Foundry. He knew destroying the state's military infrastructure would bring a swift end to hostilities.[25]

Early in 1865, the Confederacy, though crippled, remained a formidable adversary. Grant understood this and was anxious to see the Secessionists in the west "entirely broken up" before they had time to regain strength. He considered capturing Mobile an important part of his grand strategy of exerting simultaneous pressure on all parts of the South. The Mobile campaign was no side show. Under Grant's orders, the Federals allocated more than 45,000 soldiers and a fleet of over 20 warships for the invasion. He expected the attack of Alabama to begin without delay.[26]

On May 11, 1864, Federal General Edward Canby was ordered to the Gulf region, to head a newly created theater command: the Military Division of West Mississippi. The Mobile campaign would be the first major expedition under the 48-year-old's personal leadership within that new command.[27] A Kentucky native and graduate of West Point, he finished near the bottom of the class of 1839. "He seems to be a strong instance of the faithful cultivation of rather mediocre gifts,"

Union Major General Edward Canby commanded the Army of West Mississippi during the
invasion of south Alabama and siege of Mobile.
(*Courtesy of* The Library of Congress)

wrote one Union officer. "He was tall and wooden; patient and courteous, but reserved in official intercourse; of a taciturnity that was extreme and embarrassing at first approach, but changed to a simple, kindly, and easy intercourse with those who won his confidence."[28]

Canby had previously gained combat experience in the Mexican and Seminole Wars. On February 21, 1862, while he commanded the Department of New Mexico, the Confederates at the battle of Valverde defeated his forces. Five weeks later, other troops in his department, but not under his immediate command, beat the Southerners at Glorieta Pass. This victory prevented the Confederacy's westward expansion into the New Mexico Territory. An officer known for his administrative skills and prudent judgment, he was then assigned staff officer duties in Washington, DC. In July 1863, he went to New York City as commanding general to restore order after the draft riots, which had resulted in the deaths of over 100 civilians and a further breakdown of race relations in that northern city.[29]

Preparations for the overland campaign were meticulous; Canby knew launching operations against the city would not be easy. His apprehension of Mobile's strong defenses was certainly one of the reasons for the delay of the Union attack. Early Spanish and French explorers noted the "land-locked" Mobile Bay region featured natural defensive advantages. Unique geographical factors caused the Federals to be apprehensive about attacking the city earlier in the war. A vast marsh to the north of the city extending to Three-Mile Creek made it nearly impossible for the

Northerners to attack from that direction.[30] The bay also posed challenges to an invading fleet. "It has been difficult to approach Mobile at any time on account of the peculiar indentations of its water courses," reported the *Cincinnati Enquirer* on April 21, "and of the fact that an enormous sand-bar in the bay has long prevented ships, except of the lightest draft, from reaching its docks." Many of Farragut's large vessels could not get any closer than 12 miles to Mobile.[31]

Besides Mobile's natural defensive advantages, the Confederates had nearly four years to prepare the city's man-made fortifications. "The defenses of Mobile are much the strongest I have seen in the South; and the harbor is literally crammed with every kind of obstructions that human ingenuity could invent," wrote one Federal soldier. Mobile's shore batteries, sunken channel obstructions, gunboats, and deadly submerged torpedoes littering the water approaches also helped keep Farragut's fleet a safe distance away after the battle of Mobile Bay.[32] The *Philadelphia Inquirer* reported that the strength of Mobile's vast earthen fortifications would require at least 40,000 soldiers and 90 days to capture the place.[33] On October 17, 1864, the *Detroit Free Press* reported:

> Every line of intrenchments [sic] around Mobile made by [Generals] Ledbetter, Withers, Buckner and Maury will be occupied. The guns mounted are of the best quality, and those in the forts near the city are of the largest caliber. There is no point from which the city can be shelled which is not commanded by ten-inch columbiads. Brooke guns guard the upper bay, which cannot be navigated by vessels drawing more than eight feet. Any attempt will hardly be made to shell the city till the batteries below are reduced, of which such vessels are incapable.[34]

The reputation of Mobile's strong fortifications certainly influenced Canby's grand tactics of invasion. Through intelligence reports from deserters, he knew that the city's western land approach defenses featured three strong lines of earthworks with massive ditches 8 feet wide and 5 feet deep in front of them. The Southerners also removed the thickly wooded country that surrounded the city for a clear field of fire.[35]

Though work was still needed, the Southerners had confidence in Mobile's fortifications. During the summer of 1863, General Joseph E. Johnston, at the time commander of Confederate forces in Alabama and Mississippi, conducted an inspection of the formidable defenses of the city. Reportedly, he declared Mobile the strongest fortified city in the South.[36] General Pierre Gustave Toutant Beauregard, who commanded the Department of the West, also expressed confidence. After inspecting the fortifications in early 1865, he declared that Mobile could hold out.[37] On February 22, 1865, the *Daily Progress* (Raleigh, NC) reported that the defenses of the city could resist a siege for at least two months and that "a stern defense would be made."[38]

Although the garrison defending Mobile was small, they had competent leadership. The city was within the boundaries of Lieutenant General Richard S.

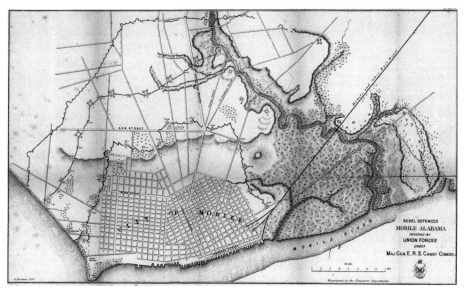

City of Mobile Defenses (*Courtesy of* Library of Congress)

Taylor's Department of Alabama, Mississippi, and East Louisiana. Headquartered at Meridian, Mississippi, Taylor, 39 years old and a native of Kentucky, was the politically well-connected son of Zachary Taylor, the 12th President of the United States. He was also the former brother-in-law of Confederate President Jefferson Davis. Earlier in the conflict, he served under General Thomas "Stonewall" Jackson in Virginia.

Taylor was well respected by many of his Confederate comrades. "He's the biggest man in the lot. If we'd had more like him, we would have licked the Yankees long ago," Southern General Nathan B. Forrest reportedly said of him.[39] He was a veteran of the Shenandoah Valley campaign, and the battles of Front Royal, First Winchester, and Port Republic. Troops under Taylor's command had also successfully repulsed the Union's Red River expedition after he was transferred to the west.[40]

Major General Maury, Taylor's District of the Gulf commander, was relied upon heavily. Maury, a Virginian, was given the overwhelming task of leading the defense of Mobile. An 1846 West Point graduate, he was a classmate of Civil War notables such as Confederate generals "Stonewall" Jackson, A. P. Hill, and George Pickett, as well as Union General George McClellan. A native of Fredericksburg, Virginia, and a Mexican War veteran, Maury was 43 years old and served with distinction in the battles of Pea Ridge, Iuka, and Corinth. In May 1863, he assumed command of the District of the Gulf with headquarters at Mobile.[41]

CSA Lieutenant General Richard S. Taylor commanded the Department of Alabama, Mississippi, and East Louisiana. He surrendered the last major Confederate force remaining east of the Mississippi River on May 4, 1865. (*Courtesy of* History Museum of Mobile)

Lieutenant Colonel Arthur James Lyon Fremantle, a British military observer who visited Maury at Mobile in 1863, described him as a "very gentlemanlike and intelligent but diminutive Virginian."[42] A *New York Times* correspondent described him as a "dapper little fellow much smaller in stature than (General Joseph) Wheeler or (General Earl) Van Dorn."[43] Although Maury was a small man, approximately 5-foot 3-inches tall, he was, as one Louisiana artilleryman noted, "every inch a soldier."[44]

Defending Mobile was the greatest challenge of General Maury's military career. His small Southern army faced an imminent and massive Federal invasion. The two corps and column under Canby were each larger than his entire garrison.[45] Although he had a head start on strengthening the vast fortifications around the city, he struggled to find enough laborers to fully complete them in time to oppose the Union juggernaut.[46] The Confederacy was unable to provide him with the number of soldiers required to adequately garrison the forts in Mobile and Baldwin counties, and he was running low on ammunition and supplies. Despite the overwhelming odds against them, Maury's small garrison would use innovative tactics and weapons to make the most of their limited resources. They would mount a spirited and stubborn defense.

Even after the battle of Mobile Bay in August 1864, Mobile retained strategic and economic importance to the Confederacy because of its railroad and river connections. The Federals certainly considered the capture of the city unfinished business. It was a critical position for the Southerners to defend and the Unionists

CSA Major General Dabney H. Maury commanded the Department of the Gulf. He was responsible for the monumental task of leading the defense of Mobile. (*Courtesy of* The Library of Congress)

to attack. Both sides were still trying to win and did not know the War Between the States was about to end. Despite the Union victories elsewhere that were foretelling the downfall of the Confederacy, the soldiers at Mobile were still fully engaged and fought as valiantly as if the result of this struggle was crucial to ultimate victory for either side.

CHAPTER ONE

Mobile is Threatened

Fourteen days, from March 26 to April 9, 1865, saw fewer than 6,000 Confederate soldiers hold off more than 45,000 determined Union soldiers at Spanish Fort and Fort Blakeley.[1] Many of the Southerners were veterans of all the principal battles in the west. Most had been wounded at least once, yet they still came to fight. In February 1865, Southern Private Phillip D. Stephenson, 5th Company of the Washington Artillery, met an old comrade on his way to defend Mobile:

> When I was on the train for Mobile, a soldier came to me and said, "Don't you know me?" I did not. "I'm Ned Stiles," said he. I was horror stricken. A skeleton he was, with the ashen hue of death upon him. He could hardly stand up. His rags were filthy and hung on him. Yet he was going to Mobile to rejoin his command! His awful wound was hardly healed, but there he was.[2]

The desperate defense of Mobile culminating in the siege of Spanish Fort and Fort Blakeley began on August 5, 1864, when Union Admiral David Glasgow Farragut, with 18 ships, including four ironclad monitors, supported by land forces under Major General Gordon Granger, attacked the Southerners guarding the lower entrance to Mobile Bay. Farragut, who had commanded the Federal sea assault on the Confederacy in the Gulf of Mexico from the beginning of the war, led his fleet past Fort Morgan's powerful batteries and torpedo-mined waters at the mouth of the bay.[3] After clearing the Confederate gauntlet, his armada defeated Admiral Franklin Buchanan's small four-ship squadron, which included the powerful but slow ironclad ram CSS *Tennessee,* in the epic battle of Mobile Bay.[4]

Following the surrender of the CSS *Tennessee,* Fort Powell, the small fort that had guarded the Grant Pass entrance into the bay, was hopelessly vulnerable to Federal gunboat fire. Convinced that a continued struggle was futile, Fort Powell's commander, Lieutenant Colonel James M. Williams of the 21st Alabama Infantry, ordered his garrison to spike their guns and evacuate at dark. To prevent the fort from falling into Federal hands, Williams had it blown up at 10:30 p.m. Two days later, on August 7, Dauphin Island's Fort Gaines surrendered. Finally, on August 23, 1864, Fort Morgan fell to the Unionists, ending all blockade-running ventures out of Mobile Bay. Farragut's important victory sealed the Port City and gave the

Union control of the fortifications at the mouth of the bay. Not satisfied with the strategic success they had achieved, General Granger was eager to complete their primary mission, the capture of Mobile, immediately after the fall of Fort Morgan.[5]

A veteran of the Mexican War, Granger previously had fought at Wilson's Creek, New Madrid, Corinth, Chickamauga, Missionary Ridge, and the battle of Mobile Bay. The 44-year-old New Yorker was aggressive and brave. "Reckless, handsome, ambitious, quick witted, and warm-blooded, he relished the pleasures as well as the honors of a soldier's life," one Union officer wrote of him.[6] Journalist William Shanks, a contemporary of Granger, portrayed him as "a man without any sense of fear—[he] is more thoroughly indifferent to the dangers of battle than any man I ever remember to have met."[7] One newspaper further described him: "In appearance General Granger was of commanding stature; in manner he was easy and natural, and was agreeable in conversation. He was a strict disciplinarian, but was in no respect tyrannical. Obedience he enforced, and he was loved by his command as well as respected by those whom the fortunes of war made his enemies."[8] During the siege of Spanish Fort, Granger regularly visited his men on the front line. "Gen. Granger in the trenches," wrote one officer from Wisconsin in his diary on April 2, "gave one of the boys all the tobacco he had."[9] Although Granger was widely recognized to be an admirable commanding general in media reports, and by the men who served under him, he was not universally admired by certain of his superior officers.

At the battle of Chickamauga, seeing General George H. Thomas in danger of being routed, Granger disobeyed orders and led his men into action in time to

Union Major General Gordon Granger played instrumental roles in the battle of Mobile Bay in 1864 and as commander of the XIII Corps during the Mobile Campaign. (*Courtesy of* The Library of Congress)

prevent catastrophe. For his actions that day, he became known as the "Savior of Chickamauga." Despite Granger's heroic exploits, General-in-Chief Ulysses S. Grant, who disliked him, instructed Major General Henry W. Halleck to tell General Canby, commander of the U.S. Military Division of West Mississippi, that he "must not put him in command of troops, for if he does it is certain to fail."[10] Fortunately for Granger, Canby ignored Grant's suggestion and gave him command of the XIII Army Corps on February 18, 1865.[11] Granger had earned Canby's full confidence during the battle of Mobile Bay, where he led land operations against both Fort Gaines and Fort Morgan. President Abraham Lincoln called Granger's cooperative effort with Admiral Farragut there a "brilliant success."[12]

Granger had actively requested permission to lead an expedition against the city even before the fall of Fort Morgan. On August 20, he wrote General Canby, "If it is the intention to make a dash on Mobile, the sooner it is done after the fall of Morgan the better." He wanted to transport his troops up the bay on steamboats, disembark above Dog River and then march on the city.[13]

Although Mobile boasted strong lines of earthen fortifications, there were a sparse number of men defending it during most of the war. In hindsight, one could argue that Granger's bold plan could have succeeded and prevented "all the work and bloodshed of the following spring."[14] At the time of the battle of Mobile Bay, the garrison had been depleted to reinforce the Army of Tennessee in the defense of Atlanta. Had the Federals known how few men defended Mobile, they could have then captured the city with minimal losses.[15] "When the army of General Granger commenced its attack upon the defences [sic] of the lower bay, there were actually no troops in Mobile or the defenses of it upon the land side," Major General Dabney H. Maury, commander of the Confederate District of the Gulf, wrote after the war. He believed that with a demonstration by Farragut's fleet on the city artillery batteries, Granger would have successfully captured Mobile without serious loss.[16]

Though the battle of Mobile Bay cleared the way for an attack on the city, Canby, in agreement with Farragut's assessment that Mobile would "be an elephant and take a large army to hold it," denied Granger's request. Though Canby still considered the capture of the city an unaccomplished objective, he believed it was "unwise to make any direct attempt upon Mobile until the cooperating land force can be largely increased."[17] Granger would have to wait eight months before Canby had enough men to launch the land campaign for Mobile.[18] As the commander of the Military Division of West Mississippi's reorganized XIII Corps, he would play a prominent role in the spring 1865 expedition.[19]

Immediately following the battle of Mobile Bay, there were fewer than 4,500 gray-coated soldiers near Mobile. Running low on ammunition and men, General Maury was desperate for reinforcements. Alarmed by the prospect of an imminent attack, he pleaded with his superiors for more men. The day after Fort Morgan fell, Maury even sent an urgent message to General Nathan B. Forrest, the legendary cavalry leader, pleading, "Come and help Mobile."[20] The Confederacy was not able to send help until after the battle of Nashville. Those reinforcements would come from the battered remnants of the Army of Tennessee.[21]

One of the first officers sent by the Confederacy to assist Maury was Brigadier General St. John R. Liddell, a 50-year-old Louisiana plantation owner. He had attended West Point briefly before being discharged in 1835 for poor academics and an alleged fight with a couple of classmates. Although he lacked extensive military training, he had proved to be a capable and hard-nosed commander at Perryville, Murfreesboro, Chickamauga, Stone's River, and the Red River campaign. His biographer, Nathaniel C. Hughes, described him as "a participator, a doer, a fully engaged human being. Liddell was a violent man. He killed."[22] General Maury needed a replacement for General Richard L. Page, who was captured in late August 1864 with the surrender of Fort Morgan. The Confederacy determined Liddell was the right officer for the job and sent him to Mobile.[23]

Liddell had only been in south Alabama a couple of months when his help was needed to counter expeditions meant to menace and test the strength of Mobile's defenses.[24] Around November 1864, Union General John W. Davidson left Baton Rouge, Louisiana, on a raid toward Mobile. Maury responded by sending his cavalry from Baldwin County to meet the threat. U.S. forces under Colonel George D. Robinson at Fort Barrancas, learning of the depleted garrison, launched a raid against Pollard Station, a vital Confederate stores depot located just north of the Alabama state line, at the juncture of the Alabama & Florida and Mobile & Great Northern railroads. Colonel Robinson's force consisted of approximately 3,000 African-American soldiers and over 200 cavalry troopers. "They devastated the country, burning houses and stripping the people, women and children, of every means of subsistence. They often ravished the women, who offered their concealed valuables without avail to these diabolical scoundrels for immunity from outrage," recalled Liddell.[25]

In December 1864, upon receiving information on Robinson's raid, Maury ordered back the cavalry as fast as he could. Although valuable time was lost, Colonel Charles G. Armistead, commanding the 16th Confederate Cavalry, still managed to move his brigade rapidly, covering 150 miles in 52 hours. Near northwest Florida's Pine Barren Creek, Armistead's cavalry caught up with Robinson's expedition on their return to Fort Barrancas. From Little Escambia [River] to Pine Barren Creek "severe fighting took place." Newspaper reports indicated Liddell's men "pursued and severely punished the Pollard raiders."[26] General Pierre Gustave Toutant Beauregard, commander of the Military Division of the West, wrote that Armistead and his mounted soldiers fought with "spirit and gallantry," killing 17 and wounding 64. Robinson was severely wounded in the engagement.[27]

In December 1864, Granger also launched a raid from Pascagoula toward Mobile's western defenses. The Federal expedition prompted Alabama Governor Thomas H. Watts to issue an appeal for reinforcements. His plea to "the Men and

Headquartered at Fort Blakeley, CSA Brigadier General St. John R. Liddell commanded the Eastern Division of the Department of the Gulf. He was captured during the assault of Fort Blakeley on April 9, 1865. (*Courtesy of Michael D. Shipler*)

Boys of Middle and South Alabama," to come to the defense of Mobile, appeared in newspapers around the state. "A large force of the enemy is approaching Mobile through Mississippi, and are now within a short distance of the city," wrote Watts. Offering to provide transportation and arms, Watts urged men to go to Mobile at once where he would personally lead them. "One more effort and our cause will be safe," he wrote, stressing the need for more men to defeat the Federal attack.[28]

On December 26, Granger's raid was forced to turn back after facing stiff resistance and supply problems. Granger's difficulties and the strong defenses of Mobile's western approach influenced Canby's decision to invade Alabama via Baldwin County three months later.[29]

Following their near destruction at the battles of Franklin and Nashville, Hood's army retreated southwest over the Tennessee River in the direction of Tupelo, Mississippi, in December 1864. The gray-coated soldiers limped into camp at Verona, Mississippi, where Hood resigned, and Taylor assumed temporary command of the Army of Tennessee.[30]

One Southern soldier summed up the state of the Army of Tennessee after Nashville in his diary entry on January 22, 1865. "Hood's Army is completely cleaned out and demoralized. This campaign has been the most disastrous of the war, and is certainly a very severe blow to us," wrote Private Robert D. Patrick of the Hunter Rifles, Fourth Louisiana Infantry.[31] Confederate morale was definitely at an all-time low.

The Confederacy continued with their struggle for independence despite their setbacks. In January 1865, after resting a few weeks at Verona, most of the Army of Tennessee was ordered to North Carolina.[32] Whereas most of the soldiers headed east, General Taylor consolidated and detached Gibson's Brigade, Holtzclaw's Brigade, and French's Division (consisting of the brigades of Cockrell, Ector, and Sears), to reinforce Mobile.[33]

On January 24, Taylor telegraphed Maury, informing him of some of the reinforcements he was sending. "10,000 men in Mobile would compel a siege by regular approaches, would occupy the Federal Troops in the Southwest for a long time," explained Maury, "and would be as much as the Confederacy could spare for such objects."[34] Maury was pleased to learn he would be receiving a considerable portion of the Army of Tennessee's artillery units. Taylor estimated nearly 1,500 experienced artillerists would be at Maury's disposal, comprised of "800 to 1000 'dismounted' artillerists" from Texas and recently exchanged prisoners from Fort Gaines who had surrendered during the battle of Mobile Bay. Believing this number exceeded what was necessary, he instructed Maury to convert the excess number into an infantry command to be used to complete the defensive earthworks. Maury and Taylor were fortunate to have the services of Colonel Samuel H. Lockett, their highly regarded chief engineer who had previously designed the famous defenses of Vicksburg. Colonel Lockett was directed to send all engineers and African-American slaves under impressment from Montgomery to Mobile to expedite the completion of the defensive works. Taylor sent Brigadier General Randall L. Gibson's veteran infantry brigade of about 600 men and mentioned General Nathan B. Forrest would send "two or three 'dismounted' batteries" to guard property and garrison Choctaw and Hanna Bluffs, north of Mobile.[35]

On January 30, Taylor telegraphed General Pierre Gustave Toutant Beauregard his assessment of the military situation that existed and the rationale behind his troop distributions:

> Sherman's movements render a victory necessary to us at once, and it will require all our means to insure it.[36] I can resist without <u>Stewarts Corps</u> and <u>cannot</u> fight a battle with it against an Army. French's Division is <u>very weak</u> but will enable me to fully <u>garrison Mobile</u> and Choctaw Bluff. The remainder of the corps should go <u>East at once</u>, to insure success there. We can thus save – communications, raise the siege of Mobile should it be invested or be prepared to meet Thomas when he advances in the spring.[37]

Due to a shortage of labor, materials, and tools, strengthening the fortifications around Mobile posed a challenge. Concerned about the slow progress on the works around the city, General Taylor sent 800 African-American prisoners, captured by General Nathan B. Forrest in Tennessee, to be employed as laborers at Mobile.[38] The African-American prisoners, some who were once reportedly slaves in Mobile, were dressed in the standard issue U.S. blue uniforms.[39]

During his defensive preparations, Maury wrote Taylor requesting clarification on whether he should sacrifice his troops to save Mobile. "The answer must be, save the troops and abandon the City," Taylor responded in a confidential letter from his Meridian headquarters on February 16, "but the practical question before us is, will the consequence of the loss of Mobile be such as to justify us in risking the loss of the garrison by attempting to hold the city? This has been affirmatively decided." Taylor knew an investment would occur before siege operations could begin. He instructed Maury to hold his position if possible. "No troops would have been withdrawn from the Army of Tennessee to reinforce your garrison, had it been contemplated to abandon Mobile," wrote Taylor. Recognizing the overwhelming odds against them, he nevertheless emphasized that a defense had to be attempted. "The longer Mobile can be held the better for the cause, as other operations of the enemy will be delayed and time afforded us to march an army to its relief."[40]

Lieutenant General Nathan B. Forrest's Cavalry was the only hope for reinforcements for the Confederates at Mobile. General Richard Taylor believed that if Forrest's troopers could defeat Union General James H. Wilson's raid into Alabama, he could then go to Mobile to help lift the siege. (*Courtesy of* The Library of Congress)

If the Mobile garrison could hold out a week, Taylor planned to send Forrest's cavalry, after they defeated Union General James H. Wilson's raid from the north.[41] "If you can beat the force in your front we can relieve Mobile," Taylor telegraphed Forrest, referring to Wilson's cavalry raid.[42]

The Confederate soldiers sent to reinforce Mobile had suffered great losses at Franklin and Nashville. "The ranks of Holtzclaw's Brigade had become decimated through the severe and arduous duties in covering the retreat of the Army," remembered Joseph Baumer, drummer with the 36th Alabama Infantry. "We were ordered to proceed to the defenses of Blakeley and Spanish Fort in the harbor of Mobile, Alabama."[43]

To make matters worse, the Southern soldiers endured a long and uncomfortable train ride on the Mobile & Ohio railroad from Verona to Mobile, where they were destined for further hardship.[44] "'Twas after Hood's defeat at Nashville, - that terrible retreat," recalled First Lieutenant James A. Chalaron during a toast at a reunion of the 5th Company, Washington Artillery, many years after the war, "and after a no less trying ride of twenty-four hours in sleet and rain on open flat cars from Columbus to Mobile, in February. Seventy-five men per car; no platform rails, no seats, 'twas barely standing room, and from the train many an exhausted soldier dropped upon the track that night."[45]

By late January, reinforcements from the Army of Tennessee began arriving and setting up camp at various locations near Mobile. "We reached Mobile the last day of January," recalled Corporal Edgar W. Jones of Company G, 18th Alabama Infantry Regiment. Soon after arriving in Mobile, Jones and his regiment were sent over to the eastern shore and took up position near Baldwin County's Fort Blakeley.[46]

Many of the soldiers sent to reinforce Mobile maintained their sense of humor despite all the horrors they had experienced. The following postwar account of First Lieutenant Charles B. Cleveland, Company K, 3rd Missouri Dismounted Cavalry Regiment, recalled a humorous incident that occurred upon arrival at the eastern shore of Baldwin County:

> When the boat arrived at the rude and imperfect wharf and we were unloading and going ashore two men too much in their cups stepped through a hole in the wharf and fell into the water beneath. One of them was [reportedly] Burr Cox, of Company G [18th Alabama] … they both went through at the same time.
>
> There was a splashing, dashing and yelling such as would put "Johnny Sand's wife" to the blush. There was plenty of piling for them to cling to until they were brought up and gotten on shore. Certainly, they were suddenly transformed into a state of sobriety. They were the wettest, towsiest, most be-drabbled, meekest, most subdued looking fellows I think I ever beheld. The sight was laughable indeed.[47]

Mobile experienced substantial rainfall during the time leading up to the invasion. On February 8, around noon, was when the 46th Mississippi arrived in the city. They quickly sought shelter from the rain. "Captain Benoit, A. A. G [Acting

Assistant Adjutant General] of Sear's brigade, secured an old warehouse where we were sheltered til 10 o'clock a.m. Sunday," Sergeant William P. Chambers, Company B, 46th Mississippi, wrote in his journal on February 8. "We also were fortunate enough to secure some old tents that had once belonged to Reynolds' brigade. They are the first tents we have had since the fall of Vicksburg."[48] Later they moved approximately 5 miles south of Mobile and set up camp near other regiments at Camp Memminger. From early February through mid-March 1865, the 46th Mississippi lived in a comfortable camp in a scenic location near Mobile Bay. From their camp, a few hundred yards from the water, the soldiers could plainly see the Yankee naval vessels in Mobile Bay.[49]

Mobile's Confederate Naval Squadron

On August 8, 1864, following the capture of Admiral Buchanan at the battle of Mobile Bay, 58-year-old Ebenezer Farrand assumed command of the small flotilla at Mobile. Having entered the old navy as a midshipman in 1823, he had 42 years of experience.[50]

Farrand had served as a commander in the Federal navy at the Pensacola Navy Yard before the conflict and was a familiar military figure on the Gulf Coast. In the early stages of the secession, when Florida left the Union, he was still serving as a U.S. naval officer in Pensacola. On January 12, 1861, Confederate militia arrived at the gates of the Pensacola Navy Yard and demanded its surrender. Farrand was a conspicuously cooperative participant in the surrender of the Pensacola Navy Yard to the Confederate militia. He was observed shaking hands with them, seemingly not surprised at their arrival. Farrand was said to have strongly influenced the aging commanding officer of the Navy Yard, Commodore Armstrong, to surrender. Once the Pensacola naval base was firmly in possession of the Secessionists, he resigned and joined the Southerners.[51]

The highlight of Farrand's Confederate service occurred in May 1862. As commander of the Confederate naval defenses at Drewry's Bluff in northeastern Virginia, his shore batteries turned back the invasion of five Federal gunboats from the James River. This victory prompted the Confederate Congress to pass a resolution expressing thanks to him "for the great and signal victory achieved over the naval forces of the United States in the engagement."[52]

Prior to the invasion, leaders of the Confederate army and navy at Mobile did not work well together. Before the fighting began, General Maury complained of the lack of cooperation given by Commodore Farrand.[53] On February 4, in a letter to President Davis, General Taylor expressed his dissatisfaction with the Mobile naval squadron calling it "a farce." He wrote that the navy's "vessels are continually tied up at the wharf; never in co-operation with the army. The payment of its expenses is a waste of money."[54]

CSA Commodore Ebenezer Farrand assumed command of the remnants of the small Confederate Navy at Mobile after the battle of Mobile Bay. (*Courtesy of* Alabama Department Archives and History)

In fairness to Farrand, he was not left much to work with after the battle of Mobile Bay. His small fleet included the ironclads *Tuscaloosa, Huntsville,* and *Nashville,* and the gunboats *Morgan* and *Baltic.* Due to shortages of men and materiel, the *Tuscaloosa* and *Huntsville* were never fully completed. These two ships were only partially armored, had weak engines, lacked a full complement of guns, and were used mainly as floating batteries. Newspaper reports indicated that the *Nashville* was "as strong as the *Tennessee* at all points at which she will be exposed in a fight."[55] The reality was the vessel was only a partially armored side wheel steamer. The *Morgan* was the lone gunboat to escape capture at the battle of Mobile Bay in 1864. The *Baltic* was a converted river boat. Once an ironclad, its armor was transferred to the CSS *Nashville.*[56]

Despite his low opinion of Mobile's small navy flotilla, the lack of cooperation between Farrand and Maury concerned Taylor. On February 22, to mount the best possible defense, he directed Maury to make a sincere effort to work with his naval counterpart:

> A divided command has, with few exceptions, always been a source of weakness, of discord, and not unfrequently of irredeemable disaster. This is the history not only of this but of all preceding Wars. The same history shows these few exceptions to have been directly attributable to the mutual concessions and sacrifices made by the several independent commanders. Indeed a proper harmony of feeling and unity of action on the part of independent and distinct forces can only be attained by the Com'der of each divesting himself of all prejudices and individual

opinions, and heartily co-operating each with the other in mutual efforts for a common cause. It is with this view I wish you to frequently meet and confer with the Naval Com'der at Mobile [Commodore Farrand].

His forces properly directed can greatly assist you in defending the city. Those forces cannot be properly directed unless some co-operative plan of action be now definitely and understandingly settled upon by that officer and yourself. On the other hand, there may be something you and I can do to assist him, providing him perhaps with necessary supplies for protracted operations. If he has not a full supply of fuel notify me and I will have it furnished. If his supply of Commissary or other stores is insufficient, now is the time to know it, in order that you may make adequate arrangements to meet these wants. It will be too late when the place is actually invested.

Be pleased also to assure him of my earnest desire to promote harmony and united action between our land and naval forces, and my constant readiness to render him every possible assistance, either by furnishing whatever may be needed to properly supply his vessels and forces, or by cooperating with him in any plans he may have for resisting or annoying the enemy.[57]

Greatly outnumbered, the Confederates were innovative in their efforts to overcome the great odds against them. On January 26, 1864, the Confederate States navy contracted 30-year-old Irish immigrant John Patrick Halligan, a civilian, to design and build a ground-breaking new vessel at the Selma Naval Foundry. Presumably named after himself, Halligan called the submersible torpedo boat the *Saint Patrick*. Upon completion, Halligan was supposed to use it to attack the Union fleet in Mobile Bay. Although he received assistance from the military, Halligan privately funded the project with the anticipation of substantial monetary rewards when the vessel proved to be successful. In a June 16, 1864, letter to General Maury, Catesby R. Jones, commandant of the Selma Naval Foundry, and Ordnance Works, wrote that Halligan's submersible vessel combined "a number of ingenious contrivances." Propelled by a small steam engine and by hand when submerged and fully capable of "raising and descending at will," Jones predicted the torpedo boat would be "very formidable."[58] On November 20, 1864, a spy named Edward La Croix reported to the Union navy the details of the torpedo boat with a length of "about 30 feet" that had sailed down the river to Mobile.[59]

The sight of the Yankee fleet in Mobile Bay, within clear view of his Confederate camps, did not sit well with General Maury. Not one to remain idle, the Virginian made considerable efforts to expedite the launching of the *Saint Patrick*. Maury's prodding was ineffective; Halligan had endless delays and was evidently not eager to test his invention against the Union navy. By early December 1864, Maury had run out of patience and wrote Secretary of War James A. Seddon that he did not believe Halligan had any intention of using his "most valuable invention."[60]

The low-profile, steam-powered vessel was supposed to be ready for action on July 1, 1864; however, Halligan, whom the navy gave the rank of lieutenant, continually delayed launching an attack on the Federal navy. Maury continually urged Commodore Ebenezer Farrand to order Halligan to launch the *Saint Patrick*.[61] Halligan had been exempted from military service during the construction of the boat. Maury, frustrated with the delays, thought "the only practical purpose the *Saint Patrick* was serving was to keep Halligan and her crew of six able-bodied men from doing military duty." [62]

On January 13, 1865, frustrated by the lack of urgency on the part of Halligan and the navy, Maury voiced his concern directly to Confederate President Jefferson Davis and requested command of the vessel. "Halligan and five or six men have now been for months exempt from service on account of her [*St. Patrick*]," he wrote to President Davis. "There has never been so good an opportunity for a torpedo boat to operate as is afforded by the fleet off Mobile." In response, Secretary of the Confederate navy Stephen Mallory ordered Farrand to turn over the torpedo boat to Maury. [63]

INCIDENT ON BOARD THE "OCTORARA," JANUARY 26, 1865.

General Dabney H. Maury ordered the torpedo boat *Saint Patrick* attack on the USS *Octorara* on January 28, 1865. Illustration originally from *Harper's Weekly* (*Courtesy of* History Museum of Mobile)

Convinced Halligan was stalling to avoid military duty, Maury removed him from command, citing lack of "nerve and capacity to attack the enemy." As a replacement, Farrand transferred the services of navy Lieutenant John T. Walker to the army under Maury's direction. Upon assuming command of the vessel, Walker discovered that Halligan had removed vital parts from the vessel's machinery. He searched and found Halligan at the Battle House, Mobile's premier hotel. Using "energetic and good management," Walker recovered the missing parts from him and then prepared to launch an attack on the Federal flagship *Octorara* in Mobile Bay.[64]

On January 28, at approximately 1 a.m., Walker, whom Maury described "as a young officer of great gallantry and merit," took the stealthy vessel into Mobile Bay where it attacked the *Octorara* "abaft the wheel-house." The torpedo failed to explode. "The greatest consternation and confusion was occasioned on the ship," Maury reported to Taylor, "so that the fire of artillery and musketry which was directed against the *Saint Patrick* failed to strike her and she returned with her crew to the protection of our batteries." Despite the failure to sink the *Octorara*, Maury recognized Walker's "fine conduct" during the expedition in his report to Taylor. During the attack, some of the *Saint Patrick*'s machinery was damaged. Walker was confident the boat would be ready by the next "dark moon." Although the *Saint Patrick* assisted in transporting supplies to Spanish Fort, no further attacks by the vessel on the Union fleet were known to have occurred.[65] Although the Unionists stopped blockade running out of Mobile Bay, the Secessionists were determined to hold the city of Mobile at all hazards.[66] Anticipating an attack, General Maury tirelessly appealed to his superiors for more men and supplies. General Taylor did his best to send him all the soldiers that could be spared for the defense of Mobile. As the *Saint Patrick* attack demonstrated, Maury was determined to employ every possible resource and innovation available to defend the city against the Federal incursion.[67]

CHAPTER TWO

Eager for the Fray

Once Confederate reinforcements reached Mobile they established military camps around the city. As they waited for the expected Yankee attack, the gray-coated soldiers regularly performed military functions such as picket duty, artillery drill, and labor on the earthen works surrounding the city. "We were not pushed, however, but allowed to be leisurely," Stephenson remembered.[1] In their free time, the Confederate soldiers engaged in various pastimes, contemplated, and discussed current issues concerning the future of their struggle.

Lieutenant Colonel James Williams of the 21st Alabama Infantry, an avid sportsman, took advantage of the excellent hunting in the Mobile Delta. In a December 19, 1864 letter to his wife, Williams wrote, "I am in a fine duck region now—have sent for my ammunition and will have a good time." Colonel Williams, who briefly commanded the Apalachee River Batteries Huger and Tracy during December 1864, was in an ideal duck hunting location.[2]

Private E. G. Littlejohn, Company G, 10th Texas Dismounted Cavalry, wrote his wife, "I just finished building me a little chimney to my shantee last night, built us a little pen of logs, covered it with a fly. We have nothing at all to burn but green pine. We learned to burn it finely. We have had a great deal of rain lately, but not much cold weather."[3] The significant amount of rainfall Mobile experienced during the weeks leading up to the invasion would play a role in the coming campaign.

Some members of the 5th Company of the Washington Artillery were accompanied in camp by their slaves who worked as cooks and body servants. For entertainment, they enjoyed banjo strumming and would have their slaves compete with one another in clog dancing "breakdowns." There was one slave named Charles who was an extraordinarily talented dancer. "He would get on the floor and with cheers and compliments and 'taffy' keep shuffling his huge feet until he would nearly drop," recalled Stephenson.[4]

Common soldiers would often receive permits from their officers to go into the city. On top of all the adversity the Confederate soldier faced, he also had to overcome extremely inflated prices in Mobile caused by the shutdown of blockade running and the strains of war. "Everything in price is beyond the reach of a private soldier," wrote Private Littlejohn to his wife on February 9. He added, "A man can eat a month's wages in a day and not half try."[5] Mobile's shops were sparsely stocked. On March 3, Sergeant Chambers commented in his diary on the inflated prices he found in the city. "We encountered nothing worthy of note. We found very small stocks of goods in any of the houses, though what was there was at exorbitant prices. We paid five dollars for a dinner of baker's bread and butter."[6] Coffee houses charged a dollar a cup with an "ironclad pie" thrown in. Stephenson lamented, "Said coffee being made of sweet potato chips toasted or wheat and other things mixed, and the pies with faintest traces of dried apple having some time or other passed that way."[7]

For a five-dollar cover charge, the Southern soldiers could watch nightly shows in a crowded theater. Not all leisure activity was expensive. They often lounged around the elegant Battle House hotel, took strolls on Government Street, or enjoyed live bands that played about twice a week in the city park. Sometimes the men would walk along the shores on the shell road where they could plainly see the Federal fleet in the bay.[8]

"When the rain does not interfere we have preaching every night and frequently during the day," noted Sergeant Chambers in his February 27 journal entry. "A missionary named McMurtry is here. He, Andrews and the three regular chaplains—Foster, 35th; Gordon, 36th; and Lattimore, 46th (with Hutson of the 39th)—frequently alternate in conducting the services. Much interest is manifested and the baptismal waters are often stirred."[9] Religious worship was indeed an important part of life for many Southern soldiers. It played a role in helping the men cope with the many challenges they faced.

The Confederate camps were also full of rumors, often false rumors. On March 22, Lieutenant Colonel James Williams of the 21st Alabama Infantry wrote his wife, "There is plenty of rumors all the time, a new one is born every minute, but nobody is excited—half my men are working in the trenches and nearly all the other half are playing marbles before the quarters like so many schoolboys."[10]

The Hampton Roads Peace Conference

On February 3, at the same time the Southern soldiers camped near Mobile, the Hampton Roads Conference was held at Hampton Roads, Virginia. The peace conference was between a delegation of Confederates under Vice President Alexander Stephens and Unionists led by President Abraham Lincoln and Secretary of State William Seward.[11]

During these negotiations, the men encamped around Mobile spent time discussing whether they should continue the fight. The Southerners were divided on the subject; some favored accepting Lincoln's terms whereas others wanted to continue the fight. Corporal Edgar W. Jones of the 18th Alabama Infantry argued that if they quit now, there would always be those who would say we could have won if we kept going. "So let's fight it out," he argued. "We will be the gainers by it, for if we get whipped it will settle the question for all time to come."[12] The graycoats also listened to speeches from their officers, reverends, and prominent citizens, whose message was there was "hope in fighting, in submission none."[13]

The Hampton Roads Conference failed to reach an agreement. On February 17, the 1st Missouri Brigade held a meeting at their camp near Mobile where they declared the terms offered by Lincoln at Hampton Roads "are such as we cannot accept, because they are so degrading in the extreme." Believing Lincoln offered the Confederacy "nothing but chains and slavery," the Missourians adopted several resolutions, all reaffirming their determination to defend their "country to the last." Preferring an honorable death to submission, they resolved to never lay down their arms until achieving independence. Their resolutions were published in the *Mobile Register and Advertiser,* the *Army Argus and Crisis,* and other papers.[14]

Arming the Slaves

Determined to strengthen their armies and overcome the setbacks they had experienced, the call for arming the slaves into regular Confederate service increased. Throughout the war, Southerners pondered the use of enslaved African-Americans on the battlefield. Deliberations occurred among political and military leaders, in the general society, in the newspapers, and among the soldiers. As the war continued far beyond initial expectations, as casualties and destruction escalated, and emotions grew more intense, the debates increased in both frequency and urgency. As soldiers encamped around Mobile, the issue of admitting African-Americans into the service was being discussed in the Confederate Congress.

Mobile's military leaders favored enlisting men of African descent. General Richard S. Taylor claimed that some slaves in Mobile were willing to fight for the South. He recounted the following conversation with one slave during an inspection tour of Mobile's fortifications: "a fine-looking negro, who seemed to be leader among his comrades, approached me and said: 'Thank you, Massa General, they give us plenty of good victuals; but how you like our work?' I replied that they had worked very well. 'If you give us guns we will fight for these works, too. We would rather fight for our own white folks than for strangers.'"[15]

During the siege of Mobile, Taylor was receptive to a proposition from citizens of Alabama to furnish slaves for military service. On April 4, he gave them assurances that the lack of communication from officials at Richmond, "on the subject of the late legislation with regard to the employment of negroes as soldiers," would not be an obstacle. Although lacking enough arms for them at the time, Taylor sought to find out how many African-Americans would be available for Confederate service on short notice.[16]

In November 1863, General Maury, to augment his depleted forces, sent a formal request to James E. Seddon, Confederate Secretary of War, to form a company of "Creoles," men of mixed race, into the Confederate service. He informed Seddon that the men were "admirably qualified" to be heavy artillerists. Maury's request was considered progressive for that time, although Seddon was skeptical and somewhat unreceptive in his response.[17] On March 23, 1865, as the Northern soldiers, often referred to as bluecoats, were marching up the eastern shore of Mobile Bay, Maury published orders in the local newspapers instructing all creoles and free persons of color to report to his headquarters to participate in the defense of Mobile.[18]

General Liddell was a conspicuous proponent of recruiting African-Americans into the regular Confederate service. He knew the South needed more men and that African-Americans could strengthen their forces. In December 1864, he wrote a letter to Confederate Senator Edward Sparrow, chairman of the Military Committee, from his headquarters at Fort Blakeley. Liddell recalled: "I took some pains to express my firm conviction that the war was going against us unless we could get foreign assistance or we could unite with the people to emancipate the slaves and put all the men in the army that were willing to join our side." Liddell claimed Sparrow shared the letter with General Robert E. Lee who agreed with him and "desired to get Negro soldiers, saying that he could make soldiers out of any human being that had arms and legs."[19]

Most Confederate soldiers came from families that did not own slaves. Yet, there were differing opinions that existed among the men regarding freeing the slaves to fight for the South.[20] On February 11, Confederate Secretary of State Judah P. Benjamin requested General Robert E. Lee, who was made commander-in-chief of all Confederate armies in late January 1865, to gauge the level of support in the army for enlisting slaves. Lee ordered his generals to pose the following question to the soldiers: "Are you in favor of putting negroes who for the boon of freedom would volunteer as soldiers in the field?"[21] In compliance with Lee's orders, in mid-February, there were brigade and division meetings held in the Confederate camps around Mobile where the pros and cons of allowing African-Americans into the army were discussed. "The Negro question is up pretty high. Some of the soldiers are in favor of it and some are opposed to it. I am in favor of anything before subjugation," wrote Jim Watson of Company G, 10th Texas Dismounted Cavalry, summing up the debate in a letter to his father on February 22.[22]

There were Southern soldiers who felt African-Americans would make valuable additions to the army. "Let their sable faces be seen in every military and civil department where they can be employed with advantage," wrote Sergeant Richard C. Beckett, a 19-year-old trooper with the 12th Mississippi Cavalry's Company B. In camp near Fort Blakeley on February 10, Beckett wrote a letter to the *Mobile Evening News* and the *Mobile Register and Advertiser* and proclaimed Southern African-Americans, "will fight better than those of the enemy." Writing under the alias "T. C.," in a letter approved by his commanding officers, Beckett suggested that the Confederacy guarantee freedom to every African-American that served honorably. He urged the Confederate Congress to act immediately:

> This is a great crisis in our struggle for independence, and there is not a moment to be lost. — Our enemy is now mustering his forces for our overthrow in the spring, and certainly it behooves us to be making counter movements to defeat his deep-laid schemes. What are we doing? What you do, do quickly. This is no time for speculation and inaction. We must act, and act quickly.[23]

Sergeant Chambers, who was against the measure, believing it was "not right," recorded in his February 17 journal entry, "There is a cry to put negroes in the army and I understand that our congress is considering the subject [...] Disguise the fact as we may, the real sentiment of this brigade and this division is for peace on almost any terms."[24] Despite some that were against enlisting slaves, those who favored the measure prevailed. One of the resolutions passed by the 1st Missouri Brigade at their February 17 meeting stated, "That if thought expedient by Congress to employ negroes as soldiers, we are favorable to it."[25] On February 18, at a division meeting, another resolution passed stated "that the best interests of the country demanded" African-Americans be enlisted in the service.[26] Recognizing the potential threat, General Grant was anxious for the invasion of Alabama to begin without delay. On February 27, he instructed General Canby to "get all the negro men we can before the enemy puts them in their ranks."[27]

On March 13, the Confederate Congress finally acted, approving the enlistment of African-American soldiers "to increase the military force of the Confederate States" and "repel invasion, maintain the rightful possession of the Confederate States." General Order 14 mandated, "No slave will be accepted as a recruit unless with his own consent and with the approbation of his master by a written instrument conferring, as far as he may, the rights of a freedman." The law required blacks "receive the same rations, clothing, and compensation" as white soldiers. The orders also mandated officers treat troops of color with "humane attention" and "protect them from injustice and oppression."[28]

Upon hearing of the decision to arm the slaves, the *New York Times* denounced it as "extremely injudicious on the part of the South, and most likely to prove speedily fatal." The *Times* wrote, "we do not believe that negroes, as a general rule, will fight for the South." The newspaper expressed the view that the Confederacy lacked enough weapons and food for them.[29]

Unfortunately for Mobile, General Order 14 was not issued until March 23, just four days before the siege of Spanish Fort began, too late to make any significant impact for the South.[30] There is some evidence suggesting African-Americans were brought over to Baldwin County to fight at the Confederate forts. During the siege of Spanish Fort, General Randall L. Gibson made repeated requests for African-American troops. In his after-action report, he mentioned on the last day of the siege "several hundred negroes who arrived that evening to be employed in the defense."[31] His repeated requests and official report suggest that he fully intended to use them as soldiers and not just as laborers.

Some Southerners felt the Confederate Congress should have acted sooner. "Many think if we had put negroes into the army at the start," remarked Kate Cumming, a Confederate nurse from Mobile, "that we should have had another tale to tell to-day; and I am confident that if we had freed the negro, we would have had the aid of foreign powers."[32]

The Restoration of General Joseph E. Johnston

The disastrous defeats at Franklin and Nashville led to Hood's resignation. Confederate President Jefferson Davis ordered Taylor to assume command of the Army of Tennessee. On January 18, after receiving the orders, he replied to President Davis. The articulate Taylor called his assignment "unfortunate for the cause." He felt compelled to advise Davis that both the army and the public wanted General Joseph E. Johnston reinstated immediately. "The safety of the country demands it," he wrote. Content with a subordinate role, Taylor expressed the view that only the restoration of Johnston would restore confidence in the people and the Confederate forces.[33]

General-in-Chief Robert E. Lee restored Johnston to the command of the Army of Tennessee in February. "I understand that Congress has at last made Gen. R. E. Lee commander-in-chief of all Confederate armies," Sergeant Chambers wrote of Johnston's return in his February 19 journal entry. "Another measure of Congress is recalling Gen. J. E. Johnston to the command of his old army. It is thought these two measures will do much to restore public confidence. I do not know what is best. I am simply resolved to do my whole duty as nearly as I can."[34] As Taylor predicted, Johnston's return to his old command lifted morale. On March 4, the *Mobile Evening News* reported the restoration of Johnston had an "electrifying effect on the country."[35] The newspaper reported, "Both citizen and soldiers rejoice over it, and see in it the omen of brighter fortunes to a sacred cause." The news inspired many soldiers absent without leave to return to their commands.[36]

Some members of the Army of Tennessee detached to Mobile wanted to rejoin their old commander in North Carolina. The officers of the Washington Artillery's 5th Company went as far as writing the following letter to Johnston: "The announcement of your reinstatement to command in the field has filled us with new hope, and stimulated our desire to serve again under you. We, therefore, pray that you will use your influence to have the Fifth company Washington Artillery fitted up as a light battery, and ordered to report to you," wrote the officers.[37]

Once General Johnston resumed command of the Army of Tennessee, he was not pleased to discover French's Division was at Mobile. On March 27, he telegraphed

General Beauregard and General Lee: "Under what authority were French's division and Gibson's and Holtzclaw's Brigades left at Mobile? If they are there by your authority and not absolutely required, please order them to rejoin their corps."[38]

Strengthening the Fortifications

General Taylor, like Maury, was concerned about the lack of progress being made on the earthen works. On February 1, he sent a telegraph to Maury, advising him to put the newly arrived soldiers to work on the fortifications at locations separate from the African-American laborers.[39]

Concerned the Union army could occupy the old Spanish Fort and silence the two water batteries on the Apalachee River, Huger and Tracy, Maury ordered the fort strengthened with the construction of a "heavy six-gun battery of Brooke rifles." He also equipped the fort with numerous artillery pieces of various calibers, including four 24-pounder bronze howitzers from a Federal gunboat captured on the Yazoo River in Mississippi.[40] The area surrounding the fort was further strengthened with obstructions such as abatis, chevaux-de-frise, and subterra shells (known today as landmines).[41]

On March 15, the 5th Company of the Washington Artillery moved from their camp south of Mobile across the bay to the eastern shore's Spanish Fort. After arriving, they spent their time planting torpedoes in their front and strengthening

Bombproofs at Spanish Fort. (*Courtesy of* Alabama Department of Archives and History)

the earthworks. To protect against Yankee artillery shells, the graycoats built bomb-proofs. Typically, these shelters were pits dug in the ground covered with two layers of logs and 4–6 feet of dirt.[42] Stephenson recalled, "One I worked upon was about 16×20 feet in dimensions and 10 to 12 feet deep." The Confederate soldiers would cut down large trees, roll them over the hole they dug, then add a layer of dirt, then add another layer of heavy logs perpendicular, then another layer of brush and dirt. The roof could be 6–8 feet thick.[43]

Grand Review

By early March 1865, most of the reinforcements from the Army of Tennessee had arrived. On the afternoon of March 7, there was a grand review and parade on Mobile's Government Street that helped further boost the morale of the men.[44] As they marched by in "double platoons," citizens lined the streets and applauded troops for their straightness. "'There goes the 5th Co. W. A.,' came whispers from the pavement, and out of the corners of our eyes we could see the smiling ladies," remembered Stephenson. "That review revealed about 10,000 men all told, scraping together as the sum total of the city's defense—the city and all of its outer posts such as Blakely [sic], Spanish Fort, etc., far down the bay to the enemy's lines." The parade lifted the soldiers' morale. Stephenson remembered after seeing themselves in the parade the troops were "much elated" and proud of their strength.[45]

Maury was less than thrilled with the appearance of some of the soldiers on parade. "We had in our company, several soldiers, who had neither coat nor pants. They were down to shirts and drawers," recalled Private James R. Maxwell of Captain Charles L. Lumsden's artillery battery. Lumsden had made repeated attempts to properly outfit his men without success. Embarrassed with their condition, he did not require the sparsely dressed men to march. Yet, he told them if they did march, their appearance would likely lead to them obtaining new uniforms.[46]

The men decided to march, in front rank, and succeeded in catching Maury's attention. "The General rode up to Lumsden and asked: 'Captain, what does that mean, those men in ranks, in that condition?'" Once the Captain explained their dilemma, Maury immediately granted him permission to send a one-man detail to Tuscaloosa, their hometown, to obtain the needed clothing.[47]

Stephenson's claim of "about 10,000 men" was an overestimate. After the war, Maury remarked, "Including 1,500 cavalry and all the available fighting men for the defence [sic] of Mobile, and all its outposts, batteries and dependencies, my force did not exceed 9,000 men of all arms!"[48] Although Maury's small army faced a massive Yankee invasion, Lieutenant James A. Chalaron of the Washington Artillery claimed "the defenders of Mobile were in no way dismayed, but on the contrary were eager for the fray."[49] Chalaron and his comrades would not have to wait long. They would soon be engaged in the last siege of the war.

CHAPTER THREE

Glisten with Federal Bayonets

"Two clouds appeared on the horizon of my department," recalled General Taylor. Union General Ulysses Grant's theater strategy called for invading Alabama simultaneously from the Tennessee Valley and from the Gulf. From the north, General James H. Wilson prepared a 10,000-man cavalry expedition against the Confederate iron foundry at Selma. From the south, General Canby was collecting a force of over 45,000 men to attack Mobile.[1]

From January to mid-March 1865, Canby collected and organized his large force for the invasion of Alabama. Fort Gaines on Dauphin Island and Fort Morgan at Mobile Point, the two coastal forts captured at the battle of Mobile Bay, were approximately 30 miles south of Mobile and were the staging points of the XIII and XVI Corps. Fort Barrancas, located on Pensacola Bay, Florida, also served as a staging area for the invasion.[2]

After his victory over General Hood at Nashville, Union General George H. Thomas, commander of the Army of the Cumberland, sent the reorganized XVI Corps under the command of 50-year-old Brevet Major General Andrew Jackson Smith south to reinforce Canby. Upon their arrival to New Orleans, Canby designated Smith's command to be known as the XVI Corps.[3]

Named after the late U.S. President Andrew Jackson, Smith was an 1838 West Point graduate and had served in the Mexican War. "Like a Viking, he voyaged through the country, descending from his boats and taking a hand in any fight where he happened to be," wrote one Union officer of Smith.[4] The Pennsylvania native proved his leadership ability at Corinth, Arkansas Post on the Arkansas River, Vicksburg, Sherman's Raid of Meridian, the Red River campaign, Tupelo, and in Missouri.[5] "We of that command always thought him invincible as a corps commander, and such a thing as defeat with him in command never for one moment entered our heads, no matter what the odds against us," remembered one soldier from Ohio who served under Smith in the XVI Corps.[6]

The confidence his men had in him was understandable, considering Smith's distinction of never being on the losing side when in command of a campaign or

Union Major General A. J. Smith commanded the XVI Corps during the Mobile Campaign. His men, largely comprised of farmers from the Midwest, were known as the "Guerillas." (*Courtesy of* The Library of Congress)

battle. At Red River, when General Nathaniel P. Banks first saw Smith's rough-looking Midwesterners, he disparagingly referred to them as "Guerrillas." Banks probably changed his opinion of Smith's troops when they saved his forces from obliteration during their retreat from the Red River. Prior to being sent to Mobile Bay, Smith had played a significant role in the defense of Nashville, where his performance earned him the brevet rank of major general.[7]

The Voyage to Mobile

General A.J. Smith's command took a long, uncomfortable boat journey from Eastport, Mississippi, north down the Tennessee River, west down the Ohio River, and south down the Mississippi River to New Orleans, where they briefly encamped at Chalmette, Louisiana. "The trip from Eastport to New Orleans, 1500 miles on board a river transport, with only the hard deck for a bed, and space of about 18 inches by seven feet, for each soldier, and no accommodation for cooking was bad enough," recalled Private Richard A. Spink of Company A, 14th Wisconsin Infantry, "but our condition at Chalmette was simply terrible. It rained every day, and our camp for two weeks was a regular quagmire. A good paper would be written on the trials and tribulations of a soldier at Chalmette."[8]

Despite the miserable conditions endured by the bluecoats, military discipline was maintained. "Then followed the assembling and reorganizing of the small detachments along the Mississippi and outlying districts," recalled Colonel Henry C. Merriam of the 73rd Infantry Regiment, United States Colored Troops (U.S.C.T.). "They were brought together in larger camps and placed under able commanders, who under General Canby's masterful orders and supervision, instituted the strictest discipline and instruction in all that goes to make up the highest efficiency in the field." Canby's insistence on discipline proved beneficial throughout the campaign.[9]

During the brief stay in the suburbs of New Orleans, the Union camps were full of rumors regarding their destination.[10] Mobile Bay, the most common rumor, was soon confirmed. From the suburbs of New Orleans, the soldiers endured cramped and uncomfortable conditions on board steamers destined for the Union-held forts in south Alabama and northwest Florida. "About noon [on] the 20th, the assembly was sounded, and we 'fell in' and marched to the [Algiers] Wharf. Got on Board the Jennie Rodgers, crossed the River to New Orleans, and layed some time at the R. R. Depot. It was almost night when we got to Lakeport, only 6 miles from the City," recalled Third Sergeant Charles O. Musser, Company A, 29th Iowa Infantry Regiment, in a letter to his father dated February 24, 1865.[11]

Sergeant Musser and the 29th Iowa traveled to the mouth of Mobile Bay on the *Clyde*, a second-class steamer with a low-pressure engine. "Crowded was no name for the way we were stowed into that old tub: 600 men all on one deck. We had about 6 inches' square to the man," Musser wrote his father. "And worst of all was about the time we got settled down, it began to rain." The soldiers crowded on the decks, endured a strong storm, and could enjoy no rest as their boat "rolled and tumbled on the waves." Many of the blue-coated soldiers, suffering from sea sickness, would lean over the ship's railing to vomit.[12] Soldiers on one Gulf steamer were given rations of dried herring. One Union officer remembered, "And those herring—how long afterward did their taste remain—and how few that ate of them, can eat them since!"[13]

Upon arrival at Mobile Bay, the *Clyde* stopped for about an hour at Dauphin Island, then proceeded across the mouth of Mobile Bay to Fort Morgan. Musser estimated 7,000 to 8,000 troops camped at Navy Point and double that amount at Dauphin Island. "Three monitors are lying off the Cove," he wrote, noting the naval presence in Mobile Bay, "and some half dozen men of War, besides about 8 or ten Mosquito Boats, there is about forty sail Vessels at anchor here, and I do not know how many steamers."[14]

Many of the Northern soldiers had never seen the beaches of the Gulf of Mexico. The white quartz sand, varied weather conditions, and surrounding environment were strange to them. "It was on the morning of February 1st that we first caught a sight of the shores of the bay as we were riding at anchor," recalled First Sergeant Thomas B. Marshall of Company K, 83rd Ohio Volunteer Infantry, on seeing the beaches off Pensacola, Florida, for the first time. "Our first thought was if we were now in Ohio we would be shivering around a red-hot stove or shoveling snow out of our paths, and as our eyes fell on the shore and saw the hillocks of white sand, we thought, sure enough it was snow and shivered in sympathy with our imagination."[15]

On February 15, Brigadier General James R. Slack, 1st Brigade, 1st Division of the XIII Corps, arrived at his camp on Dauphin Island. "I got here [Dauphin Island] this morning about 8 o'clock. Was thirty-six hours running from Lakeport here. I got very tired of the trip," Slack wrote his wife. Rough Gulf water conditions slowed the trip. Slack, who managed to avoid seasickness, wrote that the boat ride should have only lasted 12 hours.[16]

Fort Gaines and Fort Morgan

From mid-January to early March 1865, Canby collected more than 45,000 troops at staging camps set up at Dauphin Island, Mobile Point, and Fort Barrancas. Soldiers were constantly arriving, with approximately 32,000 blue-coated soldiers encamped at Mobile Point and Dauphin Island. These consisted of over 13,000 men from Granger's XIII Corps, 16,000 troops from Smith's XVI Corps and 3,000 men consisting of engineers, artillery, and cavalry scouts.[17] Granger's XIII Corps encamped at Mobile Point near Fort Morgan, whereas Smith's XVI Corps camped near Fort Gaines on Dauphin Island. On March 16, a correspondent for the *New York Times* reported: "Dauphin Island and Mobile Point glisten with Federal bayonets."[18] Although camp life on the south Alabama and northwest Florida beaches had its benefits, time spent at Fort Gaines, Fort Morgan, and Fort Barrancas received mixed reviews from the bluecoats.[19]

On March 23, General Thomas K. Smith wrote a letter to his mother describing Dauphin Island:

> A glance at the map will show you the locality of "Dauphin Island" and Fort Gaines, my headquarters for the present. It is just beyond Grant's Pass, at the entrance of Mobile Bay, about twenty-eight miles from the city of Mobile, and about one hundred and eighty miles from New Orleans. The island is not many miles in circumference, and, save on one side, the view from it is only bounded by the horizon, it has little vegetation but pine trees, and the surface is covered with fine, white perfectly clean sand, almost as free from impurities as snow. The beaches are fine, and the music of the surf is always in my earth … the air here is most delicious, and is said to be highly salubrious.[20]

On March 26, Union General Thomas K. Smith wrote a letter to his daughter, who had never seen the Gulf Coast, describing his headquarters on Dauphin Island. "My house is close to the beach, so close, that the spray of the wave sometimes wets my window pane," he wrote. "The last sound that I hear, as I turn to sleep, is the wave on the shore; the first object that greets my eye as I wake in the morning, is the wave dimpling in the calm dawn or throwing up its white caps in the freshening breeze."[21]

Upon his arrival by boat, Andrew F. Sperry, a musician with the 33rd Iowa Volunteer Infantry, noticed a line of piles, extending across the entrance into the bay, that were used by the Confederates to obstruct the U.S. fleet several months before. "Fort Morgan, which, terrible as we supposed it to be," Sperry wrote, "looked like nothing more than a long, low sand-bank mounting one or two guns, we moved on up the bay, and entered the little harbor of Navy Cove, four miles above the extremity of Mobile Point."[22] The newly arrived blue-coated soldiers saw Fort Morgan's "dismantled walls and broken brickwork" from the bombardment sustained at the battle of Mobile Bay seven months earlier.[23] "It is terribly battered up, the bombproof was burned by our shells," Slack wrote to his wife, adding Fort Morgan was a "magnificent structure."[24] Captain Stephen A. Cobb, Commissary of Subsistence of Volunteers, recalled Fort Morgan's appearance: "This magnificent fort, as the old-school warriors styled it, presented a pitiable appearance at that time. Situated at the extremity of Mobile Point, a narrow neck of low land extending out into the gulf, it is exposed on three sides to the wash of the sea … the entire fort was in ruins. Farragut had peppered it into pieces on the side toward the bay."[25]

Most of the Federals under General Canby hailed from the Midwest. The Gulf Coast beaches to many of the Northerners "seemed strange and wild," unlike any place they had ever seen. Sperry described his experience encamped on the beaches at the mouth of Mobile Bay in this excerpt from his 1866 book:

> It was glorious fun for us, while the novelty lasted, to go out and bathe in the surf of the gulf in the hot forenoon; or walk at night along the beach, where every step stirred up showers of phosphorescent sparkles, that looked as though the very sand were latent fire; or to wade for oysters in the shallow pond above the cove, and forget our baked heads and cut and bruised feet, in the tantalizing prospect of fried oysters for supper; or to gather a crowd on the edge of the little swamp, and endeavor to capture an alligator; or to watch the fairy like sailing craft and warlike steamers, as they glided to and fro, so near us. All these were pleasant at first, but the novelty would not last forever. [26]

Dr. Charles B. Johnson of Company F, 130th Illinois Infantry, arrived and encamped at Fort Morgan in early March. He described a sand dune, 20–30 feet high, near the Federal camp, overlooking the bay where the Union soldiers could see Dauphin Island and vessels in the bay. "A school of porpoises could often be seen at play in the waters of the bay," he wrote. "This to the men, nearly all of whom were from the interior, was a novel sight." Despite the novelty of the ocean view, Johnson described the region as "sterile and as uninteresting as could be imagined."[27] General Thomas K. Smith did not share the same opinion as Johnson. "All the day you can watch by its shore and never weary," Smith wrote his daughter.[28] Another benefit of coastal life the soldiers discovered was easy access to fresh water by simply digging a hole a few feet deep in the sand.[29]

Captured at the battle of Mobile Bay on August 23, 1864, Fort Morgan became one of the Union staging camps for the invasion of Alabama. (*Courtesy of* The Library of Congress)

Oysters and Sand

Ignoring their normal government-issued rations, the Northern soldiers enjoyed a plentiful supply of fresh seafood, primarily oysters, during their time on the Gulf

Coast. By wading in the water, the men would gather wagonloads of oysters.[30] "We have nothing to eat but Oysters," wrote Sergeant Musser to his father on February 24, from Mobile Point, "which we can get by the quantity by going about a half a mile around the Cove." He went on to write that the troops collected oysters by the bushel and enjoyed plenty of seafood at little cost, noting he could live well there if he had some money.[31]

Before the occupation of Dauphin Island, several families there made a living fishing and collecting oysters and burning oyster shells into lime. "Oysters and fish of the finest varieties abound and I have every facility for taking them. I have never seen oysters so fat or of so delicate flavor, and I am told that they are good and wholesome every month in the year," General Thomas K. Smith wrote in a letter to his mother. Fortunate to have a cook that specialized in the preparation of oysters, Smith wrote that his diet consisted of oysters and bread all through his time on Dauphin Island.[32]

"We arrived at Ft. Gaines in Mobile Bay yesterday and are at present encamped at Dauphin Island," wrote future Minnesota governor, Colonel Lucius F. Hubbard, 2nd Brigade, 1st Division, XVI Corps, in a March 8 letter to his aunt. "This is not the pleasantest place in the world, though I have seen a great many infinitely worse. The location is not suggestive of a very great degree of comfort, though in some respects it is desirable. The coast along the Gulf and the bay, is one vast oyster bed, hence, we enjoy luxurious living, and all at a very cheap rate."[33]

"The island is composed entirely of sand. Quite a change from a low, wet camping place to one of white dry sand," Private Spink wrote, comparing the conditions on the Alabama beaches with his previous camp at Chalmette. He went on to recall:

> I think without a doubt we enjoyed ourselves, and had as good a time from March 10th to the 20th fishing for oysters and fishing and bathing. We could go out on the sand beach for half a mile when the tide was out. Just picture yourself 15,000 of the boys of '61 and '65 running ahead of the incoming tide, I honestly believe that was the best time we ever had, and I think John Coon will agree with me, as well as many others. It would take at least 75 pages to tell of the good times we had on the Island.[34]

Despite the abundance of fresh seafood and scenic views, some of the soldiers struggled with the monotony of island life. "Very uncertain how long we shall remain here, probably for a month yet. Cannot move until the roads settle. Rained very hard last night, and the night before, and will continue raining here until about the 1st of next month," wrote General Slack of Dauphin Island.[35] Besides collecting oysters, the Northerners passed time playing baseball when the weather permitted. One bluecoat noted, however, that hot and humid weather made even baseball rather dull. Nothing of note only ball playing and that is becoming rather dull on the account of warm weather.[36]

During their stay at the coastal forts, the Union soldiers experienced the Gulf Coast's diverse weather conditions and the annoyance of quartz sand. "There was endless heat above, and restless sand below,—sand, sand, sand in everything. Mouths, noses, ears, and even eyes were filled with it, and victuals were all seasoned with the everlasting and omnipresent nuisance."[37] Conversely, the men also suffered from cold weather during the evening. "Far South as we were now, and advanced as was the season there, we were by no means beyond the reach of cold," remembered Sperry. The temperature at night sometimes became so cold that the men found it impossible to sleep because they shivered so much. "Mobile Point was an episode in our military experience; and if at first, its novelty was pleasing to some, all at last agreed that it was an excellent place to get away from," Sperry concluded.[38]

The soldiers were also frustrated because the Federal government was delinquent in paying them. In a March 7 letter to his father and sister, Musser complained, "No money and no credit on this wilderness of sand. There is some talk of paying us off soon, but that soon is forever coming, and we will move before any Paymaster can accommodate us this time."[39]

Fort Barrancas

Union General Canby was fortunate to have competent and experienced corps commanders. Like Granger and Smith, 46-year-old Major General Frederick Steele was a battle-tested Mexican War veteran who was assigned command of a column from Fort Barrancas on Pensacola Bay. Highly esteemed by his men, he fought at Wilson's Creek, Pea Ridge, Chickasaw Bayou, Arkansas Post on the Arkansas River, Vicksburg, and Camden before reporting to Fort Barrancas.[40] Born in Delhi, New York, Steele went on to graduate from West Point in 1843, where he was classmates with the commander of Mobile's defenses, Dabney H. Maury. At West Point he also became a lifelong friend of the Army's Commanding General, Ulysses S. Grant. In fact, in December 1864, Grant, who described Steele as "an admirable corps commander," asked the Federal army's chief of staff, General Henry W. Halleck, to send him up to command the 9th Corps in Virginia. Steele had already been assigned to the post at Fort Barrancas.[41] Major John F. Lacey, Steele's assistant adjutant general, described him:

> General Steele was a man of striking individuality. He was very social and kept in stock a fund of stories in which he rivaled Lincoln himself. He was small, spare built, wiry, withy and enduring. His eyes were grey and had a snappy way about them that puzzled a stranger. His hair and beard were grizzly. His voice was very peculiar and its shrill, sharp notes always attracted the attention of anyone who met him for the first time.[42]

Approximately 40 miles east of Mobile Point, General Steele collected and organized a force of 13,200 troops at Fort Barrancas. Steele's Column consisted of General C. C. Andrews' division of the XIII Corps (two brigades of 5,200 men), General John P. Hawkins's division (5,500 colored infantry troops) and 2,500 cavalry troopers.[43] Under Steele's direction, the men were kept in a state of readiness through daily inspections, drill, dress parades, guard, and other camp duties.[44] Corporal Michael A. Sweetman, Company C, 114th Ohio Volunteer Infantry, recounted camp life at Fort Barrancas: "The regiment disembarked at Barrancas, and went into camp among the pine trees about one mile from the landing. And here for several weeks Drills, Reviews and Parades kept everyone busy, and camp life was neither dull nor monotonous."[45]

When their daily duties were finished, the Northerners explored the sea shore of Pensacola. Most of the Union soldiers were fascinated by their strange coastal surroundings. "As we had never been on the sea shore before, the boundless ocean so to speak had a strong fascination for a good many of us, and we never became tired of looking at the waters," recalled Sergeant Marshall. "Then, it was a very great pleasure to stroll along the shore, especially when the tide was out, and gather what to us was new and strange forms of life—shells, star-fish, horse-shoe crabs, and all the various forms of life so common in salt water, and so seldom or never seen in the interior where our homes were." Many of the soldiers had the opportunity to explore Fort Pickens, described by Marshall as "a magnificent old fortress." Located across the bay from Fort Barrancas, Fort Pickens was the only fort in the South that had remained under Federal control throughout the conflict.[46]

Naval Reconnaissance

General Canby found a cooperative counterpart in Rear Admiral Henry Thatcher, who commanded the naval squadron in Mobile Bay. A 42-year veteran of the navy, Thatcher had served most of the war with the North Atlantic Blockading Squadron and had participated in the two battles for North Carolina's Fort Fisher. On January 15, 1865, the 59-year-old Thatcher was ordered to take command of the West Gulf Blockading Squadron after the successful capture of Fort Fisher. On February 19, he arrived at Mobile Bay and replaced Commodore James S. Palmer, who had temporarily assumed command when Admiral Farragut was sent home on furlough due to health issues. Palmer felt it was "unfortunate" to be superseded just prior to the invasion. Nonetheless, he vowed to stay on and assist Thatcher with "cheerfulness and zeal." Upon assuming command, Thatcher inherited a large fleet of vessels, including six ironclads, allocated for operations against Mobile. Soon after his arrival he quickly opened communication with Canby and offered his full cooperation toward their shared objective of capturing Mobile.[47]

The Federals believed that General Beauregard had moved Johnston's army east to face Sherman and not much of a force was left to oppose them around Mobile.[48] General Canby for some time had believed the city would fall of its own weight; the Confederates would evacuate it instead of trying to defend a blockaded seaport.[49] To further support his belief, he had received reports that the Southerners were evacuating south Alabama. On March 8, to ascertain the truth, Canby requested that Thatcher conduct a naval reconnaissance in force.[50] The admiral complied,

Union Rear Admiral Henry K. Thatcher was criticized for not ensuring adequate precautions that could have prevented the extensive torpedo damage his fleet sustained in Mobile Bay. (*Courtesy of Naval Heritage and History Command*)

ordering the decks of five light-draft gunboats cleared for action. He assigned Lieutenant Commander G. H. Perkins of the USS *Chickasaw*, an ironclad monitor, the mission to "feel the enemy" and ascertain the number of guns the Southerners had mounted in their batteries.[51]

On Saturday, March 11, Lieutenant Commander Perkins and his fleet proceeded toward the city, near the mouth of Dog River, as close as the shallow waters would permit. The *New York Times* reported that the U.S. Navy "opened their broadsides" when they reached a half-mile from the Confederate shore batteries. The Southerners responded with their heavy guns. During the heavy firing, reportedly lasting nearly three hours, the Unionists sustained only minor damage to one of the torpedo rakes of a Federal monitor. The Federal gunboats damaged some of the Confederate cannons. The Union soldiers clearly heard the cannonading at their camps at Fort Gaines and Fort Morgan nearly 30 miles to the south. The reconnaissance revealed the Confederate soldiers had not evacuated. Perkins found their defenses firmly intact and reported their intent to fight.[52]

Preparations for the Invasion

On February 24, William Wiley, a private with the 77th Illinois, wrote in his diary, "Do not think we will remain long here for the Campaign … There is some talk of us moving across the Bay to Cedar Point and move from there upon the City of Mobile."[53] Wiley and his comrades would have to wait another three weeks as Canby deliberately prepared for the expedition.

Grant was not pleased with Canby's slowness in launching the invasion into Alabama. He had intended the campaign to occupy Southern soldiers there, thus preventing them from reinforcing the forces opposing Sherman's march through Georgia. Canby was unable to launch his expedition in time to serve this purpose. "On the 27th of February, more than a month after Canby had received his orders, I again wrote to him, saying that I was extremely anxious to hear of his being in Alabama," recalled Grant in his memoirs. In the same letter Grant ordered Canby to "destroy railroads, rolling stock, and everything useful for carrying on war." He also warned him of the probable presence of the vaunted General Nathan B. Forrest in the Gulf region, whom he described as "an officer of great courage and capacity," adding he "would be difficult to get by."[54] On March 9, 1865, frustrated with delays, Grant wrote Canby the following scathing message:

> I am in receipt of a dispatch * * *[sic] informing me that you have made requisitions for a construction corps and material to build seventy miles of railroad. I have directed that none be sent. Thomas's army has been depleted to send a force to you that they might be where they could act in winter, and at least detain the force the enemy had in the West. If there had been any idea of repairing railroads, it could have been done much better from the North, where we already had the troops. I expected your movements to be co-operative with Sherman's last. This has now entirely failed. I wrote to you long ago, urging you to push promptly and to live upon the country, and destroy railroads, machine shops, etc., not to build them. Take Mobile and hold it, and push your forces to the interior—to Montgomery and to Selma.[55]

"The preparations for a general movement against Mobile seem to be about completed … We expect to leave here shortly for an offensive movement, but whether it will be directly against the city, or into the interior of Alabama, I am unable to say; but the former seems more probable," wrote Colonel Hubbard to his aunt on March 8.[56] On March 16, the last of A. J. Smith's troops finally left New Orleans for Dauphin Island. A cipher clerk's error had caused some of Smith's men to be landed at Vicksburg, causing an unexpected and unnecessary delay. Inadequate transportation from New Orleans to Dauphin Island further delayed them.[57] The next day, following the arrival of all the soldiers, Grant's impatient prodding, and Thatcher's naval reconnaissance, Canby finally launched the Mobile campaign.[58]

On March 17, the day before the expedition began, a clear and cold day, General Granger's 13th Army Corps received they would start their march at 4 a.m. the next morning. They prepared themselves by placing four days of cooked rations in their haversacks. Additionally, the troops carried 50 rounds of cartridges, two pairs of shoes, knapsack, gun, and rigging. As one soldier remarked, the weight carried was "no laughing matter."[59]

Adjutant Wales W. Wood of the 95th Illinois Regiment wrote:

> Away up the bay, hid among her strongholds, and protected by fortifications, forts and torpedoes, which guarded all avenues of approach, lay the defiant rebel city, which, thus far in the war, had eluded the visitation and grasp of the Union armies. Silently she awaited the bursting of the storm gathering at her doors, and in the stupendous preparations culminating around her, was conscious of a fate similar to that which had befallen sister cities, one by one, all along the Atlantic coast.[60]

The Northern soldiers were optimistic about the prospects of the campaign. "If our arms meet with no reverse during the pending campaigns, I shall hope to see the war ended with the present year. The army prays for such a consummation, as earnestly as our friends at home," wrote Hubbard.[61]

On February 14, a report in the *Philadelphia Inquirer* alleged the inhabitants of Mobile "are nearly all in favor of surrendering the city."[62] On March 21, the *Cleveland Daily Leader* published a report from a female evacuee from Mobile stating "there was every indication that the city would be evacuated." Such newspaper reports misled some Union soldiers to believe that the Confederates would simply abandon the city and fall back to Selma once they appeared.[63] They would soon learn that the small force defending Mobile had no intention of giving up without a fight.

CHAPTER FOUR

The Advance Commences

Prior to the Mobile campaign, General Canby gathered intelligence reports from a variety of sources on the city's defenses. Union General William T. Sherman, who was once stationed at Fort Morgan earlier in his career, was familiar with the Mobile Bay area. On August 17, 1864, Sherman found time to write General Canby even though he was busy leading the attack of Atlanta. In the letter, he suggested Canby take his forces up the eastern shore.[1]

Canby also received intelligence reports from Confederate deserters that advised him of Mobile's defenses. Captain George W. Mader, a recent deserter who had served as a Confederate engineer in Mobile, turned himself into the Federals. He told the Yankees the most efficient way to capture Mobile was to "take Spanish Fort, Batteries Huger and Tracy, first." He gave them detailed descriptions of Mobile's defenses and reiterated earlier claims that the city was the best fortified place in the Confederacy. Contradicting other reports, Mader stated that the Secessionists had not evacuated and planned to hold the place.[2]

An astute and cautious officer, Canby believed the city's defensive lines were too strong to be attacked successfully from the west. Even without Sherman's advice and the intelligence reports, he probably would have decided against assaulting Mobile's immense western fortifications. He chose to move first against Fort Blakeley and Spanish Fort, both in Baldwin County.[3] His plan was to capture the two forts located on the northeastern shore of the bay and obtain access to the waterways leading to Mobile, thus flanking the extensive fortifications of the western defenses.[4]

Canby's grand tactics entailed a three-pronged attack. His soldiers, however, would have to endure miserable conditions on their march north to Spanish Fort.[5] The XIII and XVI Corps would take different routes in their advance north into Baldwin County on the east side of Mobile Bay, moving against the Confederate strongholds of Spanish Fort and Fort Blakeley. Steele's Column from Fort Barrancas would march north, giving the appearance of heading toward Montgomery, cut the railroad at Pollard, Alabama, and then turn west to attack Fort Blakeley.[6]

Meanwhile, a large Federal cavalry force from the Army of the Cumberland, under General James H. Wilson, would move from the north against Montgomery and

Selma, occupying General Nathan B. Forrest's mounted troopers. This theater strategy was intended to be simultaneous, to prevent the Confederates from concentrating their forces against Canby. On March 17, 1865, St. Patrick's Day, after a few weeks of encampment at Dauphin Island and Mobile Point, 32,000 blue-coated soldiers advanced to the eastern shore of Mobile Bay, thus launching the invasion into Baldwin County.[7]

The March of the XIII Corps to Fish River

The movement of Canby's two corps toward Spanish Fort and Fort Blakeley was an arduous ordeal.[8] Granger's XIII Corps endured the hardest part of the movement. Constant rain and swampy road conditions slowed the initial phase of their advance. His men traveled east from Navy Cove on Mobile Point Peninsula and then moved in a northern direction. For seven difficult days, March 17–23, the XIII Corps marched nearly 45 miles through swamps and on bad roads to join the XVI Corps at the predetermined location on Fish River. The designated rendezvous point was Dannelly's Mill, approximately 19 miles south of Spanish Fort, in an area known today as Marlow's Ferry.[9]

On March 17, Private Wiley wrote in his diary, "Reveille at 3 AM. Marched at 4, marched 15 miles and camp for the night. Some eastern troops was just in advance of us. They had started in heavy marching order." Due to the massive size of the Union movement, all the regiments could not move out at the same time or cover the same distance. "It was almost noon before our forces got on the route," Musser wrote his father of the first day's march, and "we did not march over 12 miles this day. The roads [were] very bad: Sand Banks and Swamps continually. Camp No 1 [was] on the bayside and within hearing of the Breakers. The Country is covered with Scrubby Pine and Live Oak."[10]

The Union soldiers marched in an eastward direction during the initial portion of the movement. Musser wrote:

> We struck tents early next morning [March 18th]. Our regiment was the Vanguard of the Division. Roads getting worse and worse fast. We have been Traveling almost an easterly course since we started, sometimes a little south of east. We halted at noon for dinner at an old rebel Camp … 9 miles from Camp No 1. Forward is sounded soon, and again we move on. 5 miles farther and we pitch Tents on Camp no 2. The country presents almost the same appearance as the first days march: the timber a little heavier and all Pine.[11]

One Northern soldier recalled each man carried "one change of underclothing; namely, one shirt, one pair drawers, one pr socks, and one Woolen Blanket, one Rubber Blanket, an extra pr shoes, and one half of a shelter Tent," made even more uncomfortable when they got wet. They also carried "4 days rations in their haversacks, 50 rounds of Cartridges and for every 12 men, one ax, and one shovel or spade. Just think of that load," wrote Musser. When it was not raining, the days became uncomfortably hot, usually by noon, causing many soldiers to discard their extra blankets and clothes, littering the roadsides for many miles. Each night they stopped and fortified their position with a line of timber breastworks.[12]

Lieutenant Charles J. Allen, chief engineer for the XVI Corps, and a group of mounted soldiers selected from the 4th Wisconsin Cavalry under Captain Warren P. Knowles, known as "Knowles Scouts," had left on a reconnaissance mission to Fish River in advance of the XIII Corps. On Allen's return to Fort Morgan, he came across Granger and the XIII Corps on their march to Dannelly's Mill. He shared intelligence with Granger on the road conditions to the rendezvous point: "I informed him as to the character of the country and the liability of the roads—good when dry—to become impassable after heavy rain." Allen, who was brevetted the rank of captain, was recognized in General A. J. Smith's official report for his "judgment, ability and industry" and for performing "his duty excellently well."[13]

In some locations, Federal soldiers had to wade through swamps. One soldier recalled: "The whole division formed in columns closed in mass; and at the word all proceeded to roll up their pants and prepare to wade. Wade it had to be, for there was no other way of crossing."[14] Sometimes they were forced to haul artillery and wagons 50 yards by hand through mud and water. On March 19, the XIII Corps crossed Shell Bayou, which was nearly 3 feet deep and about 75 yards wide.[15] After marching 16 miles and crossing the bayou, Brigadier General Elias Dennis of 2nd Brigade, 1st Division, reported that the troops stopped and went into camp where they made coffee and dinner.[16]

Though Baldwin County was sparsely populated at the time, the Union soldiers did encounter some inhabitants during the march. Sperry recalled the following encounter on the second day of the march:

> An old negro woman, apparently half crazed with joy at the sight of the Union army she and hundreds of the race, companions in suffering, had so long prayed for, was standing near the road as the column passed her, shouting, dancing, crying and laughing, almost hysterically, in the vain effort to express her overflowing feelings, "Glory, Hallelujah!" she shouted; "Glory Hallelujah! The Lord's done heard us! Glory! Glory! There's eight thousand of us praying for you at Mobile! Go on! Go On! Glory Hallelujah!" Then the poor creature would dance, and shout and sing, cry and laugh, all at once, while the tears coursed down her worn and wrinkled cheeks as she beheld the army which to so great a portion of her race seemed the harbinger of jubilee, and almost as the coming of the Lord.[17]

On March 19, Sergeant Charles O. Musser and the 29th Iowa served as the rear guard. He described making corduroy roads in a March 24 letter to his father. "Pioneer Corps, and in fact the whole forces had to," wrote Musser, "make the roads Corduroy. This day, we build over one mile of that kind of road through a swamp. Most of the Train crosses. We move about ½ mile and form Camp No. 3."[18]

On March 20, a strong thunderstorm and hard rain swept away bridges, overflowed rivers, and turned the whole region into a massive swamp.[19] Private John W. Fry of the 42nd Company, 96th Ohio, described the roads from Fort Morgan to Spanish Fort as "nothing more than a quagmire." Wagons and artillery often sank to their axles.[20] Pioneer corps, assisted by Granger's entire force, made the roads passable by making them corduroy. One day they built over one mile of corduroy roads through a swamp for the wagon trains to cross.[21] "We went to building a corduroy road through the swamp to get our trains and artillery over," Private Wiley wrote in his diary. "Not finding any rails handy we went to cutting down the pine trees and splitting the sections in halves and laying them side by side. In this way we made two or three miles of road and got our trains over."[22] The time spent corduroying the roads significantly slowed the progress of the Federals.

Sperry recalled one camp site on route to Fish River "pitched in the midst of the endless forest of tall, straight, almost branchless pines. The ground was flat, smooth, clean and dry and the camp would have been an excellent one if only wood and water had been near." The Unionists used pine knots, quite plentiful in the area, as firewood, although they excessively smoked their food.[23]

On March 20, the Northern soldiers marched approximately 5 miles. "Across the road in one or two places lay the ugly carcasses of alligators," recalled Sperry, "which some of the advance party had killed and left there; and it was by no means nice to speculate upon the probability of having such an ungainly 'insect' some night as a bed fellow."[24] That evening the troops endured another hard rain.[25]

On March 21, Granger's troops changed direction and began marching north, covering only about 4 miles due to poor weather and road conditions. The men had to endure miserable conditions. "Today was one day that we will never forget. the [sic] rain poured down in torrents. The whole country almost flooded," wrote Musser. "About 1 p.m. it stopped raining, and we came to a halt to help the Artillery and Wagons through the now almost impassable swamps." In water and mud waist deep, Granger's men "unhitched the Horses and hitched the Prolong of Manropes and about 100 men per cannon." On some portions of the road, artillery pieces were hauled 200 yards until firm ground was reached and they could rehitch to the horses. "One may judge how the roads is [sic] where 8 large Horses can't move a 12 Pounder Napolean [sic] gun," Musser wrote. After the ordeal was over for the day, he recounted how the muddied and wet men built "large fires of Pine Knots" and "stood in the smoke until we were more like contrabands than white men."[26]

Sergeant Musser claimed the roads were the worst he'd ever seen an army march through. "The ground in most places seems firm," he wrote, "but as soon as half dozen teams goes over it, down they go to axels, and then it's 'halt,' 'front,' 'Stack Arms, Boys and help those team out of the mud.'" The work was hard; however, he claimed the men did not grumble. "I never saw as lively and light hearted an army since [we] came south, they all seem in the best of spirits and care not what comes. they [sic] are prepared to meet anything," he wrote. Musser estimated they had corduroyed up to 10 miles of road at that point in the expedition.[27]

On March 22, as they slowly moved north, the XIII Corps heard heavy cannon fire from gunboats further up the bay. The gunboats were shelling the woods where roving Confederate soldiers had been seen. At the same time, the XVI Corps was landing at the mouth of Dannelly's Mill.[28]

"It was clear and warm. The roads were fair. That day we were marching through the pine timber where the trees had been barked on the southside to get the pitch to make rosin. A fire got started in the timber and pitch and nearly strangled us but we had to go through it choke or no choke," Private Wiley recorded on March 23 in his diary.[29]

Around midday, the XIII Corps began reaching Fish River, where they found some gunboats at anchor. After a rest and meal, the 29th Iowa, around 2:30 p.m., crossed a wooden pontoon bridge over the river, laid earlier by the XVI Corps. According to Sperry, General William P. Benton ordered the bands of his division to play "Out of the Wilderness" as they crossed the bridge and united with Smith's XVI Corps on the north side of Fish River. Despite the arduous conditions they had just suffered through, the resilient men still felt confident. "We were now part of the largest army which we had ever been," recalled Sperry, adding that they felt invulnerable.[30]

Dannelly's Mill

General A. J. Smith's XVI Corps was spared the tiring march to the rendezvous point at Dannelly's Mill. Instead, on March 19 through 21, Smith's Guerrillas embarked from Dauphin Island on a flotilla of steamers and light-draft gunboats across Mobile Bay to Week's Bay, located on the eastern shore.[31] Once in Week's Bay, the Federal transports headed to the Dannelly's Mill rendezvous point located on the right bank of Fish River, about 17 miles above its junction with Mobile Bay. The Federal soldiers found Fish River to be "a very deep and narrow, as well as a very crooked stream." Gunboats accompanied the transports and shelled the woods from Point Clear to Blakeley River bar to cover the troop landing at Dannelly's Mill. Private Spink remembered "large eagle nests in the trees, some as large as a cart wheel, and the great number of eagles, and colored people by the hundreds, and all glad to see the Yankee soldiers."[32] Landing unopposed, the XVI Corps immediately went to work. They set up camp, threw up breastworks, built bridges over many streams for the passage of artillery, and maintained communication with the gunboats offshore.[33]

"From Dauphin Island we went up the [Mobile] Bay to Fish River & up the river to a place called Donnelleys Mill [sic]," recalled Lieutenant James K. Newton of Company F, 14th Wisconsin Volunteer Infantry, and "from there we marched round to this place & I think we took them somewhat by surprise. They expected us up by the other side of the Bay & in fact there was a Brigade sent to effect a landing at Dog River, but it was only a feint to cover our real purpose."[34] Once in camp

Harper's Weekly depiction of Union troops landing at Fish River. (*Courtesy of* Michael D. Shipler)

at Dannelly's Mill, the men of the XVI Corps were ordered to throw up defensive works and wait for the arrival of the XIII Corps. The feint Newton mentioned, across the bay in Mobile County, was carried out by the brigade of Colonel Jonathon B. Moore from Cedar Point to Fowl River.[35]

Feint at Cedar Point

On March 18, Canby sent the 1st Brigade of the 3rd Division of the XVI Corps, led by Colonel Jonathon B. Moore, on a diversionary demonstration from Dauphin Island to south Mobile County in the direction of Fowl River. This feint was intended to distract the Southerners and conceal the real landing and movement on the eastern shore.[36]

At noon, the navy ferried Moore's Brigade, approximately 2,000 men from the 95th and 72nd Illinois, 44th Missouri, and 33rd Wisconsin, on the vessels *Swain*, *Groesbeck*, and *Mustang* on a short trip to Cedar Point which was in plain sight of Dauphin Island. The tinclads numbers 44 and 47 shelled the woods before the troops disembarked, driving off about 20 mounted Confederates.[37] "The force sent over to Cedar Point landed without opposition," Adjutant Wood noted after the war, "though on our approach mounted men seen hastening away in the direction of Mobile." The Southern horsemen Wood observed were lookouts monitoring the movements of the Federal army.[38]

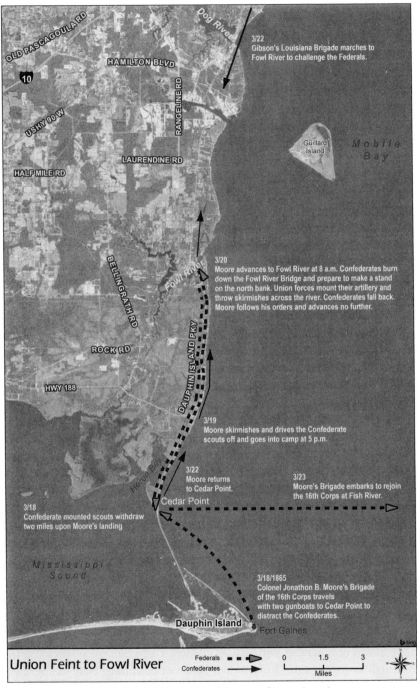

Union Feint to Fowl River (*Courtesy of* Kevin Stoots)

The Federals landed on a long narrow wharf, near the remnants of Fort Powell, which was evacuated by the Southerners during the August 1864 battle.[39] "On reaching the end of the wharf it was discovered that the planking had been torn up for a few yards, which would thus compel the men to jump a foot or two on the sand below," reported the *Philadelphia Inquirer.* Anticipating an invasion at this location, Confederate soldiers hid several large torpedoes for their unwelcome guests. Fortunately for the Northerners, an officer of the 72nd Illinois, the first regiment to disembark, discovered a partially buried land mine where the planking had been torn up. The blue-coated soldiers soon found five torpedoes in the vicinity before a tragedy occurred.[40]

"Landed on the mainland at Cedar Point where we are camped. I am on picket," Private Edward Q. Nye, Company G, 72nd Illinois, recorded in his diary on March 18. The Northern soldiers set up camp at an abandoned graycoat encampment. Many of the soldiers waded in the water collecting large amounts of oysters, which they brought back to this camp. "We got oysters by the arm load by wading into the water a short ways," wrote Private Nye.[41] He also observed the unusual appearance of the two forts and breastworks which were made entirely of oyster shells and reported to be a half-mile in length.[42]

Although the Union soldiers avoided the Confederate torpedoes, they did not escape the persistent and agonizing assault of mosquitoes. Nye wrote in his journal, "The mosquitoes are out in force. I never saw anything like it. They sting like bees. Shoe leather does not impede them in the least from boring your toes." The Federal soldiers had encountered mosquitoes during previous campaigns, but they were unprepared for the size and relentless nature of the Cedar Point insects.[43] "Oysters and mosquitoes seemed to be the chief products of the locality, and the abundance and luxury of the one were equaled only by the multitudes and inflictions of the other," Wood wrote. "While the soldiers were satisfying their keen appetites the mosquitoes were busy satisfying theirs as to soldiers; and while the boys in blue were feasting upon and filling themselves with, the delectable food, these pestiferous insects were being filled with the blood of the intruding Yankees," Wood continued.[44] The mosquitoes were relentless. Private Nye wrote in his March 19 diary entry: "Very pleasant day and one to be enjoyed but for the infernal mosquitoes, who seem bound to have their fill of Yankee blood which luxury they have not been able to procure until lately."[45]

Perhaps the most interesting soldier of Moore's Brigade was Private Albert Cashier, 95th Illinois, Company G. Cashier fought in numerous battles and skirmishes but what made him truly unique was the fact that he was a she. Jennie I. Hodgers successfully hid her identity throughout the war.[46]

Before the march to Fowl River began, Moore instructed his brigade to make as much noise as possible to deceive the Confederates into believing the Union attack was coming from that direction.[47] That afternoon, the brigade broke camp and marched north 9 miles in a line of battle. As they advanced, every 15th man carried an axe and shovel to throw up defensive breastworks. Additionally, the brigade was supported by a considerable shelling from the gunboats as they skirmished with the gray-coated soldiers in their front.[48] On the march, the bluecoats found a Southern trooper and his horse lying near each other "both dead, killed by one of the shells."[49]

"The march was continued until dusk, when the regiments camped in line of battle, in the thick pine woods several miles from Cedar Point," recalled Wood. To further his feint objective, Colonel Moore's brigade utilized deception. "Orders were here issued for the regimental bands to beat three tattoos each that evening," Wood wrote, "as well as a corresponding number of reveilles on the following morning, varying the tunes each time, in order to accomplish the deception intended. If this piece of strategy availed anything it must have convinced the enemy that a large force of twelve regiments was approaching Mobile, whereas there were only four." The band of the 44th Missouri had only recently been formed and was composed of "unskilled" musicians. "If you listened to them once you could afterward easily detect them among a thousand well-trained bands," Wood remembered. The Yankee band's noticeably poor performance may have unwittingly revealed the real intention of Moore's expedition. Wood recounted:

> At the hour designated for beating tattoo all the regiments played it through once, the musicians of the 44th performing it in their characteristic style. The second and third times the tunes were varied by the other regiments and one would have supposed that there were really so many more regiments in the Federal encampment. When, however, the 44th struck up its second tattoo and attempted by continued musical demonstrations to represent another regiment, the failure was complete and the boys throughout the different camps, unable to restrain themselves, burst forth in snouts of irrepressible laughter making the woods ring for a long distance around.[50]

The Northerners marched several miles north before stopping at dusk. The regiments then camped in line of battle in the thick pine woods.[51]

On March 20, the intelligence of the Union movement from Cedar Point reached the Southern soldiers encamped in the suburbs of Mobile. "It was reported [the Federals] were landing in force at Cedar Point some thirty miles below here," Chambers wrote in his journal on Sunday, March 21, "and Gibson's Louisiana brigade was sent in that direction yesterday [March 20] afternoon. Later reports say it is only a cavalry force that is debarking at Cedar Point."[52]

Brigadier General Randall L. Gibson of Louisiana, 33 years old, commanded Gibson's Louisiana Brigade. A lawyer before the conflict, he graduated from Yale in 1853, then attended law school at Louisiana University (which later became Tulane University) in New Orleans. He was a veteran of Shiloh, Chickamauga, Atlanta, Franklin, and Nashville.[53]

"Marched out about 2 miles this morning and laid there until noon," wrote Nye in his diary on March 20. "Skirmishing pretty near all the time. Got back to the edge of the timber (near) the point. Tonight we are camped in the woods."[54] On the same date, Lieutenant Colonel Joseph Stockton of the 72nd Illinois recorded in his diary: "Marched about three miles. Skirmishing very hard, but the enemy kept falling back. We gave them every chance for a fight, but think they had not force enough. Reached a small stream called Fowl River and halted. One of the heaviest rainstorms I ever experienced came up. All got soaking wet."[55]

On March 21, Moore's Brigade remained in camp all day due to the hard rain.[56] A Confederate scout report described the advancing Union soldiers as a small cavalry force.[57] Apparently recognizing the Federal advance to Fowl River was a feint, the Louisiana Brigade returned to camp in the afternoon.[58]

On the afternoon of March 22, with their diversionary movement completed, Moore's men returned to Cedar Point where they embarked on gunboats to rejoin the XVI Corps across the bay at Fish River. "Marched down to the landing this morning. Laid there until the tide rose in the evening when we got on transports and are now on our way towards the River. Very fine day. Heavy cannonading all day over in direction we are going. Gunboats shelling Rebs I guess," Nye recorded in his March 22 diary entry.[59]

Moore's Brigade anchored near the mouth of Fish River where they enjoyed a great feast of oysters. On the morning of March 23, they debarked and went into a camp a half-mile from Fish River. The *Mobile Evening Telegraph* reported that the Federal soldiers had left the locality—whither is not known.[60] On the same day, elements of Granger's XIII Corps also began to reach the rendezvous point.

Military Orders and Circulars

By March 22, the Confederates, understanding the strategic significance of Mobile's river and rail access, were aware of General Canby's tactical intentions. Realizing the fate of Mobile would be decided on the eastern shore, at Spanish Fort and Fort Blakeley, General Liddell sent the following ominous early morning message to Maury's chief of staff, Colonel George G. Garner:

> I now think there can be no longer any doubt upon the subject. It is sad to think of the desolation that will follow the traces of these devastating columns of Yankees. I have nothing late from the force coming by Fish River. I can only conjecture that if sufficiently large it will attempt to get possession of Spanish Fort for a base whence occupation can be given to the fleet in the bay. In carrying through the movement on Selma the use of the Alabama River is of the utmost importance to the enemy, hence I don't think we will be permitted to remain in quiet long.[61]

Liddell's telegraph indicates his understanding of Canby's intentions and the importance of defending their position. "I have no longer any doubt that the enemy is in strong force at Dannelly's Mills," he wrote in a subsequent message to Colonel Garner on the same day, "and will probably move up some distance tomorrow. Colonel Spence informs me that his enemy's pickets are at Cowpen Branch about two miles this side." Realizing the Yankee juggernaut was heading his direction, Liddell demanded labor on the incomplete fortifications at Spanish Fort and Fort Blakeley before the arrival of the enemy.[62] He also requested reinforcements "come at once, that every preparation for defense may be completed in time to receive the enemy."[63] Maury responded promptly by sending him reinforcements, approximately 4,000 men.[64]

Depredations at Fish River

The few inhabitants of south Baldwin County were subjected to harassment by foraging Northern soldiers. On March 23, the *Mobile Evening Telegraph* reported depredations committed by the Union soldiers on citizens near Fish River. The newspaper reported:

> They visited every house in the neighborhood, robbed the families of everything valuable, killed all the stock, and did all the damage they could. Their conduct towards the poor helpless families is said to be cruel. They destroyed the women's and children's dresses—even took the bonnet from one lady's head, and tore it up—searched her husband and made him take off his socks. The family that came over was robbed of everything except the clothes they had on them. Their house was burned by the brutes.

The *Evening Telegraph* source was Baldwin County resident Antonia Boyce. She reported that on Tuesday, March 21, a squad of 40 to 50 Union soldiers went to her house "in a blustering and insulting manner and commenced destroying everything on the premises." She said the blue-coated soldiers, composed mostly of Dutch and Irish men, destroyed her furniture, bed, and dresses by cutting them up. Despite begging them to spare her children's clothing, they "laughed heartily" as they cut up the apparel. The newspaper reported: "One man, when she appealed to him, remarked, 'I know its hard, madam, but it is our orders to destroy every rebel family in the country,' and they continued the job, even scattered the pins, needles, hooks and eyes, over the floor and broke even a vial of paragoris." Federal soldiers shot Boyce's horse, two cows, all their chickens, and took her husband to an outhouse and stripped him. She claimed the soldiers had planned to take them to Fort Morgan before they managed to escape. They hid in the woods before walking several miles north to Spanish Fort where the Confederate soldiers treated them kindly. Mrs. Boyce said that every family on Fish River received similar treatment before the Northern soldiers burned down their houses.[65]

For months, in anticipation of an impending attack, Maury had issued numerous orders and circulars in Mobile newspapers. Unfortunately, the threat of an impending attack was reported so often that many had grown indifferent. Maury "has by some been irreverently dubbed the Lord of Panic," wrote Lieutenant Colonel James M. Williams of the 21st Alabama in a letter to his wife.[66] Confederate Lieutenant Robert Tarleton, who was stationed in Mobile, wrote his wife, "Our city is not at all changed in appearance—the band plays in the square as usual and to judge from the display of such festive occasions, you would never suppose it is in a state of siege, although Gen'l Maury says so."[67] Even though compelling reports indicated a Federal expedition was imminent, Maury's latest orders were perceived as another false alarm by some. The following notice appeared in the local newspapers and was eventually copied and published around the country:

> Headquarters District of the Gulf, Mobile, Alabama, March 3, 1865
> Circular.
> From indications at Pensacola, and in the lower bay, it is believed that the enemy will make an early and heavy attack upon Mobile.
> As soon as the enemy effects a landing, with a view of operations against the city, the commanders of the artillery forces occupying the redoubts will cause houses, fences, trees, and other objects that may interfere with the range and effect of their fire, to be destroyed or removed.
> Persons residing beyond the defenses, and within cannon range of them, are advised to make speedy preparations for removing, with their effects, to places of safety.
> During an attack upon the city, all persons within its limits will be greatly exposed to the enemy's fire, and extreme distress may be occasioned among non-combatants, in a protracted siege, by scarcity of provisions.
> It is, therefore, urged upon all non-combatants who can go away to do so, and upon those who are compelled to remain, to lay in as large stores of food as possible.
> By Command of Major General Dabney H. Maury[68]

Maury knew from Liddell's dependable reports that the massive Federal invasion was moving up the eastern shore toward Spanish Fort.[69] As reliable accounts of the Union advance continued to come in, the editor of the *Mobile Telegraph* urged citizens to help in the coming siege: "Every man fit to carry arms must make up his mind to the necessity of carrying them." The *Telegraph* editorial emphasized the need for obeying orders from the military leaders and advised anyone not able to fight, such as women and children, to evacuate.[70]

On March 23, the *Mobile Telegraph* reported, "The city of Mobile is declared in a state of siege. Commanding Officers will see that all persons arrested by the Military authorities are held in custody until released by the same authority." All persons were prohibited from passing the Confederate lines toward the Federal army to stop desertions.[71] All drinking establishments were closed in the city to avoid unnecessary disturbances.[72] "All men capable of bearing arms are required to attach themselves to some organization for local defence [sic], immediately, or else, on failure to do so, will be considered a non-combatant, and forced to leave the city." All the stores in the city closed at 3 p.m. to give the employees, who doubled as a local defense force, time for military drill.[73] Slave owners were given notice to remove their slaves from Mobile. The military authority enrolled slaves between the ages of 18 and 45 years of age, who were not removed, as laborers around the city's fortifications.[74]

Execution of Deserters

Most Confederate soldiers had no intention of giving up without a fight. Still, there were some who chose to abandon their comrades. No sympathy for deserters was given, especially those that attempted to go to the enemy. The Southerners enforced a policy of strict military discipline until the last days of the conflict. On Tuesday,

March 14, a rainy day, they carried out a military execution of a deserter. "We had a military execution," wrote Colonel Williams to his wife Lizzy. "I had charge of it and commanded the brigade which was ordered out to witness it—the particulars I omit as I have no doubt that they would not interest you as much as they do some people—Two more will be shot here during the next week or ten days—they are deserters from my regiment [21st Alabama]."[75] On March 31, the "two more" Williams mentioned were executed at Fort Blakeley, a day before the siege of that place began.[76]

CHAPTER FIVE

At Last the Enemy were in Sight

Upon receiving confirmation of the Union advance in Baldwin County, General Maury sent General Liddell reinforcements. On March 23, the same day the XIII and XVI Corps united at Dannelly's Mill, General Randall L. Gibson's Louisiana Brigade was ordered to report to Liddell at Blakeley. As Gibson's command marched past Mobile's Battle House Hotel toward their transport boats, the smiling faces of vending girls greeted them, and they gave them apples and peanuts.[1] Once they arrived to the eastern shore, Liddell quickly directed Gibson to move south toward Deer Park, near Fish River, with two regiments of Holtzclaw's Brigade, under Colonel Bush Jones, and the 12th Regiment of Mississippi Cavalry, to observe the enemy's movements.[2] Not yet fully aware of how badly they were outnumbered, Liddell's command, particularly the contingent of horsemen under the gallant Lieutenant Colonel Philip B. Spence, did their best to obstruct the advance of the much larger Union force at their front.

On March 24, Maury sent French's Division, led by 40-year-old Brigadier General Francis M. Cockrell, to Fort Blakeley. Cockrell's troops prepared three days' rations and then went across Mobile Bay at 3 p.m.[3]

Liddell recalled his confidence in Cockrell's Missouri troops: "I was fully satisfied that this small force should not be demoralized by defeat in the field against such odds."[4] Liddell's faith in Cockrell's Missourians was well justified. They were veteran soldiers who had fought in all the major battles of the west.[5]

Cockrell maintained strict discipline and was known to drill his men up to four hours a day. In fact, President Jefferson Davis, after observing them in October 1863, proclaimed the Missourians the best-drilled brigade he had ever seen. In a drill competition judged by General Maury and General William J. Hardee in Mobile on January 8, 1864, Cockrell's men won over soldiers from Alabama, Mississippi, Tennessee, and Texas. The ladies of Mobile presented Cockrell's Missouri Brigade the prize of a handmade silk Confederate flag.[6]

Every member of Cockrell's Brigade, "from the general to the drummer boy," shared the grim distinction of having been wounded in battle, some many times,

CSA Brigadier General Francis M. Cockrell commanded the battle-hardened Missouri Brigade at Fort Blakeley. (*Courtesy of* Alabama Department of Archives and History)

yet they continued to fight. They were battle-hardened veterans of Iuka, Corinth, Hatchie Bridge, Fort Gibson, Vicksburg, Cassville, New Hope Church, Kennesaw Mountain, Chattanooga, Peachtree Creek, Atlanta, Ezra Church, and Hood's disastrous Tennessee campaign. Private Phillip D. Stephenson recalled a remarkable encounter on his train ride to Mobile with one member of Cockrell's Brigade, Corporal Edward "Ned" J. Stiles, Company E of the 1st Missouri Dismounted Cavalry. Stiles had been left for dead at the battle of Allatoona but was found by Union soldiers who nursed him. He had been exchanged and was heading back to Mobile to rejoin Cockrell's Brigade. Stephenson was horrified to see the pitiful condition of Stiles; he could hardly recognize him. "A skeleton he was, with the ashen hue of death upon him," remembered Stephenson. His clothes resembled dirty rags and he could hardly stand up. Though his wounds had barely healed, Stiles was still going to Mobile.[7]

General Cockrell had been wounded on numerous occasions and had narrowly survived many close calls during the war. At Vicksburg, he was blown up in the air by a Union mine placed under the Confederate works. At Kennesaw Mountain, Cockrell was reading a dispatch when a shell exploded near him. A piece of the shell hit him, breaking several fingers on both hands. Knowing one of his fingers would be stiff for the rest of his life, he insisted the field surgeon set the broken finger in a crescent shape so that it fit his sword handle, an apple, and a pen. He was severely wounded at Franklin and unable to lead his men at Nashville.[8]

His second-in-command, Colonel Elijah Gates, whom General Sterling Price reportedly called the bravest man he had ever known, was wounded five times during the war and had lost his arm at Franklin. Cockrell and Gates were still healing from their wounds when they rejoined French's Division en route to Mobile in early February.[9]

The short trip from Mobile across the delta to Fort Blakeley was full of unfortunate mishaps.

On March 25, Sergeant William P. Chambers recorded in his journal:

> We left the camp about 4 o'clock p.m. yesterday [Friday, March 24] and proceeded to the city (Mobile). Embarking on the *Magnolia* at about 8 o'clock p.m., we were landed at Blakely [sic] about midnight. As we neared the landing at Blakely a soldier of Cockrell's brigade, while in a state of intoxication, fell overboard and was drowned. An hour or two later two boats collided on the river and one of them was instantly sunk. It was laden with Q. M. and commissary stores principally for our brigade. It is said several lives were also lost. The collision was the result of sheer carelessness it would seem, for it was a beautiful starlight night and the boats could easily be seen for several hundred yards.[10]

After arriving at Spanish Fort on the eastern shore of Baldwin County, Private Stephenson, sensing the great odds they were up against, assessed the situation. "We felt ourselves to be in a trap as soon as we took in the situation. Tony Barrow and I sat on the parapet one afternoon soon after getting there and planned a way to escape for ourselves," Stephenson recalled. They looked out on the Mobile delta and noticed a chain of islands in the marsh that led north toward Fort Blakeley. In the event of an assault, they planned to use those islands to escape by swimming between them until reaching Blakeley. What Stephenson did not know was his commanding officers were already preparing a hidden escape route through the marshes along the same route.[11]

The 16th Confederate Cavalry/12th Regiment Mississippi Cavalry

The only force contesting Canby's massive advance was about 500 troopers belonging to the 16th Confederate Cavalry, also known as the 12th Regiment Mississippi Cavalry, part of Colonel Charles G. Armistead's Cavalry Brigade. The Confederate Secretary of War issued Special Orders 69 on March 24 that constituted the 10 companies under Colonel Armistead as the 12th Regiment Mississippi Cavalry.[12] A few troopers from Mobile and Baldwin County, members of the 15th Confederate Cavalry, were detailed to assist them as guides and scouts because of their firsthand knowledge of the area. Although vastly outnumbered, these horsemen actively scouted and harassed the advancing blue-coated soldiers.[13]

Lieutenant Colonel Philip B. Spence, a 29-year-old Princeton-educated native of Davidson County, Tennessee, led the cavalry opposing Canby's force. Before the secession of Tennessee, he crossed the state line to Alabama to join the Confederate army. Prior to assuming command of 12th Mississippi, Spence took part in the battles of Chickamauga, Belmont, Perryville, Shiloh, Corinth, Murfreesboro, and the Atlanta campaign. He also served on the staff of General Leonidas Polk until after the battle of Chickamauga.[14]

The advance of the Federal army presented many challenges to the small cavalry regiment opposing them. Prior to the Yankee advance, Spence's men enjoyed abundant rations of freshly caught seafood from the bay. "During our short service on the bay, after leaving Gen. Sherman's front in Georgia, we had commenced thinking that to be a Confederate soldier with oysters and fish for rations was not a hard life after all, and we greatly enjoyed the change from the scanty supply we received while in front of Gen. Sherman in North Alabama and Georgia," remembered Spence.[15]

Unfortunately, Union navy gunners soon ended the Confederate cavalry seafood banquet. Admiral Thatcher's gunboats shelled the woods from Point Clear to Blakeley River Bar to clear the coast of Southern soldiers. Although the gunboats did not cause much damage, they succeeded in preventing Spence's men from feasting on freshly caught seafood. "We were not long permitted to enjoy a luxurious living, as the United States navy shelled my commissary squads whenever they appeared upon the shore," continued Spence. "An old soldier would take hazardous chances to get something good to eat, and fishing was first class," added Spence, "but the heavy guns of the United States navy were more than we could stand, so we had to go back to corn bread and sorghum."[16]

USS *Milwaukee* (*Courtesy of* Naval Heritage and History Command)

Granger's men encountered "not more than 50 rebels altogether" during the march from Fort Morgan to Dannelly's Mill.[17] After March 24 the Federal soldiers began to meet fierce resistance from a small but determined force of Southern mounted troopers. On March 24, at 2 p.m., a portion of the XIII Corps, still marching to Dannelly's Mill, was attacked by the 12th Mississippi Cavalry.[18] "A party of guerrillas made a dash on our wagon train, which was stuck in the mud below Fish River," the Unionist-controlled newspaper *New Orleans Times* reported three days after the engagement, "and captured ten mules and eight drivers, and one straggler. Two mules were killed. All the wagons and stores were brought in."[19] The "party of guerrillas" referred to in the *Times* report was a small contingent of gray-coated horsemen.

Lieutenant Artemus O. Sibley, a 36-year-old Baldwin County native and member of the prominent local mill-owning family, led the attack.[20] He belonged to Captain Thomas C. Barlow's Company C of the 15th Confederate Cavalry. Due to Sibley's extensive knowledge of Baldwin County, he was detailed to assist the 12th Mississippi. Reporting from a rural area called Greenwood, he informed General Liddell of his successful attack. His report differed from the *Times* account. He wrote that they killed eight mules to take away their means of transportation and captured 21 prisoners. "I learn from prisoners General A. J. Smith has a command somewhere on western shore, intending to operate with this against Mobile," reported Sibley. He also suggested to Liddell that further cavalry attacks would be effective on the rear of the Federal column.[21]

Granger's after-action report also differed from Lieutenant Sibley's account. "As the supply train of General Veatch's division was approaching Dannely's [sic] Mills on the 24th the advance wagons were struck by a small party of guerrillas," reported Granger, "the rear guard a brigade being at the time working the main body of the train over a bad piece of road. No wagons or stores were destroyed or injured. Eight teamsters and 14 animals, however, were captured."[22]

To Spanish Fort

On March 24, Canby's partially reunited force remained in camp at Dannelly's Mill for a day, waiting for the remainder of the XIII Corps to arrive. "I must say that this is the pleasantest soldiering we have seen since we have been in the field. Our present camp is in a beautiful river grove," wrote Corporal Otto Wolf, Company F, of the 117th Illinois Infantry, in a letter dated March 24, 1865, to his parents. He continued, "One of the nicest I have ever seen with plenty of good water and all that is needed to make a good camp. I would be perfectly satisfied to remain here the rest of my time if by so doing the war would close just as soon."[23]

In the early hours of March 25, the final phase of the march to Spanish Fort and Fort Blakeley commenced "led by Canby in person." Although the advance began early, the XIII Corps' 3rd Division, who set out behind the XVI Corps, did not strike their tents until noon. "As large an Army as this can't move fast. The road was very good, but we were nearing a stronghold of the enemy. Consequently, we had to feel a little ahead," explained Sergeant Musser.[24]

Canby issued strict orders forbidding personal foraging on the march. Only when necessary were authorized foraging parties permitted under the supervision of a responsible officer, who was supposed to issue receipts for any item confiscated. On the first day out from Fish River, one soldier asked an officer about the order against foraging. "Can't a man forage?" he asked. The officer clarified the orders against any personal foraging. "Well then what in the hell is the use of being a soldier?" the soldier asked in disgust.[25]

After marching several miles, the 95th Illinois reached Deer Park where "the troops bivouacked for the night and fortified."[26] Most of the Union troops did not have the luxury of sleeping under shelter. "We made but about six or eight miles that evening, and then camped so far ahead of the wagons, that they did not come up that night. The consequence was," wrote Sperry, recalling the evening of March 25, "that many a poor officer, whose blankets and provisions were in the train, had to lie down supperless, on the bare and chilling ground, and take what little sleep he could, by the warmth only of the half tended pine knot fires."[27]

One Baldwin County legend involves the old Methodist church, now a local museum, located in the present-day city of Daphne. As the Federal soldiers marched toward Spanish Fort, they reached the area known today as Daphne around dusk. Several tired bluecoats went to the church looking for a place to rest. Baldwin County historian Florence Dolive Scott recounted the following in her 1965 book:

> They learned that Mrs. Edmondson, a leading member and widow of the church's builder, was the custodian of the keys. Several of the blue-clad soldiers rapped at Mrs. Edmondson's door and asked, "Are there any Rebs in here?" "There certainly is a Reb in here!" The soldiers were somewhat taken aback, but they asked courteously if they and their men could sleep in the Church. She granted them the privilege on the condition that nothing in the church is disturbed. Next morning, the same soldiers returned the keys and truthfully assured Mrs. Edmondson that everything in the Church was being left exactly as it had been found. As they were leaving, one of the soldiers remarked that "You can never say you haven't had a big congregation in your church; every pew and aisle was packed with sleeping soldiers."[28]

On March 26, the bluecoats again marched out early, moving slowly through a forest of towering pine trees. One officer of the 72nd Illinois Infantry described the roads on this portion of the route as "bad owing to the nature of the soil, which was sandy loam." Supply wagons regularly sank in the sand down to their hubs.[29]

The Southern troopers also contributed to the slow progress of Canby's army. The Unionists met stiff resistance from Spence's horsemen. "The advance was constantly disputed by the enemy, generally with a small force of cavalry," recalled Allen. He continued, "The enemy, knowing the country, avoided close quarters, but from every advantageous position poured in a fire, causing upon several occasions the deployment of our leading regiments."[30] They kept up a "continual fusillade," making an occasional stand when they found strong positions. The much larger Union force drove them back to the vicinity of Spanish Fort. As they fell back, Spence's troopers burned rosin and turpentine plantations causing enormous flames. One federal officer remembered the flames as "strong and high."[31] Spence described the fires set as "hotter and larger" than the ones set by Sherman on his march through Georgia. He recalled, "I brought no distress upon any citizens except possibly those who owned this valuable product at the time. There were but few inhabitants between Fish River and Spanish Fort."[32]

On the march to Spanish Fort, Federal soldiers captured a telegraph office and several dispatches that revealed the extensive intelligence the Secessionists had gathered. Besides harassing the massive Federal column in their front, the Southern cavaliers had kept their commanders informed of enemy movements. The seized dispatches showed that the Confederates knew when the Federal soldiers began their movement, where they camped, how they were armed, and the types of artillery they were bringing.[33]

During one of the skirmishes with the 12th Mississippi, a future Minnesota governor was wounded. On March 25, Colonel William R. Marshall, the popular commander of the 7th Minnesota Infantry and 3rd Brigade of the XVI Corps, was on his horse in front of his brigade when he was shot in the neck near Deer Park. "About noon the skirmishing began and we were all badly shocked by Colonel Marshall (who still commanded our brigade) being wounded by a ball passing through his neck," wrote John Danielson, Company G, 7th Minnesota Infantry Volunteers. The severe flesh wound entered the left side of the back of his neck, narrowly missing his spine. After his wound was dressed, the men cheered as he remounted his horse and passed along the lines.[34]

Although vastly outnumbered, Spence's troopers fought bravely, forcing Canby's soldiers to move cautiously and fortify each night. Early in the evening of March 26, Musser wrote they stopped within 2 to 3 miles of Spanish Fort, made a line of breastworks, and remained vigilant all night.[35] Spence remembered with pride, "The average march from Fish River to the investment of Spanish Fort was less than two miles per day, my command remained in front of the enemy until Blakely [sic]."[36]

"At last the enemy were in sight," recalled Private Stephenson. Thatcher's fleet appeared first as ship after ship came up the bay toward Spanish Fort.[37] The U.S. land forces then approached D'Olive Creek, located about a mile and a half south of Spanish Fort, around noon on March 27. The Confederates, underestimating the size of Canby's force, decided to meet the Unionists in the field at D'Olive Creek. The gray-coated soldiers formed a line on the high ground north of the creek, where they expected to meet one corps of Federals.[38]

"Soon the pop, pop of our pickets' guns in the interior drew our attention. Their firing grew into volleys, as well as the answers," Private Stephenson recalled of the arrival of Union forces near Spanish Fort.[39] The 1st and 3rd Divisions of the Union XIII Corps moved as a separate column toward Spanish Fort, bridging and crossing the two forks of the D'Olive Creek. The arrival of the XVI Corps to the right of the XIII Corps surprised the Southern defenders and threatened to outflank them.[40] "Our men soon came into view, slowly falling back and retiring to the line already marked as their permanent fighting posts," remembered Private Stephenson. The vast force of well over 30,000 Federal soldiers then began their methodical investment of the fort.[41]

As the Federal army neared Spanish Fort they confronted a deadly Confederate weapon that would inflict many causalities. "When within about five hundred yards of the battery the advance caught two men, laying torpedoes, along the road, between Danby [sic] Ferry and the Spanish Battery," reported the *Nashville Daily Union* on April 14, "but not until several men and horses had been killed. A Colonel, whose horse trod on one, was literally blown to pieces, both man and horse were killed instantly."[42]

Confederate Private Eli Davis, Company A, Lewis's Battalion of Alabama Cavalry, in an account of the first day of action, wrote, "We fought them until they forced us back into the ditches of the fort."[43] The overwhelming size of the advancing Federal army, over 30,000 men, soon became apparent, forcing the Confederates to abandon their plan to fight the Unionists in the open field. The graycoats fell back into the protection of Spanish Fort and Fort Blakeley.[44] General Liddell assumed command of Fort Blakeley, while General Gibson was given charge of Spanish Fort. General Maury described the two Louisiana generals as "gentlemen of birth and breeding, soldiers of good education and experience, and entirely devoted to their duty."[45]

The Gibraltar of the Southwest

Spanish Fort was a strong earthwork originally erected by Spaniards more than a hundred years earlier.[46] Situated on high hills, the fort was located on the eastern shore near the bay, and in plain view of the city. On March 28, General Slack, in a letter to his wife Ann, compared the terrain around Spanish Fort to that of a more famous earlier battle. "The ground around the fort is quite hilly, somewhat like Vicksburg," he wrote.[47] The Union-controlled *New Orleans Times-Democrat* also made comparisons to Vicksburg when it declared Spanish Fort the "Gibraltar of the Southwest."[48] The defensive lines of the fort ran in a semicircle, approximately a mile and a half from end to end. Resting on a high bluff overlooking Blakeley River on the extreme right was the strongest position at Spanish Fort, redoubt 2, also known as Fort McDermott.[49] Its left flank terminated at a large marsh at Minette Bay. The Secessionists thought that the marsh was so dense they only needed a picket line there. Maury considered the marsh impassable, a miscalculation that later proved costly.[50]

Sperry described the terrain around the fort as ideal for a siege: "Deep gullies, separated of course by ridges or knolls of earth, formed a rough likeness to concentric circles which, connected by the heavy breast-works of logs and dirt, constructed in

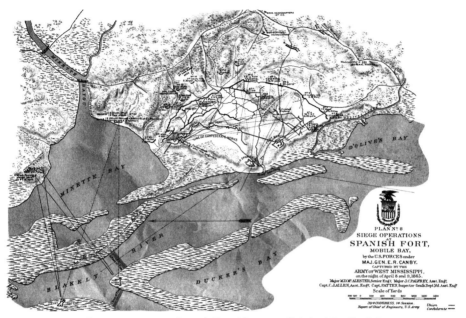

Siege operations at Spanish Fort (*Courtesy of* Michael D. Shipler)

profusion in an almost incredibly short time, constituted our parallel lines of approach and defense." He added, "To aid the fitness of the place, an excellent and copious brook ran at a convenient distance, and good springs gushed from the little hills."[51]

Despite its commanding position, a significant amount of work was still needed at Spanish Fort. Before the attack, work on the fort had progressed sluggishly due to a lack of laborers.[52] "Such was the extent and incomplete condition of the defenses at Spanish Fort when, on assuming command, I carefully inspected them," General Gibson explained. "It was apparent that an immense work with the spade, pick, and ax was before us, and that some decisive measure must be adopted to prevent the large army already upon our front from coming upon us vigorously or by an onset. At once the main body was disposed along the rifle-pits and set hard at work, though there was quite a deficiency of tools." He continued, "Spades, axes, and every available instrument that could be of service in any way, were kept busy night and day from the commencement to the close."[53] Corporal Jones, whose position with the 18th Alabama Infantry was near the middle of the works, recalled, "But little effort had been made to build fortifications. So we at once went to work preparing to make the place as secure as possible."[54]

The Spanish Fort Garrison

The actual size of the Spanish Fort garrison, due to the troop transfers, varied throughout the siege. Estimates of the fort's strength ranged from 1,800 to approximately

3,400 men.[55] Three brigades defended the works at Spanish Fort. When the Federal investment began, the garrison consisted of General Bryan M. Thomas's Brigade, Gibson's Louisiana Brigade, and Ector's Brigade. Under the cover of darkness on the evening of March 30, Brigadier General James T. Holtzclaw's Brigade left the Blakeley Wharf on steamers and headed south on the Blakeley River for Spanish Fort. They were sent to relieve the Alabama Reserves under General Bryan M. Thomas. After being relieved, the Alabama Reserves were transferred to Fort Blakeley, an unequal exchange that cost the Spanish Fort garrison "400 muskets."[56]

To Gibson's dismay, the strength of Spanish Fort's garrison was to be further reduced by the transfer of Ector's Brigade, commanded by Colonel Julius A. Andrews, to Fort Blakeley. After learning of Maury's decision, Gibson called a council of war with his brigade commanders—Colonel Francis L. Campbell, Colonel Bushrod Jones, Colonel Isaac W. Patton, and General Holtzclaw—to inquire their opinion of holding their position with the reduced force. The officers all agreed that they would not be able to hold the fort if the Federal soldiers assaulted the works. On April 1, Gibson telegraphed Maury of their collective opinion and pleaded to keep Ector's Brigade. Despite the crippling reduction of men, he made a point to say the garrison would nevertheless remain steadfast in their duty. "Let me assure you of one thing[:] whatever force is left here shall make a defense that will reflect no discredit upon our army. Every officer and man will do his whole duty," he wrote.[57]

CSA Brigadier General Thaddeus Holtzclaw was second in command at Spanish Fort. (*Courtesy of Alabama Department of Archives and History*)

General Liddell, who also regretted Maury's decision to withdraw troops from Spanish Fort, tried to console Gibson. "Greater credit will be due General Holtzclaw and yourself by holding out gallantly with your small force," Liddell messaged Gibson, "and no one will more readily accord this credit to you, General Holtzclaw, and your garrison than myself."[58] Maury evidently reversed his orders and allowed Ector's men to remain at Spanish Fort.[59]

General James T. Holtzclaw, second in command under Gibson at Spanish Fort, was "an accomplished and earnest officer."[60] Before the conflict, he worked as a lawyer in Montgomery, Alabama. In 1860, he was selected first lieutenant in the Montgomery True Blues and had faithfully served the Confederacy since its infancy. On January 12, 1861, he was with the militia that greeted Commodore Farrand at the capture of the Pensacola Navy Yard and Fort Barrancas. Soon after, he was appointed a major in the 18th Alabama Infantry and continued to be promoted until he reached the rank of brigadier general in the summer of 1864. Holtzclaw was shot through the lungs at Shiloh, a wound feared to be fatal; yet he returned to duty 90 days later and went on to become a prominent leader at many battles.[61]

"Granger appeared before Spanish Fort, and [A. J.] Smith moved up to within four miles of Fort Blakely [sic]. The next day a good portion of the latter's command was withdrawn to operate against Spanish Fort with Granger. One division was left to threaten Blakely [sic] until Steele should arrive," reported *Harper's Weekly* on May 6, 1865.[62]

Batteries Huger and Tracy

The Southerners constructed two artillery batteries, Fort Huger and Fort Tracy, to guard the entrances to the Apalachee and Blakeley Rivers. The forts were located approximately 1,700 yards from Spanish Fort and between 300 to 500 yards apart from each other. The channels immediately south of the Huger were closed by "seven to ten rows of piling" and heavily planted with torpedoes. These obstructions prevented Thatcher's fleet from passing the forts and isolating Spanish Fort from Fort Blakeley and Mobile.[63] Liddell noted that the two marsh batteries could not be attacked until Spanish Fort and Blakeley had been captured.[64]

In early 1864, after the fall of Vicksburg, General Leonidas Polk created the 22nd Louisiana Consolidated Regiment of Volunteer Infantry by ordering the consolidation of the remnants of several Louisiana units—the 3rd, 17th, 21st, 22nd, 27th, 29th, and 31st Louisiana Infantry Regiments.[65] Colonel Isaac W. Patton commanded 22nd Louisiana at Huger and Tracy. A native of Fredericksburg, Virginia, he had moved to New Orleans after he served under General Zachary Taylor as a second lieutenant in the 10th United States Infantry during the Mexican War. At Vicksburg, he was shot in the hip and taken prisoner of war. Patton was almost killed again in Mobile before the siege even began. The *New York Times* published a report from a deserter that

Patton was shot at "for indulging in the luxury of making love to some other man's wife." The woman's husband, who was intoxicated, shot at Patton seven times, but he managed to escape injury.[66] Patton was one of six brothers that faithfully fought for the Confederacy. One of his brothers, General George S. Patton I, commanded the 22nd Virginia Infantry Regiment of the Army of Northern Virginia. George was the grandfather of the famous World War II general, George S. Patton III.[67]

Fort Huger, located on the point where the Apalachee and Blakeley Rivers met, was named in honor of Lieutenant Commander Thomas B. Huger, C. S. N., who was killed in 1862 at the battle of New Orleans.[68] Major Washington F. Marks of the 22nd Louisiana Artillery commanded the battery, which was described as a "first class sand or earthwork" featuring four projecting parts, built at an angle, called bastions. Companies B and K of the 22nd Louisiana Artillery and Company C of the First Mississippi Light Artillery, totaling approximately 200 men, garrisoned the fort. The armament was said to consist of three Brooks guns, five 10-inch columbiads, and four 8-inch Dahlgrens.[69]

Fort Tracy was named after Brigadier General Edward D. Tracy, who was killed at Port Gibson in 1863.[70] Lieutenant Colonel John T. Plattsmier, Company I of the 22nd Louisiana, commanded Fort Tracy. The garrison of Fort Tracy had between 60 and 120 men from Companies G, H, and I of the 22nd Louisiana Artillery. Battery Tracy's armament included two Brooks guns, one 10-inch columbiad, and three 8-inch Dahlgrens.[71]

The Spanish Fort garrison was in for one of the most intense and trying experiences of their lives. Laboring and fighting day and night, Gibson's brave garrison would valiantly defend their key position for nearly two weeks against a relentless Federal besieging force.

CHAPTER SIX

Held with Great Pertinacity

Spanish Fort and Fort Blakeley were the primary obstacles obstructing the Federal expedition. Spanish Fort was considered by many the "Key to Mobile." There was a widespread belief that once this fort fell, Mobile would be nearly defenseless—the city would fall.[1] The sparse number of men defending the fort were primarily from the battered remnants of the Army of Tennessee. Many had fought in the major battles of the western theater and now faced another hard fight against overwhelming odds.[2]

Many Federal soldiers believed that once they appeared, these outnumbered and likely demoralized Southerners would evacuate; they could not possibly have any fight left in them.[3] "This work will delay us but a short time," a correspondent with the *New York Times* wrote of Spanish Fort.[4] Although the bluecoats expected little resistance, they would soon encounter a desperate struggle. Against all odds, for nearly two weeks, the Southern soldiers stubbornly held their position at Spanish Fort.

The Siege Begins

Alden McLellan, First Lieutenant in Brown's Light Artillery, remembered, "Our works were invested by a strong force of Federals, and the siege was on."[5] During the investment, after the fortifications were reconnoitered, Canby "promptly" declined XVI Corps Commander General A. J. Smith's request to charge Spanish Fort. He reasoned there was plenty of time and resources to execute a successful siege instead of unnecessarily sacrificing lives in a direct assault.[6] Obviously, Canby learned from the mistakes of other commanders that had resulted in the senseless slaughter of so many brave men in earlier campaigns. His cautious approach to siege warfare is an example of how military tactics had evolved during four years of Civil War. The tactics used during the campaign for Mobile closely resembled a World War I battle.[7]

The Federal army quickly invested Spanish Fort and proceeded with siege operations. On March 27, Colonel Stockton wrote in his diary, "Heavy firing and skirmishing all day. We are now in front of Spanish Fort, a strong earthwork thrown up by the rebels to guard Mobile. The monitors are at work on the water front and the army has it surrounded in the rear. It is bound to fall; only a matter of time."[8]

By noon on March 27, the besiegers had advanced to within close range and finished the investment of Spanish Fort.[9] Breastworks were thrown up and the Federal army settled in for a siege, keeping the Spanish Fort garrison under constant pressure. The Southern soldiers responded with fierce resistance. Batteries Huger and Tracy and the gunboats in the delta "completely enfiladed" the right of A. J. Smith's line, killing and wounding several men in the 3rd Division of the XVI Corps. To protect their exposed men, they had to build traverses on their right.[10]

The Northern soldiers, both officers and enlisted men, were determined to capture Spanish Fort. They continually worked on their breastworks and approaches day and night. At one point in the siege, officers of the 3rd Division of the XVI Corps would man the trenches as the enlisted men slept. Digging trenches in front of a fortified position was uninspiring work. The besiegers' thoughts inevitably dwelled on the possibility of being hit by a sharpshooter or being crushed by an exploding artillery shell. Endless hours of laboring under such conditions was exhausting and depressing.[11] The Federals issued whiskey rations to boost morale in these fatigue parties. "The men really needed some stimulant to recuperate their strength. No matter what our temperance reformers preach, (If they don't practice) I insist, a little whisky, judiciously given, does the men good, aye, more, is beneficial to their health, which must be somewhat impaired by their late almost superhuman exertions," wrote a correspondent from the *New Orleans Times-Democrat.*[12]

Initially, Yankee skirmish lines were relieved during the day. Soon it became apparent the cover of darkness provided a safer opportunity to relieve those in the advance rifle pits. "Heavy details were kept on the skirmish line," remembered Sperry, "and relieved in the day time. This was all wrong." Sperry continued, "Several men were wounded while being thus relieved; and soon the details refused to be relieved in the daytime, preferring to remain in their shallow lines, and holes of partial safety, rather than risk the full exposure of their persons so near the rebel works, for the mere sake of coming back to camp."[13] The Federals changed the time for relieving the skirmish lines.[14] Sergeant Musser explained in a letter to his father that skirmishers were regularly relieved "at dark every night so that the rebs can't see the movements."[15] This change reduced the number of casualties significantly.[16]

Federal Field Hospitals

Over the course of the long conflict, the Federal army developed an efficient system for caring for their wounded. Each division had a field hospital located safely in the rear of the trenches. Wounded soldiers were taken on stretchers to the field hospitals, which were furnished with "bunks, bed sacks" and capable of caring for up to 200 men. They were not crowded, as steamers regularly transported the badly wounded to hospitals at New Orleans. Thorough measures were taken to maintain sanitary conditions in the field hospitals. "At the suggestion of medical officers immediately upon the closing in of the troops around the fort," reported Dr. Charles B. White, Medical Director of the XIII Corps, "sinks were dug and attention paid to those sanitary precautions which might serve in the case of long siege to prevent or delay the appearance of those disorders which so frequently occur in the camps of besieging troops." Few of the wounded died in the field hospitals. Those killed in action were buried in marked graves in division burial grounds.[17]

Starke's Landing

The heavy Union troop movement north from Dannelley's Mill left the road "entirely destroyed," jeopardizing the supply line. On Tuesday, March 26, with rations nearly depleted, Canby ordered 39-year-old Brigadier General Joseph Bailey to supervise the construction of a wharf approximately 5 miles south of Spanish Fort. Bailey took charge and quickly organized two pontoon landings. "If the latter kept a diary," wrote Major Benjamin C. Truman, "a glance at its pages will show that during one week's time he had four fights, a hundred wrangles, slapped the faces of three steamboat Captains, and nearly killed (with hard work) some three hundred members of the Ninety-seventh Colored." Bailey's autocratic leadership style worked. The following day, Starke's Landing, as it was known, was completed. The wharf significantly expedited the transportation of rations, reinforcements, artillery, and other supplies from Fort Gaines and Fort Morgan needed for the siege. Starke's Landing also allowed the Unionists to transport their serious causalities for medical attention by water quickly.[18]

Torpedoes

The Confederates relied heavily on torpedoes, known today as sea mines, in Mobile Bay to impede the progress of the Union navy. "The fleet was unfortunate in having to combat the most practical and thorough torpedo system in the world," remembered Union Colonel Charles S. Hill, "and in waters admirably adapted to their uses for both offensive and defensive operations."[19] The effective use of torpedoes succeeded in causing the Union soldiers to proceed in a slow and cautious manner. According to Union General Thomas K. Smith, the torpedoes made the navy "timid and wary in the management of their ships."[20] In fact, nowhere else in the war were torpedoes more effective than Mobile Bay.

"Our torpedoes were very rude," wrote General Maury after the war. "Some were demijohns charged with gunpowder. The best were beer-kegs loaded with gunpowder and exploded by sensitive primers. These were anchored in every channel open to an enemy."[21] Submerged just below the surface, the muddy waters prevented Union sailors from seeing the torpedoes.[22] General Thomas K. Smith wrote, "A vessel in passing over them produces the necessary friction, and the explosion, if immediately underneath the vessel is generally sufficient to blow a hole through the bottom and sink her."[23]

"On the eastern side of the bay, however, between the shore and a small island, runs another channel, which might be used to pass around these obstructions, but this is disputed by a strong shore battery [Battery Huger], and it has been literally sowed with torpedoes," reported the *Philadelphia Inquirer* on March 31. "So thick are they that a small boat containing the surgeon and a petty officer from the Tuscaloosa, who were rowing over them hunting ducks, by accident exploded one of them and was blown to atoms."[24]

"The Navy cannot cooperate with the army on account of torpedoes in the Bay," wrote one Union army officer.[25] The torpedoes in Mobile Bay were remarkably successful in preventing the Federal navy access to the rear of Spanish Fort. "The enemy's fleet lay six miles down the bay, just out of reach of us. They were afraid to come closer for two reasons," recalled Corporal Jones. "The bay was full of torpedoes and our siege guns were dangerous if they got in range. We would have been in a box if the fleet could have approached, for it would have been in our rear. As it was their shots fell short by about 200 yards, and they seemed never to be able to throw them any nearer to us."[26]

On March 27, the U.S. monitors *Milwaukee* and *Winnebago* moved up the bay to within 1½ miles of Spanish Fort. The monitors fired on the Confederate steamer *St. Nicholas* as supplies were unloaded at the landing below the fort. The *St. Nicholas* withdrew up the Apalachee River.[27] While the *Milwaukee* was returning to the fleet, there was an explosion. When the smoke cleared, the bow of the *Milwaukee* was up in the air. The powerful double-turreted ironclad had struck a torpedo and within three minutes had reached the bottom of the shallow water.[28]

"I am very sorry for it, as she was one of our most efficient boats," wrote General Slack, referring to the loss of the *Milwaukee*, in a March 28 letter to his wife. He continued, "her decks are out of water."[29] The *Milwaukee*'s bow and half the wheel-house remained above the shallow water where it went down. Following her sinking, Admiral Thatcher sent Lieutenant J. N. Giles and other members of the *Milwaukee* ashore where they established the "Naval Battery" at Spanish Fort using guns salvaged from the sunken monitor. Thatcher later commended Giles for his "zeal and gallantry" at the "Naval Battery."[30]

The Confederate torpedoes continued inflicting damage on the Yankee fleet. "The channel was full of them. This was apparently why our leaders left our rear so exposed. Farragut respected those torpedoes and advanced but little beyond his sunken ship during the whole siege," remembered Confederate Private Phillip D. Stephenson.[31]

On March 29, in an area that had already been dragged thoroughly, another fell victim to a drifting mine. The *Osage* was a single-turreted ironclad monitor that had participated in 26 engagements during the conflict. Strong eastward winds were causing the monitor *Winnebago* to come up close to the *Osage*. To avoid a collision with the *Winnebago*, the *Osage* weighed anchor and moved to a safe distance, when

USS *Osage* (*Courtesy of* Naval Heritage and History Command)

a torpedo exploded under her bow at 2:40 p.m. The blast made an 8-foot-square hole in her hull, which caused her to sink. Her bow and forward deck, however, remained visible above the shallow water.[32] Four sailors were killed and eight wounded in the blast. After removing her turret and guns, the navy raised the ironclad from the shallow waters.[33]

On March 29, Admiral Thatcher narrowly escaped the explosion of one torpedo. Seated on the deck of his flagship, he supervised as two sailors examined a torpedo they had "scooped up" from the bay. The sea mine was supposed to have been emptied of its powder. When they unscrewed the percussion nipples, the torpedo exploded and injured them both. Thatcher, seated only a few yards away, was fortunate to be unscathed.[34]

On April 1, Sergeant Musser wrote his father, "Our monitors are moving up slowly today feeling for torpedoes and occasionally throwing a shell at the forts."[35] Despite their caution, yet another Federal vessel hit a submerged torpedo. "The ironclad *Rodolph* was sunk while towing a scow with apparatus for raising the *Milwaukee*," recalled Master Mate Waterman, "and four of her crew were killed and eleven wounded."[36] The *Mobile Advertiser and Register* reported, "Blown Up—A Yankee ship in the enemy's fleet was blown up yesterday by a torpedo. This is the third one that has gone up since the attack on Mobile began."[37]

"Our navy, in this siege, has not displayed much enterprise or great gallantry. An excuse may be found in the demoralizing effect of the torpedoes that sunk

Illustration of the sinking of the *Osage* and *Milwaukee* from *Harper's Weekly* (History Museum of Mobile)

three of their best ships," wrote General Thomas K. Smith.[38] Torpedoes sank more Yankee vessels in Mobile Bay than any other place in the conflict. The Confederate torpedoes in Mobile Bay had a crippling effect on Thatcher's fleet. Morale was low after sustaining such heavy losses. "There is considerable dissatisfaction with (Admiral) Thatcher among the officers on his inactivity," wrote Second Assistant Engineer George P. Hunt, an officer of the USS *Metacomet*, in a letter to his future wife Cordelia Eames. Hunt added, "I suspect Washington will send relief down here for the Admiral when they hear of three vessels lost and four aground."[39]

The Union navy usually equipped their vessels with "torpedo fenders" as a safeguard against sea mines. This apparatus consisted of a thick rope stretched between two spars attached to the front of the boat. They were designed to detonate mines before they could strike the vessels. However, Admiral Thatcher allegedly failed to ensure that the *Osage* and *Milwaukee* had torpedo fenders. The two ironclads "were exploded on successive days, whence it appears that the warning of the first was not sufficient" a *New York Times* correspondent pointed out. Although he claimed both vessels "had their rakes down," Thatcher was criticized for failing to take necessary precautions.[40]

In a postwar report to Jefferson Davis, Maury noted that a total of 12 Union vessels, including "three ironclads, two tinclads and seven transports," were destroyed by torpedoes.[41] He pointed out that after the *Osage* and *Milwaukee* were sunk by torpedoes near the Apalachee bar, the fleet were no longer effective participants in the siege. "Now and then a few shots were fired at ranges of about three miles. But no casualties or other inconvenience resulted from these demonstrations," wrote Maury.[42] Despite having a weak naval squadron, torpedoes had enabled the Confederates to effectively neutralize the Federal fleet during the campaign.

Notable Occurrences at Spanish Fort

On the first evening of the investment, a company of Union skirmishers were positioned a hundred yards in advance of their regiment in a turpentine orchard. On the dark and rainy night, General Granger, his chief commissary, Captain Stephen A. Cobb, and an orderly carrying the corps flag rode along the skirmish-line filling in gaps with regiments where needed. "This daring act called out a shower of bullets, and the orderly was shot through the face, and is not expected to live," wrote one correspondent.[43] Granger responded by ordering his skirmish-line to return fire, but his reserves mistakenly thought he had ordered them too, causing the entire regiment to fire. The mistake had gone unnoticed by Granger who had focused his attention on the gray-coated soldiers. As he rode down the skirmish-line, he gave the order to fire low. Hearing the order, a wounded soldier with a blood-covered face, trickling in the fire-light from an ugly wound in his cheek and neck, said, "'General, they are firing a little too low back there,' pointing to the reserve; 'I got that shot from the rear.'"[44]

At Spanish Fort, a correspondent from the *New Orleans Times-Democrat* reported an incident which demonstrated General A. J. Smith's strong countenance: "Once a piece of shell shrieked within a few inches of his head. He coolly puffed his Havana, not deigning to make a remark about the 'close shave' which made half a dozen darkies seek, with remarkable celerity, their bombproof covers."[45] Smith's calm and brave demeanor surely inspired his XVI Corps "Guerrillas."

One day, Yankee sharpshooters menaced the gray-coated soldiers from a position up a tree. "Three of them [Federals] climbed a sweet gum tree, the only tree in front nearer than one mile, and at one o'clock they fired on us," remembered Confederate Captain Eli Davis, Company A, of Lewis's Battalion. "We located them by the smoke of their guns coming out of the leaves. We fired on them, and two fell out like squirrels; the other came down and ran as I never saw a man run before."[46]

On Saturday, April 1, Master Mate George S. Waterman recalled the remarkable accuracy of the *Lady Slocomb* cannon manned by the 5th Company of Washington Artillery at Spanish Fort's Battery Blair:

> The Fourteenth Indiana Light Artillery was worrying over our columbiad with its fifty-pound shells. About 10 A. M. one of the shells struck a limber of this Hoosier Battery, and as it carried eighty pounds of powder ignition was instantaneous, and the limber chest flew to pieces, killing one and wounding five. My schoolmate, Corporal Charles W. Fox, sighted this columbiad "Lady Slocumb [sic].[47]

"Oh! It was shocking spectacle," exclaimed a correspondent from the *New Orleans Times-Democrat*.[48] A reporter from the *New York Times* who witnessed the incident called the devastation inflicted on the 14th Indiana Battery "the most fatal effect which I have known to result from a single shot during this war." The reporter further described the carnage the *Lady Slocomb* caused:

> One poor fellow was burned and blackened into a ghastly and shapeless mass. Others were scattered about, dreadfully mangled, writhing in fierce agonies, some with arms and others with legs blown off; and one, more unfortunate than all, with an arm and both legs torn away. Another remained standing after the shock, but the fiery flame of powder had seared his eyes as though a bolt from Heaven had passed over them. Thick darkness wrapped him forever, and putting out his quivering hands before him, as if to assure himself, he wandered dimly over former recollections. "Is it already night?" [49]

Soon after this devastating shot, the 1st Indiana Battery fired two shells from a 30-pound Parrott that disabled the *Lady Slocomb,* breaking off the right trunnion of the cannon and killing three men who manned it. Expecting an assault, the Washington artillerymen managed to prop up the big gun and reload it with canister. A replacement cannon was brought up under the cover of darkness on April 6; the *Lady Slocomb* was placed upon the ground where it remained for 26 years. [50]

The same day the *Lady Slocomb* was disabled, a "swamp hawk" flew between the opposing lines. "While the Seventh Minnesota was on duty in the advance trench in the daytime, a bird came and lit some yards in and between their line and the confederates. Many shots were fired at the bird, and it soon dropped to the ground," wrote General C. C. Andrews, who commanded the 2nd Division of the XIII Corps. Private William Rowe, 7th Minnesota, Captain Buck's Company D, "jumped over the works and ran out in plain sight of the Confederates, picked up the bird and returned unmolested to his place in the trench." [51] A Southern officer was seen giving the order to "cease firing" as the young Minnesotan jumped over the breastworks to collect the bird. As the brave Yankee returned to his lines, he removed his hat in recognition of the soldiery courtesy shown him by the Confederate soldiers. Just before disappearing in the trenches, he also took the opportunity to taunt the graycoats by shaking the bird over his head at them. [52] Records indicate Rowe, who came from Ramsey County (St. Paul area), Minnesota, was only 16 years old, the youngest member of Company D at the time of the siege of Spanish Fort. Considering Rowe was mustered into service on February 11, 1865, Spanish Fort was his first engagement. His youth and inexperience help explain his brave but foolish behavior. [53]

Rowe was fortunate; the Confederate defenders at Spanish Fort were usually not so kind toward overconfident Yankees. Two soldiers from Wisconsin who needlessly exposed themselves paid dearly for their carelessness. One man from the 35th Wisconsin stood in the open on the bank in the rear of the sunken battery of the 6th Michigan. When his comrades warned him that he would be shot, he replied: "The ball isn't molded yet that would hit me." Shortly after his arrogant claim, a bullet hit him in his right elbow, a wound that cost him his arm. [54] On April 2, the seventh day of the siege, an officer of the 33rd Wisconsin paid the ultimate price, killed "by foolishly exposing himself." [55]

As the bluecoats advanced their breastworks to within musket range, Southern sharpshooters posed a deadly threat. "The sharpshooters during this siege used wooden embrasures and sand bags instead of 'head logs,' which had become so popular with our marching and fighting armies," noted Maury.[56] The wooden embrasures helped the sharpshooters inflict casualties on the bluecoats. The *New York Times* reported: "WILLIAMS, of the Fortieth Missouri, lifted his head up to peep over at the enemy a day or two ago, and it was instantly blown away."[57] From the cover of trees in Spanish Fort, Confederate sharpshooters, armed with Whitworth rifles, shot several men in Carr's Division who were located on the extreme right of Spanish Fort, near Minette Bay. "One officer, a captain," remembered Union Lieutenant Charles J. Allen, "belonging, I think, to Carr's division, was shot through the heart."[58] Such fierce resistance forced the Federals to realize the gray-coated soldiers had no intention of giving up without a fight.

The Union sharpshooters also inflicted casualties on the Southerners inside Spanish Fort. Although the Confederates used half-inch-thick steel plate screens to close the embrasures as protection from the Yankee snipers, several causalities still occurred.[59] Adjutant William S. McNeil of the 1st Alabama Artillery Battalion recounted the circumstances of the April 3 death of a member of the 21st Alabama near the center of the fortifications of Spanish Fort:

> Sergeant Fitz Ripley, of the Twenty-first Alabama, a man of generally genial disposition, had waked up that morning in an unusually depressed state of mind and had informed some of his friends he was firmly convinced that his name would be on the list killed for that day. Neither argument nor ridicule moved him and all that long day he had walked among us with the aspect of a doomed man; yet now the day was done and he stood safe among us, but still silent. Someone in the party undertook to rally him about his presentiment, which he received good naturedly, and rising to his full height, he threw his arms back, in an attitude of a man stretching himself, remarking: "well, boys, this morning I was as sure —." He never finished the sentence. We all heard the thud of the bullet as it struck him full in his expanded chest.[60]

On Friday, March 31, Colonel William E. Burnet, Maury's chief of artillery, was killed at Spanish Fort. Burnet, who came over from Mobile to help establish a new battery, was shot in the head by a sharpshooter as he inspected the enemy lines with General Gibson. "His loss at such a time was severely felt," remembered Maury.[61] The son of former Texas President David G. Burnet and a West Point graduate, he was the highest-ranking Confederate officer killed in the siege of Mobile. "He was a man of rare attainments," recalled Maury, "of extraordinary military capacity, of unshrinking courage, and pure character."[62]

The death of Burnet led to a fight between Commander George W. Harrison, Captain of the CSS *Morgan*, and Captain John W. Gillespie, an ordnance officer from Maury's staff.[63] Harrison had refused a request from Maury to take Burnet's body on board the *Morgan* until he could send a different boat to bring it to Mobile. He even ordered Maury's staff officer, Captain Gillespie, who delivered the request, to leave his ship. Maury managed to find another boat to transport Burnet's body to the city where he was buried on April 2. The next day, Gillespie and Harrison had an altercation. Second Lieutenant Robert Tarleton, 1st Battalion, Alabama Infantry, shared details of the fight in a letter to his girlfriend, Sallie B. Lightfoot. He wrote:

> A very rich thing occurred here today. I told you about Capt. Harrison's ordering an officer to leave his ship. This officer was Capt. Gillespie, who won the undying gratitude and admiration of this community by administering a dose of corporal chastisement to the unpopular captain. Poor dog—everybody gives him a kick. Gen'l Maury told him very plainly what he thought of the affair and this evening he was relieved from the command of the *Morgan*. Gen'l M[aury] and Commander Farrand witnessed the affair between him and Gillespie and observed a most "masterly activity" Jack is in much glee about it. describes with much gusto the tableaux—Capt. H[arrison] upon his back. G[illespie] choking him with one hand and making hostile demonstrations on his phiz with the other. H[arrsion]'s legs kicking up frantically towards Heaven.[64]

Holloa Yank

In some locations, Union soldiers worked their lines up as close as 60 feet from the Southerners.[65] "We fired so lively that they dare not show their heads over the works. We were so close that they could not depress their cannon enough to touch us & some of the boys in front of one of the portholes silenced the Gun it contained," wrote Union Lieutenant James K. Newton, in an April 2, 1865, letter to his mother.[66]

As the advanced skirmish lines of the Northern soldiers approached the garrison works, the opposing trenches became so close that conversations took place between opposing soldiers. "A miniature commerce in coffee and tobacco was at least much talked of," Sperry of the 33rd Iowa recalled, "if not carried into actual effect; for as there were no sutlers' shops allowed with this expedition, tobacco had now become almost as scarce with us, as coffee among the rebels."[67]

Often the intent of the conversations between the enemies was to antagonize. When a Union soldier addressed a Confederate, he would call out "Holloa Johnny." Mocking their Northern accent, the gray-coated soldier would sarcastically reply, "Holloa Yank." Both sides were guilty of insulting and antagonizing each other. "One day, in front of [Fort] McDermett [sic]," General C. C. Andrews recounted, "a federal soldier had called out to the confederates several times, but got no answer. Finally, in good earnest, he asked why they so refused to answer. The confederate replied, 'Because you all insult us so when we talk with you.'"[68]

Confederate artillerymen also did some antagonizing. There was one big cannon at Fort McDermott, probably a 6.4" Brooke rifle; the Northerners referred to it as "Dog Towser," which literally means "large dog" or a "large rough person, especially full of energy." The "Dog Towser" wreaked havoc on the Federal lines and "was extremely annoying by its fire."[69]

Contemporary illustration of Fort McDermott (*Courtesy of* Alabama Department of Archives and History)

The opposing lines at Spanish Fort became so close in some places, such as redoubt 3, that the Southern soldiers could use primitive hand grenades. The graycoats were observed hurling "rampart grenades" at their enemy.[70] The grenades had an unsettling effect on the besiegers. "We feared only their small shells thrown by hand but their fuse was not very good," recalled Lieutenant T. J. Hunt, Company B of the 10th Minnesota.[71]

There were many narrow escapes from the clutches of death during the siege. "In that part of the line which Company D occupied, there was a stump of a tree," remembered Sperry, "which had been cut down for the breast-works. One day a number of men were standing around it, chatting, when a shell came over, and cut into two a musket sticking in the ground nearby, stuck the stump and passed on without hitting any person."[72]

The following account by Corporal Jones describes how the garrison avoided artillery shells at night:

> We could see the shells at night by the time they got a few feet from the gun's mouth; the fuse lighted could be distinctly seen, and the shell could be dodged. It was our custom to wait until we saw the shell start on its decent [sic] and run down the line until after the shell had done its work and return to our places.
>
> These races occurred at regular intervals of fifteen minutes. We finally dug holes in the ground and covered them with big logs and dirt, and under these logs into the ground we would dart when a bomb was fired. Dr. Shephard generally lay in the pit, but all the same he would dodge when a missile went by. To me this was amusing, and I would laugh on the sly, but the doctor saw me, and said: "Jones, I don't see anything funny about this business, and want you to hush it."[73]

The Federal artillery barrage was tremendous. "The music of bird and bee, the soft sighing of the summerlike breeze through the pines, the gentle murmur of the Bay, and all the soothing—the sublime, soul-inspiring harmonies by which Nature moves," wrote Union Captain John N. Chamberlin of the 1st Louisiana Native Guard, "were drowned in the tremendous roar of artillery and, Pandemonium seemed to be let loose upon earth."[74]

Canby's cautious siege tactics resulted in comparatively fewer casualties at Spanish Fort than in earlier battles of the war. Still, there were many men on both sides who did not survive the siege. Lieutenant Sol Thompson from Tuscaloosa County, a member of the 18th Alabama Company E, died an agonizingly painful death. "A piece of shell tore off one shoulder and opened a hole into his lungs. I looked into the wound and saw the lungs and heart. What suffering he endured for a while, but not long. He was soon dead," remembered Corporal Jones. Before he died, Thompson begged his comrades to kill him, so he could be put out of his misery.[75]

Gumtree Mortars

"Cohorn [sic] mortars were freely used and after the enemy's sharpshooters had closed in they frequently cleared them out of their pits," wrote General Maury, who had "about forty" made in Mobile's foundries. To augment these portable conventional mortars, both armies made wooden mortars from gum tree stumps for use in their excavated trenches. "Cohorn mortars were very useful, especially to us, because of the great scarcity of ammunition," Maury noted.[76] Their short-range gumtree mortars were hollowed out to 8- and 10-inch caliber and lined with sheet iron and hooped with iron.[77]

"The mortars are feared more than anything else. They throw shell 120 pounds which come plump [sic] down on one," wrote Colonel Thomas H. Herndon of the 36th Alabama.[78] There were niches in the walls of the earthworks that the Southern soldiers could sit in, seemingly protected on three sides. One unfortunate Alabamian met a particularly gruesome end when a Federal mortar shell, on its descent, struck him as he was sitting in one of the niches. The shell crushed his head and appeared to explode in the middle of his chest. "He was literally blown into bits, scattered to the four winds," recalled Jones. "I recollect joining in the hunt for the fragments of his body, but little of it was found."[79]

The Unionists also employed gumtree mortars. These primitive ordnance pieces were used in the advanced trenches to project shells into the fort.[80] The *New Orleans Times-Democrat* described the wooden mortars as "small but destructive engines of war."[81] Six wooden mortars were made for each of General A. J. Smith's two divisions at Spanish Fort, ingeniously built by Minnesotans of Wellman's Pioneers. The Union mortars were derived from 15-inch sections of sweet gum trees that were 12 inches in diameter, with the bore 9 inches deep. The barrels were bored with a

Both Union and Confederate forces used gumtree mortars during the siege. This mortar was made by Minnesota soldiers from Baldwin County, Alabama gumtrees. (*Courtesy of Minnesota Historical Society*)

2-inch auger, then reamed to size [4 inches] and strapped with iron. Conventionally bored with a powder chamber and vent, they launched many 12-pound shells into Spanish Fort. Pleased with the effectiveness of the gumtree mortars, Smith reported they "rendered excellent service."[82]

The Very Flower of the Western Army

One Northern newspaper reported, "Spanish Fort proved to be much stronger than was expected."[83] Before the invasion, some Federals believed the Southern army at Mobile would evacuate once they appeared. They soon realized the reality of the situation. "As to Mobile, in my judgment, it is going to be a long siege. The general impression was that there would be a speedy evacuation, but the attack has been so long delayed, that the enemy have had full opportunity to fortify and are making a most obstinate resistance," observed Union General Thomas K. Smith.[84] The vigorous defense led to erroneous reports of the size of the Spanish Fort garrison, ranging from 6,000 to 15,000 men.[85] "In fact the officers and troops comprising the garrison were remnants of many historic campaigns," wrote Union General C. C. Andrews, "and possessed no small share of culture and spirit."[86] General Maury described the Spanish Fort garrison as "the very flower of our Western army."[87] In an April 5 letter to his Aunt Mary, Colonel Hubbard of the 5th Minnesota further described the determination of the Confederate defense of Spanish Fort. "We are considerably astonished at the character of the obstacles," he wrote, "and the determination of the opposition with which we meet. The position against which the army is now operating is a very formidable defensive work, strongly garrisoned, and held with great pertinacity."[88]

Despite the unexpected level of resistance, the Northerners were equally determined to achieve their objective. "If there are any righteous or wicked left in Mobile," wrote one Union officer, "they had better get out of it for we intend to take the city if it takes us all summer to do it."[89]

CHAPTER SEVEN

Steele's Column

On February 28, 1865, Major General Frederick Steele took command of over 13,000 men at northwest Florida's Fort Barrancas.[1] As the XIII and XVI Corps advanced to Spanish Fort, Steele's Column, as it was known, would execute a feint movement toward Pollard, Alabama, designed to make the Secessionists believe their objective was Montgomery. After cutting the Mobile & Great Northern rail line at Pollard they would head west to complete the investment of Fort Blakeley.[2]

General Steele was a conservative democrat who allegedly opposed emancipation. Before his assignment at Fort Barrancas, Steele held a command in Little Rock, Arkansas, where he sponsored the conservative *National Democrat* newspaper. His backing of the paper was controversial because the publication openly supported the maintenance of slavery and the campaign of a planter for Arkansas governor.[3] Horace Greely, the radical editor of the *New York Tribune*, assailed Steele's leadership at Little Rock. In his book, *The American Conflict,* he wrote that Steele "never struck one hearty blow at the Rebellion where he could, with a decent regard for appearances, avoid it." Greely claimed Steele "identified in principle and sympathy with the enemy on every point but that of Disunion, his powerful influence was thrown against the Emancipation policy of the Government … [and] he was a sorrow and a scourge to the hearty, unconditional upholders of the Union."[4]

Contrary to Greely's assertions, Steele actively recruited African-Americans from Arkansas into regiments. In fact, his column from Pensacola relied heavily on the nine regiments of General Hawkins's division, one of the largest deployments of African-American soldiers in the war. Major John F. Lacey, one of Steele's staff officers, noted the general "treated these troops [African-Americans] with confidence and found them faithful and brave."[5]

Steele's command included two cavalry brigades under Brigadier General Thomas J. Lucas, three brigades of General John P. Hawkins's U.S. Colored Troops, and two brigades and artillery under Brigadier General Joseph F. Knipe. Also, General C. C. Andrews's 2nd and 3rd Brigades and artillery of the 2nd Division of the XIII Corps were attached to the column."[6]

The Long March

On March 10, Steele's Column received orders to prepare rations and march out of Fort Barrancas the next morning for nearby Pensacola. "It was a very fatiguing march, the roads being quite swampy, making it difficult even for the infantry, to say nothing about the cavalry and artillery. We reached our destination about 4 P. M. and found a most desolate city," recalled Sergeant Marshall. "Ashes where houses used to stand; skeletons where the lumber had been taken to assist in tent making; while only about twenty families had habitable dwellings. Most of the time here was spent fishing in the bay for oysters, which were very palatable."[7]

From March 12 to 20, the bluecoats encamped at Pensacola. Most of the residents of the city had evacuated earlier. Corporal Michael A. Sweetman, Company C of the 114th Ohio Volunteer Infantry, remembered finding Pensacola an almost deserted town. On March 21, Steele's men left Pensacola and began their march toward Pollard, Alabama, just north of the Alabama state line. They marched north through the piney woods along the Florida & Alabama railroad.[8] On the first day of the march, Steele's Column experienced the same storm that delayed Granger's XIII Army over in Baldwin County. Sergeant Marshall recounted how they overcame the adverse road conditions caused by torrential rain during the long march:

> On one occasion, while crossing a branch of a river, the running water had made it much softer, where a battery essayed the passage. When the lead horses had got across where they could barely touch hard ground, the other four horses were belly deep in the mire, and some of them on their sides, while the gun itself was dragging in the mud. The team had given up, but one hundred men then hitched a long rope to the tongue and at the word, horses, gun and all walked right out of the mud to solid ground. This was repeated time after time as long as there was a team or piece of artillery that wanted to cross. At one time two gangs of men, each with a wagon and team in tow, ran a race across an open place in the forest, going at a trot, one of the wagons with all four of the wheels on top of the ground, the other with two on one side cutting clear into the hub. It was exciting but very laborious. At a place called Perdido, all the teams had to be roped through. This kind of labor made the march a very fatiguing one, as on this day we made but four miles and for several days the distance made was from two to eleven miles.[9]

For the first few days of their march from Pensacola, Steele's troops moved slowly, meeting light resistance from the Confederate cavalry at their front on the first two days of the northward march. On March 23, they reached Pine Barren Creek and found a bridge the Confederate soldiers had destroyed and encountered the first inhabitants, a single mother of a young boy and girl. The women's oldest son was serving in the Federal army. Her husband was hung as a traitor by the Secessionists.[10]

On March 24, the bluecoats built a new bridge 300 yards long for the artillery and infantry to cross over the creek. The next day, General Lucas's troopers led the way in the advance north. Lucas, described by one Indiana soldier as "a splendid looking man," soon engaged his horsemen in a running skirmish with Colonel Charles G. Armistead's Confederate cavalry brigade, specifically the 8th Alabama Cavalry under Colonel Charles P. Ball.[11]

CSA Brigadier General James H. Clanton commanded the cavalry force that opposed Steele's Column in northwest Florida. He was seriously wounded and captured during a skirmish at Pringle's Creek, Florida on March 25, 1865. (*Courtesy of* Michael D. Shipler)

Brigadier General James H. Clanton, Ball's commander, was at his rear. A 38-year-old University of Alabama graduate, Clanton was a Mexican War veteran and had worked as a lawyer in Montgomery before the war. In 1862, Major George G. Garner, General Braxton Bragg's assistant adjutant general, advised General Daniel Ruggles, his commander at Corinth: "Colonel Clanton is gallant to rashness, and may require some little advice to caution."[12] The Alabamian may not have been a cautious man; however, he was conspicuous for his bravery when he opened the battle of Shiloh and fought at Farmington, Booneville, Atlanta, and other engagements.[13]

In early January 1864, Clanton had arrested members of the "Peace Society" within his command that had deserted near Pollard, Alabama. Despite his decisive actions, General Joseph E. Johnston believed the mass desertion proved "Clanton's incompetency." Alabama Governor Thomas Watts and others defended him in letters to General Leonidas Polk, who at the time oversaw the Department of Alabama, Mississippi, and East Louisiana. Watts wrote that Clanton was "a dashing, gallant officer."[14]

Skirmishing just south of present-day Century, Florida, the Union Cavalry faced stubborn resistance from the Secessionists at Mitchell Creek. Despite being vastly outnumbered, the Southern horsemen harassed and annoyed the Yankees. According to Private James M. Dunn of the 97th Illinois Volunteer Infantry, "The rebs were found at every ford, behind logs & fences."[15] On March 25, 1865, gray-coated troopers made stands against the Federal juggernaut at Mitchell Creek, Cotton Creek, and Canoe Creek before falling back to a small stream called Pringle's Creek, known today as Pritchell Mill Branch Creek.[16] Colonel Ball decided Pringle's Creek was not a strong enough defensive position and retreated. Unknown to him, General Clanton's Brigade came up and decided to make a stand at Pringle's Creek. The brigade, about 500 men, was under the interim command of Washington T. Lary's Sixth Alabama Cavalry. Clanton himself had not yet arrived from Pollard, Alabama. Lary's men set up a makeshift breastwork of fence rails on the north side of Pringle's Creek.[17]

As the Union mounted soldiers advanced, they drove back the Confederate troopers until Clanton arrived and promptly ordered a halt. Lary informed him that they were being flanked, yet the general insisted they "must fall back in order" and commanded his horsemen to "dress up on the colors." Lieutenant Algernon S. Badger of the Union's 1st Louisiana Cavalry led his men in a gallant charge. Within 15 minutes of the start of the fight, Clanton, after shooting and wounding a Federal officer, was shot in the back as he tried to escape.[18] The rest of Clanton's men were chased to the Escambia River. Unaware that the center of the bridge was torn up, they bounded into the powerful stream and escaped to the opposite shore or were drowned. The others fled into the swamps. In his official report, Steele credited the "skill and boldness" of the troopers under General Lucas for their "most gallant style" in taking the Southern horsemen by surprise at Bluff Springs.[19] The Unionist that captured the flag of the 6th Alabama Cavalry, Private Thomas Riley, Company D, 1st Louisiana Cavalry, was awarded the Congressional Medal of Honor.[20]

Clanton's wound was severe and prevented him from traveling. He signed a parole for himself and was left with a Dr. Grigsby, a Confederate surgeon, who cared for him and the other wounded at a small house near Pringle's Creek. Despite reports he was mortally wounded, Clanton fully recovered.[21]

By the evening of March 25, Steele's Column reached the Escambia River. The next morning, they crossed the Escambia River and arrived at Pollard, where they destroyed 1,000 yards of the Mobile & Great Northern railroad for the "moral effect," cut the telegraph line, and burned a railroad bridge and three buildings that had been used as Confederate Commissary and Quartermaster buildings.[22]

General Lucas relied heavily on Lieutenant Colonel Andrew B. Spurling of the 2nd Maine Cavalry. Spurling, 32 years old, led the 2nd Brigade of Lucas's West Florida Cavalry Division into Alabama in advance of Steele's Column. His objective was to carry out Grant's orders to "destroy railroads," thus preventing reinforcements from Montgomery coming to the aid of Mobile and disrupting the Confederacy's ability to communicate.[23]

On the evening of March 23, Spurling singlehandedly captured three Southern troopers, an engagement that earned him the Congressional Medal of Honor. A little after dusk he came suddenly upon three Confederate horsemen 6 miles from Evergreen, Alabama. "They attempted to escape and two of them were wounded and all were made prisoners," Spurling wrote in his after-action report. One of the three captured was Lieutenant John W. Watts of the 7th Alabama Cavalry. He was the 18-year-old son of Alabama Governor Thomas H. Watts and was a staff officer of General James H. Clanton.[24] Later that evening Spurling men cut the Alabama & Florida railroad and the telegraph wires about 5 miles above Evergreen. Without losing a man, Spurling succeeded in capturing two locomotives and 14 cars loaded with government stores. From one of the trains destined for Mobile, Spurling reportedly captured 100 soldiers, including seven commissioned officers, and $25,000 worth of Confederate postage stamps. On March 26, his cavalry rejoined Steele's Column at Pollard.[25] Spurling's raid ensured the Confederates would not be able to send reinforcements from Montgomery via the Mobile & Great Northern railroad.

In addition to the delays caused by skirmishing the Confederates, inclement weather slowed the advance of Steele's Column. Hard rainfall caused many of the roads to be impassable, forcing the Federals to lay over 25 miles of corduroy road. "It was a very difficult march on account of the roads, our longest day's march was 17 miles, the shortest 5 miles," wrote Private Henry W. Hart, 2nd Independent Battery of the Connecticut Light Artillery. "We had to make corduroy roads about one third of the way," Hart continued, and "about two thirds of the way was through yellow pine swamps. Many times we had to pull horses and guns out of the mud and mire with ropes."[26]

On March 27, Steele's men changed direction, marching west in torrential rains along the Mobile & Great Northern railroad. They reached Canoe Station, which had been headquarters of Colonel Armistead's Cavalry Brigade, the same day. During the long march from Fort Barrancas, inadequate food supplies became an issue plaguing Steele's Column. "The whole region was as bare of food supplies of all kinds as were our haversacks and trains," remembered Colonel Henry C. Merriam of the 73rd U.S.C.T. He clarified, "We had undertaken a march of nearly one hundred and fifty miles on eleven days supplies. It would have been sufficient except that there was inadequate allowance made for accidents and delays."[27] The Confederates left corn at the abandoned Canoe Station depot, and some local citizens brought up ox teams to carry it off. Unfortunately for the locals, when the hungry blue-coated soldiers arrived they confiscated all the corn and slaughtered the ox teams to feed the men.[28]

The corn and oxen confiscated at Canoe Station did not solve the hunger issue plaguing Steele's Column.[29] Private Dunn recorded in his diary, "Men were so starved that we would eat raw corn left on the ground by Cavalry horses." On March 29, in desperate need of subsistence supplies, Steele left Weatherford's plantation and marched 17 miles to reach Stockton, Alabama. Upon their arrival there on March 31, the hungry soldiers found enough food to last them for a few days. "We live high tonight, plenty of fat pork & beef which I enjoy sure," wrote Dunn.[30] Private Hart described how they foraged to overcome the lack of rations on the long journey: "Short on rations on account of the supply train throwing out rations to make them light, we was allowed to take what we could find for men and horses. The

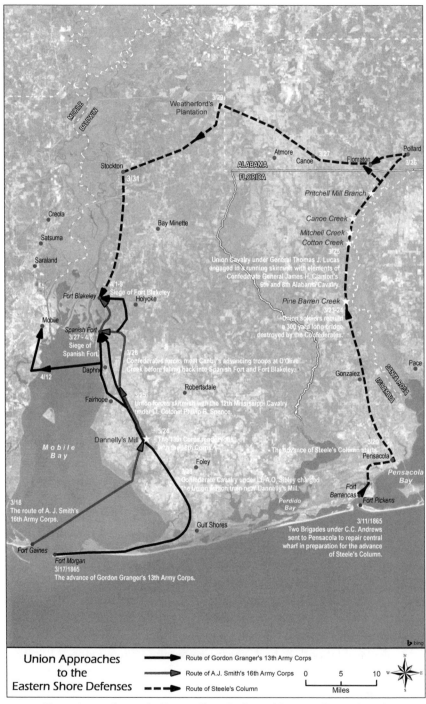

Union Approaches to the Eastern Shore Defenses (*Courtesy of* Kevin Stoots)

result was we had all we could eat. We lived better than ever before, on chickens, pigs, and fresh beef. We traveled days and cooked nights. We found abundance of corn for our horses."[31]

Despite Greely's claim that Steele was an enemy of emancipation, his African-American soldiers seemed to embrace him. On April 1, toward the end of the long march, an incident occurred illustrating the desire of two runaway slaves to communicate directly with Steele at Stockton. Major Lacey, writing in an attempt to portray their speech, recalled:

> I remember that two negro refugees were brought to my tent by the pickets. They told me that they must see "de gineral hisself," and I could not induce them to tell anything to a mere Assistant Adjutant General of the staff. It was two o'clock in the mornin but I went to the General's tent and called him out. He came to the tent door and asked the "contrabands" what they wanted. He did not look like a General as he stood there thinly clad at the foot of his cot, at the tent door. One of them said: "Is you do gineral?" General Steele assured them that he was indeed General Steele and again asked them what they wanted. "Well," the negro replied, "we done just come to tell you that we was hyah."[32]

On April 1, Steele's men began the final phase of the march from Stockton to Blakeley. Along the way, some Federal soldiers enjoyed destroying private property. Apparently happy to cause as much destruction as possible, Private Dunn wrote in his diary that the Federal soldiers burned "4 or 5 large houses & one saw mill. I am glad of it."[33] That morning heavy firing was heard at Spanish Fort coming from the direction of Fort Blakeley, about 4 miles north. This noise signaled the arrival of General Steele from Pensacola. "Quite a large train loaded with rations was sent to him from here day before yesterday. You know he started from Pensacola," wrote Lieutenant James K. Newton, Company F, 14th Wisconsin Volunteer Infantry, in an April 2 letter written in front of Spanish Fort to his mother.[34] Corporal Michael A. Sweetman, Company C, 114th Ohio Volunteer Infantry, recalled, "Thus, after two weeks of marching, in which only about 100 miles were traveled, but of which fully one-third was over corduroy roads built by the prisoners and soldiers as they advanced, the army of Gen. Steele had reached its objective point."[35]

Although Fort Blakeley was invested the same day as Spanish Fort, the siege was not pushed until Steele's arrival.[36] Spurling's troopers, sent ahead of Steele's Column to find the best route to Holyoke, encountered the 46th Mississippi on picket duty, approximately 4 miles from Blakeley. He ordered the 2nd Maine Cavalry to dismount and deployed them on both sides of the road to fight on foot. The Yankee horsemen advanced as they continued exchanging fire with the Confederates. Spurling reported that the graycoats stubbornly fell back for more than a mile, "contesting every inch of the ground," seeking protection behind fences and anything else that provided cover. At an opportune moment, Spurling ordered the 2nd Illinois to charge, successfully routing the graycoats, capturing a portion of them. "Two companies of the Second Illinois Cavalry pursued the fugitives within a half a mile of the enemy's works at Blakeley from which a sharp fire was opened with artillery," he reported. Spurling's men captured 74 prisoners, including three commissioned officers, most were members of the 46th Mississippi Infantry. The Union cavalry succeeded in capturing the 46th Regiment's flag, eight horses, mules, and "70 stands of arms." During the fight, one Union soldier was mortally wounded, another slightly injured in the foot by a torpedo explosion, and four horses were killed, all from the 2nd Illinois Cavalry. After halting the troopers in a good position, Spurling soon received support from Hawkins's Infantry and additional horsemen from Lucas's Cavalry. After driving the Southern soldiers into Fort Blakeley, Spurling ordered the captured prisoners to "dig up the remaining torpedoes on the road."[37]

Steele's command was warmly received upon completion of their long and arduous journey. When General Steele arrived in front of Fort Blakeley, General Peter J. Osterhaus, Canby's chief of staff, was there to meet him. On April 2, Private Dunn wrote in his diary that Osterhaus very cordially greeted him and said, "I'm so glad we're altogether [sic]."[38]

Fort Blakeley

Blakeley was once a bustling town several years before the war, but yellow fever epidemics coupled with high land prices led to its downfall. "The town of Blakely [sic], so far as we could discover, existed almost solely in name," recalled one bluecoat. "We were told that there had once been a number of fine houses there, and that the town was a well-known watering-place for the beauty and fashion of Mobile. No semblance of such prestige now remained." Two roads led to Blakeley, the Stockton road from the northeast and the Pensacola road from the southeast.[39]

Major Truman, 2nd Division of the XVI Corps, further described Blakeley for the April 24 edition of the *New York Times*:

> Blakely[sic] is a small town, above the mouth of the river of that name, located on the eastern shore, about four and a half miles due north of Spanish Fort, and twelve miles northeast from Mobile. When this town was elevated its projectors calculated that Mobile would be thrown in the shade in an amazing short time. True it is, that Blakely is better located as regards health, and the eastern channel can float larger craft than the western. But really, Blakely is just no place at all; and were it not for our later victory a mile from its centre [sic], no one out of Alabama would know that such a place existed.[40]

Soon after the battle of Mobile Bay in August 1864, General Maury sent a small force to occupy Blakeley to prevent the Unionists from cutting off communication between Mobile and the batteries Huger and Tracy, and thus open the Apalachee River to the Union navy.[41] Fort Blakeley featured nine redoubts constructed on a 3-mile-long semicircle of continuous earthworks with 4–5-foot ditches. The earthworks of the fort ran south to north, with both flanks resting on high ground near the Tensaw River. The garrison was armed with coehorn mortars and over 40 pieces of artillery

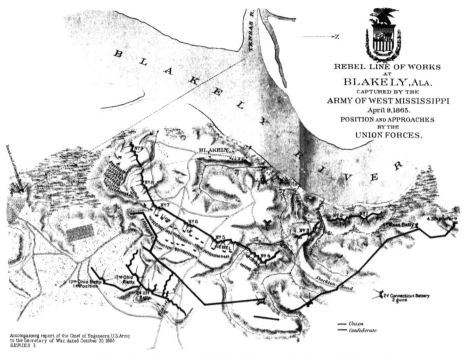

REBEL LINE OF WORKS
AT
BLAKELY, ALA.
CAPTURED BY THE
ARMY OF WEST MISSISSIPPI
April 9,1865.
POSITION AND APPROACHES
BY THE
UNION FORCES.

Rebel line of works at Fort Blakeley (*Courtesy of* Library of Congress)

of various caliber.[42] "The rebel works at Blakely [sic] were the last built of all the defenses of Mobile, and were not so strong as the works below," wrote Truman.[43]

The Fort Blakeley garrison consisted of three brigades and fluctuated between 2,800 and 3,500 men, not large enough to man the vast fortifications adequately.[44] "The rebel works at Blakely [sic] were extensive, as indeed the rebel works in Alabama always were," remembered Sperry, "always such as would require a force from two to ten times as great as they could ever have, to properly man them." He added, "We had for ourselves full learned that earthworks, to be effectively available, must not be too extensive for the force likely to defend them."[45] Although the Confederates had designed the fort to be garrisoned by a much larger force, there simply were not enough troops available at this stage of the conflict. Successive Confederate defeats at the battles for Atlanta, Franklin, and Nashville, and the Army of Tennessee's operations in North Carolina, had substantially decreased the number of able-bodied men to garrison the vast fortifications around Mobile.

To compensate for the shortage of men, Liddell strengthened Fort Blakeley with obstructions. "The fort was a strong earthwork surrounded by a strong abates [sic] of fallen trees, fallen with their tops from the fort and their limbs all turned up and sharpened and also three of [sic] four lines of shividefrize [sic: Cheval de frise]," Private Wiley recorded in his diary. Torpedoes had been liberally planted all around the works by the Southern soldiers. "The ground around the fort was just latterly [sic] planted full of torpedoes," wrote Wiley.[46] Private Dunn noted in his diary: "The devils have planted their infernal machines everywhere."[47]

Investment

In his official report, General Steele described the investment of Fort Blakeley. He arranged Hawkins's Division on the right, "from the Tensas [sic] River to near the Stockton road, Andrews' division extended from Hawkins' left to near the Pensacola road." Early the next morning, Brigadier General James Veatch's Division arrived from Spanish Fort and was positioned to the left of Andrews. Soon after Veatch's arrival, General Garrard's 2nd Division of the XVI Corps, also from Spanish Fort, came up and completed the investment.[48]

Once the bluecoats completed the line of investment, orders were given to the troops to immediately entrench themselves, and soon they were hard at work with their spades and shovels. From April 2 to 9, the Northern soldiers worked night and day on their breastworks. Despite having a limited supply of tools, the Union soldiers completed over 3,000 yards of earthworks and entrenchments as they were subjected to a barrage of shot and shell from the gray-coated soldiers. Colonel William T. Spicely, 2nd Brigade, 2nd Division of the XIII Corps, reported: "In the prosecution of this work the zeal displayed by the men …is worthy of mention."[49] With the end of hostilities in sight, the Yankees were motivated to capture the works as quickly as possible.

Liddell ordered a series of sorties to disrupt the progress of the advancing Northerners. On April 6, at 3:30 a.m., he sent out an attack against a working party of the 15th Massachusetts. Despite some sharp fighting for about an hour, the Southern soldiers failed to dislodge the Union skirmishers.[50] On April 7, Liddell sent out another sortie, just before dawn, against the advance line of troops—the XIII and XVI Corps. The Northerners repulsed the sortie with considerable loss to the garrison.[51] On April 8, he ordered yet another attack at 1 a.m. The fighting was intense for about half an hour; however, the Confederate soldiers were again repulsed. Later that morning, the Southerners opened their artillery for about an hour. The barrage did little to deter the progress of the Federals.[52]

Notable Occurrences at Fort Blakeley

Private Alfred Hill, Company E, 6th Minnesota Volunteer Infantry, 2nd Division of the XVI Corps, recalled the hazards they experienced even when over a mile away from the Confederate works:

> About a mile and a half to the eastward of the rebel works immediately defending the town are some private graves among the pine trees, apparently the commencement of a cemetery, but without fencing or other general improvements. The tomb of one of General Marion's

men, Godbold, is there; and immediately to the north of it a couple of rods, a local family, the Wilkinsons, have a little plot of land, about fifteen paces square, surrounded by a low brick wall.

Here, shortly before sunset on the 3rd of April, the brigade encamped, the Sixth Minnesota being a couple hundred paces distant from the brick graveyard, to the east and southeast of it. The troops were told to pitch no tents, light no fires, but lie on their arms, keep as quiet as possible, and await further orders.

On two or three occasions shells reached the brigade camp, one of which cut off a thick pine near to Godbold's grave, but did not injure either living or dead. These shots were provoked by men climbing the tall pine trees to get sight of the enemy's works.[53]

The Union soldiers managed to dig their trenches to within 80 yards of the Confederate advanced rifle-pits. Early in the siege, the proximity between the lines led to conversations between Cockrell's brigade and the opposing Northern soldiers. When they were not firing at each other, the Confederate pickets would ask the Federals questions such as how many men they had, how long they had been in the service, if they got paid, had good grub, tobacco, and whiskey.[54] Sometimes brief truces occurred where soldiers on both sides would meet halfway between the lines to trade coffee for a newspaper or tobacco. "When the truce was ended and both sides started back to their works, the Rebs would call out: 'Say, Yanks, if you all git in first, don't shoot till we uns git in,'" remembered Lieutenant Colonel Charles S. Hill, 10th Kansas Infantry. "Nor did they; but woe to the head that showed itself a half minute after."[55]

During the siege, there were many remarkable examples of bravery and coolness in the face of enemy fire. On April 4, the third day of the siege, one such instance occurred. General Steele's chief of staff, Lieutenant Colonel Luther H. Whittlesey of the 11th Wisconsin, was observing the enemy on the front line, near the 52nd Indiana. To get a better view, he "advanced 50 yards in front of the skirmish line to an old log building, which had been used as a barrack, and climbed upon the rafters." The Confederates took notice and opened their artillery shells in his direction. "Shells exploded above and around him," General C. C. Andrews recounted, "and through the house beneath, yet he continued to write in his note-book as if nothing was happening, till he had finished his observations, and then descended and left."[56]

On April 6, General Maury ordered Lieutenant Colonel Spence's 12th Mississippi out of Fort Blakeley to Mobile for outpost duty.[57] One company of the Southern cavalry was apparently still creating problems for the Northern soldiers near Blakeley. On April 8, to address the issue Steele ordered Lieutenant Colonel Spurling and about 30 men from the 2nd Maine Cavalry to intercept Captain W. I. Deupree's Company D of the 12th Mississippi, who were still lurking in their rear. Traveling in the direction of Stockton, Alabama, 8 miles from Blakeley, Spurling and his troopers "disguised themselves in confederate uniforms." Believing they were Confederates, the locals informed him Captain Deupree and Lieutenant D. L. Fitzgerald with "12 men, would be at a certain house at 1 p.m., to capture some 'Yankees' who were in the habit of visiting there." With this valuable intelligence, Spurling's mounted soldiers

Union Major General Frederick Steele commanded the column out of Fort Barrancas that attacked Fort Blakeley. (*Courtesy of* The Butler Center for Arkansas Studies)

went to the house, "attacked them, killed one and wounded one, and captured the Captain, Lieutenant, and seven men."[58] Although local citizens often made efforts to assist the graycoats, it backfired on this occasion.

An incident of interest involving Steele occurred during the siege of Fort Blakeley. An avid animal lover, the general lost his beloved horse Sigel when the animal broke away from an orderly who was leading him. The horse ran straight into the Confederate lines at Fort Blakeley, causing the general much grief.[59]

CHAPTER EIGHT

We Respectfully Decline to be Relieved

The Spanish Fort garrison courageously defended their position despite the overwhelming odds against them. Confederate Captain Eli Davis, Company A of Lewis's Battalion, recalled, "I went through the fight at Missionary Ridge and New Hope Church and other hard battles, and from the time the fight at Spanish Fort commenced until the end it was as hard as I was ever in."[1] How was the besieged garrison able to hold out for 13 days against a numerically superior force? The answer can be found in the character of the soldiers who fought there and the support they received from citizens in Mobile. They were courageous and determined men led by a gallant and able commander.

The Fall of Selma

Shortly after the siege began, General Taylor telegraphed General Maury to assure him of his intention to send General Forrest to assist in the defense of Mobile after defeating Union General James H. Wilson's raid coming from the north.[2] The soldiers defending Mobile eagerly awaited news that the "Wizard of the Saddle" was once again triumphant and would soon arrive to help lift the siege. With limited means of communication, many false rumors regarding Forrest's efforts against Wilson circulated. In an April 3 letter to a wounded comrade not with his regiment in Mobile, Captain Albert C. Danner, quartermaster of the 1st Missouri Infantry, wrote that this is "a great country for rumors." He wrote of hearing several conflicting reports, some of which included Forrest meeting and defeating Wilson, Wilson routing Forrest at Selma, and Forrest being near Tuscaloosa still trying to find Wilson's mounted soldiers.[3]

On Thursday, April 5, the painful truth reached Mobile. Selma, site of the important Confederate arsenal and naval foundry 150 miles to the north, had fallen on April 2. Forrest's small force, estimated to be 4,000, many not even soldiers, was routed by Wilson's much larger command of 13,000 troopers.[4] The next day, Canby ordered a 100-gun salute fired at Spanish Fort in honor of the Union victory at Selma.

"I regret the fall of Selma. I presume the people of Mobile are quite despondent. It is no use. We will have to fight it out. I believe Mobile will prove a big job for the Yanks. The Yankee gunboats are now firing a salute. I fear they must have heard some good news," wrote Confederate Private Mark Lyons, Company K, 22nd Consolidated Infantry Regiment, in an April 6 letter to his wife.[5] "The importance of Selma to the rapidly sinking cause of the Confederacy cannot be over-estimated," the *New Orleans Times-Democrat* reported. "Its capture, as a precursor to the surrender or evacuation of Mobile, has a sound moral effect upon our cause here."[6] The somber news meant Mobile was on its own and could no longer expect reinforcements.[7]

Remarkably, despite all the setbacks and adversity faced during the long war, the willingness of many Southern soldiers to fight remained strong. Maury recounted one incident illustrating the fortitude of the men defending Spanish Fort:

> I went into the works to see Captain Slocumb [sic], the commander of that company [Washington Artillery], relative to relieving them by a fresh battery from Mobile. I told him they had been overworked and needed rest, and other companies not yet engaged stood ready to take their place. He replied: "Appreciating, General, your consideration for my men, I desire to submit the question to them before consenting to our being relieved." He soon came back and said: "General, the company, grateful for your kind intention, desire to hold this position to the end. We respectfully decline to be relieved." And they held it.[8]

Brigadier General Randall Lee Gibson

One of the reasons the besieged garrison at Spanish Fort held their position for so long was the strong leadership of Randall L. Gibson—a wise and resourceful commander with an inspiring leadership style, respected and admired by his men. On March 30, he issued the following circular to the garrison of Spanish Fort:

> I. The brigadier general commanding, desires to express to the troops the admiration of their valor and endurance and his entire confidence in their ability to defend this position.
> II. Thousands of anxious hearts turn toward you.
> III. Let every officer and man resolve to do his whole duty to stand firm at his post and to make the enemy pay dearly in blood for every inch he may advance and by the blessing of Heaven, we shall continue those successes which so far, with scarcely any loss, crowned your efforts.[9]

On March 31, Gibson instructed his officers to be vigilant and push the men to work hard on strengthening the fortifications. "Press forward the work upon their outer lines to awaken their officers to the necessity of vigilance and energy at this hour," Gibson ordered his brigade commanders. "You must dig, dig, dig, Nothing can save us here but the spade. There are plenty of them if you will gather them up. A siege train will open upon this position and the main works should be worked upon during the day as well as the skirmish line when it can be done."[10]

The construction of bomb-proofs was intended as a place for soldiers to go for safety and rest. Still, there was little time for rest. "Spades, axes, and every available instrument that could be of service in any way," wrote General Gibson, "were kept busy night and day from the commencement to the close."[11] Corporal Jones of the 18th Alabama Infantry recalled, "We had no opportunity to sleep, only as a fellow would drop down and go to sleep without being told. In fact, we were supposed to be always on duty. There was no time announced to eat or sleep. You just did things as you could."[12]

The Spanish Fort garrison lacked the men necessary to properly man the fortifications. "We did not have enough to man the fort as it ought to have been done, not by half," wrote one soldier of the 18th Alabama. "We had only men enough to fill the trenches three or four feet apart."[13] An innovative commander, Gibson sometimes utilized unique methods to deceive the besiegers into thinking the garrison was larger than it was. "Special parties were detailed to lay off a long line of battle as far in advance of the position as they could go," wrote Gibson in his after-action report, "and to make camp-fires along its whole length; and other devices were employed to create an exaggerated impression of our numbers, and to conceal the exact locality of our positions."[14]

Although discouraged, Gibson made the effort to remain positive for the sake of the morale of his men. "The eighth day has closed without important results. The situation remains unchanged except that in the first day's action the enemy succeeded in pushing back my skirmish line at certain points for a short distance, has erected heavier batteries and is using 8 and 10-inch mortars," he reported to Maury on the evening of April 2. "But our losses become smaller every day," he added, "our ability to cope with him greater, and the confidence of the officers and men grows stronger and stronger."[15]

Gibson's toughness surely inspired his men. "Some days before the battle ended he received a sharp wound, but did not go off duty nor let his name go in the report of wounded," wrote General Maury.[16] His personal example seemed to influence the Spanish Fort garrison to maintain a positive attitude despite living in adverse conditions. "I am entirely well," Colonel Thomas H. Herndon of the 36th Alabama Infantry wrote his wife from Spanish Fort. "Very dirty, of course, as I have to live in the ditches, without an opportunity to change my clothing or do more than wash my face & hands & this very scantily."[17]

George S. Waterman, a Confederate navy officer from New Orleans, described a chance meeting with General Gibson during a visit to Spanish Fort. As he and others searched for the location of their friends in the Washington Artillery's 5th Company, they came upon him examining the Federal lines with field glasses. Gibson informed Waterman and his comrades where the Washington Artillery was located and then kindly invited them to sit down beside him. He was about to walk toward redoubt 3, where the Washington Artillery was positioned, and offered to lead them there. "Unmindful of the bullets, he raised his glasses to survey the enemy with characteristic nonchalance for several minutes," remembered Waterman. "A bullet

CSA Brigadier General Randall L. Gibson was praised by Confederate and Union leaders for his skillful defense of Spanish Fort. (*Courtesy of* Alabama Department Archives and History)

angrier than the others skipped past his ear, over our heads, and struck the tent at about the height of a man seated in a chair." One bullet barely missed his head and struck a nearby tent, prompting the soldiers inside to scramble out to see what was going on. Gibson then guided the men to their destination. "While there was grim humor in his cautious reference to the hill country, with its sharpshooters in the treetops, as well as on the hilltops, we reached the old parade ground, which had been made bare as a floor," wrote Waterman. "Here we made a stand, the General straight as an arrow, while his 'colleagues' looked 'two ways for Sunday.'" When they came within 150 yards of their journey's end, they bid the general farewell. Gibson wished them a happy arrival and returned to his observation point.[18] Waterman's recollection reveals the courage and coolness displayed by Gibson during the siege.

Gibson was a problem solver, as he demonstrated when plagued with ammunition shortages. He offered the men "a leave of absence for thirty-six hours to every man who turns into the ordnance department twenty-five pounds of lead or an equivalent twenty-five solid shot and shell or six mortar shells, allowing one man only from each command to be absent at a time." To prevent abuse of this incentive and ensure the missiles had come from the enemy, he also informed the garrison, "Any man detected in destroying serviceable cartridges either our own or such of the enemy's that fall into our hands will be severely punished and deprived of the privilege of the order."[19] His incentive of granting furloughs to any soldier who could gather up the specified number of spent cartridges was effective. "The enemy poured a constant stream of lead into our lines," he recalled, "gave every man who would bring in so much lead paroles of twenty-four hours to visit Mobile. A number of enterprising fellows eagerly pursued traffic and greatly enjoyed the reward."[20]

Private Stephenson of the Spanish Fort garrison further expanded on the benefits of gathering spent cartridges. "Another recreation during the early part of the siege was to gather bullets and other forms of lead in the open space behind us," Stephenson recalled. "This lead was sent back to Mobile for remanufacturing into cartridges and he who gathered a certain amount got a furlough of a day or so into the city. The soldiers did not hesitate to risk their lives while not in action roaming around in the exposed open ground behind us gathering bullets. A furlough was a furlough."[21]

Gibson understood the importance of morale and motivation. One day, he announced to the troops that he would "give any officer or soldier who captures a prisoner leave for twenty-four hours."[22] The following message from Gibson to his officers is another example of how he sought to inspire his officers:

> I wish to say to the officers of the command that the present picket line must be held. It will never do to give it up. They must use words of encouragement and cheer to the men on this duty. Tell them that in case the enemy attempts a sudden dash or a serious assault, to remain in their pits and so fight – that this will be the safest course and the only one which ensures success; tell them that the main line can fire on the enemy, every man and every field-piece, without hurting them. Abattis is preparing to go to the front of them, and the works must be made strong enough to resist artillery. Push forward the digging everywhere. Our main works must be made strong enough to resist sixty-four pounders. Encourage, stimulate your men on picket. It is morale that defeats a charge, it increases as the great Napolean [sic] said, a resisting power tenfold. Let this order be read by every regimental commander. Everything depends upon the company officers when fighting in works. They must use persuasion, and when this fails, follow General Lee's orders – using force.[23]

To prevent desertion and, in his own words, "giving information to those who seek to destroy our lives and homes," Gibson issued orders forbidding soldiers from going beyond the main line of works. He ordered officers and men to fire on and arrest anyone attempting to go to the enemy and promised a furlough of 30 days to any man who arrested a deserter. He ordered secret police organized in each company to "detect them, and kill them at once."[24]

Privately, in his correspondence to Maury, Gibson pointed out that his soldiers "are wider apart than they ever were under Johnston or Hood."[25] Despite the manpower shortages, he was determined to mount a stiff defense. He worked vigilantly to keep his garrison alert and ready to repel any attack the bluecoats might initiate. On April 5, he issued the following circular from his headquarters at Spanish Fort:

> The idea is prevalent that these works will never be assaulted. It is made the imperative duty of every officer to see that his men are so arranged that in the twinkling of an eye they may fall

into their proper places; that the works are adapted to allow every gun to be concentrated, and fired under the head logs; that his picket-line is equally prepared and protected. The picket-line must be held. Regimental commanders must see that the pickets in their immediate front are encouraged and hold their lines. Brigade commanders will be expected to charge and dislodge the enemy immediately from their picket-lines, should he attempt to dash on them, and to occupy them. Whenever there are indications of an assault, and always when heavy shelling begins, officers must see that their men put on their accouterments and have their guns in hand. It is ordered that after shelling, or in case of an assault, every officer and man yells as loud as possible.[26]

Gibson was persistent in requesting support from General Maury. He actively sought gunboat support, howitzers, axes, and spades. Moreover, he insisted African-American soldiers were needed to strengthen his garrison. "To defend the place you must let me have the axes and negroes. Have you any negro troops?" he messaged Maury on April 5 at 1:30 p.m. "I would be glad to get some." An hour and a half later, Gibson sent Maury another message stating he would make "good soldiers of all the negroes" sent to him.[27] In his original after-action report, he also noted that almost "all the Negro servants of the officers participated in the defense of the works—one or two of whom were wounded." Gibson capitalized the word Negro in his original handwritten report, something he was rarely known to have done in his life. It is also noteworthy that these men were given arms at a time when there was not enough to provide for all the white soldiers.[28]

Sorties

Gibson, like Liddell at Fort Blakeley, ordered several sorties, sudden attacks from the fort, to keep the Northerners off balance during the battle of Spanish Fort. Wasting no time, he ordered an attack on the first day of the investment.[29] "To gain time, and by show of confidence and boldness to make the enemy cautious," he wrote in his after-action report, "I resolved to attack him before daylight the next morning." Gibson reported the surprise sortie was launched early in the morning by a detachment of 550 men from the Louisiana Brigade under Lieutenant Colonel Robert H. Lindsay on the Federal picket line in "gallant style." The sortie succeeded in capturing a few prisoners, many arms and accouterments, and killing two and wounding several of the 47th Indiana. He also stated the raid succeeded in making the Yankees move cautiously, investing the fort instead of making a direct assault.[30]

Two days later, March 29, he ordered a second, less successful, night sortie. "There was an alarm last night," wrote Colonel Stockton of the 72nd Illinois in his diary, "a party of Rebs made a sortie on a working party of the XIII Corps."[31] The Federals were digging advance rifle pits in General James C. Veatch's front. Corporal Haydock, of the 33rd Iowa Infantry's Company E, heard a sudden "heavy rattling of musketry" and "loud cheering" on his left. The sentry on horseback watching the movement of the Southerners, known then as a vedette, warned his comrades three times, without flinching, despite the rapidly approaching sortie. With no chance of retreating, Sergeant Joseph A. Redpath, in a reassuring tone, ordered: "Fix your bayonets, men; and when they come up, punch back." The working party fired their guns, successfully repelling the sortie. "The enemy had determined to capture our skirmish line that night, as we had crawled too close for their gunners to work their guns," recounted Haydock. "But our boys convinced them that night Mobile was a doomed city."[32] Despite Haydock's assertion, the Southern defenders still had much fight in them and were not going to give up easily.

"They attempted to deceive our men by driving a lot of cattle out ahead of them thinking that we would not see their men until they would get close enough to surprise and capture our pickets but their ruse didn't work as they expected our men seeing their game," Private Wiley recalled. "The fatigue men fell back to the rifle pits and our skirmishers let loose on them and scattered fresh beef all around there and the rebels seeing that their game had failed soon gave it up and fell back to their works."[33] Captain T. G. Carter, Company K, 7th Regiment of Minnesota Volunteer Infantry, remembered, "The next morning it was ascertained that a large drove of cattle had in some way gotten between the two lines, and it seems that both sides supposed an assault was being made. All of the cattle were killed, and it seems that the Federal fire killed and wounded some of the Confederates."[34] After the war, Southern Corporal Edgar W. Jones disputed the accounts of cattle between the two lines. "There has been a lot said about both armies at Spanish Fort charging a lot of cattle which appeared between the line in the night time and that many cattle were killed, and that the stench became terrific," he wrote. He added, "Nothing of that sort ever occurred under my observation. I never heard of any cattle being shot under such circumstances, nor was there ever a stench that came to my nostrils. I am certain that such a thing did not occur after the siege set in."[35] Multiple sources claimed there was cattle between the lines despite Jones's claims.

On March 30, Gibson's most successful sortie occurred. Captain Riley B. Stearns, Company K, 7th Vermont, had assumed a skirmish line in front of Confederate Battery Three. Stearns's men had advanced their line by digging 25 yards to within 150 yards of the works and were causing much annoyance for the garrison. To deal with Stearns's encroachment, Captain Clement S. Watson of Company K, 25th Louisiana Regiment, and a member of General Gibson's staff, volunteered and led a sortie against the skirmish line of Captain Stearns. At sunset, Lieutenant A. C. Newton, Company E, 4th Louisiana, and 30 men formed the sortie group. Before attacking, the Confederates started a fire of slashings and brush which blew smoke over Captain Stearns's position. Using the smoke cover, Watson and his men assaulted the 7th Vermont's position, killing several and successfully capturing Stearns and 21 of his men.[36] "The charge was so sudden and vigorous that we could offer but little resistance," wrote Stearns in his April 16 official report. "I gave the command to fire, which was obeyed by the majority of my men, but the next instant every man had at least one musket at his head with a summons to surrender. I found two muskets and a revolver pointing at me, with a request to come out of the pit. I accepted the alternative thus offered," he reported.[37]

Following his capture, Stearns was taken to Gibson's tent where he was offered "a frugal repast, consisting of cold fowl, cold water, with tin table furniture."[38] A true Southern gentleman, Gibson was complimentary, saying his part of the line was "particularly annoying" and "he had never seen troops stand shelling" as he and his men had endured. The captured Federal soldiers were subsequently sent to Mobile, then on to the stockade at Meridian, Mississippi.[39] On April 2, Gibson, pleased with the results of Watson's sortie, wrote Maury recommending his promotion to the rank of major "for the singular skill and valor with which he conducted a sortie against the enemy on the 31st instant."[40]

Despite the sorties, each night the blue-coated soldiers continued digging their advance lines closer to the Confederate works. "The enemy has gradually but rapidly drawn his lines around us," wrote Colonel Thomas H. Herndon of the 36th Alabama Infantry, on April 6, 1865, in a letter to his wife. "He is now within 200 or 250 yards of us and has made considerable progress in a new parallel some 40 or 50 yards nearer."[41]

The Cover of Darkness

Communication with headquarters at Mobile was maintained throughout the battles at Spanish Fort and Fort Blakeley via telegraph and evening boat dispatches. "Communication is still kept up with Mobile by way of Blakeley; but the latter place is also invested & guns have been planted between here & there which make it rather precarious & dangerous," Colonel Thomas H. Herndon wrote to his wife during the siege. "Mobile can still be communicated with by small boats to Fort Huger & then in the same way to the city," he added.[42] Another Confederate soldier stationed at Spanish Fort described the water routes used by the Confederates to travel to Mobile: "The sole approach to the city through the bay was a narrow and tortuous channel marked out by stakes which ran zig zag across to Blakely then down to Spanish Fort."[43]

One of the Confederate dispatch bearers was Joseph Baumer, a soldier with Company C of the 36th Alabama Infantry. "After being supplied with a sturdy oarsman and skiff which carried me to the west shore of 'Pole Cat Bay,'" recounted Baumer, "I was from there on familiar from early boyhood with the intervening morass between it and Mobile River, which I succeded [sic] in crossing in safety and without having been detected on my delicate mission ... I returned the same afternoon on a blockade runner to battery McIntosh, and under cover of the ensuing night eluded the picket boats and was safely landed in the morass near the Fort."[44] Southern soldiers were transported by boat to and from Spanish Fort under the cover of darkness via this route. The transport vessels would travel between the fort and city as quietly as possible. "Even then the Yankees would sometimes fire at the boat and throw over shells dangerously near her, but I think it was never hit," Corporal Jones recalled. "The fleet of Yankee gunboats continued to amuse themselves from day to day by throwing shells at us that did not reach us. They were in plain view, but too far off, and afraid to venture near on account of our torpedoes; so our transports had nothing to fear except the land batteries, and they could only fire at the noise."[45]

Both sides used the cover of darkness to safely carry off the wounded and dead from the field. The Confederates transported their dead and wounded from Fort Blakeley and Spanish Fort at night by boat to hospitals in Mobile. "The dead and wounded were respectfully and tenderly received and cared for each night, as they arrived in the steamers from the scene of action," recalled General Maury.[46] William L. Cameron, a young officer with the *Nashville*, remembered that Southern vessels located on the Tensaw River "provided boats and crews to go to Spanish Fort and exchange fresh men for wounded and worn out ones from the fort," although there were very few fresh men available.[47]

Chaplains at Spanish Fort

Father Isidore Francis Turgis, a highly regarded New Orleans Catholic priest, was chaplain of Gibson's Brigade. On April 7, Turgis and Father Andrew Cornette, a French Jesuit priest and scientist who taught at Mobile's Spring Hill College, exposed themselves to great danger when they went across the bay to serve as chaplains at Spanish Fort.[48] Writing in third person, Father Cornette recorded in his journal: "Rev. Turgis, of New Orleans, chaplain of the troops at Spanish Fort, asks for Father Cornette. The bombardment of the fort continues night and day. Father Cornette boards a steamboat at night, and under fire of the besiegers, lands at the fort about midnight."[49] In his official report, General Gibson acknowledged the risks Father Turgis took and the service he provided to the Spanish Fort garrison. "The Reverend Farther Turgis shared our dangers and hardship," Gibson reported, "and gave the consolation of religion whenever the occasion offered along the trenches and in the hospital."[50]

Father Henry Semple, a student at Spring Hill College at the time of the battle of Spanish Fort, recalled one narrow escape Fathers Turgis and Cornette survived at Spanish Fort. "As I have often heard, a shell from a monitor was planted near the two," remembered Semple, "and exploding under the earth, buried both in the sand. So they got their heads out of their graves with the aid of the spades in the soldiers' hands."[51] After the siege, Father Cornette justified the risks he and Father Turgis took, asserting the Catholic religion was known better to the men defending Spanish Fort. He also claimed that the Protestant sects lost an opportunity for not being with the troops at Spanish Fort and Blakeley.[52]

Soldier Support Groups

As the fighting at Spanish Fort and Fort Blakeley raged on, a sad scene occurred during a regular service at Mobile's Trinity Episcopal Church, ensuing while punctuated by distinct battle reverberations. Four soldiers in worn and faded gray uniforms entered the church unannounced. The female-dominated congregation stared as the gray-coated soldiers walked down the aisle with a pine coffin containing a fallen soldier from Spanish Fort on their shoulders. After placing the coffin before the chancel, the tattered Confederate soldiers sadly and silently stood at attention as the minister began the burial service. "We had no tribute to pay but tears," lamented one of the women who was in attendance that day and whose husband was defending the city at the time. After the service, some women were slow to leave the church to go to their empty homes. At the church doors, a melancholy conversation ensued: "Oh, listen to those guns. All that I have in this world, my only boy, is there," said one woman. "And my husband is there, too," replied another.[53] The female residents of Mobile did not remain idle as the soldiers at Spanish Fort and Blakeley risked their lives.

"When at last the enemy came to possess their city, the spirit of the people arose to the occasion," recalled General Maury. "During the sieges of Blakeley and Spanish Fort, every sort of support and encouragement were given to the commander and the troops."[54] Committees were formed to gather provisions for the troops fighting at the Baldwin County forts, such as the "Ladies Society of Loyal Confederates" and the "Soldiers Hope Society," which helped boost the morale of the besieged garrisons. On April 9, the following report appeared in the *Mobile Advertiser and Register*:

> A very liberal contribution in money and provisions is being made here for the relief of the defenders of Spanish Fort and Blakely. W. G. C.
>
> Supplies for the Soldiers – The Ladies Society of Loyal Confederates has appointed a Committee to canvas the city for contributions of provisions for our troops in the trenches, and that they will be given systematically the city has been divided off into districts, giving each district one day of the week.
>
> Such contributions as each person may feel to make will be gladly received, on the days appointed, at the Pioneer Express rooms, from 10 A. M. to 2 P. M., by a committee of ladies appointed to receive them.[55]

The Soldier's Hope Society made a tobacco-bag full of provisions for one of the soldiers fighting at Spanish Fort. On Thursday, April 6, young Mary D. Waring, a member of that society, wrote, "It was filled with everything which these war times was capable of sending, and have no doubt that it was appreciated by our brave Confederates – just the name sends a thrill of pleasure through my whole frame."[56]

One of the beneficiaries of the soldier support groups was Private James L. Ray of Company A, 10th Texas Dismounted Cavalry. On April 1, as he fought at Spanish Fort, Ray, aka "Chub," wrote the following request that was published in the *Mobile Advertiser and Register*:

> Notice – I, a private, of Company A, 10th Texas, Ector's Brigade, French Division, 24 years old, 6 feet high, gray eyes, auburn hair, light mustache, will bind myself to wed young lady of Mobile who will be so kind as to send me a plug of tobacco, to chew while fighting the Yanks. You must remember that in fighting I have to bite my cartridges, and get powder in my mouth, which is an unpleasant taste. They can send it by the Commissary of my regiment, or mailboy of the brigade.[57]

The newspaper advertisement was successful. "The next morning, while I was reading a paper I overheard Captain House of the 14th Texas reading something out in front of me which sounded familiar, and so I went to where he was, and he said that the author of that article need not be ashamed of it, for he had two mighty plugs of tobacco for the author of it," recalled Ray. He continued, "And I remarked that 'for the sake of the tobacco I would Daddy the article,' and so he gave me two fine plugs of tobacco and a nice sweet little note from his cousin, Miss Charlotte D. Punch, which was highly appreciated And [sic] I kept count of the tobacco which that ad bought me and it amounted to 137 plugs of tobacco."[58]

On April 4, Ray sent to the *Advertiser and Register* this remarkable letter of thanks to the women of Mobile:

> On picket, Spanish Fort, April 4, 1865
>
> Messrs. Editors: With powder-burned face and sore shoulder from the backward movement of my rifle. I have concluded to rest a little, and while resting I will amuse myself by dropping you a line. But, stop right here, I will take a chew of tobacco, for I have plenty and of the finest article, and I did not buy it, nor steal it, nor draw it, but I have it. We are having a fine time here sharp shooting with the Yankees, though we never put our head above the breastworks, for the atmosphere is unhealthy too high up, but we have headlogs to shoot under which the boys call "skull crackers." We have another game we play over here; it is a game I used to play when a boy, but there is not altogether so much fun in it now as there was then. It is a game called "Antay Over." We play it here with shells from a mortar gun. The one that catches it is the one that is caught out and not the one that throws it.
>
> We have generally about two artillery duels each day, and they make things happen when they get at it. Everything is comparatively quiet at night.
>
> Ten thousand thanks to the ladies of Mobile for sending us that provision, they sent us last night. I think I was the hungriest man on the "map." You ought to have seen with what eagerness I devoured those eggs, meat and cake. While eating my heart ran out in thankfulness to the fair daughters of the fair city. I was proud that I was a soldier battling for the rights of ladies as those.
>
> I shall have to close. The shells are coming too fast and my mind is too much centered on "Number One," and my nerves too unsteady to write. You know that bombshells are very demoralizing if they are not so dangerous.
>
> More anon, Chub.[59]

Although appreciative of the provisions the women of Mobile sent, Ray found himself in a moral dilemma. Years later, he recalled:

> I decided that I would try it again. And so one day I wrote another little slip for the *Mobile Register* with regard to something to eat, and very next day there came a large wooden box filled with boiled ham, cakes, pies and other good and wholesome foods, and we sure did enjoy it, and have never ceased to love the dear women of Mobile.

After a few days' reflection over the proposition to wed the young lady who would send me a plug of tobacco, I saw that I was in a critical condition, and began to study up some way to get out of the difficulty. The thought struck me that up in Utah, Brigham Young had an institution that believed in plurality of wives, and so I wrote another article for the Mobile Register proposing to the young ladies who had sent me the tobacco, that we would all have to go to Utah in order to comply with my promise, as we could not carry it out in these United States. And as none of them accepted the proposition I was relieved of my promise.[60]

"The people of Mobile had evinced during the whole war a deep devotion to the cause of their country," recalled General Maury. There existed some pro-unionist sentiment in the city; however, there were also countless examples of support for the Confederate war effort that validated Maury's claim.[61] The supplies and delicacies distributed by the women of Mobile to soldiers like Private Ray boosted the morale of the besieged garrisons. This generous backing helped the Confederate soldiers hold their position for almost two weeks despite the overwhelming odds against them.[62]

CHAPTER NINE

The Treadway

For nearly two weeks Spanish Fort "was held by seventeen hundred muskets, and less than three hundred artillerists," wrote General Maury.[1] By April 8, the besieged garrison was struggling to hold their position against the intense Yankee bombardment. Unknown to many of the men defending the fort, Maury never intended the garrison to be lost and took measures to evacuate them at the last moment.[2]

"The roar of the storm I can illustrate only by comparing it to the breaking of a hundred thunder storms at once," wrote one soldier of the 95th Illinois in a letter to his hometown newspaper.[3] All day long the Federals fired their big guns and mortars into Spanish Fort. The relentless pounding of their big guns took its toll on the fortifications and garrison of Spanish Fort. "What a day that was!" remembered Private Stephenson. He recalled:

> Think of seventy-five or a hundred guns massed in that contracted semi-circle around us. Think of those huge mortars belching forth their monstrous contents. Think of the fleet in our rear pouring its fire into our backs. Suddenly the demoniac storm burst forth and it ceased not for a moment through all the interminable day. The very air was hot. The din was awful it distracted our senses. We could hardly hear each other speak ... It was though [sic] the "the Pit" had yawned and the uproar of the damned was about us. Men hopped about, raving, blood bursting from ears and nostrils, driven stark crazy by concussion.[4]

"Every time one of these guns went off the earth seemed to give way," remembered Corporal Edward Jones of the 18th Alabama, "and I seemed to be lifted six inches from the ground and allowed to fall back rather suddenly."[5] The earthworks offered little protection against "those huge descending bombs." Many of the men scattered in the open space behind the works and focused on dodging mortar shells. Stephenson became adept anticipating where the shells would land. "I had found out that by watching the bomb as it left the mortar and, after describing the curve, began to descend, I could tell pretty near where and when it would strike," he recalled. His fellow soldiers would look to him to guide them out of harm's way. His officer would say, "Sing out, Stephenson, and tell us which way to run!"[6]

One Union officer, Lieutenant T. J. Hunt, Company B of the 10th Minnesota, recorded his observations of the Secessionists inside Spanish Fort. He noted seeing two gray-coated soldiers holding up either side of a pole used to suspend sand bags. This contraption covered the opening in the earthworks where they fired their cannon, shielding the men while they loaded. They were, however, left exposed when attempting to fire their big gun. Lieutenant Hunt noted that they probably had 50 sharpshooters fired at the opening when the sand bags were lowered. "No man could escape deadly missives; they could not aim their cannon; they shot wild," he wrote. The barrage of Union sharpshooting limited the Confederate artillerists' ability to aim their cannon properly.[7]

Lieutenant Hunt claimed the besiegers were anxious to attack the fort. "We were in at the death. Our blood was up; no man thought of the rear; we felt like finishing the work there and then," Hunt recalled. The Confederates knew they could not hold out much longer.[8] The relentless bombardment of Spanish Fort was clearly heard 4 miles to the north at Fort Blakeley.[9] General Liddell, who maintained regular communication throughout the siege, telegraphed General Gibson that he would send all the boats he could get in anticipation of evacuation.[10]

The Assault of Spanish Fort

On Saturday, April 8, General Maury went to Spanish Fort to assess the situation for himself. "I took Colonel Lockett, Chief Engineer with me into Spanish Fort," recalled Maury, "that we might determine what progress the enemy had made with his mining operations and how much longer it would be safe to keep the garrison in the place." He believed the Federals would not be able to assault Spanish Fort successfully before Wednesday and instructed Gibson to prepare his garrison to march out after dark on Tuesday night. Later that evening, soon after his return to Mobile, Maury received an urgent telegraph message from Gibson indicating the bluecoats had assaulted the fort and threatened to cut off their route of evacuation.[11]

General Eugene A. Carr, commander of the 3rd Division, XVI Corps, believed Spanish Fort's northern flank was vulnerable. To ascertain the practicality of an assault, General A. J. Smith, Carr, and Colonel James L. Geddes, Brigade Commander of the 3rd Brigade, 3rd Division, XVI Corps, cautiously moved up to the advanced trenches for a closer look at the Confederate left flank. They all agreed the position was weak and could be turned. Colonel Geddes was then given permission to lead an assault.[12]

Geddes ordered Lieutenant Colonel William B. Bell forward with the 8th Iowa Regiment at sundown. Taking advantage of the tremendous cannonading, Bell and the Iowans carried out the assault at 6:10 p.m., through a supposedly impassable swamp, to flank the extreme left of Spanish Fort. On that cold night, the Yankees advanced through the swamp, approximately 200 yards wide, full of deep water and mud while under heavy fire.[13] "It has been understood that they carried narrow strips of plank or rails or poles and threw them across the turf," recalled Corporal Jones, "and thus got so far in that they had us on the flank, and before he knew it they were pressing us from that direction, and to such extent that we were unable to hold them in check long." Due to lack of time and the belief the swamp was impassible, no substantial defensive works were constructed by the Southerners there except for a few logs.[14]

The Confederates were caught by surprise when the 8th Iowa attacked the end of their line and toppled the bluff by about 6:30 p.m. "They got through that marsh, however, and pushed back the feeble picket line we had there, got to the bay between us and Blakely [sic], thus cutting us off," remembered Private Stephenson of the assault.[15]

"With deafening yells" they "charged through the swamp" and turned left up a steep bluff behind the Confederate breastworks. This position was held by North Carolina and Texas soldiers of Ector's Brigade under Colonel Julius A. Andrews and Captain Robert L. Barry's Lookout Battery, a Tennessee artillery company.[16]

Ector's Brigade defended their position vigorously. Although vastly outnumbered, some of them refused to surrender. "They fought to the last moment, and then, with the words, 'I never will surrender' on their lips, met death in a fearless manner," noted General C. C. Andrews.[17] The assault up the bluff behind the Confederate lines rolled up the end of Ector's Brigade for about 300 yards, up to the position of Barry's Lookout Battery.[18]

General Carr reported 245 casualties in his division during the siege, most occurring during the flanking assault on the bluff. The 3rd Brigade under Geddes suffered the most, 106 causalities, 51 reported by the 8th Iowa. Lieutenant Henry Vinyard, who commanded Company G, 8th Iowa, was one of the officers killed while leading his company in the attack. He was shot in the left arm and suffered a fractured left thigh, an injury which proved fatal. "Pay no attention to me," Vinyard told his men as they gathered around him when he went down, "Boys—move on."[19]

Sergeant Edgar A. Bras, Company K, 8th Iowa Infantry, earned the Congressional Medal of Honor during the assault for capturing the flag of one of the Texas Regiments of Ector's Brigade. It is probable he captured the flag from the standard bearer of the 32nd Texas Dismounted Cavalry.[20] The surprise attack led to the immediate capture of nearly half of the 29th and 39th North Carolina Regiments, a portion of the 32nd Texas, and a detachment of the Lookout Battery, nearly 200 prisoners. The captured Southerners were quickly sent to the rear and off the bluff.[21]

Geddes, convinced the Confederates were taken by surprise, ordered the 124th and 108th Illinois to attack directly across the steep ravine, occupying the remainder of Ector's Brigade. After capturing the commanding position, the Unionists dug rifle pits with a line of defenses perpendicular to the main works, near Barry's Lookout Battery. They also positioned two captured artillery pieces on the Confederates and stopped there for some time.[22]

The staff officer assigned to Canby's staff directly by General Grant, General Cyrus B. Comstock, urged A. J. Smith to push his men forward. Troubled by the darkness, Smith declined and said, "Let me do it my way, & I will have the fort by 10 am tomorrow."[23]

While the 8th Iowa assaulted from the swamp, the Yankee batteries and gunboats in the bay opened fire. The purpose of the artillery bombardment, which one bluecoat described as "simply awful, and never to be forgotten," was to prevent the Confederates from sending reinforcements to their left. "The charge at the right was a surprise to the rebels, and as it effectually flanked their position, threw them into confusion, and completed the demoralization our shells must have commenced," wrote one soldier of the 95th Illinois.[24]

Despite the intense bombardment, the Southerners made an immediate attempt to restore their line. Soldiers from the 39th North Carolina Regiment and 20–30 men of the 14th Confederate Texas Dismounted Cavalry led by Captain James A. Howze tried to dislodge the 8th Iowa. "He gave the word charge," recounted Zacheriah W. Bailey, a soldier of Ector's Brigade, "and the boys gave the Rebel yell and charged. Here I saw our brave young flag bearer, Billy Powers, go down. This checked us. Someone gathered up the colors and we retreated. This was the last gun we fired."[25]

A reaction force of provost guards from Gibson's headquarters carried out another counterattack. One of the leaders of that charge, First Lieutenant Alfred G. Clarke, provost marshal of Gibson's Brigade, was mortally wounded. "Louisiana has not lost during the war a truer man or a more thorough-going soldier," Gibson wrote in his report.[26]

Although the Confederate counter charges failed to regain the captured position, their efforts allowed the hard-pressed Spanish Fort garrison enough time to accomplish a remarkable evacuation.[27] The counterattacks were costly, though; General Carr reported his men buried 26 Southerners the following morning and Gibson reported another 45 wounded.[28]

The failure to construct strong connected works along the swamps on the Confederate left flank was pointed out by Union General C. C. Andrews. "Their works there were disconnected and their occupants were captured in detail," wrote Andrews. "More industry and care there would have enabled them to repulse the attack, or would have prevented the attack that was made."[29] General Maury admitted the lesson learned from the assault at the northern border of Spanish Fort. "No commander should ever rely upon the reports of country people about marshes, nor even of engineer officers," he wrote about a year after the Mobile campaign. "But if the movements or safety of his command may depend on the practicability of a marsh, sharpshooters should be deployed over it. In many cases they will find their way over swamps and marshes which have been before considered impenetrable."[30] The lack of adequate fortifications at the northern flank was due to the incorrect belief that the swamp was impassable. This miscalculation led to the fall of Spanish Fort.

In his after-action report, A. J. Smith made special mention of the gallantry and grit displayed during the assault by Colonel Geddes, who led his men despite suffering from illness.[31] His decisive action allowed the Federals to capture a key position inside Spanish Fort. Ironically, the regiment that figured most prominently in the assault, the 8th Iowa along with Geddes, had been captured by General Holtzclaw's former regiment at the battle of Shiloh in 1862.[32]

The Secret Escape Route

Before the siege began, Maury ordered Gibson "not to hold Spanish Fort for a moment after the garrison was in danger of capture; not to risk, in the defense of an outpost, forces intended to occupy and defend the stronghold and the works around Mobile." Maury could not risk having the entire garrison captured.[33] When Gibson realized that the Federal force was too large to be driven back and could cut off their route of retreat, he carried out Maury's orders and began the withdrawal of his troops. "It was always difficult and delicate to decide," Gibson wrote in his after-action report, "but I thought the moment had at length arrived, contemplated by my instructions, when, however painful to the devoted defenders, the position had to be given up."[34]

On April 8, at 9 p.m., Gibson telegraphed Maury, "I am beginning to retire by treadway. Hope to lose nothing but artillery. Will have a guard at the landing, so as to hold fast to the last moment."[35] Before leaving, he ordered the cannons spiked, carriages disabled, and remaining stores issued. In his official report, the general from Louisiana noted that the wounded, infirmary corps and "several hundred negroes" were carefully removed first before the rest of the garrison evacuated. He specifically mentioned that the "several hundred negroes" who had arrived that evening were "to be employed in the defense." Considering Gibson had previously requested "negro troops," it is conceivable that they were sent over to fight as Confederate soldiers.[36]

"It was pitch dark when our troops got well into position on our right, and firing upon both sides, had in a great measure ceased," wrote Major Benjamin C. Truman, a staff officer for Kenner Garrard's 2nd Division of the XVI Corps. "The rebels, at intervals, were exceedingly quiet, when all of a sudden occasionally, they would break out with a fire from their artillery and musketry from right to left." General Carr was heard to say, "I believe they are evacuating."[37] The graycoats were baffled why the Unionists did not continue to push forward. "It was only a few hundred yards from us, and we could see them moving about in the moonlight. Why they did not come right on and take us too we could never understand," recalled Private Stephenson.[38]

The darkness of night prevented the cautious Federals from knowing the importance of the position they had gained, easing the Southerners' stealthy escape. "If it had been a clear night, our gunboats, and even our Parrotts, on our right, would have prevented this thing," claimed Major Truman. Despite suspicions the garrison was leaving, the Northerners failed to follow up and press their advantage quickly enough to capture the entire garrison.[39] General A. J. Smith's cautious decision not to push forward allowed the bulk of the garrison to escape. This delay and the darkness of the night gave Gibson enough time to evacuate most of his garrison safely via a secret, narrow treadway plank, hidden in the marsh.[40]

"A plank road was made on trestles across the marsh to him to secure the retreat of his troops," wrote General Maury on the preplanned escape route to withdraw the troops at that last moment.[41] "These measures were well known to General Gibson and others of his officers and men, by whom they had been prepared and by whom they were executed with complete success," recalled Maury.[42]

Construction of the treadway bridge started before the Union investment of the fort. Accounts on the width of the treadway varied from between 1 and 4 feet wide. Maury described it as being "three or four feet above the marsh" and approximately 1 mile in length. The treadway ended on the Apalachee River opposite Battery Tracy.[43]

At approximately 10 p.m., the soldiers, after spiking their guns, quietly prepared to escape after receiving whispered orders to evacuate. During the preparations to leave, the cherished battle flag of the Washington Artillery's 5th Company was sewn around the body of Orderly Sergeant John Bartley.[44] Unaware of the preplanned escape route, the common soldiers were "bewildered," and wondered how they could possibly escape the Yankees surrounding them. Directed toward the delta in their rear, they moved out quickly. Colonel Thomas H. Herndon was reportedly the last man to leave the trenches of Spanish Fort.[45] In remarkable detail, Private Stephenson recounted the successful escape from Spanish Fort:

> Did the enemy see us? They ought to have seen us. On that run to the beach, we ran directly across the line of fire of Farragut's ships.
> We reached the edge of the steep bluffs overlooking the bay and caught up with our men. What next? Behold the head of the column seemed to melt gradually into the earth, and as we moved up to supply their place we understood their disappearance. The face of the bluff was precipitous and creased with great fissures opening out upon the water. The head of our column had disappeared down one of these! We followed pell mell, right down the almost perpendicular sides of the gorge clinging to vines, saplings, rocks, anything to keep our hold, down, down, until we reached the bottom, fifty feet or so below. And there, to our amazement we found the beginning of a Treadway.

Lieutenant James A. Chalaron of the Washington Artillery remembered, "With shoes removed and all articles productive of noise or glitter left behind, with muskets carried low down to hide their sheen from the keen eye of the foe's pickets, in single file, the garrison threaded down the bluff to the sea marsh, where a plank Treadway led toward the boats that were stationed to pick up our escaping force."[46] The Southerners quietly followed the treadway, "which ran from a small peninsula from the left flank across the river, and over a broad marsh to a deep channel opposite Battery Huger." Although within range of the Union's heavy batteries, "high grass" helped conceal their escape on the narrow treadway. Private Stephenson further described the hidden escape route:

> The treadway first debouched upon the beach, then turning to the right, it went up the shore quite a distance. Just how far I cannot say, but I know we passed so close to the enemy's pickets stationed in the marsh that we could hear them talking, and right under the nose of their battery. Finally the treadway turned and struck out into the bay. The water was shallow and we walked just above the water's surface. Suddenly a shot came. It was from that battery! Imagine our consternation, but it was not repeated for some time. It was evident they did not see us, but were merely firing periodically across what they supposed to be the channel in order to prevent any succor reaching us ... We came to the end of that treadway at last. It ended on one of those very islands by which my comrade Tony and I had planned to escape. A chain of them, as I had said, ran up the bay some six or eight hundred yards from the shore.[47]

At the end of the bridge several flat-bottomed riverboats were assembled to ferry the garrison across the river.[48] Once the graycoats reached the end of the treadway, they could see in the darkness the outlines of the steamers their commanding officer had sent over for them. The soldiers jumped off the treadway where it ended on the island, into the marsh. Knowing the Yankees were nearby, the soldiers were in a desperate situation, floundering off the swampy shore of the Apalachee River, waist deep in mud. "It was a bog. I do not know how far down I would have gone had it not been for a friendly log. I grabbed the end of it with both hands, pulled myself upon it, ran out to the other end, and tried the mud again. This time I did not go so deep," recounted Stephenson.[49]

"The irresponsible Dr. Sheppard was in the crowd with a jug of whiskey. He was not a very good jumper, and being burdened with his jug he soon became hopelessly mired," remembered Corporal Jones, who escaped with the 18th Alabama Infantry, one of the first regiments to leave on the treadway. "He called for help and told the boys that he would divide up with them when he got out. The boys pulled each other out, when one would miss the tussock, at which he jumped and sank waist deep in the mud and water." They were covered in black mud when they made it to the boats that transported them to Mobile.[50]

Father Andrew Cornette, one of the Jesuit chaplains from Spring Hill College ministering to the Spanish Fort garrison, referring to himself in the third person, described the escape in his diary: "General Gibson determines to evacuate the fort. The evacuation is effected between eight o'clock and midnight. Father Cornette escapes with Father Turgis in a boat at 12:15 a.m.; at 12:20 a.m. the fort is taken and at 1 o'clock it is in flames, lighting up the retreat of the fugitives."[51]

A Yankee battery noticed the gunboat Private Stephenson was on and took some shots that came dangerously close. Still, the boat continued to steam up the river and made it safely to Fort Blakeley.[52]

Not all the graycoats escaped by boat. The evening of April 8 was especially dark, which slowed the movement of the evacuation. To get all the troops to safety before daylight, Colonel Bush Jones led some of the men up to Blakeley using an alternate evacuation route through the marsh. Earlier in the siege, as an extra precaution, the route was determined to be feasible and staked out by engineers and men from the 9th Texas. "This marsh was quite practicable for infantry by that time," recalled Maury. He noted the flood had subsided and the ground had dried. Had the enemy known this they could have placed troops and batteries there. This would have flanked the Confederate left and cut off their escape route.[53]

There are conflicting claims on who ordered the construction of the treadway plank that saved most of the Spanish Fort garrison. In a postwar account, Maury gave himself credit for the creation of the foot bridge. "I had caused a plank road or bridge about one mile long to be made on trestles from the left flank of the lines of Spanish Fort," he claimed, "over the Bayou Minette and the marshes, to a point opposite Battery Huger; and General Gibson's orders were to save his garrison, when the siege had been protracted as long as possible without losing his troops, by marching out over this bridge."[54]

Liddell's recollection differed from that of his commanding officer. "I used every effort to make possible and practical infantry connections, but had much trouble and very little time to affect my object," he wrote after the war. "Obstacles were often designedly thrown in my way, as the work was considered by General Maury to be superfluous. The time did come, however, when he was glad to avail himself of what I had accomplished. It eventually saved the garrison of Spanish Fort."[55]

Despite precautions taken, the Federals captured approximately 500 Confederate soldiers. During the bombardment, some of the gray-coated soldiers had sought refuge deep inside the bomb-proofs and did not know their comrades had evacuated. The bluecoats surprised the Southerners when they were dragged out of their bomb-proofs with the demand "Surrender, boys, at once."[56] Gibson was not pleased with the capture of these men. "It is to be hoped and presumed that these accidents will be satisfactorily explained," he wrote in his official report. "I deeply deplore the capture of even a part of these brave men."[57] Gibson knew the Confederacy could not afford to lose those soldiers.

Joseph Baumer, a musician with Company C of the 36th Alabama Infantry, only 18 years old at the time, was one of the unfortunate soldiers who did not escape. "A 300-pounder bomb exploded near me," recounted Baumer, "and I must have been unconscious for some time when I was aroused by a strapping tall Yankee who proceeded to question me as to the number of our troops who escaped from their clutches." The bluecoat, a soldier of Brigadier General James D. Veatch's Division, "rudely ordered [Baumer] to fall in with some other prisoners."[58] Not all the Federal soldiers were rude to their Southern prisoners. Another captured soldier, Private Milo W. Scott of Captain Robert L. Barry's Company, Tennessee Light Artillery, also known as the Lookout Battery, wrote in his diary, "Myself and others captured at 12 M Night. Treated very kindly."[59]

Federals Take Possession of Spanish Fort

Shortly after 11 o'clock, the Union soldiers began to realize that the fort was evacuated. As they advanced from their entrenchments, they discovered several dead graycoats, some big guns spiked, and most of the garrison vanished.[60] First Sergeant Lauren Barker, Company A, 28th Wisconsin Infantry, recalled:

> Some of the 27th Wis. Boys were on the skirmish line near the fort, and as the firing grew less and seemed to stop they thought the fort must be evacuated, so three of the men crawled over to it at 11 o'clock p.m. and found all gone but two or three men and the rebel flag. One of the men took down the flag, and they crept back to the rifle pits, and that 27th Wis. man put that flag in his knapsack and brought it to his home at Sheboygan, Wis.[61]

Colonel Geddes informed General Carr, at 11:30 p.m., that there were no soldiers left in Red Fort and that he believed the rest of Spanish Fort was also evacuating. Carr responded by directing Geddes and his other brigade commanders, Colonel Lyman Ward and Colonel Jonathon B. Moore, to advance on the fortifications. Private Richard A. Spink, Company A of the 14th Wisconsin Infantry, recalled that just before midnight "the entire division moved up behind a strong skirmish line, and without resistance climbed over the parapets of Spanish and Red Forts."[62]

When the bluecoats discovered the fort evacuated, they were overcome with joy that the long siege had finally ended. Several eager members of the 33rd Iowa who were resting in camp to the rear "tumbled out of bed, and went up to see the fort by moon-light."[63]

"I was in the charge the night the fort was taken, and was sent after we got inside of the fort with a squad of men to pick up anything I could find," recalled Private Austin Y. Barnard, Company I of the 94th Illinois Infantry. After capturing a Confederate picket of six men and reporting to Colonel John J. McNulta, the soldiers of the 94th Illinois found "some hardtack and sowbelly to eat."[64]

Due to the darkness of the night, there were incidents of friendly fire. As soldiers of the XVI Corps entered Spanish Fort, they were mistaken for Confederates by their comrades of the XIII Corps. "After we had complete possession of the fort we were fired upon by troops of the Thirteenth Corps for half an hour," recounted Corporal Frank P. Eckert, Company G, 124th Illinois Infantry, "before they could be made to understand that the fort was ours by officers and men standing on top of the rebel works and shouting to them to cease firing."[65]

"We had a great joke on the 13th Corps," recalled Lieutenant James K. Newton, Company F, 14th Wisconsin Volunteer Infantry. "After our men had got inside the fort they mounted the breastworks & gave a cheer: the 13th Corps thought the Rebs were going to make a charge, & they began to fire at a great rate into our own men. They felt rather sheepish when they found out who they were firing at. The Gunboats too, threw one 11-inch shell into the fort after we had occupied it, but did no damage that I am aware of."[66]

Immediately after the capture of Spanish Fort, adjutant Wales W. Wood recalled some of the Northern soldiers were so "enthusiastic they got ahead of the regimental line in its advance to the bay." Wood described an incident involving Jim Barry, an Irish immigrant from Company E, of the 95th Illinois:

> As we caught up with him he was sitting on a keg of tobacco, under a tree, and from the proud feelings that animated his patriotic heart, voiced in his peculiar Irish witticisms, he appeared to think he had captured the whole Confederacy, and holding up and saluting me with an extract of his booty, he exclaimed: "Adjutant, will ye have a plug of tobaky?" The offer was so ludicrous that "Jim" received no reprimand, and no arrests were made of the few who outdistanced the regiment on this occasion.[67]

The night of the evacuation, friendly fire resulted in tragedy for one Federal soldier. Using a skiff, two blue-coated soldiers being held as prisoners at Fort Tracy managed to escape. "Reaching the main land they moved cautiously along the shore; but some of the federals having followed down after the retreating garrison, heard the rustling of the bushes, and thinking it was some straggling confederates, challenged them to surrender," recounted Andrews in his postwar account. "Presuming the demand came from confederates, the fugitives made no answer, whereupon they were fired on, and one of them was instantly killed. The other cried for quarter, and soon found himself among friends."[68]

Upon occupying Spanish Fort, the Northerners examined what the Confederate soldiers left behind. They found the graycoats had "left all their Artillery behind, among which are 7 seven inch Brook rifles. One very fine 30 pound parrot made by the rebels at Selma and marked March 1865," wrote Captain Chamberlin.[69] The evacuation was "so hasty" that several guns were left unspiked.[70]

They saw the destruction they had caused to the fort during the nearly two-week siege. They found the ground marked with "deep holes" from the artillery shells and shot. "Numbers of our men who were off duty wandered over the work and picked up many a memento of this crushing defeat to send to the dear ones at home," reported a correspondent from the *New Orleans Times-Democrat*. Inside Spanish Fort was littered with "pieces of shells," cartridge boxes, broken muskets, disabled gun carriages and cannon.[71]

The Unionists also discovered the generous portions of food prepared by Mobile's support committees for their garrison. "Our boys found a large quantity of commissary stores, which they appropriated without the forms of army regulations," wrote one Illinois soldier. A *Times-Democrat* correspondent reported, "Our men have fared well sumptuously to-day, sweet potatoes in abundance, hams, corn meal, flour and tobacco, (the latter far superior in quality to ours) were in every tent. The 'Johnnies' had plenty to eat, the prisoners says that their provisions were cooked in Mobile." Evidently, there was plenty of proof of the support the women's groups in the city had provided the besieged garrison.[72]

"Blood stained clothes were lying about in profusion," the *Times-Democrat* reported. The besiegers also found and buried the Confederate dead who were left where they had fallen.[73] The loss of life at Spanish Fort was comparatively less than similar battles earlier in the war. By the time of the Mobile campaign, it appears the commanding officers learned from the appalling casualties of earlier campaigns. Canby, believing time and manpower were on his side, chose cautious siege tactics over a large-scale assault of Spanish Fort.

"Since our ill-fated charge on the fortifications at Vicksburg hardly a man in the Regt can think of charging again without shuddering & tho we would charge if we were so ordered, it would not be with the spirit & belief in our success, in which every charge should be made," wrote Lieutenant Newton. "I don't believe we have that one General here who would risk a charge—that one Osterhaus—I'm sure A. J. Smith—or Old Dad, as we call him—wouldn't."[74] One Union soldier at Spanish Fort, referring to an earlier battle, wrote, "It was charge! charge! charge! Here a little more good sense is shown, and a regard had for human life; and the end approaches much more rapidly."[75] The soldiers, who had surely lost many comrades to such tactics, recognized and appreciated Canby's cautious approach.

"The losses reported up to the evacuation were 73 killed, 350 wounded, and about half a dozen missing. I have not been able to get the exact number of casualties on the evening of the evacuation," reported Gibson on April 16. "I estimate our loss to have been about 20 killed and 45 wounded, and 250 captured, making a total loss of 93 killed, 395 wounded, and 250 missing, out of a force of less than 2,000 men, contending for two weeks against two corps d'armee and a large fleet, with over seventy-five cannon on land and nearly as many on water."[76] The low casualty rate is remarkable considering the massive besieging force and the tremendous bombardment the garrison endured. This is a testament to the strength of the Confederate fortifications and Gibson's skillful leadership.

Although casualties were relatively low, the fighting at Spanish Fort was nevertheless an unforgettable experience. Colonel Ryland Todhunter, Assistant Adjutant for Ector's Texas Brigade, who fought at virtually every major battle in the western theater, proclaimed, "no engagement exceeded Spanish Fort in severity."[77] The *New York Times* reported: "The whole scene, as presented on our occupation, was most dismal indeed, and shows what an awful ordeal the poor misguided fellows went through during these two weeks of incessant storm of shot and shell. Really, what that garrison passed through during their struggle to hold Spanish Fort may be easier imagined than otherwise."[78]

A year after the siege, Maury admitted that garrisoning Spanish Fort may have been a mistake. "We expended daily from twelve thousand to thirty-six thousand rounds of rifle cartridges; our supply was not great," he wrote. This great expenditure of ammunition left little for the defense of Mobile after the fort fell.[79] "If the Eastern Shore were to be occupied at all, a strong work at Fort McDermott would accomplish the object sought," he reflected. In an 1866 *New Orleans Daily Crescent* article he wrote:

> It was, perhaps, an error to fortify or occupy the position of Spanish Fort. No batteries from these bluffs could seriously harm batteries Huger and Tracey [sic]. The battery near Bayou Minette bridge was in as good a position as could have been selected upon that site; it was 2700 yards from battery Huger, and bombarded Huger and Tracey [sic] for twelve days without causing serious loss or any damage.[80]

Nevertheless, leaders on both sides of the conflict acknowledged Gibson's "spirited" defense and skillful evacuation. Union General C. C. Andrews praised Gibson, describing him as "competent and active, and [as inspiring] his troops with enthusiasm. He was highly complimented by his superior officers for his conduct during the siege."[81]

General Richard Taylor wrote:

> Fighting all day and working all night, Gibson successfully resisted the efforts of the immense force against him until the evening of April 8, when the enemy affected a lodgment threatening his only route of evacuation. Under instructions from Maury, he withdrew his garrison in the night to Mobile, excepting his pickets, necessarily left. Gibson's stubborn defense and skillful retreat make this one of the best achievements of the war. [82]

Despite all the disadvantages, Gibson's skillful leadership inspired his men to hold their position against a numerically superior siege force for nearly two weeks. "General Gibson displayed great courage and capacity during this brilliant operation," wrote General Dabney H. Maury.[83] He added, "I consider the defense of Spanish Fort by General Gibson and the gentlemen of his command one of the most spirited defenses of the war."[84] Maury also justly recognized Gibson's brave men: "The men under his command represented every State of the Southern Confederacy. They had been more than four years in active service. They fitly closed the career of the Confederacy by an action so brilliant that had it taken place two years sooner it would have greatly exalted the prowess of the Confederate troops."[85]

CHAPTER TEN

It was a Glorious Sight

Exasperated by the escape of the Spanish Fort garrison, General Canby turned his attention on Fort Blakeley. On April 9, 1865, leaving a brigade behind at Spanish Fort, he sent reinforcements to General Steele at Fort Blakeley.[1] General Peter J. Osterhaus, Canby's chief of staff, ordered General Granger's 3rd Division and General A. J. Smith's 1st and 3rd Divisions to move out "with all possible dispatch" from Spanish Fort to join the investing forces at Fort Blakeley and "to be put in readiness for an immediate assault." The augmented besieging force then proceeded to increase the bombardment of Fort Blakeley.[2]

On the approximately 4-mile march north to Fort Blakeley, the Northern soldiers received welcome news from Virginia. One of Canby's staff officers rode by the marching troops, informing them that the Confederate capital had fallen seven days earlier. "Boys, Richmond has fallen," the officer on horseback announced to every regiment he passed, which resulted in loud cheers from the men. "Brig. Genls., staff and all," wrote Union Sergeant Musser to his father, "would off with their hats and give three Cheers for Grant and Sherman."[3] Although the war was not over yet, the Federal soldiers knew the end was near.

The pontoon bridge the Yankees crossed over Minette Bay was visible to the artillerists at Fort Tracy. Colonel Isaac W. Patton, the commander of Fort Tracy and Huger, promptly notified General Liddell via telegraph that heavy columns of blue-coated soldiers from Spanish Fort were seen marching his way.[4]

False Reports of the Fort Blakeley Garrison Escaping

On the morning of April 9, the besiegers of Fort Blakeley received the news of the escape of the Spanish Fort garrison. "The effect upon us all was very depressing," recalled Colonel Merriam, "for the failure to capture that garrison, after spending half a month digging them out, meant that these troops had abandoned a position no longer tenable, only to fall back to stronger fortifications covering Mobile, there to be again besieged, probably under conditions less favorable to us."[5]

The Spanish Fort garrison did not remain long at Fort Blakeley. Maury ordered them to be sent by steamboats, as soon as possible, for the immediate defense of the city. "Ominous enough it looked while we were there. We thought we were in for it again. Indeed, we were marched ashore and remained there long enough to make fires at the landing and hung around for an hour or so," remembered Private Stephenson of his brief stop at Fort Blakeley. "On the hill only a few hundred feet above us were our works, and sharp firing was heard (it was one or two a.m. I judge), and balls splattered about us viciously. Our fate was evidently in suspense and 'stay' or 'go on to Mobile' plainly balanced each other. Finally, we marched aboard again; the boats turned toward the city, and we left Blakely [sic] to its fate."[6]

The departure of the Spanish Fort garrison created a somber mood within Fort Blakeley. "On the morning of the assault on Blakely [sic] the Spanish Fort garrison marched in on our right, down to our landing and took transports for Mobile," recalled Captain Orlando F. Guthrie of the 1st/3rd Missouri Dismounted Cavalry. "Then we knew we were 'gone up' unless the enemy deferred the attack on our position until the transports (steamboats) could return for us."[7]

Granger notified Canby that lookouts from a tree observatory spotted a gunboat loaded with Confederate troops heading to Mobile.[8] Shortly afterward he sent another message to Canby, stating, "Another rebel gun-boat coming from Blakely loaded with troops. The enemy has about a dozen row-boats, a sloop, a covered scow, one small propeller, near Forts Huger and Tracy."[9] These reports led the Northerners to erroneously believe the men they saw leaving on the boats were the Fort Blakeley garrison.

Soon false rumors that the Fort Blakeley garrison was escaping circulated through the Union trenches. "The enemy's skirmish line yielded less stubbornly today and the artillery fire was not so heavy as formerly. This caused a general belief that the place was being evacuated and fears were entertained and expressed that the prize was slipping through our fingers," wrote Colonel Hiram Scofield, commander 2nd Brigade, 47th Colored Infantry, in his after-action report.[10] "General Benton sends word that he believes the enemy is evacuating the works in our front, and that his skirmishers are creeping up to ascertain," Captain F. W. Emery, assistant adjutant of the XIII Corps, messaged Colonel Bertram of the 20th Wisconsin. "The general desires that you also move the skirmishers up cautiously and ascertain the truth or error of this report."[11] Fearing the campaign would be prolonged if the garrison successfully evacuated, the bluecoats were determined not to let them escape.

Canby sent a message to Steele to ascertain if the rumors were true and if so to prevent the evacuation. Steele replied that two boatloads of troops were observed heading toward Mobile, indicating an evacuation. Concerned the Fort Blakeley garrison was escaping, orders were given to the artillery to throw shells over the parapets.[12] Still frustrated by the escape of the Spanish Fort garrison the previous night, Merriam recalled, "To me it appeared that the escape of the garrison in our front also would be simply disgraceful."[13] The Federals failed to realize the gray-coated soldiers they observed on the boats were the garrison of Spanish Fort. Nevertheless, Canby and his generals knew the rest of the men inside of Blakeley could not escape until those boats returned. This knowledge motivated them to push forth plans to directly assault the works and prevent the escape of the garrison.[14]

The Assault of Fort Blakeley

Unknown to the opposing forces at Fort Blakeley, approximately 800 miles to the northeast a monumental event had taken place just a few hours earlier. Meeting at the village of Appomattox Court House, Virginia, General Robert E. Lee surrendered the largest army of the Confederacy, the Army of Northern Virginia, to General Ulysses S. Grant. News of the capitulation would not reach Mobile for about a week.[15] At the same time Lee and Grant finalized the terms of surrender at the McLean House, General Steele, concerned the garrison of Fort Blakeley was evacuating, issued orders for an attack to begin at 5:30 p.m.[16]

Before the main assault of Fort Blakeley occurred, General Hawkins's African-American soldiers attempted a charge in front of the redoubts 1 and 2, which were located at the northern end of the Confederate line of works. Sergeant Benjamin H. Bounds of the 4th Mississippi Infantry Regiment, Company F, remembered the pre-attack:

> About two thousand of the negro troops dropped into a deep hollow nearby. Being unable to get a shot from my position, I stepped upon the breastworks. I saw a negro about twenty steps away with his gun on me. I threw my gun to my shoulder as quickly as possible. But he fired first. The ball knocked off a piece of skin on my left hand and raised a red streak on my cheek. He then turned to run when I put a belbium ball through the cross of his suspenders and dropped him dead on the spot. We soon dislodged them from that position when I got his gun—a fine English rifle and thirty nine rounds of cartridges.

Bounds, who was 25 years old at the time, and his comrades managed to repulse the initial attack of the 68th U.S. Colored Troops, forcing the African-Americans into a ravine until the main assault occurred.[17]

At approximately 5:15 p.m., the Yankee artillery opened on the Confederate lines "most terribly," recounted General Andrews, who was present at the front. He added, "The bombardment was terrific."[18] The Secessionists, conserving their limited supply of ammunition for the expected attack, did not return fire. "Everything in the fort was still as death; not a man could be seen, not a gun fired," wrote one Federal.[19] At approximately 5:30 p.m., the order came for Union cannons to cease firing and the Confederate soldiers wondered what was happening. Suddenly loud cheers were heard from the bluecoats as they rushed from their trenches towards Blakeley's fortifications.[20] The graycoats opened fired on the assaulting Northern soldiers "with terrible effect."[21]

Union assault of Fort Blakeley–*Harpers Weekly* (*Courtesy of* Michael D. Shipler)

Witnesses verified that the Federal corps commanders behaved gallantly during the assault. After issuing orders for the charge, General Steele went into the trenches with the 34th Iowa Infantry. According to Major Lacey, as the assault commenced Steele "drew his sword and leaped over the protecting earth-works as nimbly as he had once done at Chapultepec (Mexico), and rushing forward and with his staff entered the enemy's defenses under a heavy fire. The scene was an inspiring one."[22] One soldier from Iowa recounted his observations of General A. J. Smith, the XVI Corps commander, during the charge: "'Old A. J.' was there, and you can bet he went into that fight with the boys, right at their heels, encouraging them with his peculiar phrases."[23] General Gordon Granger, commander of the XIII Corps, had also come up from Spanish Fort and was there for the charge.[24] One newspaper correspondent reported his observations of Granger:

> There are doubtless some general officers who, when a fight is raging, consider their own lives so precious to the army and the country, that they never come under fire, but always snuff the battle from afar. To this class Gordon Granger does not belong. Twice before the storming of Blakeley, I had seen him upon the field; and at both Chickamauga and Chattanooga he did not hesitate to stand erect at the post of danger; heedless of the death which he regarded it his duty to face. I found him at Blakeley the same soldier still.[25]

"Soon we heard a yell and increased firing by the rebs. We looked over the works and our entire line from right to left was charging the reb works," wrote Private Henry W. Hart, 2nd Independent Battery, Connecticut Light Artillery. "It was a glorious sight, a line of 15,000 men marching steady into the jaws of death."[26] Union Colonel Hiram Scofield reported, "The spirit and enthusiasm of the troops could not be excelled. Men actually wept that they were placed in reserve and could not go with their comrades into the thickest of the fight."[27] The Confederates opened on the Northern soldiers from all their batteries, causing them to waver at one time.[28] Corporal Michael A. Sweetman, Company C, 114th Ohio Volunteer Infantry, wrote:

> At sight of our advance the rebel forces increase their efforts. Solid shot and shells go screaming and shrieking through the air, and the crashes of the latter as they explode and send their death-dealing missiles in all directions are heard on every side. Grapeshot and canister, with their peculiar swish and swirr, confront and envelope us, and the numerous and omnipresent minie-ball, with its vicious, spiteful ping, adds its no small amount of nerve-disturbing force to the pandemonium of fearful sounds.[29]

First Sergeant Carlos W. Colby, Company G, 97th Illinois, was severely wounded in the charge and crawled into a rifle pit with other wounded men. He recalled:

> Near us, behind a stump, was a big fellow crying out lustily, "Go on; we will whip them?" He had repeated this two or three times, when a comrade with a broken arm asked him what was the matter with him that he did not go in. His reply was that he had been stunned by a bursting shell. "Well," said the comrade, "you have good lungs; now try your legs toward the fort, or I will put a hole through you." With that he brought his gun to his shoulder and cocked it, resting the muzzle on his elbow with the hand hanging down. "Go," was his command, "before I let daylight through you." And he went. The last we saw of him he was going over the fort.[30]

"The distance from our intrenchments [sic] to the rebel works was from a quarter to three-quarters of a mile, and over a flat, level bottom, which had been heavily timbered, but the trees had been felled in such a way as to best obstruct our advance," recalled First Lieutenant Thornton G. Capps, Company E of the 122nd Illinois Volunteer Infantry. "Besides this, before we reached the intrenchments [sic] of the enemy we had to tackle a double line of abates [sic] and a thick line of torpedoes buried in the ground and attached to wires stretched from stump to stump."[31]

"The fire from the rebel batteries was most terrible for a short time, but failed to check the advance of our intrepid troops, who, under a murderous fire of grape and canister overhead, and torpedoes under foot, tore away the elaborately constructed abatis and chevaux de fries, swept over the ditches, and, at the point of the bayonet, carried the whole line of works," reported the *Cincinnati Enquirer*.[32] "The Rebs had cut down all the trees in front of the breastworks and sharpened all the limbs so that it was nearly impossible to get over them besides having two lines of Abattis all around the Fort," recounted Private Otto Wolf, Company F, 117th Illinois Volunteer Infantry. "Well our regiment charged over it all in about fifteen minutes after the starting, charged right over the Breastworks and all the way down to the Tensaw [sic] River which is about a mile back of the breastworks."[33]

The 2nd Divisions of the XIII and XVI Corps and a division of African-American soldiers primarily carried out the assault. "The colored troops behaved with marked gallantry in the assault although repulsed in their first assault they rallied under a heavy fire and charged the second time and with complete success," recalled Captain Chester Barney, Company E, 20th Iowa Infantry Volunteers.[34] Private Furman Stubbs of Company D, 37th Illinois, remembered one young African-American soldier who miraculously survived a torpedo explosion and continued his charge toward the fortification. Stubbs wrote, "A torpedo was exploded, and sent the youngster up in the air about 10 feet, and he came down and ran right along behind them."[35]

Sergeant Marshall described how his regiment made it over the Confederate fortifications:

> Lieutenant Colonel Baldwin caused part of his regiment to return the fire of the garrison while the rest made an opening through the abattis. The colors, carried by Sergeant D. E. Meyers, were flying conspicuously, and both flag staffs were shot in two, and the colors riddled with bullets. As soon as a passage was opened through the abattis, Colonel Baldwin gave the order for the regiment again to advance. This was done with a dauntless spirit. The men, with their bayonets, pried an opening through the next line of abattis, then rushed forward, bearing their flying colors, and, though still encountering numerous obstructions, in the nature of wire lines, were soon on the redoubt. Captain Geary of the Eight-Third, was among the first to mount the parapet, but a private soldier is said to have been the first over them.[36]

"The line of defenders was too long and thin to admit of reinforcements being drawn from any part of it. The men behaved as well as men can," wrote General Maury.[37] Initially, the famed Missourians under General Cockrell held their position with many Federals surrendering to them; however, there was no way they could repulse the massive tide of Northern soldiers assaulting all along the rest of the line. "Lieutenant Colonel Baldwin was soon on the parapet; and, seeing that most of his regiment was ready to mount the works, he jumped down inside, and cried out, 'Surrender,'" recounted Marshall. "The commanding officer inquired, 'To whom do we surrender?' Baldwin answered, 'To the Eighty-Third Ohio.' Then the officer said, 'I believe we did that once before,' referring to a somewhat similar occasion at Vicksburg."[38] Indeed, many veterans on both sides had faced each other before fighting their last battle at Fort Blakeley.

There were many scenes of desperate fighting and remarkable courage when the bluecoats made it to the breastworks. Leading his men over the parapets and into the fort, Lieutenant Angus R. McDonald of the 11th Wisconsin Infantry was immediately shot. Sergeant Daniel B. Moore, Company B, 11th Wisconsin Infantry Volunteers, remembered a gray-coated soldier "rushed up and wounded him in the thigh with his bayonet, and was about to thrust once again into the Lieutenant's side when I shot him, and then fought with the butt of my gun over the body and kept them all off until the position was taken." Moore was wounded in the head with a bayonet, but managed to avoid a more serious lasting injury.[39] He was one of the 14 Northerners who earned the Congressional Medal of Honor for distinguished gallantry during the attack.[40]

In some areas of the line, "the fighting was hand to hand, our infantry using the bayonet and clubbing muskets, and the rebel artillerymen wielding sponge-staffs and handspikes."[41] General Andrews recalled several Confederate soldiers "with muskets, remained outside of the works, refused to surrender, and maintained a cool and desperate struggle till they fell."[42] Private John N. Brown of the 69th Indiana recounted the following incident involving one Confederate officer who defiantly chose to fight to the death:

> A few minutes after the surrender the colorbearer of 97th Ill., with the flag, had a hard time in getting thru the obstructions with the colors, and was the last one of his regiment to come over the breastworks. He planted his flag in front of the regiment and a line of the enemy standing in front of him, with grounded arms. The minute the flag was planted up a gun rebel Lieut. G. S. Moore picked up a gun and shot the colorbearer dead. Moore was shot at the same time. I saw them fall.[43]

There were accounts of graycoats continuing to resist after the Federal soldiers were inside the fortifications. Confederate First Lieutenant Charles B. Cleveland recalled, after surrendering, the bluecoats came up and began firing. "After yelling no quarter to the damn Yankees," Captain Joseph H. Neal of the 1st Missouri's Company A and four other men were gunned down. "I had been placed in command of Company C, the color company, and, seeing that our chances for life were small," recalled Cleveland, "ordered the men to grab their guns and go at them. This we did, killing all who had come over. Our flag was still ours and I took it from the staff and gave it to one of the men, who afterwards gave it to Colonel Gates. We then surrendered to the 154th New York Regiment." After surrendering, Cleveland was granted permission to bury the dead before being turned over to the XIII Corps.[44]

Author Paul Brueske with Historic Blakeley State Park Interpretative Ranger Brian DesRochers examining Fort Blakeley's Redoubt # 4 (*Courtesy of* Pam Swan).

The Missourians were the only men General Liddell believed could be "relied upon thoroughly."[45] To their right, manning redoubts 5 through 9, were the Alabama Reserve Brigade under General Bryan M. Thomas. Supposedly the weak link of the garrison, many of these soldiers were less than 18 years of age. Missouri Captain Orlando F. Guthrie thought the inexperienced Alabamians "would get excited when the assault came, and shoot the tops off the trees and the Yanks would bulge right in on them."[46] To the credit of Thomas's Brigade, they fought valiantly and inflicted a substantial number of causalities on the bluecoats.[47] At redoubt 6, the 10th Kansas met particularly fierce resistance from the 63rd Alabama. "The furious fire that had beset them, made them cluster in a group," wrote General C. C. Andrews, "and they entered the works more as a column in mass than a line." Several of the outnumbered Alabama soldiers chose to fight to the death rather than surrender to the troops from Kansas. When Captain Robert W. Wood of the 10th Kansas demanded one captain to surrender, the Southerner grabbed three muskets and repeatedly fired at him, missing each time. Corporal Augustus Shultz of Company A finally shot the defiant graycoat in the head.[48]

"Sergt. John J. Gray aimed a twelve-pounder James rifle, charged with canister," wrote Second Lieutenant E. W. Tarrant, Tarrant's Battery of the Alabama Light Artillery, "directly down the line and sent the contents hurtling through the crowded ranks of the enemy." Tarrant added, "The resulting casualties were great; and the enemy were so enraged that they could scarcely be restrained from wreaking summary

CSA Brigadier General Bryan M. Thomas commanded the Alabama Reserves at Fort Blakeley. (*Courtesy of* Alabama Department of Archives and History)

vengeance upon our small force, claiming that we fired upon them after we had surrendered, which, of course, was not true." He claimed that Sergeant Gray fired the last shot at the battle of Fort Blakeley.[49]

"During the excitement of surrendering a federal officer stepped up to Lt. Colonel Steve Cooper of Howard County, Missouri, and demanded his sword, which was then offered him, point first, 'Reverse it!' was the order, and Col. Cooper threw the sword away as far as he could, saying 'Go and get it, I hand nothing to a federal soldier,'" remembered Captain Guthrie.[50]

There were also claims of Northerners firing after the surrender. Confederate Lieutenant Joshua L. Moses, in command of part of the South Carolina's Culpepper Battery, was killed during the assault. Reportedly, his last words were, "For God's sake, spare my men, they have surrendered." Moses is believed to be the last Jewish officer to be killed in the long conflict.[51]

There were allegations that African-American soldiers under General Hawkins committed atrocities during and after the assault.[52] "The very devil could not hold them, their eyes glittered like serpents, and with yells & howls like hungry wolves they rushed for the rebel works," wrote Union Lieutenant Walter Chapman of the 51st U.S.C.T. in a letter to his parents. A comparatively small number of graycoats were captured by Hawkins's colored troops after they piled over the breastworks. Federal after-action reports indicated the reason for this was that the Confederates ran over to surrender to white Federal soldiers, to avoid being "butchered" by the African-American troops. Chapman claimed they took no prisoners and "they killed all they took to a man."[53] Union Private Wiley further described the scene he witnessed in the following account in his diary:

> The colored troops were so worked up [sic] by the time they got in the fort that their officers couldn't control them. They set up yell [sic], "Remember Fort Pillow" and were determined to do as the rebels had done with the colored troops at Fort Pillow. Kill them, surrender or no surrender! They had to bring up a division of white troops to stop them.[54]

After the African-American troops rushed over the Confederate works, they were in a "great rage," accusing the Confederate soldiers of having fired upon them after surrendering. According to Confederate Captain Edward W. Tarrant, Tarrant's Battery of Alabama Light Artillery, "they shot Captain Lanier, thought we were to be butchered in cold blood, so I passed word along our line that if another man was shot I would seize a musket, as would every man of us, and we die fighting to the last. The officers of the negroes, however, succeeded in getting control of them, and there were no more outrages."[55]

By 6 p.m. the noise of battle had ceased, a white flag was visible, and the U.S. flag was raised over the fort. "Thus, on the evening of the 9th of April 1865, took place the battle of Blakely [sic], which, like that of New Orleans in 1815, was fought after the necessity for it had passed away," recalled Private Alfred Hill, Company E, 6th Minnesota Volunteer Infantry.[56] The brave men fought as if the war effort depended solely on them. At the time, they had no way of knowing that Fort Blakeley would be the last major battle.

"It was certainly the most exciting and fatiguing eighteen minutes that could possibly be crowded into any one's life," recalled a soldier of the 83rd Ohio. "We made all the noise we could, and the exertion of our lungs, added to that of the rest of the body, sapped our strength very rapidly. Some lost their voices entirely, and did not regain them for several days."[57] On April 21, the *Cincinnati Enquirer* reported: "The success of the assault was manifested by the vociferous cheers of the troops, and for many minutes their demonstrations of joy exhibited no signs of relaxation or discontinuance."[58]

Being the first regiment to plant colors on an enemy's breastwork was a source of pride and glory. For many years after the war, in newspapers and other publications, there were numerous conflicting claims as to which regiment was the first to plant their colors on the Fort Blakeley breastworks. "There is not a particle of doubt, that our colors were the first that were planted on the enemy's breastworks," remembered one soldier of the 83rd Ohio Volunteer Infantry. Soldiers of the 76th Illinois, 94th Illinois, and 73rd U.S.C.T. also made claims to be the first on behalf of their regiments.[59] It is difficult to ascertain the truth. "Where the lines was so long, and where every division, brigade, regiment, company and man tried so hard and did so well, it is impossible to tell where the mantle should fall," wrote one newspaper correspondent who witnessed the assault.[60]

"Thus ended the assault and capture of Fort Blakely [sic] with its garrison of four thousand men and forty heavy guns," remembered Colonel Merriam. "It lost much attention and public appreciation through the overshadowing event transpiring in Virginia on the same day—the surrender of Lee—but its place in history as the last assault of our great and bloody Civil War, will always be assured."[61]

CHAPTER ELEVEN

The Jig was Up

Many Confederate soldiers attempted to retreat through the woods in the rear of the fortifications, toward the Tensaw River, closely pursued by the besiegers.[1] Some of the fleeing soldiers made it to the river, got on logs, and attempted to float downstream to be picked up by gunboats off shore. Approximately 150 soldiers of the garrison reportedly escaped to safety, whereas others were shot or drowned.[2]

Private Samuel P. Combs, Company G, 29th Iowa Volunteer Infantry, wrote, "Many a Johnny had to nip the dust. Lots of them ran into the bay and were drowned or shot by the colored troops. We tried to stop the killing of the rebels, but had to stand back, for the colored troops had blood in their eyes and meant to have revenge for the murder of their comrades at Fort Pillow."[3]

The *Nashville*, *Morgan*, *Huntsville*, and *Tuscaloosa* were positioned off the shore on the Blakeley River with their guns aimed at the fort.[4] Anticipating the imminent assault, all guns were loaded with grapeshot and canister. The soldiers, armed with double-loaded muskets, were to wait until they could see the whites of the enemy's eyes, fire, and then retreat. William L. Cameron, a young naval officer on the *Nashville*, remembered there was a plan in place to rescue the garrison at the time of the assault:

> Upon the retreat of our men and the advance of those of the enemy left standing after the fire from the fort, the guns from the vessels were to open upon the enemy with grape and canister. In the meanwhile all boats from the fleet, with flatboats, etc., were out in front of the bank, ready to rescue our men, who had orders after their first volley to run for the bank and jump into the water.
>
> We expected to see our infantry running toward us and to hear the roar of the guns from our vessels firing over our and their heads; but something had happened "not on the program." The commander of the fort [Liddell], it seemed, concluded to fire another round at the enemy, as the slaughter from the first had been so great; but those behind came over the bodies of their comrades in the ditch, and before anybody knew anything the Yanks and Rebs were so mixed up that the vessels dared not fire their guns. And then there came with a rush of our poor fellows, closely followed by the enemy. Our men jumped in the water. Many could not swim, and those who could were an easy mark for the negro soldiers, who fired at them from the bank and at us in the boats. We picked up all we could and quickly retired to our respective vessels, where we landed them and returned for more. I do not know how many

CSS *Nashville* (*Courtesy of* Naval Heritage and History Command)

were rescued; but many were drowned, some killed in the water and some on the shore, and the rest surrendered.[5]

Once Lieutenant John W. Bennett, commanding the CSS *Nashville*, discovered the Northerners were assaulting the fort, he moved his vessel close to the shores off Blakeley and rescued some of the garrison. From one of the escaping soldiers, Bennett learned Liddell was on the beach trying to escape. He sent a gig to rescue him; however, the bluecoats had already made it to the shores of the river and their fire forced him to abort the rescue attempt. "It was inexpressibly painful to me to abandon the attempt of his rescue," reported Bennett. "The boats of the squadron rescued from the water between 150 and 200 of the garrison."[6] Reportedly, General Liddell "was up to his neck in water and was fired at several times before being allowed to surrender."[7]

Taken prisoner by a Captain Julian, Liddell noted he was "treated with some show of respect." He later recalled, "Some officers of my staff were captured with me, others at points where they were on duty at the time the enemy entered the works. Generals Cockrell and Thomas were apprehended unhurt, with most of their staffs."[8] The day after he was captured, Liddell had a meeting with Canby, who he admitted treated him with "consideration and courtesy."[9]

First Lieutenant Alden McLellan of Brown's Light Artillery recounted his attempted escape from Fort Blakeley once the Union soldiers came over the works:

> I made a run for a wharf to get planks to escape upon, I throwing down four planks. The steward took two, and I ran down to get my planks, but another fellow was floating off on them. By this time the Federals were on the bluffs of the river, about two hundred yards off, and were firing at every object in the river. Some of the shots struck quite near me. I concluded not to take a plank ride just then, and was busy fastening a twenty-dollar gold piece in the lining of

my cap and dropping my watch into my bootleg when a Federal called out: "Say, you fellow with a green shirt on, come up or you will get hulled (shot) next time."

McLellan obeyed, making his way to the bluff where several of his comrades became prisoners of war.[10]

Lieutenant George W. Warren, Company A, 3rd and 5th Missouri Infantry, was one of the few fortunate enough to escape. "We saw in a moment the jig was up," recalled Warren.

Seeing the futility of resisting the overwhelming tide of charging bluecoats, Warren and several of his comrades instinctively ran for the Blakeley wharf, a half-mile to the rear of the fort.

When he got to the wharf, Warren immediately jumped on board a flatboat, which was heavily loaded with some sort of freight. Captain Upton M. Young of the 3rd Missouri, General Cockrell's aide-de-camp, and approximately 40 men followed. Warren shouted to those on the riverbank to cut the boat loose, but no one helped. He then leaped into the water and quickly cut the thick mooring rope with a dull knife and was dragged aboard by a fellow soldier. After floating off with the river current, someone shouted to them that the boat was loaded with gunpowder and would blow up once the bluecoats started firing at them. Panic-stricken, some of the men jumped overboard to try to swim to the shore, but at least one drowned. Those remaining on board dumped the cases of artillery powder into the river.[11]

As the current rapidly took them away, they watched helplessly the humiliating capture of their comrades on shore. "We saw Colonel (James) McCown put his white linen pocket handkerchief on the end of a ram-rod, step in front of his little squad of men," recalled Warren, "and waving this emblem of submission, surrender the Third and Fifth regiments of infantry." Federal soldiers fired at Warren's boat as it slipped away. Although musketry hit it several times, the oak gunwale protected the men who were lying flat. "We at last passed beyond their reach," remembered Warren, "even with artillery, and as the current was carrying us into the channel that led around under the guns of Spanish Fort, we concluded to cast anchor and trust to the chances of being picked up by friendly boats." Around 11 p.m. on April 9, they were picked up and transported safely to Mobile.[12]

The Aftermath

"We have stormed the entire line of works, and our troops are now in full possession," Steele wrote in a dispatch to Canby soon after Fort Blakeley was captured.[13] The commanding general thanked him and responded, "God bless you and your brave men and the good cause for which we fight."[14]

Following the fall of Fort Blakeley, there were instances of acquaintances prior to the war meeting once again. Captain Orlando F. Guthrie, a graycoat from Missouri, recalled, "An old schoolmate of mine in federal blue, Marcus Cox, of Bloomington, Ill., came up and shook hands with me, and we had a long talk about old days."[15] A correspondent from the New Orleans *Times-Democrat* reported: "A Confederate came up to General Granger and said, 'General, I am glad to see you; do you know me?' He proved to have been one of the employees of the General in 'those good old times,' I believe, at Fort Laramie."[16] First Sergeant John Corkery, Company D of the 1st Missouri Infantry, recalled meeting an old friend from St. Louis. "One of our guards was Joe Emmet [t] of St. Louis, now famous as 'Our Fritz,' who recognized me," Corkery recounted, "marched with me a couple of miles while we exchanged news about friends in each army. Joe knew every St. Louis boy in our regiment."[17]

Not everyone was happy to see each other after the fight. "More of our men were slain after the surrender than in the battle," Sergeant Bounds claimed. "Finally the white officers bunched us in squads of forty or fifty each and placed guards around us as close together as they could with fixed bayonets facing outward to protect us from the infuriated mob."[18]

There were accounts by Northerners that seemingly corroborate some of the accusations.[19] "Some of the Louisiana men [U.S. Colored Troops], however, made an attack on the prisoners and were with difficulty restrained from injuring them," wrote Union General C. C. Andrews. Federal officers of the 68th U.S.C.T. tried to restrain the enraged African-American soldiers. In their effort to save the prisoners, Captain Fred W. Norwood was wounded in the knee and Lieutenant Clark Gleason was mortally wounded, dying several days later.[20] After this incident, the officers regained control of the men from Hawkins's Division. Andrew F. Sperry of the 33rd Iowa wrote, "No display of feeling against the prisoners were allowed to be manifested; there was no sign of 'crowing' over a fallen foe, no taunting or insult allowed or attempted; but we could often hear expressions of the deepest hate and vindictiveness from dusky lips when away from the line of guards."[21]

Yet General Andrews claimed the prisoners were generally treated humanely. "A colored soldier of the 50th regiment found his former young master among the prisoners. They appeared happy to meet, and drank from the same canteen," he recalled.[22]

"A large and valuable amount of war dispatches, 50 beeves and 75 sheep, and a large amount of commissary stores were captured," the *Times-Democrat* reported. "There was tobacco, corn and meal, 'hard tack,' hams, salt, sugar, molasses, vinegar, etc. A good haul." The correspondent observed dead and wounded, "wearing gray as well as the blue uniform, lying around" the works. Federal ambulances soon arrived to take all the wounded to hospitals and bury the dead.[23] The day after the assault, Union doctor Johnson entered Fort Blakeley and later recounted his observations:

Passing into Blakely [sic] early on the morning of April 10, it having been surrendered at 5 p.m. the day previous, an opportunity was given to see things pretty much as the Confederates had left them. One thing that interested the writer greatly was some captured haversacks containing Johnny's rations. The meat was such as cur [sic] man would never have tasted unless reduced to the verge of starvation and the bread seemed indescribably poor, and of such character as a Northern farmer would hardly feed to his hogs. It seemed to been made from meal of which more than half was bran, and after being made into small pones—"dodgers,"—had been apparently cooked in the ashes and given about the appearance that two or three days sun-drying would bestow.

That men would consent to live on such food, and with scarcely any pay, daily encounter the vicissitudes of army life, and when occasion called, cheerfully risked their lives in battle, is a high tribute to Southern hardihood, pluck and courage.[24]

Four years of conflict had devastated the Confederacy's resources and limited their ability to provide decent food to their men. Despite lacking access to quality nourishment, the garrison of Fort Blakeley courageously carried on and did their best to hold their position against a numerically superior force. The Union doctor's account acknowledged the character of the courageous Southerners and the conditions they willingly endured for a cause they believed was noble.

The day after the capture of Fort Blakeley the prisoners were marched down to Spanish Fort. "We observed in all about 3,000, of whom very many were especially noticeable from their extreme age or youth," remembered Chaplain Richard L. Howard of the 124th Illinois. "They were Thomas's Alabama Reserves, and truly, as was often said, both the cradle and the grave had been robbed to furnish them."[25]

Sub-terra Shells

The Confederate sub-terra shells—and mines as they are known today—had a devastating effect during and, unfortunately, after the battles of Fort Blakeley and Spanish Fort.[26] "Our men suffered more by these devilish things than by rifle fire," wrote Private Henry Hart.[27] Even before the assault of Fort Blakeley, the sub-terra shells wreaked havoc. "A staff officer, riding the other day, woke up from a state of insensibility to discover himself fifteen feet from the roadway, and the mangled remains of horse that had been blown to atoms, he by strange chance, escaping with the temporary loss of his senses and the bruises of his fall," General Thomas K. Smith wrote in an April 4 letter to his wife. Made of 12-pounder shells and equipped with a mechanism that triggered an explosion when stepped on, sub-terra shells were a "great annoyance" to the Union soldiers. "They were planted in ruts of roads, and even in the path leading to pools of water where our men would be likely to go to quench their thirst," remembered Major Charles Allen. Typically marked by forked twigs and "a piece of cloth to warn their own men," the Southerners planted sub-terra shells in front, outside of the abatis and obstructions, of both Spanish Fort and Fort Blakeley.[28] "Every man feels that he is literally walking on the thin crust of a volcano," wrote General Thomas K. Smith.[29]

There was an immense number of torpedoes planted around Fort Blakeley.[30] Often during the siege of Fort Blakeley, sub-terra shells exploded as bullets and shells hit the ground in front of the fort.[31] "We had quite a number killed by torpedoes," wrote Connecticut artillerist Private Henry W. Hart in a letter to his wife the day

Union Major General C. C. Andrews commanded the Second Division of the XIII Corps.
Andrews wrote the book entitled *History of
the Campaign of Mobile* shortly after the war.
(*Courtesy of* The Library of Congress)

after the fall of Fort Blakeley. During the assault, the Northern soldiers sustained
horrifying injuries. "A captain had his leg blown off the first step he took after
leaving the rifle pits to charge," wrote Private Hart. "Another had both legs blown
off besides his private parts was all blown off."[32]

After the fort fell, the explosion of the sub-terra shells continued to inflict
casualties. "We have heard about 50 explode since the fight," wrote Hart.[33] Federal
officers surrounded Colonel Elijah Gates and asked him to point out where the
torpedoes were planted. He replied, "I don't know where they are, and by the Lord
Harry if I did I would not tell you," recalled Captain Guthrie of the 1st/3rd Missouri
Dismounted Cavalry. They threatened to take him along, and he said, "All right, I
have the satisfaction of knowing you will be blown up with me."[34]

In his official report, General C. C. Andrews recalled the issues caused by torpedoes
around Fort Blakeley after the assault and gave his views of the weapon:

> It required great care in withdrawing the prisoners from the fort to avoid loss of life on account
> of these torpedoes. I sent out a detail of prisoners last night with a Confederate officer who knew
> the whereabouts of the torpedoes to take them up. The detail was also at work today and some
> seventy have been taken up or exploded. In regard to this system of warfare, I cannot omit here
> to observe that it seems inhuman on this account that after a battle is over it may be out of the
> enemy's power to prevent the disaster which they are calculated to produce as in this instance
> non-combatants searching for the wounded and the dead were liable to destruction. And it
> sounded hideous indeed, last night hours after the battle had ceased, to hear these explosions
> and to feel that those were being torn to pieces, who were searching for the dead and wounded.[35]

The morning after the fall of Fort Blakeley, Steele ordered the prisoners to dig up the torpedoes "under a penalty of being marched in a body, back and forth until all had been exploded."[36] Private Dunn noted in his diary: "All is quiet except torpedoes. The prisoners are gathering them up and exploding them. Genl. Steele gave them written notice that if a private was wounded one of their officers should hang; that if one was killed, two would be hung. It excited much anxiety amongst them."[37]

On April 10, Canby sent a message to General Grant informing him of the results of the battles at Spanish Fort and Fort Blakeley. "Thirty one pieces of artillery were found in the Blakely [sic] works and thirty seven at Spanish Fort," he reported. "The prisoners at Blakely will reach 3,000. Generals Liddell, Cockrell and Thomas included; at Spanish Fort 583 prisoners, making a total of about 4,000, including those captured by Steele on his way from Pensacola. One gun boat surrendered but subsequently escaped. Our losses are severe in Garrard's, C. C. Andrews, and Hawkins divisions."[38] Andrews reported 127 Union soldiers killed and 527 wounded at Fort Blakeley.[39] Union Private Dunn commented on the casualties in his diary: "Our loss has been light compared with the value of the results. We believe we now have the key to Mobile and the Confederacy is certainly on its expiring couch. Long may it expire!"[40]

Maury was criticized for his decisions regarding the defense and evacuation of Fort Blakeley. "No dishonor can attach to any of the garrison of Blakeley on account of this disaster," wrote General Maury a year after the war. "From their veteran general down to the beardless boys of the young Alabama Reserves, they behaved with the devotion of the soldiers of the Confederacy."[41] Despite the praise of General Liddell and his men, he was not pleased with his order to withdraw the Spanish Fort garrison. In his postwar memoirs, he wrote:

> Our lines at Blakely [sic] could not be filled by one half, except by placing the men about one yard apart which gave no volume to the fire from the line. General Maury, however, declined to allow me to retain the troops that had escaped from Spanish Fort. He sent them all in transports and blockade runners to Mobile in sight of the enemy's boats from the Bay, who could not fail to perceive the weakness of the remaining forces in the works. In fact, they thought that we were evacuating the places in total.
>
> I believe if General Maury had permitted me to keep the Spanish Fort garrison, I could have repelled this assault. The weight or volume of fire would have been sufficiently heavy and deadly to have driven back the assaulting columns. As it was my line was nothing more than a good skirmish line, whose fire was entirely too weak. I know that General Maury did all in his power, but it was impossible to hold the defenses with such inadequate forces.[42]

"Maury intended to withdraw Liddell during the night of the 9th," recalled General Taylor. "It would have been more prudent to have done so on the night of the 8th, as the enemy would naturally make an energetic effort after the fall of Spanish Fort; but he was unwilling to yield any ground until the last moment, and felt confident of holding the place another day."[43]

Some Federal officers also criticized Maury's handling of Fort Blakeley. In his book on the *History of the Campaign of Mobile*, General C. C. Andrews wrote it was a "mistake to keep the garrison at Blakely [sic] an hour after the fall at Spanish Fort. Every possible means should have been used to remove it before an assault could be made."[44] Union Colonel Charles S. Hill offered a blunt criticism: "That the entire Blakely [sic] garrison was captured was due to their own stupidity, as it was almost absolutely certain that the besiegers would assault and carry the works the day after the fall of Spanish Fort."[45] There were reasons Maury was not able to evacuate the Blakeley garrison in time to avoid their capture. Shortly after the war he wrote, "It seems to be an error not to remove the garrison of Blakeley to Mobile as soon as Spanish Fort was abandoned. It would have been difficult to do this after day dawned, and up to that time all of Spanish Fort garrison had not been transferred from Blakely [sic] to Mobile."[46] In another postwar account, Maury further defended himself: "I could not have brought away the garrison of Blakely [sic] till after dark on the 9th, and the enemy had been so very cautious I was not anxious about waiting one day longer."[47]

Although there were a few more skirmishes that occurred later, Fort Blakeley proved to be the final large-scale battle of the war. One Union soldier stated, "It is now a matter of history that the 9th of April 1865, so auspiciously opened by the surrender of Lee at Appomattox, was no less appropriately closed by the capture of Blakeley."[48] Occurring just hours after the surrender of the Army of Northern Virginia at Appomattox Court House, the assault of Fort Blakeley on April 9, 1865, ended the last siege of the war. The campaign was full of acts of heroism and intense fighting. The men that fought there were as courageous as soldiers anywhere in the conflict. Although some of these brave men may not have realized it at the time, the capture of this key position sealed the fate of Mobile.

CHAPTER TWELVE

Evacuation

The capture of Fort Blakeley and Spanish Fort opened the back door of Mobile to the Yankees. The estimated 4,500 Confederate troops left, roughly half the original number of men before the siege, could not possibly defend the city with any hope of success. General Forrest, whom General Maury depended on for succor, had been defeated at Selma. Furthermore, the tremendous expenditure of ammunition defending Spanish Fort and Fort Blakeley left the Confederates with few options.

"When Blakeley fell, there was so little ammunition left that an attempt to withstand a siege in Mobile would have been entirely unjustifiable," wrote Maury.[1] "Blakely [sic] captured with most of the garrison. Many were shot or drowned. Evacuation of the city ordered," one Mobile resident recorded in her diary, "but this, the darkest hour of all: Richmond captured, Petersburg surrendered, Mobile about to be evacuated."[2] One Southern soldier summed up the situation: "The only thing now to do was to evacuate Mobile. Many citizens also wanted to leave."[3] Faced with an overwhelming Federal force poised to assault Mobile, Maury had little choice but to abandon the city.[4]

On April 10, after ordering the works dismantled and cannons spiked, Maury began evacuating the remnants of his garrison north toward Meridian, Mississippi.[5] "Gen. Maury's ill-appointed, worn out, half starved army of 8,000 men [inaccurate estimate], fell back slowly toward Meridian on the Mobile and Ohio railroad," recalled Lieutenant Colonel Spence. The evacuation route of the Mobile & Ohio was the only unbroken rail line from Mobile northward into the interior. In a telegraph sent during the evacuation, Taylor emphasized to Maury, "Unless you have surplus transportation, troops must march and transportation used for moving stores."[6] Maury apparently did have adequate surplus transportation as the infantry went by rail up the M&O.[7] Besides the Mobile & Ohio railroad, the Confederates used wagons, horses, and steamboats to evacuate.[8]

"This morning, we were much startled by the ringing of the alarm-bell," Mary Waring, a young resident of Mobile, wrote in her diary on April 10, "the object of which was to call troops together to prepare for evacuation."[9] Mobilian Mary E.

Brooks recounted, "I was awakened early one morning by an unusual noise in the street, and running to my window I looked down upon a body of troops resting on the march," she recalled, "sitting on the sidewalks and on our steps. On inquiring into the meaning of it all, I was told that they were leaving Mobile to make a stand farther up the country."[10] Another resident, B. B. Cox, who was a young boy at the time of the evacuation, added, "As fast as they could get away from the city every man that looked like a soldier left."[11] The graycoats were intent on a swift evacuation.

On April 11, the evacuation continued. Major Richard C. Bond of the 1st Louisiana Artillery informed his command at Mobile's Battery Gladden that they were about to be evacuated. "It is no fault of ours," he wrote in a general order. "The enemy, with his large fleet, idle at the moment, has not dared to approach within range of our battery." Bond tried to console and encourage his men. "I know that there are no cowards or faint-hearted among you," he wrote. "It is easy to be gay and confident after victory; none but the really brave and true are firm and obedient under misfortune." To further encourage them, he wrote that they would soon join two revered Southern leaders "who have never known defeat," General Richard S. Taylor and General Nathan B. Forrest.[12]

William Rix, a Unionist businessman from Vermont living in Mobile during the war, wrote the city was "in pandemonium." He added, "The fleet of steamboats was delayed, at the last moment, by the desertion of pilots and especially firemen who were negroes." Confederate squads went out in the streets and pressed laborers to assist in operating the steamboats so that they could get the fleet started up the Alabama River.[13]

One of the keys to the successful evacuation was the efforts of the gallant Lieutenant Colonel Spence and the 12th Mississippi Cavalry. On April 6, Maury withdrew Spence's horsemen from Fort Blakeley for outpost duty around Mobile. For the next week, Spence and his troopers would have little time for rest.[14] After the fall of Blakeley, before leaving Mobile, the mounted soldiers were ordered to trade out their worn-down horses for fresh ones belonging to private citizens, an assignment unpopular with the residents of Mobile. The *Mobile Daily News* reported: "Many horses and mules were impressed and carried off for the Confederate artillery service and other purposes." During the evacuation, Spence's cavaliers performed many tasks, including reporting on the Federal army's movements, establishing courier lines, destroying railroad bridges and trestles, and covering the trains and soldiers as they headed toward Meridian.[15]

"I was ordered on out-post duty and remained in front of the besieging army until the city was evacuated," recalled Colonel Spence.[16] On April 10, Spence was ordered to report to General Gibson, who was in command of Mobile during the evacuation. Gibson informed Spence that all infantry and artillery would be withdrawn during the night. "You better withdraw your more distant pickets and dispose them nearer, so that when you leave your present position you will have them in hand," instructed Gibson. "Keep scouts out pretty well and at daylight make this your headquarters and occupy the city. Much will be left to your own discretion." Gibson instructed Spence to remain in Mobile as long as possible, without risking any part of his command being captured, and to prevent any disorder in the town.[17]

On April 12, Maury messaged Gibson from Chunchula, Alabama: "Impress on Spence the importance of <u>destroying bridges and trestles</u> as he retires. The general commanding will go to Citronelle, and the trains will take from the wagons there whatever freight can be transferred, so as to lighten up the wagons," he wrote. "We will wait here till the next train comes up and send one back to try and get Colonel Lindsay and men. There is a car of corn and rations for Spence at this station." On the same day, Maury also messaged Spence directly: "You must keep close to the enemy and not give up ground unless forced to do so." Maury instructed him to send news on the Federal movements, to send a scout to Oven Bluff, to burn all trestles and bridges between Mobile and Citronelle after the Confederates' trains passed, and to send orders to the quartermaster on what was needed.[18]

Maury praised Spence's performance in the defense and evacuation of Mobile. "Colonel Spence was one of the most efficient and comfortable out post commanders I ever had to deal with. He always took what was given to him and made the most of it. He was devoted, active, brave and modest, and did his whole duty to the very last day of our existence as an army," he remembered.[19]

The Confederate ironclad warships *Huntsville* and *Tuscaloosa* lacked the engine power to travel upriver against the strong currents of the Mobile and Tombigbee Rivers. Instead of attempting to tow the vessels, Commodore Farrand ordered both ships scuttled in the Mobile River. The crew and materials from these two vessels were divided among the remaining Confederate ships. Before embarking, the navy yard was burned. Farrand's small fleet, the ironclad *Nashville*, the ram *Baltic*, the gunboat *Morgan* and the steamers *Black Diamond* and *Southern Republic*, the blockade runner *Virgin* then successfully escaped up the Alabama River.[20] As the remnants of the Southern navy proceeded up the narrow and crooked Alabama and Tombigbee Rivers to Demopolis, their long and wide vessels would occasionally run into the banks. "That night was a sorry one for all of us," remembered William L. Cameron, an officer aboard the Confederate ship *Nashville*.[21]

Batteries Huger and Tracy

Throughout the siege, Batteries Huger and Tracy had a shortage of ammunition, just 200 rounds for the Brooke guns and about 300 for the 10-inch guns. Maury ordered the commander of the two forts, Colonel Patton, to conserve the low supply of ammunition for an emergency. "There was no more to be had in the Confederacy," wrote Maury of the ammunition shortage. "Therefore, the garrisons covered their guns with merlons against the batteries on the Eastern Shore, and built bombproofs for themselves."[22]

After the fall of Fort Blakeley, the garrisons of the two marsh batteries sprang into action. "Fort Huger [and Tracy] now had some use for her heavy guns to turn upon Spanish Fort, occupied by the enemy," remembered General Liddell. "The batteries were ordered to open fire, holding nothing back, and to hold their position until receiving orders to retire."[23] For two days after the fall of Fort Blakeley, Huger and Tracy defiantly held out, covering the evacuation of troops from Mobile.[24] The two batteries were finally able to unleash their fury since they knew they were soon leaving. "As the guns upon forts Huger & Tracy boom out with heavy roar, the sound fills my heart with bitter sorrow," wrote Mobile resident Laura Pillans.[25] They relentlessly fired more than a dozen heavy guns at the Union-occupied Spanish Fort. From Huger, repeated shots plowed up the earth and caused significant damage at Fort McDermott.[26]

On April 11, Huger and Tracy continued to relentlessly shell the Federals during the day. The same day, Canby ordered a surprise evening attack on Fort Huger with 600 men. Around sunset the last gun was fired from the Confederate batteries.[27] By that time, Maury had managed to evacuate the bulk of his forces from Mobile and sent word to Colonel Patton to evacuate the water batteries under the cover of darkness that Tuesday evening. After holding out against the combined firepower of Admiral Thatcher's naval force and the Union land batteries, the two swamp batteries were found abandoned. "These troops, in all about 300 Louisianans, remained in the presence of the enemy's army and fleet, ten miles distant from Mobile, whence they knew no succor could reach them, and continued to receive and return the fire of the constantly increasing batteries planted against them," wrote Maury, "until after dark of the 11th, when in obedience to orders of the General commanding, they dismantled and abandoned their works and retired upon the city, reaching Mobile after daylight of the 12th."[28] Before leaving the artillerists spiked their cannons and then successfully escaped with their small arms and ammunition, using a treadway plank in the rear of Tracy.[29] "From Tracey [sic], reaching out to its rear for near two miles," remembered Maury, "another bridge had been constructed, to Chocolate Bayou, on deep water range to Mobile and far beyond range of the enemy's guns."[30]

On April 11, at 11 p.m., receiving word Huger and Tracy were abandoned, men of the 114th Illinois [pontoiners] entered the works and inscribed their names on the fort. The next morning, the garrisons of Tracy and Huger, without a single casualty, were among the last to leave the wharf of Mobile for Demopolis.[31]

The two batteries on the Apalachee River were the "last defenses of Mobile to yield."[32] Both sides noted the supposed historical significance of the batteries. General C. C. Andrews claimed: "It was the last day for great guns in Mobile Bay—the last for the war."[33] Likewise, Maury wrote: "These garrisons fired the last cannon in the last great battle of the war for freedom of the Southern States."[34] Yet, both Maury and Andrews were mistaken; the cannons fired from Huger and Tracy were not the last of the conflict. Five days later, heavy artillery was used at the battles of Columbus and West Point, Georgia.[35]

"Tis over. The last gun has been fired—the last soldier has marched out [of Mobile]. Ere another sun shall have set, the flag of the enemy will be floating over this city—a hostile band be playing the airs most distasteful to our ears—and a file of soldiers exalting in our defeat, be marching up our beautiful street," wrote Ann Quigley, Head Mistress of the Mobile public school, Barton Academy, in her diary on April 10. "And our own brave ones—where are they? Hundreds lie sleeping in the damp tangled marshes of the Eastern Shore—hundreds are suffering in hospitals while the rest, exhausted by two weeks unavailing efforts to defend our city, are making their way to other fields of carnage & slaughter."[36] After watching the last of the Confederate soldiers leave, Laura Pillans sadly wrote, "Perhaps I shall never look upon a gray coat again."[37]

Cavalry Skirmish at Little River Bridge and Eliska, Alabama

As the Southern artillerists at Fort Huger and Tracy covered the evacuation of their comrades, approximately 60 miles northeast of Mobile, a cavalry skirmish occurred at Little River Bridge and Eliska, Alabama.[38] On the morning of April 5, U.S. General John T. Lucas, with a command of 1,500 troopers, moved out from near Blakeley with orders to occupy Claiborne, on the Alabama River, to "cut off the retreat from Mobile by that route."[39]

On their way to Claiborne, the Federal horsemen encountered a small contingent of the 15th Confederate Cavalry under Lieutenant Colonel Thomas J. Meyers and Captain T. C. English's company of mounted infantry at the southern border of Monroe County, Alabama.[40] The Southern horsemen were sent there to guard the Alabama River "above Choctaw and establish a courier line to Demopolis" during the Confederate evacuation from Mobile.[41] Estimates of the number of mounted soldiers under Myers and English ranged from 200 to 450 men.[42]

Myers had assumed command of the 15th Confederate Cavalry, while Colonel Harry Maury, a cousin of General Dabney Maury, was recovering from an injury in which a horse reportedly kicked him.[43] Captain English happened to be the brother-in-law of noted Union General George B. McClellan. He reportedly rode into this fight on McClellan's personal saddle, left behind by the general on a prewar visit.[44]

Lucas had hoped to surprise the Secessionists there, but intelligence of his advance had already reached them. A couple of miles past Mount Pleasant, Alabama, they suddenly came upon the Southerners posted strongly behind swampy ground and for about 20 minutes fighting was fierce.[45] "Harry Davis the flag bearer was shot in about 20 feet of where I was at," wrote Confederate Private C. H. Driesbach of English's Company, "and getting off his horse, sat down by a pine tree and was last seen holding the flag aloft."[46] Lucas ordered the U.S. 1st Louisiana Cavalry to charge, forcing the vastly outnumbered Southerners to retire. They were pursued for a few miles, but many escaped through the woods.[47]

In his after-action report, Lucas reported three officers and 73 men captured, along with two battle flags, many small arms, and 500 bales of Confederate cotton. His troopers sustained 13 causalities (10 soldiers wounded and three killed), whereas the graycoats suffered seven men wounded and three killed.[48]

Following the fight, Lucas moved into the nearby town of Claiborne and occupied it without resistance. "So hurried was the rebel retreat through the town that they did not inform the people on their side of the river of the change which had occurred in the troops occupying this place," reported Lucas, "and an enrolling officer and several soldiers crossed the river in a flat we sent them and fell into our hands." On April 15, after capturing several more Southern horsemen at nearby Claiborne following the skirmish, Lucas and his men remained in the vicinity until heading back to Fort Blakeley.[49]

A Day of Strange Transition

By April 12, exactly four years to the day the War Between the States began, the Confederate army successfully evacuated Mobile. Early on that Wednesday morning, the last gray-coated soldiers left the city on steamboats, blockade runners, and gunboats headed north on the Alabama River.[50] One resident remembered April 12 as a "day of strange transition in our city."[51] Laura Pillans wrote in her diary, "The last company of infantry marched out this morning at 6 A. M., and a small detachment of cavalry is preparing to follow & then we shall be at the mercy of the captors."[52] Mary D. Waring awoke feeling "deserted and desolate." She noted in her diary, "All our troops got off some time during the night and the city is entirely 'free of gray coats' except some few scouts who will decamp upon the entrance of the enemy."[53]

During the evacuation, Taylor instructed Maury, "No stores must be left in Mobile except in case of absolute necessity, and ordnance stores under no circumstances."[54] Maury, who had anticipated a long siege, had denied citizen solicitations for the stored rations necessary to feed his garrison. Unable to transport all the stores to Meridian, he opened excess commissary stores for the needy.[55] Spring Hill College, one of the beneficiaries, was granted 100 sacks of corn.[56]

After the last Southern soldier marched out of the city, disturbances broke out as citizens fought over the abandoned food and supplies.[57] Women were seen carrying axes, hammers, and hatchets in the streets heading to Commerce Street to break in and help themselves to the Confederate Commissary stores.[58] Waring wrote, "Quite a commotion has sprung up, down the street, and the people threatened with a mob." She observed poor women "endeavoring to carry off as much as possible—each one tries to be first, and consequently much scuffling and rioting ensues."[59] Citizen William Rix observed, "Women and children staggered through the streets under loads of sabers, and bayonets and Springfield rifles." He continued, "The unique finale of the day's doings was the knocking open of boxes of rockets and signal torches … The wonder was that the mob was not self-quelled by being blown to atoms."[60] A volunteer guard of armed citizens was able to restore order until Federal soldiers arrived.[61]

Burning Cotton

Before the land campaign began, Confederate officials prohibited citizens from bringing cotton into the city. They did not want their cotton stores bolstering the coffers of the invading Union forces. Taylor had ordered all the cotton burned if they were forced to evacuate Mobile.[62] A substantial amount of cotton was confiscated from private citizens and transported to an area north of the city called the Orange Grove, where it could be safely burned in case of an evacuation.[63] Taylor emphasized in a telegraph to Maury, "See that no mistake occurs in orders about the cotton" during the evacuation.[64]

Once the Confederate infantry and artillery evacuated, a regiment of Colonel Spence's 12th Mississippi carried out Taylor's order to torch the cotton as they left. Reportedly, Mobile Mayor Robert H. Slough, the city council, and most of the citizens of Mobile were strongly opposed to the burning of their cotton. They were prepared to prevent it when the time came.[65] "As smoke rolled up, telling the tale of wantonness," remembered Rix, "the fire bells of the city rung out the warning, and citizens rushed to the rescue. Out of the 20,000 bales only some 2,100 were destroyed."[66] As Maury explained in a letter to General Beauregard after the war, at the time of the cotton burning his primary concern was evacuating his men "who were almost the last hope" for the Confederacy. Nonetheless, he was "mortified and annoyed" by his failure to destroy all the cotton.[67]

Meridian, Mississippi

In accordance to General Taylor's instructions, Maury moved his command to Meridian, Mississippi "on the line of the Mobile and Ohio railway."[68] Upon arrival at the Confederate headquarters at Meridian, Lieutenant Daniel Geary, a brigade ordnance officer, found "everybody and everything in great disorder and confusion."[69] Despite the chaotic conditions, the remnants of the Mobile garrison and Forrest's mounted soldiers, who also fell back to the same vicinity, were still, amazingly, prepared to continue the fight for their cause.[70]

General Taylor wrote that the small army of fewer than 8,000 men "held in readiness to discharge such duties as the waning fortunes of the 'cause' and the honor of its arms might demand."[71] In an April 13 letter to his sister, James H. Hutchisson, Company E of the 2nd Battery of Alabama Light Artillery, wrote, "The talk is that we take up our line of march for Virginia which state I do not believe we will reach for I think the whole country is full of Yankee troops and flying Confederates to the latter number of which I expect we will soon be added."[72]

Shortly after arriving, Maury moved his small force into camp near Meridian at Cuba Station, Alabama. Corporal Jones recalled, "Again we settled down to wait results. We had plenty to eat and there seemed no disposition to drill or do anything of the kind." He added, "Rations were given without stint." At their camp, they began hearing rumors of General Robert E. Lee's surrender at Appomattox Court House, Virginia. "Most of us thought that these rumors were wild and without foundation, but there seemed to be an air of mystery about everything," remembered Jones. The defenders of Mobile were beginning to realize their long struggle was over.[73]

CHAPTER THIRTEEN

Your City is Menaced

With Batteries Tracy and Fort Huger found abandoned, General Canby shifted his attention to the immediate occupation of Mobile. "I do not intend to be stopped by torpedoes," Canby declared in a dispatch to Union General Joseph Bailey at Starke's Landing the day after the fall of Fort Blakeley. Thatcher's navy, in full cooperation, thus focused their efforts on the dangerous task of removing torpedoes from the route across the bay to Mobile.[1]

"The floating torpedoes, which the rebels sent adrift, had already been cut off by stretching a great net across the narrow channel, and it remained only to remove those which had been sunk between our fleet and a point up to which the rebel fleet had itself found it necessary to pass," reported a correspondent with the *Cincinnati Commercial* on April 9, 1865. Torpedoes were abundant in the Blakeley River channel. During the day, about 20 torpedoes were removed. This allowed the wooden gunboats to begin moving cautiously up the Apalachee River and over toward the city.[2]

In anticipation of Batteries Huger and Tracy falling, Canby had requested all transports be retained at Starke's Landing to ferry troops across the bay.[3] On April 11, the Federals saw rocket flare signals from the marsh "sent up by people in the city" that indicated the Confederates were evacuating.[4] Canby promptly ordered arrangements to bring up supplies and soldiers for the occupation of Mobile. He sent the 1st and 3rd Divisions of the XIII Corps under General Granger on an 8-mile march down from Blakeley to the wharf at Starke's Landing, located 4 miles south of Spanish Fort.[5]

On the moonlit night of April 11, the 33rd Iowa Infantry, "in high spirits, singing and laughing," marched back down toward Spanish Fort. The march proved to be "exceedingly tiresome."[6] Brigade Commander Colonel Conrad Krez, 27th Wisconsin, had acquired the reputation of always taking the wrong road. Sperry recalled a frustrating experience with Colonel Krez on the late-night march from Fort Blakeley down to Starke's Landing. "When all were tired to the last extreme of unmurmuring endurance, of course the worthy brigade-commander must lose the road," remembered Sperry. "Against the advice of his staff-officers and others, and in default of precautions which ordinary common sense would have provided, he led us off on a wrong track, and had to waste perhaps an hour of marching, before we were finally set right again. The curses of the tired soldiers were loud and deep."[7]

Krez's Brigade and others did not reach Starke's Landing until the early hours of April 12. "After a most fatiguing night march the brigade arrived at the wharf on the morning of the 12th instant," reported Colonel Krez. After considerable delay, Krez finally succeeded in boarding the 33rd Iowa on the *General Banks* and the 77th Ohio and 28th Wisconsin aboard the tinclad, *No. 46*. They were the last brigade to embark.[8]

After finally making it aboard the steamers, they pushed off from the pier and anchored in the bay. In the morning, at about 7 a.m., Granger's men proceeded by boat to Mobile County.[9] A thick fog cover during most of the 6-mile journey added to the anxiety of the soldiers on board. "It was feared that in crossing the bay some torpedoes might be encountered," Lieutenant William H. Bentley recounted, "but no accident occurred."[10]

The cautious Union officers expected to meet resistance upon landing on the shores south of Mobile. Fearing an attack as they disembarked, the officers wanted to get the men ashore and "form in line" as quickly as possible. Private Wiley observed a major of the 23rd Wisconsin with a thick German accent instructing his men on the boat. "We were somewhat amused at the Major as he went from company to company giving them their instructions," he wrote. "He would come to a company and [say] 'Now poys you youst listen to me whin we gets on shore you youst brake for de land.'"[11]

"As we approached that point, several of the gun boats in our front, the Steamship Metecommet [sic], at about half mile from shore, threw a shell over the shore, when a white flag was shown," wrote General Slack in a letter to his wife.[12] One Union soldier recalled, "Metacomet's forward 100 pounder rifle sent a shell into the garden of a man named Ferguson, where a sand battery had been on the western shore." Contrary to the claims of Andrews and Maury noted in the previous chapter, the shell fired from the *Metacomet*, not Batteries Huger and Tracy, was likely the last big gun fired in the siege of Mobile.[13]

General Granger crossed the bay in the steamer *General Banks*. Sperry, who also rode on the *General Banks*, recounted:

> The morning was foggy; but soon the sun shone out merrily upon the rippling waters, and lit up a scene of military splendor such as we had never beheld. Transports and gun-boats, in single or double lines, with signal-flags rising and falling, and colors proudly flying from the mast-head, moved slowly but majestically across the bay. One or two of the gun-boats were provided with machines for raising the torpedoes with which it was feared the course was strewn; but no trouble occurred. As we neared the western shore there was a greatly-increased display of signal-flags. One gun-boat advanced some distance ahead of the fleet, and threw a single shell as challenge to the shore; but no answer came. Again the signal-flags waved bravely. The gun-boat on which were there head-quarters of the fleet now moved nearer to the General Banks, and the portly

USS *Metacomet* (*Courtesy of* Naval Heritage and History Command)

and bedizened form of Admiral Thatcher appeared majestic on her deck. Turning dignifiedly toward our boat, with a slow and rotund pomposity of manner that words could not convey, he called out "I propose to shell the shore." "By —, you'll shell a flag of truce if you do," profanely answered General Granger. The ludicrousness of the situation became apparent when on looking shoreward we saw that this tremendous array of "fleet, armies, and artillery" was thus to be brought to bear against a solitary negro, whose feeble hand waived a white kerchief tremblingly.[14]

The two divisions of the XIII Corps landed on shore at Catfish Point about 11:00 a.m., near the mouth of Dog River and the Magnolia race track, approximately 5 miles south of Mobile.[15] Granger's men met no opposition at landing since mainly women, children, and elderly men was all that remained in the city.[16] "Sent a boat ashore and learned the city was evacuated," wrote Slack. "Immediately the landing began. Water was so shallow we could not get in very readily, but we soon got off, and were second to land." He continued, "Everything was joy and hilarity. When we expected to land under a desperate fire, found no enemy to resist us. Landing was very slow, but was done as speedily as possible."[17] The 8th Illinois Regiment of infantry was the first to disembark and form in line. They immediately began the march to Mobile after the other regiments reached the shore.[18]

"Colonel Grier got the part of the regiment ashore from the Transport J. M. Brown and started for the city on double quick and left orders for the companys [sic] C and H to follow up as soon as we got ashore," Wiley recounted. "But our boat not being a flat bottom like the transports we could not get within twenty feet of shore and we could not youst brake for de land until we constructed piers or foot walks to get ashore on and we had to move then double quick to catch up with the rest of the regiment before they reached the city."[19]

Mayor Slough Surrenders Mobile

Mobile's Mayor Robert H. Slough left around 11 a.m. to surrender to the approaching Union soldiers, riding down the Bay Shell road in a carriage with a large white flag of truce flying above it. Prominent businessman Caleb Price and Dr. George Ketchum escorted him. They were followed by a second carriage with city aldermen C. P. Gage, Dr. Josiah Nott, and Cleveland Moulton. Price and Moulton were alleged to have Unionist business ties that could presumably help facilitate a peaceful transition. Moulton, who was a local militia recruiter, was rumored to have shielded Union sympathizers from service.[20]

After proceeding a short distance, Lieutenant Colonel R. G. Laughlin of the army and Lieutenant Commander S. R. Franklin of the navy, officers assigned by Granger and Thatcher, met the mayor and his delegation just south of the city limits, where they issued a written demand for surrender.[21] The following is the written correspondence between Mayor Slough and the U.S. land and naval forces:

HEADQUARTERS, LAND AND NAVAL U.S. FORCES,
   MOBILE, ALABAMA, April 12, 1865.
   MAYOR SLOUGH, Mobile, Ala.
   Sir: Your city is menaced by a large land and naval force. We deem it proper to demand its immediate and unconditional surrender.
   Very respectfully, your obedient servants,
   Major General GORDON GRANGER.
   Acting Rear Admiral H. K. THATCHER.

MAYOR'S OFFICE,
   CITY OF MOBILE,
   April 12, 1865.
   Gentlemen:
   I have the honor to acknowledge the receipt of your communication at the hands of Lieut. Col. R. G. Laughlin, staff of Major General Granger, Commanding 13th Army Corps, and Lieut. Commander S. R. Franklin, U.S. Navy, staff of Admiral Thatcher, demanding the immediate and unconditional surrender of this city.
   The city has been evacuated by the military authorities, and its municipal authority is now under my control. Your demand has been granted, and I trust, gentlemen, for the sake of humanity, all the safeguards which you can throw around our people will be secured to them.
   Very respectfully,
      Your obedient servant,
      R. H. SLOUGH,
      Mayor of the city of Mobile.[22]

As the U.S. troops marched north toward Mobile on the "beautiful road of oyster shells," they were awed at the sight of the abandoned defensive works, said to be the strongest fortifications in the Confederacy. "I think I never saw at any other place

Mobile Mayor Robert H. Slough met the advancing Union forces on April 12, 1865 on Bay Shell Road. (*Courtesy of* Library of Congress)

so extensive & strong works. Those would be stronger if the soil were less sandy but as it was nothing was left undone that skill could devise & labor execute."[23]

Many Mobilians were alarmed as the blue-coated soldiers approached the city. "Started to the graveyard but a gentleman sent me word I had better get back home at once for that the Yankees were coming into town," resident Laura Pillans wrote in her diary. "I hastened back as fast as I could but my heart was convulsed with irrepressible emotion."[24] Considering the destructive fate suffered by other captured cities, her feelings of distress were understandable.

Example of the breastworks that existed around Mobile, Fort Blakeley, and Spanish Fort. (*Courtesy of History Museum of Mobile*)

"'The Yankees are coming,' was the word passed around the city," remembered B. B. Cox, who was just a young boy at the time. "The old bell in the guard house tower pealed forth in thunderous tones and everything that had a steam bellowed forth the notification. Cox recalled being frightened because they had been educated that the Yankees had horns and tails and they did not know what was going to happen to them.[25]

As Mayor Slough surrendered Mobile, U. S naval personnel were busy hoisting the U.S. ensign in the city. After they had planted the U.S. flag at the island Battery McIntosh, these sailors went on a gig commanded by Acting Master J. B. Williams of the ironclad *Cincinnati* to Mobile. "They found no opposition to their landing, and hoisted the ensign they carried on the roof of the Battle House, climbing up on each other's shoulders to get to the flagstaff on the roof," recalled Ambrose S. Wight, who had served as clerk to the commander of the *Cincinnati*. "Twenty-five minutes after our ensign was hoisted a party cavalry came tearing in, their horses all in a foam. They went up to the roof of the custom house, across the street from the Battle House, and the first thing they saw was our flag and our men across the way." The mounted soldiers, likely a detachment from General Veatch's command, were chagrined.[26] Nevertheless, they proceeded in hoisting the U.S. Flag over the custom-house, city hall, the post office, and the market.[27] Young resident William Fulton recounted:

> At 2:30 o'clock, as I was walking out on the gallery I saw some soldiers dressed in blue going along Royal Street. I called Ma, and she said that they were Yankees who had come to hoist the flag of the dis-United States over Mobile and I ran after them and followed them till they

stopped at the Battle House, where they went in; and having eaten dinner they went on top of the house and hoisted it. They took off their caps and there were eleven of them. They walked along Royal street and stopped at the Battle House without directions from anyone at all. They were perfectly unconcerned while marching through the city as if they had been here a month.

Just before they raised the hated gridiron, Mayor Slough returned with a Yankee officer in the carriage. They stopped in front of the Custom House and Mayor Slough made a short speech to the crowd which had gathered around; telling the citizens to go to their homes and to behave quietly as possible. The mayor then went with the Yankee to the Manassas Club room where each got a cigar and returned into the carriage smoking. They drove down the bay to meet the other carriage and some more of the accursed yankee officers. About an hour after one of the Yankee generals accompanied with his staff rode along Conception St. He was followed by the carriages and an ambulance filled with yankee officers... The despicable gridiron was then raised over the Market. In a little while the officers were riding all about the city. As one group passed by me, I gave them three hearty groans.[28]

Enthusiastic Reception?

After successfully landing most of his troops at Catfish Point, Granger ordered the steamer *General Banks* to transport him up to the Mobile wharves off Government Street. Stephen A. Cobb, a staff officer for Granger, described the perilous journey through an obstruction-filled channel lined with torpedoes that were "simply immense" and "planted everywhere".[29] Captain Dane, the captain of the vessel, hailed from Maine but had lived in the South for many years. He had remained a loyal Unionist throughout the conflict. Dane had served in the Red River campaign, where he was taken prisoner but managed to escape back into Union lines. One of Granger's staff officers recalled the voyage: "Turning to him, Granger says, 'Captain Dane, can you put this boat into Mobile?' Giving his reply the full weight of his great will in the laconism of impending and probably destruction, he answered, 'Yes, or sink it.'" Dane proceeded to head the *General Banks* north toward the city. Most of the passengers on board had little hope of making it to their destination. The vessel made it safely past the obstruction- and torpedo-filled waters to debark at the Government Street wharf. The boat trip was noteworthy considering six Union ships were sunk by torpedoes in the same area over the next few days.[30]

Arriving safely at Mobile's Government Street wharf at approximately 4:00 p.m., Granger reported that he received a "warm reception."[31] He then sent a message to Canby stating, "The citizens are more than happy at our arrival and give us every information required."[32] Upon his arrival Granger also made a brief speech at the Custom House, reportedly stating that it was a free country; however everyone needed to be off the streets after dark.[33]

"The scene of our visitors were loud in their demonstrations of gladness at our coming. Some were silent—a part with malice and hate, others too overjoyed to give utterance to their feelings," recalled Cobb. "To depict that scene in its true colors is like painting the rainbow. Down the cheeks of old men coursed tears, in channels that had been dry for years. For nearly half a decade of years the banner at the mast-head had not waved in pride of Mobile."[34] It is reasonable to question whether the tears Cobb observed running down "the cheeks of old men" could have been tears of sadness for the fall of Mobile and the Confederacy.[35]

Prior to the siege, the *Philadelphia Inquirer* reported on the alleged sentiments of the people in Mobile: "Thousands, it is said, are ready to throw off the accursed yoke of military despotism which has kept them down for so long a time, and return to the protection of a Government they deserted."[36] The Unionist newspaper report was exaggerated and not necessarily accurate.

"I see by the northern papers that General Canby, who captured Mobile, says he has received a heartier welcome from the Mobilians than he has any place he has taken yet. How can the people there so soon forget their dead? Why, even the enemy can't respect us when we can be guilty of such heartlessness," remarked Confederate nurse Kate Cumming, who was not present when the blue-coated soldiers arrived, on the reports of the welcome they received upon entering the city. Later, when Cumming returned to Mobile, she learned the newspaper reports were misleading.[37]

"5 P. M. The Yankees after being received with loud hurrah by assembled traitors who rushed to the wharf to greet their friends hoisted the hated evil banner of tyranny over the 'Battle House' & then marched quietly to the suburbs," Laura Pillans wrote in her April 12 diary entry.[38] "You ought to have seen the negroes when the Yanks came in," wrote one resident in a letter to a family member. "They were all so delighted that they ran down to see them."[39]

In a letter to his sister, dated April 12, young William Fulton noted seeing "negroes" and some "white people" rushing down the street to greet Granger's boat, the *General Banks*, "shouting and hurrahing" as it docked at the foot of Government Street. Fulton wrote, "They shook hands with the detestible [sic] Yankees and were invited by them to go on the boat."[40] As Granger's report and Cobb's account asserts, there were citizens, primarily from the poorer classes, that were glad to see the arrival of the besiegers.[41] However, the accounts of Waring, Pillans, Fulton, and others provide compelling evidence contrary to the notion that Mobile was a predominately pro-Union city.[42]

"No unpleasant demonstrations were made by either the citizens of Mobile or by our soldiery upon the occupation of the daughty [sic] city. All the public buildings and stores were closed, and the private residences looked like houses of mourning," Major Truman reported in an article published on the cover of the April 24 edition of the *New York Times*. The Union blockade and the subsequent siege certainly contributed to food shortages in Mobile. Truman described the condition of the people as "in extreme want, the poorer classes of which immediately besieged our soldiers for something to eat."[43] It is possible, as Truman alluded, that some of the poorer classes, who were in "extreme want," hurried to the Unionists simply because they wanted food.[44]

A strong testament contrary to reports of Mobile being predominately pro-Union came from a reliable source—Federal General Thomas K. Smith. "You will hear that there is Union sentiment in Mobile, perhaps that not more than ten per cent of its people are secessionists," wrote Smith, "but my word for it, that not a man, woman, or child, who has lived in Mobile the last four years, but who prays death and destruction to the damned Yankees."[45]

The Northern press also noted the anti-Union sentiment that existed in Mobile. "The Mobile people are quite sore, and are at present only loyal because they have to be," wrote a *New York Times* correspondent.[46] In another *New York Times* report, a woman who had lived in Mobile since the start of the war but left prior to Canby's expedition was interviewed. She claimed that there was "no Union sentiment 'among the intelligent classes'" and that only "poor white trash" wanted a return to the Union.[47]

There were many residents who detested the mere sight of the bluecoats on the streets of Mobile. "The commonest, dirtiest looking set I ever saw," wrote Mary D. Waring of the Northern soldiers in her journal entry of April 13, 1865.[48] On the same day, Laura Pillans likewise wrote in her diary, "From my window I see the yankees pass constantly. A most hated sight." She did begrudgingly admit the good behavior of the blue-coated soldiers, noting, "They have only conducted themselves according to the rules of civilized warfare, but they are so seldom accustomed to act with such moderation that some of our people seem to be carried away by such unexpected treatment."[49]

The Bands of the U.S. Army

The Northern soldiers marched through the city with their bands playing Yankee Doodle.[50] "Everybody except the white folks, turned out to see us," recalled Sperry, who was a musician with one of the U.S. Army bands on that march.[51] "The bands played most beautifully, and the boys cheered most loudly," Union General James Slack described in a letter to his wife. "Streets were crowded, windows and doors were filled, everything was calculated to cheer the boys and inspire them with good feeling."[52]

The Union bands failed to leave a good feeling with some residents. In a letter to her son Gillist, resident Riketta Schroeder wrote, "I have not seen any demonstrations of rejoicing, but heard very distinctly the hurrahs & bands of music as the troops entered, it was very humiliating to hear Yankee doodle instead of Dixie altho' I hear they play that often."[53] Schroeder's feelings of humiliation are another example that the Union army were considered unwelcome intruders by many in the city.

Resident B. B. Cox recalled the Yankee bands as they entered Mobile:

> I stood at the corner of Monroe and Conception street and here is what we saw: about ten fifers and ten drummers proceeded [sic] the invading army they were dressed in blue uniforms, double breasted frock coats blue pants, high black soft hats, hooked up on the side with a brass pin with a feather in it, with guns at a right shoulder and fixed bayonets which glittered in the sunlight. They looked as if they did not expect to do any fighting and wanted to put up a good appearance, which they did.[54]

William Fulton's first impression of the Yankee troops differed. "A regiment of the house-burners marched through the streets of Mobile to the tune of 'Yankee Doodle,'" he wrote. "They came in very quietly with the poorest bands in the army." Fulton noted they had no brass instruments when the first regiments entered the city. A couple of hours later more brigades arrived complete with a brass band "playing Columbia, Yankee Doodle, and Columbia the Gem of the Ocean."[55]

Most of the soldiers camped in the outskirts of town. The higher-ranking officers went into the city for accommodations. General Granger and his staff, including Generals Andrews, Veatch, Dennis, and Slack, registered at the Battle House Hotel. Hoping to enjoy a good meal, the officers reportedly only found corn bread and bacon.[56] Apparently, the stay at Mobile's finest hotel was nevertheless a pleasant one. "I went out to Battle House and got a bed, with clean linen sheets, and assure you slept most soundly. Marched all the night before without a wink of sleep, moved all day, and you may be assured was tired," Slack wrote his wife.[57]

The Last Confederate Cavalry Raid

Granger immediately suspended the existing four newspapers of Mobile. He author-ized E. O. Haile, a Unionist correspondent from the *New Orleans Times*, to publish a daily paper. Under the auspices of the army of occupation, Haile immediately moved into the office of the late *Mobile Register and Advertiser* and began work on the *Mobile Daily News*, which he first published the day after the city was occupied.[58] On April 13, Mobile's new Unionist-controlled newspaper reported:

> Disgraceful—Last evening [Wednesday, April 12] after the surrender of the city, and before the guard had been stationed throughout the town, a few drunk and mounted men dashed through the streets and gobbled up, or rather kidnapped, some two or three men belonging to General Veatch's division. Such acts are not only disgraceful, and can not only result in no good to the captors, but are likely to be followed by very unpleasant consequences, not only to the perpetrators but to the people at large, in as much as it may necessitate the taking of measures which will circumscribe their privileges. For the credit of the city and its people let us hear of no more of this.[59]

The "few drunk and mounted men" referred to in the *Mobile Daily News* report was a raid carried out by elements of Colonel Spence's command, the 12th Regiment Mississippi Cavalry. "That evening at sundown, while half the town were sitting in the plazas and balconies in the sweet fancy of security, their attention was called to the dust of cavalcade rising in the air far up Jackson Street. Soon a company of cavalry in the well-known gray were galloping at a dashing speed by their doors, halting occasionally to pick up and mount behind them a sentinel in blue," recounted Rix. The raid succeeded in capturing two men of General Veatch's 3rd Division of the XIII Corps. Rix noted, "After making a detour through a part of the city they retreated again through the orange grove to the fastnesses of the swampy bottoms of the north."[60] Years later, one of the Confederate troopers involved in the raid recalled capturing a sentinel "out of the Battle House barber shop and another one out of McGill's shoe shop on Dauphin street and carried the prisoners out behind them on horses."[61]

The prisoners, likely members of the 8th Illinois Infantry, were subsequently sent to Maury's headquarters near Meridian. Spence later erroneously claimed they were "the last Federal prisoners ever captured by a confederate force." On the contrary, the last Union prisoners fell into Southern hands at the battle of Palmito Ranch in Texas, on May 13, over a month later.[62]

The Federal army wasted no time implementing control in occupied Mobile. "In a few days order will be restored and fears of the people vanished," declared the Unionist *Mobile Daily News* in its first edition.[63] Brigadier General George L. Andrews was appointed provost marshal and quickly established a provost guard to protect public and private property. The commissary riot and cavalry raid on April 12 prompted him to issue several orders restricting citizen behavior. Residents were warned not to assemble in large numbers on the streets.[64] The mayor and civil leaders were given authority to maintain order among the citizens. Andrews issued orders forbidding any persons "to ride or drive through the streets of this city at a faster galt [sic] than a moderate trot, except in the case of absolute necessity."[65] Admiral Thatcher, to protect "loyal inhabitants," positioned a few gunboats in front of the city.[66]

Not all orders placed restrictions solely on the residents. "The citizens of South Alabama may consider themselves fortunate in having their interests committed to the hands of the noble, true hearted Granger," one Unionist newspaper wrote.[67] Granger also warned his own men "not to disturb people or property in or near Mobile. Many of the people are strongly Union, and troops will not be permitted to discriminate in treatment of citizens."[68] He issued strict orders prohibiting pillaging, straggling, unauthorized foraging, and marauding. Enlisted men were forbidden from entering private homes unless so ordered. The provost guards were authorized to arrest violators and punish them to the fullest extent of the law.[69]

"On entering upon their duties in the city as Provost Guards the excitement consequent upon the change of rulers had measurably subsided, and was accepted by the citizens in a spirit of seeming good will and friendliness," recounted Captain Chester Barney, Company E, 20th Iowa Infantry. "This resulted in securing them against scenes of pillage usually attending the entrance of an army into a captured city and placed our men at once upon terms of friendly relations with the inhabitants."[70] Although the Federals sacked many Southern cities, Canby and Granger prevented Mobile from suffering the same fate.

The first issue of the *Mobile Daily News* on April 13 regretfully reported "depredations and misdemeanors" committed by U.S. soldiers on the first day of occupation. The newspaper reporter attempted to assure residents that further incidents would likely not occur. "The officers commanding are determined that order and the laws shall be maintained, and we hope for the credit of our service, that our troops will conduct themselves in such a manner as shall reflect credit upon them and the service in which they are engaged," the article stated. The report indicated that the offending soldiers were arrested and would be punished.[71]

As Granger worked to re-establish order in Mobile, Thatcher's naval squadron continued to perform the dangerous task of blowing up and removing the numerous obstructions and torpedoes from the bay, rivers, and the main ship channel. Despite sweeping the channels with tugs using chains, the torpedoes continued to cause destruction. During the removal operations, the Union tug *Torpedo*, the gunboat *Scotia*, and a launch of the *Cincinnati* were sunk in the Blakeley River.[72]

On April 13, the second day of Yankee occupation, at 8 a.m., in honor of the Union victories at Richmond and Petersburg, Virginia, and Mobile, Canby ordered a 100-gun salute fired from Mobile, Blakeley, and Spanish Fort.[73] In the words of Captain Cobb, "Thus the last city of importance in the Kingdom of Jeff Davis had ceased to be of the Southern Confederacy."[74]

As portions of the XIII Corps occupied Mobile County, the XVI Corps prepared for a long march from Fort Blakeley into the interior of Alabama. At the onset of the campaign, A. J. Smith's "Guerrillas" traveled by boat up the Fish River, thus avoiding the grueling march to Dannelly's Mill that Granger's XIII Corps had endured. On April 13, Canby ordered the XVI Corps on an arduous 170-mile march north to occupy the state capital of Montgomery. The 13-day march of the XVI Corps went through the villages of Burnt Corn, Midway, Activity, Greenville, and Sandy Ridge before arriving at Montgomery.[75]

Canby remained at Fort Blakeley until the departure of the XVI Corps.[76] Cavalry leader General Benjamin H. Grierson then accompanied the Kentuckian to Mobile. "It was my first visit there, and I was much pleased with the appearance of the place. General Canby was in excellent spirits and much elated over his success," Grierson remembered. Immediately after landing, Canby set up headquarters at Mobile's Custom House.[77]

The Last Fight

On April 13, the 3rd Division of the XIII Corps, General William P. Benton's command, was ordered to march to the Mount Vernon Arsenal, approximately 30 miles north of Mobile. The Federals had received intelligence that the Confederate rearguard was at Whistler, about 6 miles northwest from Mobile, destroying property at the railroad manufacturing and engine shops there.[78] "Our brigade had scarcely time to rest after stacking arms upon arrival in camp near the city," recalled Private John W. Fry of the 96th Ohio, "when we were ordered to 'be ready to move at once, with 40 rounds of ammunition per man; MORE FIGHTING AHEAD,' when we had fondly supposed that there was not an armed rebel within many miles of

Mobile."[79] Even though General Maury's small army had evacuated, the bluecoats remained in an offensive mode.

Crowds gathered on the streets of Mobile as the 3rd Division marched through the city on their way to Whistler Station. The band of the 77th Illinois was at the head of the column playing patriotic tunes such as "Yankee Doodle."[80]

After leaving the city, General Benton sent out foraging parties to search for cattle and poultry. The Northerners found geese, turkey, and chickens. "As General Benton was riding at the head of the column, a soldier caught a chicken just in front of him," recalled Lieutenant Bentley. "He had an axe in his hand, and dropping on one knee whacked oft' the chicken's head exclaiming vehemently, 'I'll show you how to bite me.' The General laughed heartily and rode on." As the 3rd Division moved forward that afternoon, Benton instructed his men to leave the chickens with their knapsacks until they returned. A couple of men from each company were left behind to ensure the chickens did not get away.[81]

The last skirmish of the campaign, one of the last fights of the War Between the States, took place in a wooded area near Whistler Station on the Mobile & Ohio railroad at the Eight Mile Creek. There, the bluecoat advance caught up with Maury's rearguard, Spence and his 12th Regiment Mississippi Cavalry, about 250–300 men including 15–20 troopers detached from the locally raised 15th Confederate Cavalry serving as guides.[82] "We left Mobile as the enemy was coming in and camped the first night at Eight Mile Creek about seven miles north of Mobile," recounted Private William Cato, a member of Company G of the 15th Confederate Cavalry detailed to the 12th Mississippi. The Southern horsemen stayed at Eight Mile Creek until about two o'clock the following day to cover the retreat and give their baggage wagons and artillery as much time to get away as possible. Around 2 p.m., Federal soldiers caught up with them and a lively skirmish occurred.[83]

Colonel Henry M. Day of the 91st Illinois Infantry, commander of the 3rd Division's 2nd Brigade, complying with General Benton's orders, took his regiment and the 29th Iowa and moved toward Whistler at brisk pace. As they neared Whistler, Day deployed four companies of the 91st Illinois as skirmishers. "Upon the arrival of our advance, they found some rebels here who had set fire to the buildings," wrote Lieutenant Bentley. As the skirmishers pushed forward, they met fierce resistance on the left of the railroad from Spence's troopers. "The Ninety-first Illinois were immediately ordered up on double-quick, and pushed forward to support the skirmish line, which was closely engaged," Colonel Day wrote in his after-action report. The 29th Iowa came up and took a position to the left of the 91st Illinois. They promptly received additional support from the 7th Vermont and 50th Indiana led by Colonel William C. Holbrook.[84]

Lieutenant Colonel John B. Reid of the 77th Illinois, who was very excited, hastily rushed his men on to confront the Southerners. In his excitement, he forgot to order them to load their guns. The brigade commander, Colonel David P. Grier, noticed the mistake, dashed up and said to Reid, "Don't get excited, keep cool, halt your men and have them load their guns. Never rush into a fight with empty guns." Private Wiley wrote that Colonel Reid "looked like he was pretty badly sold out"; however, he did stop his men and ordered them to load their guns before continuing forward.[85]

The 91st Illinois struggled through the swamp, "waist deep in the mud" in some places as they pursued the Confederates who made a stand from behind some trees.[86] "We had quite an open field to pass over before we reached the stream and the rebels rattled it to us pretty lively as they were sheltered behind the timber," recalled Wiley. As the blue-coated soldiers pushed forward, they found the Southerners had already started many fires to burn the Eight-Mile Creek Bridge. The Federals moved up quickly to the front and an intense fight ensued.[87] "We had quite a warm affair of it, too," recalled Spence.[88]

After setting fire to the bridge, the Southern cavaliers "posted on a slight eminence beyond." Spence formed his men in a solid position "and made as stubborn resistance as possible for so small a force against a large, well-equipped and victorious army."[89] After an intense four- to five-minute fight, Colonel Day ordered Captain Augustus P. Stover, 91st Illinois Infantry Volunteers, "with twenty men of the skirmish line," to charge over the bridge. The outnumbered Confederate troopers were driven from the bridge and the fire was put out.[90]

The Southern mounted soldiers proved to be too quick when the Federals attempted to outflank and apprehend them. Spence's men successfully escaped but not before seriously wounding three soldiers of the 91st Illinois. The Northerners attempted to chase them "for about a mile and a half." After the swift Confederate cavalry split up into squads, galloping off in different directions, Day determined a further pursuit futile.[91]

"My loss in this engagement was one killed and six or eight wounded. I fell back from Whistler to Citronelle, partially destroying the railroad: The Federal Army made no effort to follow. Doubtless Gen. Canby knew the war was over, and did not desire to be the cause of more bloodshed and suffering, and possibly thought we had suffered enough," Colonel Spence remembered.[92] Spence's reflection illustrated the realization of soldiers on both sides that the conflict was essentially over.

The "one killed" mentioned by Spence was Private John Randall, Company G, Mobile Dragoons, 15th Confederate Cavalry. Randall, reportedly no more than 16 years old, was a member of the scouting party detached to the 12th Regiment of Mississippi Cavalry. He was the last Confederate soldier killed in combat in the Mobile campaign.[93] Private Cato, a fellow trooper, remembered, "He fell where the residence of Mr. Liversage stands." Cato, who was captured a few days later, wrote that Randall was buried the same evening by the Federals "about two hundred yards north of Eight Mile Creek bridge." Later, his body was moved by his family and buried at the Magnolia Cemetery in Mobile.[94]

The New Orleans *Times Picayune* reported that the Federal expedition to Whistler resulted in the seizure of "five locomotives, a number of cars with all the machinery in the shops at the station, and the destruction of two distilleries."[95] Not all the liquor from the distillery was destroyed. Evidently, the Northerners salvaged some of it for personal use. After the skirmish, the blue-coated soldiers went into camp at the Mobile & Ohio Station, where they were issued some "commissary." Private Wiley noted in his diary that some of the men did not drink, whereas others took a "double portion" and became quite intoxicated. He wrote, "John Vanardall of Co K and some others got the Jim Jams and yelled and howeled [sic] all night and some us felt like getting up and shoot them."[96] Some of the Northerners knew the campaign and the war were nearly over and took the opportunity to indulge themselves.

From Whistler, Benton's command proceeded further inland to garrison the abandoned Mount Vernon Arsenal. Meanwhile Spence's men continued to scout and picket the country from "the Mississippi to the Tombigbee Rivers."[97]

As Mobilians abruptly transitioned back to life under Federal rule, both sides prepared for continued hostilities. Yet there was a growing realization among the opposing forces and the citizens of Mobile that the end of the war was very near.

CHAPTER FOURTEEN

All Our Joy was Turned to Sorrow

After the fall of the forts on the eastern shore, elements of Canby's forces occupied Mobile and marched into the interior of Alabama toward Montgomery. The remnants of the Mobile garrison regrouped and prepared to continue the struggle at their camps near Meridian, although some viewed further resistance as futile and chose to desert. Meanwhile, thousands of Confederate soldiers languished at island prisoner camps. Profound news that changed everything would soon reach them all.

Lee's Surrender

On April 9, General Robert E. Lee's surrender of the Army of Northern Virginia to U.S. General Grant at Appomattox Court House, Virginia, took place a few hours before the assault on Fort Blakeley.[1] Seven days later, April 16, news of the surrender finally reached Mobile. Lee's surrender led to varied reactions of the Union and Confederate soldiers.

At noon on April 17, 1865, General Canby ordered his commanding generals near Mobile to fire a 200-gun salute at their respective locations. Granger was ordered to fire 50 guns from four batteries in Mobile. Steele was instructed to fire 100 guns at Spanish Fort and 100 guns at Fort Blakeley in Baldwin County. General Smith, at Dauphin Island, was told to fire 100 guns at Fort Gaines and 100 guns at Fort Morgan.[2] "The 21st and 26th New York Batteries each fired one hundred guns in honor of the great victories achieved by Grant and Sherman in the east," wrote Lieutenant Bentley. "Rumors were also current that the Trans-Mississippi Army had surrendered. So much good news coming so soon after their own victories made the boys feel jubilant."[3]

"Lee's surrender to Grant is unquestionably equal to abandonment of the Southern Confederacy," wrote General Slack, "as General Lee was the government in fact, and the only power that held it together."[4] Not all the bluecoats were pleased with the lenient terms given to the Army of Northern Virginia. Private James Lockney of the 28th Wisconsin resented the generous surrender terms Grant gave Lee:

Oh can this be? Can our loved comrades who fill so many, many, southern graves lie still while those ten thousand southern leaders, the most desperate & devilish in design, of any like band that ever led a de*erded [sic] people in a desperate & bloody effort to establish a despotism in which all who were poor of whatever color were to be subject to the proud, wealthy & aristocratic. I have long said that I would prefer to fight out the whole matter in a dispute rather than that Davis, Breckenridge & c. should be admitted to the rights of citizenship within these U.S.[5]

News of the surrender took more time to reach the XVI Corps on their long march to Montgomery. A. J. Smith's "Guerrillas" received the news around April 19 when a courier caught up with them.[6] Officers and common soldiers were overwhelmed with joy. "Everybody cheered and shouted until they were hoarse," remembered Colonel Hubbard. "The men disregarding orders and discipline, fired a salute with their muskets on their own account. They pulled and hustled each other about, stood on their hands, rolled in the dirt and were guilty of innumerable other absurd performances; indeed, they were positively frantic for a while."[7]

"As we were marching along today we saw an officer riding rapidly and waving his hat. As we were the rear regiment," recalled Colonel James Stockton, "I halted to see what was the matter. He announced to us the surrender of Lee's army to General Grant. How the men cheered. The flags were unfurled, drums beat and all were exulting at the news as it meant the ending of the war and our getting home."[8] Impromptu celebrations such as this were a common reaction to the news of the surrender of the Confederacy's principal army.

There was a melancholy mood at the Secessionist camps around Meridian, Mississippi, when rumors of Lee's surrender reached them.[9] Some of the men who had defended Mobile still held out hope that the rumors were false, but others knew it was true. "The surrender of Lee is not doubted here and our cause is looked upon as gone," wrote Lieutenant Robert Tarleton. "This is the bluest place I have seen [Demopolis] and I shall be glad to get away from it today."[10]

"We hear that Genl. Lee and his army have surrendered to Genl. Grant," wrote Captain Clement S. Watson. "If so our struggle, for the present, is at an end and a few years of slavery will be our doom. I have an abiding faith however in the final achievement of our independence."[11] Despite a series of demoralizing and devastating reverses, Watson and many others still believed their cause would ultimately prevail.

Soon the rumors were confirmed. Feeling that "something unusual was about to take place," Holtzclaw's Brigade assembled. They stood at attention in front of their leader Colonel Bushrod Jones, who was elevated upon a box when he addressed them. There was silence as he told them of Lee's surrender. Many brave men bowed their heads and wept in sorrow. "I remember that when I fully realized what the news meant I drew apart from the throng, and seated on a log I wept as I had not done for many a day," remembered Corporal Jones. "It seemed that it was impossible, that it could not be, and how were we ever to endure Yankee domination," he added.[12] After enduring years of hard fighting and sacrifice, Jones and several of his comrades found it hard to accept their struggle for Southern independence had failed.

Prisoners of War

Conditions in Civil War prison camps, both in the North and the South, were known to be harsh. Approximately 4,000 prisoners of war, captured in the battles around Mobile, were sent to prison camps on the Gulf Coast. High-ranking officers such as generals Liddell, Cockrell, and Bryan Thomas were sent to Dauphin Island, where they were treated with courtesy. Most of the Confederate prisoners were sent to the infamous Ship Island, off the Mississippi coast, where there were numerous reports of cruel treatment.[13]

"I remained a prisoner six weeks on Dauphin Island, under General T. Kilby Smith, who treated me with much respect and kindness," General Liddell wrote of his experience. He was grateful to General Smith for allowing him to move about the island freely. On May 16, 1865, Liddell was paroled and traveled to New Orleans.[14] His stint as a prisoner of war was pleasant compared with the conditions his men had to endure.

After the fall of Blakeley, the captured Southerners were marched to Spanish Fort where they were held for a few days. They were then sent by gulf steamers to Ship Island, a narrow island about 7 miles long surrounded by saltwater.[15] "It was there we suffered," remembered Private Dallas M. Morton, Company H, 63rd Alabama Infantry.[16]

At the Ship Island prison camp, officers and enlisted men were held in separate camps approximately a half-mile apart. African-American troops commanded by German officers guarded the prisoners.[17] "Their officers were mostly foreigners who came to learn the art of war for the pay," remembered Captain Guthrie of Missouri, "and seemed generally to be pretty good fellows and heartily disgusted with the negroes."[18] Colonel Ernest W. Holmstedt, a German who spoke broken English, commanded the Ship Island prison camp.[19]

To get fresh water, the Southerners dug holes, sank cracker barrels, and fresh water seeped in. "In two days it got brackish," recounted Captain Guthrie, "then we shifted our well five or six feet and got fresh water again."[20] Private Morton added, "The sea breezes would come at night and we would almost freeze to death. Just had one thin blanket to use."[21]

According to numerous Confederate accounts, soon after arriving on the island, the African-American guards began harassing them. "When we landed we were halted, and the men were passing a short distance from us when a tall Arkansan held up his hand and called out to his captain: The bottom rail is on top," recalled Lieutenant Alden McLellan of Brown's Light Artillery. The guard then made a lunge at him with his bayonet, striking the man's hip. The prisoner jumped, pressing his hand to his hip. Apparently, relations with the guards did not improve.[22]

The guards, likely themselves former slaves, were alleged to have treated the Southerners cruelly. Numerous prisoner accounts claimed they were in some cases violent. Each day the captured Southerners would be marched miles from their camp to the east end of the island to cut wood for cooking. They would then make the difficult walk back through deep and hot sand while carrying the wood. When the men dropped from exhaustion, the guards would reportedly prod them with their bayonets if they did not get up as ordered. "Each day, as the men grew weaker, more would drop down from weakness and more would get the bayonet," remembered First Sergeant John Corkery, Company D, 1st Missouri Infantry.[23]

Sergeant Corkery recalled another incident: "Doc Stearns, a jolly good fellow, called 'Doc' because he always had a remedy for the sick, was standing at the commissary with arms resting on his hips, when 'Black Frank' yelled, 'git down date arm,' and plunged a bayonet into him."[24]

"We were guarded by negroes and was cruelly treated. They killed one man because he walked out of his tent and shot at another because he was washing his clothes in the lake. When this was done, had it been that we could have had guns we would have put an end to the negroes on this island," wrote Private Morton.[25] Private James A. Braxley, Company B, 63rd Alabama Infantry, confirmed Morton's account: "One killed one morning, the other about sunset in the afternoon. I can not [sic] recall the particulars of the first, but I was an eyewitness of the killing of the last, who belonged to some command whose camp was immediately next to that of our regiment." He continued, "This man about sunset, had picked up his blanket, went to the door of his tent, and began to shake the dust out of it, when he was shot dead by one of the negro sentinels."[26]

Private William A. Gibson, Company H, 35th Mississippi Infantry, recounted one of the killings referred to by Braxley: "Very early one morning just before day a Texan arose and shook his blanket. A negro sentinel wanted to know what he was doing. The Texan replied, 'I am only shaking the dust out of my blanket.' The reply to this response was a musket shot from the negro, by which the Texan fell dead." Both Gibson and Braxley claimed the guards were never held accountable for the two shootings.[27] In another earlier shooting by one of his guards, Colonel Holmstedt reported that it "had a good effect on the surviving undisciplined crew."[28]

Colonel Elijah Gates of the Missouri Brigade had enough of the unprovoked shootings. "One night a campfire was blazed up by the wind and the sentries fired at it, wounding three men. Col [Elijah] Gates went to Col. Holmstedt and told him if we were to be killed for nothing we would very soon give him a chance to kill us for something. This stopped the shooting," remembered Corkery.[29]

Desertion

While the Southern soldiers languished at Ship Island, desertions among their comrades near Meridian were increasing. On April 15, Canby issued orders in the local newspapers enticing deserters to come into the Federal lines. He made it known that they would be allowed to safely return to their homes without fear of being conscripted into the Federal army. The *Mobile Daily News*, newly established by the Unionists occupying Mobile, reported that deserters were "rapidly availing themselves of the liberal terms offered them by Major General Canby." The Federal Provost Office kept busy processing the numerous Southern soldiers who daily came into the city.[30]

On April 23, Southern Sergeant William Chambers wrote in his journal, "When the rolls were called this morning it was found that a great many had departed during the night. Some say three hundred men are gone. I know that five men of the brigade are not accounted for."[31] The realization the war was lost became apparent to many Southerners. "Hard as it is to say it, we have failed," Chambers wrote in his April 24 journal entry. "It is painful, it is humiliating to write the record; after all, we must give it up and own that we are whipped! A thousand reflections are suggested by the facts." He added, "I really doubt whether one thousand men of this whole force will cross the Alabama River. It seems to be a settled fact that the days of the Confederacy are numbered."[32] On the same day, Granger reported to Canby that General Maury was at Cuba Station with 2,000 men and had been much criticized for 'the disgraceful surrender of Mobile.'"[33] Despite Granger's comments, Maury, who had pre-standing orders from General Taylor to abandon the city versus risking the capture of his garrison, had little choice but to evacuate and his men knew it.[34]

Desertion also plagued the Confederate navy. Many of the Confederate sailors were European-born, sometimes described as soldiers of fortune. Perceiving a difficult situation, some chose to desert during the evacuation north on the Alabama River rather than risk imprisonment at Ship Island. "We did not care to get too close to a bank, as the sailors, knowing that the 'jig was up,' would jump ashore and leave us," remembered one Confederate naval officer. "One night we were obliged to 'tie up' to the bank, and a guard of some ten marines was placed on the shore to keep the men on board. As I now recall, the next morning the whole guard and a lot of men had gone."[35] Those who deserted, most of whom had faithfully served the Confederacy in numerous engagements, realized further effort was futile.

Despite the hopeless situation, Confederate officers tried to curtail desertion. "The attention of officers of all grades is called to the desertions taking place in some of the commands," General Gibson wrote in a General Order on April 15. "This is a time when every officer should be vigilant and attentive to the wants of his men and exercise measures at once to prevent the worst of military crimes—desertion," he added. Gibson offered "a furlough of 40 days to any soldier who helped detect and convict a deserter."[36] On April 25, in camp at nearby Gainesville, Alabama, General Forrest also appealed to his troopers: "It is the duty of every man to stand firm at his post and true to his colors," Forrest wrote to his men. "Your past services, your gallant and heroic conduct on many victorious fields, forbid the thought that you will ever ground your arms except with honor."[37]

Despite the efforts of Gibson, Forrest, and other officers, some Southern soldiers who had long fought bravely for independence finally had enough. They knew the struggle was over and left for home.

Lincoln's Assassination

On April 14, Abraham Lincoln was assassinated at Ford's Theater in Washington, DC. About a week later, news of Lincoln's death reached southern Alabama. "We all felt joyous, and of good cheer, at the prospect of a speedy peace, and that we would soon be home to enjoy that rest and quiet which all so much need. This horrible news came upon us so unexpected, so unlooked for, that we hardly know what to think or say ... the papers say Wilkes Booth shot Mr. Lincoln. Presume he is the Booth who has created some sensation upon the stage," wrote General Slack.[38] Colonel Lucius F. Hubbard echoed Slack's sentiment: "But all our joy was turned to sorrow, and our rejoicing to the deepest mourning upon our arrival [to Montgomery on the 25th]."[39]

Upon learning of Lincoln's assassination, Canby ordered flags displayed at half-staff and "half hour guns to be fired from sunrise until sunset, and minute guns from 12 a.m. to 1 p.m. at each post." Union staff officers wore crepe on their arms and a dirge, or somber song, was played at each regimental headquarters in south Alabama. Except for guard duty, General William P. Benton, commanding at Nanna Hubba Bluff, ordered all duties suspended.[40] "We got the sad news during the day of President Lincoln's assassination," wrote Private Wiley. "It raised a terable [sic] feeling of indignation in the regiment as Abraham Lincoln occupied a chief place in every true soldiers heart." Wiley wrote that when Confederate deserters came in and learned of Lincoln's assassination, they appeared "pretty badly scared." Possibly to avoid retaliation from the Union soldiers, they condemned the murder.[41] Sergeant Musser wrote: "They [Southerners] all feel sorry that President Lincoln was murdered. They say that he was more of a friend to them than the Villain Davis was."[42]

After receiving the shocking news, the rhetoric of the Federals turned to talk of vengeance. The Federal soldiers expressed sadness, anger, and felt "terribly vindictive." Slack wrote, "The sad news has cast a gloom over everything, and the deep muttering of an incensed people foretell the most terrible retribution."[43] Some of the Northerners regretted that the conflict was ending soon, feeling Lincoln's assassination called for retribution. Union Colonel Lucius F. Hubbard wrote: "Woe be to the people of the south, if hostilities again commence. In President Lincoln they lost their best friend."[44]

Sergeant Marshall wrote, "All felt that it was fortunate that we had not known of it the day of the charge or probably there would not have been a live rebel left behind their breast works."[45] Sergeant Musser believed retribution should be focused on the Confederate leadership. "Ah, the whole south will curse the day that that diabolical murder was committed," he wrote. "Revenge will be had, and it will be bloody vengenance [sic]. It is wrong to retaliate upon the rebels in the ranks, but the leaders Should hang. Every one of them should suffer the Penalty due a Traitor."[46]

From his Confederate headquarters at Meridian, Mississippi, General Taylor informed his men of Lincoln's assassination. The men were silent at first, shocked by the news. Then they asked if it was possible that any Southerner could have committed the crime. "There was a sense of relief expressed when they learned that the wretched assassin had no connection with the South, but was an actor, whose brains were addled by tragedies and Plutarch's fables," remembered General Taylor.[47]

Although Southerners typically held President Lincoln in contempt, most believed his murder would lead to vindictive persecution. "Should these reports prove true," Confederate Sergeant William P. Chambers recorded in his journal, "and they seem well authenticated, I am fearful the war will be prosecuted more barbarously than ever, for I have a poor opinion of the moderation of such a man as Andrew Johnson who, it is reported, was installed as President on the 15 inst."[48]

Allan Pinkerton, of the U.S. Special Service, was charged with the task of capturing Lincoln's assassin, his conspirators, and the fleeing Jefferson Davis and members of the Confederate cabinet. Canby's chief of staff, Major General Peter J. Osterhaus, issued orders to all commanding officers in the division to provide support to Pinkerton in the event the fugitives attempted to escape to their vicinities.[49]

On April 20, rumors of a pending Rebel attack to retake the city alarmed Federal authorities in Mobile. The rumor, circulated by deserters coming into the city, was that a large force led by General Nathan B. Forrest was headed to Mobile. The U.S. forces were immediately put on high alert and spent an anxiety-filled evening waiting for the feared cavalry leader and his troopers. The rumors of an imminent assault proved to be false.[50]

CHAPTER FIFTEEN

The Final Surrender

After General Lee's surrender, it was not certain that the remaining Confederates in the field would stop fighting. Even though Secessionist leaders had fled Richmond after the collapse of Lee's army, a vast Confederate-held territory remained. Southern armies in North Carolina, Alabama, and the trans-Mississippi remained intact, and it was far from obvious to the Union leaders that they would not continue to resist.[1] In Alabama, the Unionists were not convinced that the army under General Richard Taylor would surrender. To stop further destruction and bloodshed, on April 11, 1865, John A. Campbell, Assistant Confederate Secretary of War, wrote a letter to Taylor detailing the state of the dying Confederacy. He requested General-in-Chief Grant forward the letter to Taylor via General Canby in Mobile.[2]

In the message, Campbell, who had resided in Mobile before the conflict, explained the situation: both Petersburg and Richmond had fallen; Jefferson Davis and his cabinet had evacuated; and General Lee had surrendered the Army of Northern Virginia. He also shared the generous terms Grant gave Lee. Campbell, who had met with President Lincoln on April 3–4, also conveyed his generous surrender conditions. "His indispensable conditions are the restoration of the authority of the United States and the disbanding of the troops and no receding on his part from his position on the slavery question as defined in his message in December and other official documents—all other questions to be settled on terms of sincere liberality," he wrote. "He says that to any State that will promptly accept these terms he will relinquish confiscation except when third persons have acquired adverse interests." Campbell ended the letter by advising Taylor "to cease hostilities."[3]

Despite having confirmation of Lee's surrender, Taylor was not yet ready to give up the contest. "The surrender of Lee left us little hope of success," he recalled, "but while [General Joseph E.] Johnston remained in arms we must be prepared to fight our way to him. Again, the President [Jefferson Davis] and civil authorities of our Government were on their way to the south, and might need our protection."[4] Cut off from direct communications with the Confederate government and the Secretary of War, Taylor had to make his own decisions.[5]

At the Confederate camps near Meridian, Taylor organized the remnants of the Mobile garrison as rapidly as possible. He sent Maury to nearby Cuba Station, Alabama, to restructure his small army into a division of three brigades in preparation of joining General Joseph Johnston's Army of Tennessee in North Carolina. His forces encamped close to the railroad station and waited for further orders as Taylor prepared transportation for them.[6] On April 22, Sergeant William P. Chambers remarked in his journal, "I think our destination is the army of Gen. Johnston in North Carolina. It seems like following a 'forlorn hope' and it is with extreme reluctance that the men will go. I feel despondent, yet I will try to do my whole duty, leaving the issue in the hands of Him who 'doeth all things well.' "[7] Incredibly, Chambers and the remnants of the Mobile garrison, although understandably reluctant, were still willing to continue their struggle for independence.

To further complicate matters for Taylor, Confederate currency was deemed nearly worthless. In the last days of the Confederacy, Southern officers had a difficult time purchasing supplies and services with their currency. One captain said with a laugh that he could not even "get his one shirt washed for $1000 of it!" He was forced to share his rations with the laundress in exchange for having his shirt washed. The New Orleans *Times Picayune* reported that Taylor had to issue his officers double rations—one ration to eat and the other ration for bartering.[8]

The Armistice

On April 14, Taylor, via Major James R. Curell, his assistant commissioner of prisoner exchange, began corresponding with Canby. Initially, the subject of communication was prisoner exchange. Communication between the two generals soon turned to the issue of surrender. On April 22, Taylor suggested a personal meeting through Curell, "although informal in its inception and character," at a time and place Canby selected.[9] Curell also conveyed Taylor's desire to avoid "any unnecessary sacrifice of life, and particularly any further and useless destruction of property, entailing sufferings which may be avoided upon helpless women and children."[10]

Union General Gordon Granger, suspicious of Curell's intentions, warned Canby, "That spy, Curell, is back again, pretending to have business, but did not bring a line from Dick Taylor. I hope you will shut down on all such barefaced espionage."[11] On April 26, however, Canby, apparently disregarding Granger's comments, replied to Taylor via Curell: "I shall be pleased to meet you for the purpose of conference at any point you may designate in the neighborhood of the city. As soon as you have indicated the time I will send an officer of rank to meet you and conduct you to the place of meeting."[12]

As Taylor and Canby corresponded, Granger was busy gathering intelligence on the location of the 12th Mississippi. He planned operations to capture Colonel

Spence's command near Citronelle. On April 24, he sent a message to Canby, who was in New Orleans at the time: "I think orders should be sent Steele to move on Demopolis as rapidly as possible. It is their last depot of supplies. I shall push Bentons [sic] cavalry across from Nanna Hubba Bluff and strike the Mobile and Ohio Railroad at Deer Park, in order to pick up a small rebel picket and railroad stock at Citronelle and Chunchula." Likewise, Admiral Thatcher was preparing to attack the Confederate vessels on the Tombigbee.[13]

On April 27, Curell notified Taylor: "General Canby appoints Magee's farm, twelve miles from Mobile, and Saturday, 29th instant, at noon, as place and time for your interview. I have replied that I did not expect you could arrive until evening. He will be here himself at noon. I will remain here until you arrive."[14]

There was a stark difference in the appearance of the two parties that met at the farmhouse of Jacob Magee in Kushla, Alabama. Taylor, with one staff officer, Colonel William Levy, arrived on a hand car powered by two African-Americans. Canby, in contrast, was escorted by a brigade with a military band and several staff officers. Taylor recounted the meeting in his postwar memoirs:

> General Canby met me with urbanity. We retired to a room, and in a few moments agreed upon a truce, terminable after forty-eight hours' notice by either party. Then rejoining the throng of officers, introductions and many pleasant civilities passed. I was happy to recognize Commodore James Palmer, an old friend. He was second to Admiral Thatcher, commanding United States squadron in Mobile Bay, and had come to meet me. A bountiful luncheon was spread, of which we partook, with joyous poppings of champagne corks for accompaniment, the first agreeable explosive sound I had heard for years. The air of "Hail Columbia," which the band in attendance struck up, was instantly changed by Canby's order to that of "Dixie"; but I insisted on the first, and expressed a hope that Columbia would be again a happy land, a sentiment honored by many libations … the party separated, Canby for Mobile, I for Meridian.[15]

Following the meeting, the two generals made efforts to promptly notify their men of the ceasefire agreement, issuing orders to stay within their respective lines.[16] "There is no more fighting for us during this war, and how thankful I am for it," wrote Union Sergeant Musser.[17] During the armistice period, the Federal Steamer *Mustang*, en route to Montgomery, landed to obtain wood. Once ashore, the crew of the *Mustang* encountered the 15th Confederate Cavalry, which approached them under a flag of truce. The officer commanding the cavalry party informed the Federals that they were under strict orders not to attack any boats on the river during the armistice.[18]

The truce period was not without incident. Due to the vast wilderness and remote locations in rural south Alabama, notification of the ceasefire agreement was not always effectively communicated. On May 1, after the armistice between Taylor and Canby, Union troopers "burned the depot, some freight and tore up rails" west of Selma, in Dallas County, Alabama, at a place called Harrell's Crossroads. The destruction was said to be retaliation for Confederate soldiers firing on Federal transports on the Alabama River. Via courier, Confederate Lieutenant Colonel Samuel Jones brought the depredation to the attention of General Steele, and requested him to notify his command of the ceasefire terms so that such occurrences would not take place again. Jones assured Steele that any firing on transports that may have occurred was unauthorized. In the spirit of the armistice, he also requested Steele to remove his mounted soldiers from Cahawba.[19]

Citronelle

On April 30, Canby notified Taylor that he had received "official notice that the suspension of hostilities agreed upon between Generals Johnston and Sherman has been disapproved by the President of the United States and annulled." The Presidential rejection of the terms offered Johnston by Sherman meant Canby must resume hostilities after 48 hours. Canby then proposed surrender under the same conditions Grant offered Lee at Appomattox Court House. "Frankly what I would not say if I did not believe that circumstances of both armies were such that you may accept them for your army without reproach from any quarter," Canby wrote Taylor. He expressed his desire to end the fighting without further bloodshed and destruction of property.[20]

The generous terms Canby offered included free transportation home to all soldiers, officers allowed to keep their side arms and private horses, and paroles to be administered by Confederate officers with no Union soldiers present.[21] Taylor believed the terms Canby offered did much to "soothe the pride of the vanquished" and "were generous."[22] On May 2, Taylor wrote Maury to share his thoughts on surrender. He informed Maury that General Lee's surrender and other "disasters" to their cause made it his duty to surrender. "Indeed, recent events make it due to the soldiers and citizens of this department, whose future welfare depends upon my action, that I shall make every effort to secure an honorable and speedy cessation of hostilities," wrote Taylor. He emphasized to Maury the importance of their force staying together in an organized state and to "present as bold a front as possible" to help enable him to acquire the best possible terms for all his men. "Unless the troops remain intact and are relieved from service by some general agreement between Confederate and Federal commanders they will be hunted down like beasts of prey, their families will be persecuted, and ruin thus entailed not only upon the soldiers themselves, but also upon thousands of defenseless Southern women and children," he wrote. Taylor requested Maury stress his views to the officers and men.[23]

The next day Taylor again wrote Maury, further justifying his decision, and sharing the proposed terms of the surrender. He requested Maury convey to his men that surrender was not "the consequence of any defeat they have received at the hands of the enemy, but is simply, so far as we are concerned, yielding upon the best terms and with a preservation of our military honor to the logic of events."[24]

Taylor maintained the Southern cause was a just one; however, given the surrender of the Armies of Northern Virginia and Tennessee, it necessitated negotiations with the Unionists "to secure such terms as secure the military honors of all of us, best provide for the future protection of private rights of my officers and men, and stop the further effusion of blood in what will then be a hopeless cause." He felt "dodging and running" from the Northerners might prolong the conflict longer but would ultimately be a futile effort and would end in being forced to accept an unconditional surrender.[25]

Before General Hood left Meridian for the Trans-Mississippi Department, Taylor had consulted with him and concluded that the vast flooding of the Mississippi River (with an average width of 35 miles) made it nearly impossible to cross over a large body of troops to the Trans-Mississippi Department. "If I see the slightest hope of withdrawing my army," he wrote Maury, "or any considerable portion of it, at any cost, to some other field of operations, and then prolong the struggle with the shadow of a chance of final success, I will most certainly make the attempt. In the present condition of affairs such an attempt will not only be useless, but criminal on my part."[26] Under the circumstances that existed, Hood agreed with Taylor to the proposed surrender and would advise General Kirby Smith in the Trans-Mississippi to adopt the same course of action upon his arrival there.[27] Maury also supported Taylor's decision, remarking the terms offered "were very liberal and kindly on Canby's part, who gave free transportation over the railroads to the Confederates of all our armies who were making their weary way back to their unhappy people."[28]

Taylor recalled, "There was no room for hesitancy. Folly and madness combined would not have justified an attempt to prolong a hopeless contest."[29] Still, some soldiers at Meridian were not ready to quit fighting. "I was engaged in getting up a command of mounted men with the idea of leaving for Mexico," remembered Captain Albert C. Danner many years after the war. "We would go West, cross the Mississippi River, fight if necessary and do all the damage we could do to the 'Yanks' as we went." Danner planned to offer their services to Mexican Emperor Maximilian when they arrived. Once Taylor learned of this plan, he "put an end to it as he was bound to do." In hindsight, Danner recognized Taylor's wisdom. "We would have in all probability, become outlaws and I am very thankful now that I was not permitted to carry out my plans," Danner wrote in his 1904 memoirs.[30]

On May 3, Taylor notified Canby that he would surrender his force, the last Confederate army east of the Mississippi. The following day the two generals, along with Confederate Commodore Farrand and Union Admiral Thatcher, agreed to meet near the Mobile & Ohio railroad in Citronelle to finalize the surrender.[31]

The only surrender held outdoors took place at "one of the most beautiful and picturesque" locations on the Gulf Coast. Under a large oak tree at the homestead of Dr. Joseph Borden, Taylor handed his sword to Canby.[32] Afterward, the two generals formally signed papers which formalized the surrender of all Confederate forces east of the Mississippi River and west of the Chattahoochee River.[33] Taylor used a "steel point pen, lashed to an althen twig with white cotton thread," which was indicative of the condition of the army he represented; in contrast, "a plain goose quill" was used by Canby.[34] The New Orleans *Times-Democrat* concluded, "The last considerable force in opposition to the authority of the United States east of the Mississippi has laid down its arms, on the same terms as were accepted by Gen. Lee."[35]

Dr. Borden, showing his southern hospitality, prepared a feast for his uninvited guests. Despite his generosity, the Federals told Borden to provide "one animal (horse, cow, or mule) weekly until he was rid of his surplus in that line."[36] After the official surrender proceedings ended, General Canby took the two-hour train ride back to Mobile, departing Citronelle at 10:30 p.m. The entire trip caused him to be absent from the city for 16 hours.[37]

General Benton's Division was busy at Nanna Hubba Bluff (northeastern Mobile County), building a fort to cut off the retreat of the Confederate navy, when they learned of the surrender. Upon hearing the news, Benton rode up to his men who were working on the fort and reportedly said, "Boys, the war is over, throw down your spades and let the Fort go to H***. we [sic] don't want it." The Federal steamer *Octorara*, anchored there, fired her guns, shaking the ground, as the men cheered loudly. "All the wild savages in the far west can't make Such [sic] a noise," wrote Sergeant Musser to his father.[38]

Cut off from communication with the Confederate government, General Taylor's decision determined the fate of his men and the civilians within his vast department. He could have reorganized the remnants of Maury's and Forrest's commands into a guerrilla force and continued to fight. Considering the cover that Alabama and Mississippi's vast wilderness provided, he might have been able to prolong the conflict for years. In the best interest of his men and the future of the country, Taylor wisely concluded the bloodshed had to stop and decided it was hopeless to resist any longer.

"Coming as it does at the heels of the capture of Charleston, Wilmington and Richmond, the surrender of the armies of Lee and Johnston, and apparently without connection with them, it resembles the rattle of earth thrown upon the coffin of the extinct Confederacy," a reporter from the *Cincinnati Enquirer* wrote of General Taylor's surrender.[39] Yet his command could take pride in the fact that they were the last considerable force to surrender east of the Mississippi River. Although General Kirby Smith's Trans-Mississippi Department formally surrendered three weeks later, one could argue Citronelle was the last actual surrender. Bearing in mind most of Smith's army had already disbanded, the May 25 surrender in New Orleans was merely a formality to "clear the records."[40]

There were six Confederate defenders of Mobile that evidently did not surrender. On September 19, 1866, over a year after the capitulation at Citronelle, six graycoats hiding in a cave near the earthworks by Mobile's jail were discovered. A chain gang was removing the earthworks when they were astonished to find the gray-coated soldiers hiding in a cave. "Much against their will," the defiant men were taken into custody. They were believed to be members of the "Alligators," a group that had vowed to never surrender. Likely supported by locals, the die-hard Southerners reportedly had been in hiding there ever since the fall of Mobile.[41]

CHAPTER SIXTEEN

You are No Longer Soldiers

Although the war was over, there was still a lot to do: Confederate property was transferred to the United States, and paroles and transportation home were given to the former Secessionists who had to re-acclimate as U.S. citizens. Unfortunately, Mobile and its Federal occupiers would suffer through a tragic munitions explosion shortly after hostilities ceased.

General Taylor observed that the conflict left the people of Alabama and Mississippi suffering under "deplorable" conditions. He requested General Canby limit the number of Federal troops sent to the interior and suggested stationing them where supplies were plentiful, "that trade would soon be established between soldiers and people," recalled Taylor, "furnishing the latter with currency, of which they were destitute—and friendly relations promoted." He praised Canby for his cooperation and for his concern for the citizens of Alabama and Mississippi.[1]

"I had various occasions to see General Canby on matters connected with the surrender," he wrote, "and recall no instance in which he did not conform to my wishes."[2] During the surrender negotiations, General Taylor found Canby "liberal and just-animated by an honest desire to do all in his power to prevent unnecessary hardship and suffering."[3] Taylor admitted, "The terms of surrender demanded and granted were consistent with the honor of our arms; and it due to the memory of General Canby to add that he was ready with suggestions to soothe our military pride." Canby "most considerately" provided Taylor and his two horses transportation on his boat to New Orleans.

General Maury also expressed his high regard for the Kentucky general. Prior to the outbreak of the war, Maury had commanded Federal troops in New Mexico. When he resigned from the Union army to take a military commission in the Confederacy, Canby was sent to replace him. Before Maury left for Richmond, he met with Canby to explain how he distributed the troops of that department. He then transferred his house and office to him. Ironically, after the fall of Mobile, Canby once again replaced Maury. "Just four years afterward, I left him my office in Mobile, he and I having closed the great war after the long-contested battle of Mobile, with mutual respect for each other," remembered Maury.[4]

In addition to adopting Taylor's suggestions, Canby directed generals Granger and Steele to call on and adhere to Taylor's advice regarding movements of their troops. "Strange, indeed, must such confidence appear to statesmen of the 'bloody-shirt' persuasion," Taylor wrote in his memoirs.[5] On May 6, Taylor issued General Orders no. 54 in which he openly praised Canby to his men:

> The intelligent, comprehensive and candid bearing, pending the negotiations, of Major Gen. Canby, to whom I have surrendered, entitle him to our highest respect and confidence. His liberality and fairness make it the duty of each and all of us to faithfully execute our part of the contract. The honor of all of us is involved in an honest adherence to its terms. The officer or man who fails to observe them is an enemy to the defenseless women of the South, and will deserve the severest penalties that can disgrace a soldier.[6]

To facilitate a peaceful transition, Taylor did his best to influence his men to honor the terms of surrender. Had more considerate Unionists like Canby existed elsewhere, the resentment many Southerners felt toward the Yankee occupiers would likely have been lessened. The newly reunited nation was fortunate to have men like Canby and Taylor setting an example for peaceful cooperation.

In accordance with the terms of surrender, property belonging to the Confederacy was transferred to the U.S. government.[7] The 18th Alabama was ordered to guard public stores and government property at Demopolis until the Union army could arrive. For two weeks, Corporal Jones protected the stores, which "consisted of meat, flour, clothing, hats, shoes and many other things too numerous to mention. These things were in large quantities." Taylor's men continued to guard this property until the transfer to the Federal authorities was completed.[8]

General Taylor took seriously the responsibility of protecting public property and transferring it to the Federal authorities. "I regret to inform you that I find a disposition existing on the part of citizens to plunder the public property," he wrote in a message to Canby. In the same letter, he requested A. J. Smith and other Union generals to send an increased force of guards to points such as Demopolis and Cuba Station, where valuable stores were located. He assured Canby that "every effort will be made to identify and arrest the instigators of these lawless proceedings, and if arrested they will be turned over to the U.S. authorities for punishment."[9]

Corporal Jones remembered the citizens of Demopolis did not understand why they could not have the stores, instead of handing them over to the Unionists. Soldiers had to prevent citizens from attempting to remove bales of cotton, which lay around Demopolis, and they endured constant appeals from "women, men, officers, soldiers, negroes and all sorts of people" for items of the public stores. One evening a mob gathered outside of the building that Jones and his regiment guarded. "I told the crowd that the men had loaded guns and that they were instructed to shoot and they would, but if they would go and get an order from the colonel, they might have all that was in there so far as I was concerned," Jones recalled. "They dispersed and did not return."[10]

The 18th Regiment anxiously awaited the arrival of Yankee gunboats, which were coming up the river to relieve them. "Finally we heard 'a mighty noise down the river where the Lincoln gunboats lay,'" Jones remembered, "as the old song we sang in those days went, and as the boat, which was nothing but a transport, was landing at the wharf. We packed up and marched away."[11] Upon the arrival of the U.S. troops, the Confederates peacefully transferred all their stores to the Federal government. "Public property was turned over and receipted for," Taylor later noted, "and this as orderly and quietly as in time of peace between officers of the same service."[12]

Commodore Farrand ordered his fleet down the Tombigbee River to Nanna Hubba Bluff. On May 10, he surrendered his small command, consisting of 112 officers, 285 enlisted men, and 24 marines. The vessels and the inventory of naval stores on board were then turned over to the Union navy.[13] A correspondent aboard the *Cincinnati* at the time described the remnants of the Confederate fleet:

> The iron-clad Nashville (a formidable looking vessel, but which, on inspection, did not prove as much as her appearance would warrant,) the Morgan (a very fine vessel, unfortunately built of green timber and having a high-pressure engine, rendering her unserviceable for sea service,) the Black Diamond (a small high-pressure river boat,) the Baltic (formerly a ram, now a powerful tug-boat,) the Heroine (a beautiful and fleet iron blockade-runner,) and the Southern Republic (flag-ship, a large double-decker, side-wheel, high pressure boat,) composed the vessels to be turned over by Commodore Farrand.[14]

After the vessels were surrendered, the Southern and Northern sailors happily fraternized.

Some of the Confederate officers reunited with old messmates they had served with in the navy before the war. William L. Cameron, a Southern officer of the *Nashville*, recalled being an "honored guest" and "drinking iced wine and smoking Havana cigars," with young Federal officers on board the ironclad USS *Cincinnati*. "That night the Southern Republic, loaded with officers and crews of the captured Confederates, steamed down the romantic Tombigbee," remembered Cameron, "all hands cheering the United States fellows as she passed, and someone was playing on calliope, 'O, ain't I glad to get out of the wilderness'!"[15]

Although the former enemies openly fraternized, there were reports of hostile feelings between former Southern soldiers. Shortly after the surrender, one newspaper reported that violent threats were made against Commodore Farrand and other Confederate naval officers. The threats allegedly came from individuals, "workmen and others," who felt treated unfairly by the officers during the Confederate administration of Mobile.[16]

Parole

On May 8, by the conditions of surrender, Taylor designated Confederate officers to receive paroles of their men at Meridian, Gainesville, and Jackson.[17] At 8 a.m. that day, the remaining soldiers of the 18th Alabama Infantry were ordered to fall in for the last time. After roll was called, Colonel Peter F. Hunley spoke to his Alabamians near Meridian, giving an address that brought many of them to tears:

> Fellow soldiers, I have caused you to parade and answer roll-call for the last time. Henceforth, you are no longer soldiers, but citizens—citizens of a down trodden country. But, fellow soldiers, you leave a record behind you of which you can well be proud. The Eighteenth has left a blaze of glory in its wake. As you have been true and brave on the battlefield, let me exhort you to be honorable and loyal as citizens at home. I feel that this is a sad parting, but is mixed with a joyous prospect at the home life again. I want to thank you men for the loyalty and courtesy you have always shown me as your Commanding Officer. You will now march with me into the town, where you will turn over your guns and receive your parole.[18]

The same day at Meridian, Mississippi, General Randall L. Gibson, who had served his brigade in various leadership roles on more than 20 battlefields since the beginning of the struggle, issued a heartfelt farewell address. "Throughout all the scenes of this eventful revolution you have been fully tried, and now retire with the consciousness of having achieved a character for discipline, for valor, and for unselfish patriotism of which you may be justly proud," said Gibson in his speech. "There is nothing in your career to look back upon with regret." He added, "You have not surrendered and will never surrender your self-respect and love of country."[19]

To ensure a peaceful transition, Canby made efforts to ensure the placement of disciplined soldiers and discreet commanding officers to receive paroles from the gray-coated soldiers.[20] "The Federal troops were kept well in hand, were not allowed to insult us," recalled Private Stephenson, "and they showed no disposition to do so. There was no marching out, lining us up opposite the Federal forces, and our general surrendering his sword to the victor, no pomp and parade of triumph. We saw very little of the Federal troops." The consideration and courtesy Canby's men showed during the surrender was recognized and appreciated by the Southerners.[21]

The paroles were full of delays and took a long time to administer. Some frustrated soldiers, undoubtedly anxious to get home to their families, grew impatient and left without them. Evidently, the delays were caused by the numerous deserters coming in to claim parole. "At first no obstacle was thrown in their way, but they have become so numerous that Gen. Taylor advised that no more paroles be given them," Sergeant Chambers jotted down in his journal. "He is reported as saying that he surrendered 8,000 men, and 20,000 men are claiming paroles."[22] The presence of deserters from the Confederate army seeking their paroles "exasperated" the graycoats who had faithfully served to the end. Private Stephenson remembered:

> Some were beaten, some ridden on rails, some had their heads and beards shaven—one side only, etc. Our friends the enemy looked on and enjoyed it as much as we did and never interfered. Brave men always feel the same about such things. Much of this took place in the middle of town where everybody could see. I see one picture now—a big fellow astride a rail held high up by a number of hands, yells of derision and contempt all about him.[23]

As Stephenson's account illustrated, in many cases those who remained loyal resented those who had not. The remnants of the brave garrison of Mobile surely knew how much stronger their defense would have been had they not been abandoned by the deserters.

General Maury recalled the "deepest gloom" experienced on his final day of service for the Confederacy. "The little army of Mobile had held steadfastly together with the dignity of men who had risked all from a high motive, and we stood by each other to the last," he recalled. Maury added, "My own deep sadness was cheered by the sympathy of the noble men who had been my comrades." He recalled that "the Louisiana band, the only one left in the army" gave him a final farewell serenade.[24]

"Thus ends the Confederacy! I have loved it well and given my best service to establish it among the nations of the earth," Sergeant Chambers wrote in his journal. "But it has all been in vain so far as national independence is concerned. I seem to realize more and more that God's hand is in it and that He has ordered it well," he continued. Chambers understood General Taylor had little choice but to surrender: "To have continued the struggle would have been madness—nay, it would have been murder." He added, "No other army was surrendered on better terms than we are."[25] General Taylor, an intelligent and reasonable man, knew continuing the struggle was futile. He was no longer willing to risk the lives of his brave soldiers. Although saddened by the outcome of the conflict, Sergeant Chambers and his comrades knew Taylor had made the right decision.

Honorably, Canby organized transportation home for the Confederate soldiers.[26] He received orders from the Federal government that prohibited paroled Confederate soldiers from Missouri, a state which remained loyal to the Union, from returning to their homes."[27] When confronted with these orders, Canby appealed directly to Secretary of War Edwin Stanton. "I am much embarrassed by the instructions received not to allow prisoners of war who belong to the loyal States to return to their homes," he wrote. "I shall have some 2,000–3,000 paroled Missouri troops, which I do not know how to dispose of, and I respectfully ask that necessary instructions or authority may be given. If allowed to remain in this portion of the country on parole, they will be an embarrassment both to us and the people."[28] The Northern leaders, who were resentful and vindictive toward soldiers, from loyal states, which sided with the South, had put Canby in a difficult position. He knew the Missourians, if they were not permitted to return to their homes, would be destitute should they remain in Alabama and Mississippi. Having these homeless and penniless men in his department would be a further negative reflection on the Federal government and would make the reunification of the nation more difficult.

The Southern soldiers held at Ship Island were sent to New Orleans.[29] On the boat trip, Confederate prisoners observed the disrespect one white Federal soldier showed toward an African-American counterpart. "The white soldiers were not friendly to their colored comrades," recalled Southern Lieutenant Alden McLellan of Brown's Light Artillery. The African-American troops were required to stay at the bow of the boat, segregated from the white soldiers. McLellan observed an African-American approach a white soldier on guard duty to relieve him. "The white guard, who was leaning on his gun, looked at the relief in a very surly manner and said, 'Stand there,' and walked off trailing his gun."[30]

The prisoners of war were marched on shore and stopped for a while on a side street in New Orleans. "In the meantime the ladies of New Orleans, Rebel sympathizers, found out that a lot of hungry Confederates were clamoring loudly for a breakfast; and in a short time they had chartered every café on both sides of us and had started the waiters to us with hot rolls and coffee," remembered an Alabama artillery officer. "But this was more of a treat than the guard could complacently endure, so the waiters were unceremoniously halted short of our ranks." The brave women defiantly passed the guard with trays of food to feed the famished Southern soldiers. Remarkably, after enduring three years of Yankee occupation, many women of New Orleans remained loyal to the Confederacy.[31] From New Orleans, the graycoats traveled to Vicksburg, where they received paroles and were given free transportation back to their homes.[32]

In the days that followed the surrender, trains arrived daily in Mobile with Taylor's paroled soldiers. "The paroled officers and men of Taylor's army are overrunning Mobile," reported the *Cincinnati Enquirer*.[33] "The men of both armies fraternized," recalled Union Lieutenant Charles Allen, "as a general rule, and one would not have supposed, from simply observing them, that they had ever been enemies."[34] Although many left as fast as they could get transportation home, Sergeant Musser described the paroled Southerners as "quite sociable and willing to let bygones be bygones and once more be Americans." On the streets of Mobile, graycoats and bluecoats could be seen talking about the war and "joking [sic] as if they had not been trying to kill each other only a short time before."[35] The initial stages of the reunification and the healing of the nation were seen in the Port City through the fraternizing of the men who had fought each other bitterly for four long years.

There were some lingering issues between the Federal occupiers and the paroled Southern soldiers. General Slack wrote his wife that he was having difficulty with "impudent and saucy" paroled soldiers who had made their way back to Mobile. The Southerners, likely not having any other clothes, continued to wear their gray uniforms in town. In his letter, Slack stated if the paroled troops did not remove the "treasonable suits" from their "traitorous backs" he would have them arrested. He added that he "would just as soon see them carrying round a rebel flag. In the city they carry their side arms, sword and revolvers. Our officers and men are becoming very much incensed about it, and soon it will lead to trouble."[36] Slack's letter suggests that, despite some fraternizing between Union soldiers and ex-Confederates, there was certainly some resentment remaining. In a letter to his wife, General Thomas K. Smith, headquartered at Dauphin Island, shared his thoughts on future struggles. He wrote that the Confederates would not "go home contented" to "ruined plantations" and abandoned cities that they would have to rebuild without the aid of slave labor. He believed the Southerners would be overcome with bitterness, likely leading to future conflicts.[37]

Despite the understandable tension that still lingered, there was hope that the United States could become truly united again. "In my judgment, there is just one hope for us now, and that is a war with a foreign power that would have the effect of uniting the belligerents, I have now prisoners with me, three generals and their staff, Liddell, Cockrell, and Thomas," he wrote. "I guarantee that I can enlist all or the major part of them to go with me to Mexico or Canada to fight under the stars and stripes."[38] Similarly, one newspaper correspondent covering the surrender ceremony at Citronelle noted: "The opinion was freely expressed that should the United States become involved in a war with a foreign power she would find a large number of her late enemies side by side with her in the defence [sic] of the principles of our common country."[39] Thirty-three years later there were former Confederates who served the United States during the Spanish-American War.[40]

The Magazine Explosion

Mobile's buildings, the homes and businesses comprising the Port City, managed to escape the conflict unscathed. Shortly after the final surrender the city would suffer more destruction than Vicksburg had in the siege of 1863. "Providence ordained that Mobile should pay the penalty of her great political offence [sic]," wrote Union Captain Stephen A. Cobb. On May 25, at 2:15 p.m., a tremendous explosion of 200,000 pounds of gun powder and shell occurred at Marshall's Warehouse, the Federal army's primary ordinance depot. The warehouse was located downtown near the Mobile River.[41]

"It is probably the greatest explosion ever occurred in the U.S.," declared one bluecoat in a letter written to his sister the day after the detonation.[42] The explosion was possibly the largest the world had ever seen up to that point in time. The tremendous force of the blast cracked the massive granite of the Custom House, destroyed every pane of glass of the Custom House and Battle House on Royal Street, and even shattered windows at the village of Spring Hill, 6 miles distant.[43] "John Kavanaugh, a paroled Confederate soldier, was killed instantly on board the steamer *Kate Dale* by the concussion alone. "Not a mark was visible upon his body," one newspaper reported. Another man "was blown off the wharf and his leg broken, at the foot of Church street [sic], nearly or quite a mile from the scene of the great disaster."[44] The explosion was felt and seen at Dauphin Island's Fort Gaines, nearly 28 miles south of Mobile. At first, General Thomas K. Smith thought it was thunder when the explosion shook there. "At night, I discovered a bright light in the north and feared for a while that a steamboat was on fire," Smith wrote, "but just at this moment the mystery has been solved by the intelligence brought me that the magazines at Mobile have been blown up, half the city destroyed."[45] One Union soldier, who was camped 3 miles from Mobile when the explosion occurred, remembered, "The smoke mounted up in a dark, thick mass and then spread out like

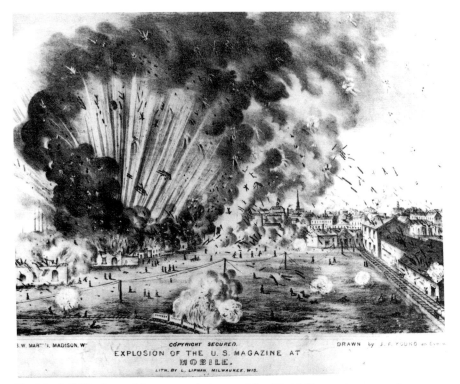

COPYRIGHT SECURED.
5.W. MAR I. MADISON, W   DRAWN by J. F. YOUNG
EXPLOSION OF THE U. S. MAGAZINE AT
MOBILE.
LITH. BY L. LIPMAN, MILWAUKEE, WIS.

The Marshall Warehouse Magazine explosion on May 25, 1865 caused a tremendous amount of destruction in downtown Mobile. (*Courtesy of* History Museum of Mobile)

an immense umbrella or mushroom, and through it could be seen broken timbers and debris of all kinds flying in every direction."[46]

General Slack, who was in town, was waking up from a nap when the explosion occurred four blocks away. "The windows of the room in which we were lying came tumbling in," he wrote his wife, "the shattered glass of one window falling all over our bed." At first, he thought the Confederates were attacking in the streets. Shells continued to explode as voices cried out for help. People trapped under buildings were literally roasted alive. Slack witnessed the unimaginable chaos and destruction. "Five or six steamers lying at the wharf were shattered into atoms, and two of them burned," he wrote. The next morning, Slack walked through the ruins, which he wrote could not be described by words, but "has to be seen to be fully appreciated."[47] Captain Cobb reported: "Men, women and children were rushing in fright through ruins and clouds of lurid dust. The groans of the dying and wounded, rising in volumes so as to almost drown the sounds of the still exploding shells and the falling walls, added to the ghastliness of the scene."[48] The next morning, General Granger, through a dispatch, informed Canby, who was at the time in New Orleans, of the

The aftermath of the explosion (*Courtesy of* the History Museum of Mobile)

tragedy. The commanding general directed Granger to have all medical officers in the area to provide aid and to issue rations to the affected families.[49]

The loss of life and property was shocking—an estimated 300 people killed, eight city blocks of buildings leveled, and approximately 10,000 bales of cotton destroyed.[50] An estimated 80 acres of downtown Mobile lay in "complete ruin." Massive fires broke out fueled by large quantities of cotton and rosin. "For days afterward, friends, in delving among the ruins for the missing, would find the bodies of persons till then supposed to be living," recalled Cobb. "The stench in the vicinity of the disaster soon became intolerable."[51] Shells continued to explode for three days.[52]

On June 2, eight days after the explosion, Chief Justice of the United States Supreme Court Salmon P. Chase, who had earlier served as Lincoln's Secretary of the Treasury, visited Mobile. In his journal, Chase wrote: "Rooms at the Battle House windows shattered by great explosion on 25." He also noted that many lives were lost and "8 to 10 squares completely destroyed."[53] The reason for the explosion was never fully known, although carelessness of workers who were unloading munitions was suspected.[54]

To the Confederates, General Taylor's surrender and the subsequent parole of his men was a sad conclusion to their four-year struggle for Southern independence. General Canby ensured his soldiers showed respect toward the Southerners. Likewise, General Taylor made remarkable efforts to enable the transition of his department back into the United States. The honorable and considerate leadership of Taylor and Canby helped overcome the tragedy of Mobile's magazine explosion and begin the process of reunifying the United States.

CHAPTER SEVENTEEN

A Grand Period to this Rebellion

The understudied Mobile campaign may not rank as high in importance as the battle of Mobile Bay or the Atlanta campaign, yet it was still a significant part of the war. The city held the distinction of being one of the last important places in the South which was captured. "It was the last to be attacked of the rebel strongholds—for the Texas ports are not worth account—and was by a few days the last to fall. It falls a prize to the valor of our brave army and navy, and not as a trophy of diplomacy," wrote one Northern newspaper reporter on the fall of Mobile.[1] Its possession gave the Union control of every strategic point in the Confederacy and, as another newspaper declared, "put a grand period to this rebellion."[2] Even though many people today think of Robert E. Lee's surrender of the Army of Northern Virginia as the end of hostilities, the last siege on the Gulf Coast helped ensure a complete Union victory.

The fall of Mobile and subsequent surrender of General Richard S. Taylor's forces marked the final chapter of the Confederacy. On May 27, 1882, Lieutenant James A. Chalaron of the Washington Artillery's 5th Company, who joined General Randall L. Gibson's Louisiana Brigade during the defense of Spanish Fort, gave a toast at an Army of Tennessee reunion. His toast summarized the entire war experience of the Washington Artillery and ended with his recollections of the siege:

> In Spanish Fort of Fourteen days with Gibson, and the last to spike our guns that night of evacuation. Rescued from out of the sea marsh of Blakely [sic] river the Fifth company is in Mobile again, where McIhenny and Miller had preceded them to be buried. This siege has fitly crowned our military experience. The town is doomed. We march away, as light artillery, refitted and complete.
>
> The end has come when Lee's surrender is announced. Our own soon follows. We furl our flag in tears, and Slocomb leads us home to weeping households, desolated households, desolated firesides, and ruined estates.[3]

Courageously, although vastly outnumbered, the defenders of Mobile determined to fight it out. The courage and sacrifice demonstrated by the Confederate soldiers was even sometimes recognized by Unionist newspapers. "These men, who, through family influence, education, or belief in States Rights Doctrine, sacrificed in many cases, fortune, position and old ties, enduring all manner of hardships to take up arms in what they sincerely thought was right," wrote a New Orleans *Times-Democrat* columnist. "We cannot but respect their feelings, as much as we deplore their mistaken notions impelling them to turn against that Government and flag, under which they were born." The columnist went on to express the hope that with time the country would once again become united.[4]

Despite all the hardships and dangers, Confederate Captain Albert C. Danner considered his experience fighting for the South "the best four years" of his life. "We took no heed of danger, were willing and expected to give our lives for the defense of constitutional government," he wrote.[5] Dedication to their cause and loyalty to each other motivated the Southern soldiers to defend Mobile through the final days of the conflict. Their nearly two-week stand at Mobile against the numerically superior Federal force was admirable.

Thirty-four years after the war, when asked by a reporter about the distinction of having fought in one of the last battles, the gallant Colonel Philip B. Spence of the 12th Mississippi paused and then expressed pride in the role he and his men played in a cause they believed to be righteous. He also took the opportunity to comment on the country being reunited. "Those who are yet living, after so many years have passed, are loyal and true," said Spence, "and their children and grandchildren are as loyal and true to the Union and to the flag of the Union as any of the gallant boys in blue who fought under Granger and the Stars and Stripes against us who wore the gray in that memorable engagement." To further his point, Spence referred to the "'Yank' and 'Johnny'" that were then fighting together in the Spanish-American War.[6]

There were also many examples of determination and heroic deeds by the Federal soldiers, such as the arduous march of the XIII Corps and Steele's Column and the assaults of Spanish Fort and Fort Blakeley. Undaunted by the formidable and deadly obstacles in their path, the besiegers bravely persevered to capture the eastern shore forts and ultimately Mobile.

Apart from New Orleans, in terms of commercial importance, wealth, and population, Mobile was considered a rival to any other city in the south.[7] Bagging Spanish Fort, Fort Blakeley, and Mobile was therefore considered a magnificent success by the Northern press. The *New York Times* pronounced, "The civilian observer, even the most practiced, looks in vain for a capital error in the Mobile campaign, unless it be in the too careless maneuvering of the fleet among the torpedoes. The whole history of the war will scarcely present a more unique, dramatic and faultless campaign than the one just completed with such splendid results."[8]

General Canby's leadership in the Mobile campaign was praised. The *Burlington Weekly Hawk-Eye* wrote, "Few isolated campaigns in history more signally demonstrate that successful war is organized and waged more by the man than by the musket, by the genius of one man, rather than by the bayonets of thousands."[9]

Federal officials in Washington also praised Canby's successful expedition. On May 16, 1865, U.S. Secretary of War Edwin Stanton wrote him a congratulatory letter that was delayed due to the overwhelming public grief in Washington over the assassination of Lincoln. In the letter, Stanton recognized the "military skill" Canby displayed to overcome the "extensive preparations" of the defenders of Mobile. "These operations were accompanied by circumstances of difficulty and discouragement and without the aid and support enjoyed by forces less remote from the great depots of supply," wrote Stanton. "But the brilliant success of your achievements has exercised an influence that cannot be overestimated in breaking the rebel power destroying all hopes and bringing their cause to ruin." He also noted in the letter that "no officer enjoyed more highly than yourself, the personal esteem and confidence of the late President Mr. Lincoln and that to his latest moment he watched the operations of your army with great interest."[10]

Despite all the praise General Canby received, his leadership in the Mobile campaign did not escape criticism. Confederate General Dabney H. Maury questioned Canby's grand tactics after the war. Maury claimed he was relieved when he found out the Union attack would be in Baldwin County. He was surprised to learn the reason Steele's Column moved from Pensacola to cut the rail lines at Pollard was to prevent their escape to Montgomery. He never planned to use this route to evacuate his garrison. Maury believed the Federal attack would have been shorter and easier had they attempted landing on Dog River and invested the city. Considering the city was level and exposed and that there were nearly 40,000 non-combatants within their lines, it would have made the defense very difficult. "Had Canby not made the indefensible blunder of landing his army at Fish river to attack Mobile, the sending of Steele's corps towards Pollard would not have been a blunder, for then I might have been forced to try to bring out my garrison on that side, and to lead it to Montgomery, and have had to drive Steele from my path or surrender to him," Maury wrote.[11]

Maury's critique failed to acknowledge the deterrent effect of the strong earthworks surrounding Mobile. Canby had received credible intelligence reports, including advice from General William T. Sherman that led him to invade the eastern shore.[12] With the information Canby had at the time, it appeared the easiest route was to move first against Spanish Fort and Fort Blakeley.[13] The Unionists, however, did not anticipate the obstinate resistance or the crippling effect of the torpedoes they encountered.[14] Furthermore, the route Steele's Column took allowed them to cut the Mobile & Great Northern line. This did more than just prevent a potential escape route. It is also barred Confederate reinforcements from being sent to Mobile from that rail line.[15]

Union staff officer General Cyrus B. Comstock wrote disapprovingly of Canby's over cautiousness in his diary. He described the movement against Mobile as "slow and sure," pointing out several instances where the campaign was needlessly delayed.

Comstock recognized Canby as a "good man & safe," but lacked "experience enough with large bodies of troops to act rapidly & take risks." He wrote that Mobile should have been taken sooner, considering the size of the Union force.[16] Comstock failed to recognize the factors that probably influenced Canby's "slow and sure" movement. Inclement weather, strong fortifications, deadly land and sea mines, and the unexpected fighting tenacity of the Confederate defenders contributed to his cautious movements.

General-in-Chief Grant, who had wanted to send an expedition against Mobile earlier in the conflict, wrote a scathing critique of Canby's expedition. In his memoirs, Grant was critical of Canby's slowness and wrote the war was "practically over" by the time Mobile was captured. "It finally cost lives to take it when its possession was of no importance," he wrote, "and when, if left alone, it would within a few days have fallen into our hands without any bloodshed whatever." Although he recognized the success of Canby's operations, Grant concluded they were "without any good result" and pointed out that "much valuable property was destroyed and many lives lost at a time when we would have liked to spare them."[17]

General Grant's overly negative assessment of the siege of Mobile failed to acknowledge some of the objectives that it accomplished. Canby's expedition succeeded in tying down the Confederate soldiers in the region, thus preventing them from reinforcing their armies in the west. His forces captured nearly 5,000 prisoners, including four generals, 300 plus commissioned officers, many flags, over 230 artillery pieces, and a huge amount of army materiel and naval stores. Mobile gave the Unionists a base to operate into the interior of Alabama and access to the Alabama and Tombigbee Rivers, albeit too late to make a significant difference in the outcome of the conflict.[18]

We now know that General Lee's surrender of the Army of Northern Virginia left the Confederate forces still in the field little hope of success. Union leaders at the time, however, did not know for certain that the remaining Southern forces would lay down their arms. Even after General Lee's surrender, President Jefferson Davis intended to keep up the contest, and numerous Southern forces and vast Confederate-held territory remained with which he could potentially do so.[19] General Canby's invasion of Alabama ultimately led to the final surrender of the last intact force east of the Mississippi, thus guaranteeing the end of the war. The siege and capture of Mobile was indeed one of the important final Union victories that put the nail in the coffin of the Confederacy.[20]

Epilogue

Violent Deaths

On April 11, 1873, General Canby was murdered at a peace conference in northern California. At the meeting, Modoc Indian Chief Captain Jack demanded that Canby remove his troops. After the general responded that only the President of the United States had the power to remove the soldiers, Captain Jack and his men attacked them. Canby was shot in the face, under the left eye, by Captain Jack. Although badly wounded with a broken jaw, the general managed to stagger to his feet and run several yards before being shot in the back. Only one of the four Federal commissioners escaped. Canby and the other two commissioners were brutally killed and stripped. He was the highest-ranking U.S. Army officer in history to be murdered by a Native-American.[1] When informed of the murder, General William T. Sherman, in his customary manner, ordered retaliation against the Modocs. He instructed Canby's replacement to "make an attack so strong and persistent that their fate may be commensurate with the crime. You will be fully justified in their utter extermination." Several days after the slayings, Captain Jack and his accomplices were captured. Months later they were executed, hanged by the neck until dead. The tribe was then banished to the Indian Territory.[2]

Southerners often felt animosity toward the leaders of invading U.S. forces. For instance, General Sherman is still vilified in the South for his destructive march through the state of Georgia. After Canby's murder, one Southern newspaper, the *Athens Northeast Georgian*, headlined a story titled, "Captain Jack and Warriors Revenge the South by Murdering General Canby, One of Her Greatest Oppressors." Evidence suggests many citizens near Mobile, and even Confederate officers who fought against him, would have objected to the tone of the newspaper report. "Narrow perhaps in his view, and harsh in discharge of duty, he was just, upright, and honorable, and it was with regret that I learned of his murder by a band of Modoc savages," wrote Southern General Richard Taylor.[3]

Many years after the conflict, the high regard one south Alabama citizen held for Canby became known nationally. In 1923, 69-year-old Baldwin County Judge Charles Hall, who lived near Fort Blakeley as a young boy, wrote to then President Harding. "General Canby was in command of the Federal army at Fort Blakeley, in

Baldwin County, Alabama," Hall wrote the President, and "my father and I went to Blakeley to see General Canby to ask him for something to eat, as everything my father owned at that time was destroyed by the Federal soldiers." Hall continued, "General Canby gave us food when we were hungry." Judge Hall asked President Harding for the location of Canby's cemetery, so he could have a wreath placed upon his grave. Moved by the request, Harding directed the War Department to ascertain the burial place of Canby, which was determined to be Indianapolis. The report of Hall's remarkable request was published in newspapers around the country.[4]

Although agitated by Canby's slowness during the Mobile campaign, General Grant acknowledged his "pure" character and service during the war. In his memoirs, he declared Canby "was an officer of great merit" possessing "great talent and learning" and "superior efficiency" as a staff officer. "There have been in the army but very few, if any, officers who took as much interest in reading and digesting every act of Congress and every regulation for the government of the army as he," wrote Grant. He noted that Canby's knowledge of Federal regulations and laws made him a "most valuable staff officer."[5]

It should also be noted that Canby issued orders insisting his men conduct themselves in an "orderly" manner when they occupied Mobile. He also generously provided paroled Southern soldiers transportation home after the surrender. His considerate behavior left a good impression on some residents in Mobile as well. The family of Confederate Major William Ketchum, whose home in Mobile was commandeered for Canby's personal lodging, reportedly maintained friendly communication with the general after the war.[6] In honor of his memory, cities in Yellow Medicine County, Minnesota, Modoc County, California, and Clackamas County, Oregon, are named "Canby." There are also streets in Mobile and Spanish Fort named after him.

Canby was not the only general involved with the Mobile campaign to be violently murdered in the years after the conflict. Three other generals, Southerners St. John R. Liddell and James H. Clanton, and the U.S. Army's Joseph Bailey, were also gunned down in the postwar years.

Upon his return to Louisiana, Liddell resumed his long-standing feud with a neighbor, Lieutenant Colonel Charles Jones, who had served with the 17th Louisiana Infantry. The exact cause of the bitter Liddell-Jones family feud is unknown, although it likely began in 1847. On February 14, 1870, as he dined aboard the riverboat steamer *St. Mary* on the Black River in Louisiana, Liddell was shot to death by Jones and his two sons.[7]

After his parole, Clanton resumed his Alabama law practice. In 1871, he represented the State of Alabama in a suit against the Chattanooga & Alabama railroad. On September 28, 1871, the case brought Clanton to Knoxville, Tennessee, where he was introduced to an intoxicated Colonel Dan Nelson, who had served in the U.S. Army during the war. Soon after being introduced, a misunderstanding led Clanton to challenge Nelson to a duel on the street. As Clanton's friend tried to calm him down, Nelson ran into a nearby saloon and returned with a double barrel shotgun. Nelson proceeded to shoot Clanton to death in the street.[8] A city in Chilton County, Alabama, is named in Clanton's honor.

Bailey was responsible for building and supervising the construction and operations of the Federal wharf at Starke's Landing south of Spanish Fort. Following the conflict, he was elected sheriff of Vernon County, Missouri. In 1867, Bailey was shot and killed as he tried to apprehend cattle thieves. The murderers were never captured.[9]

Prominent Political Careers and Public Service

Several of the Confederate and Union leaders involved in the Mobile campaign continued to serve their country as elected officials or political appointees.

Three veterans of the campaign for Mobile went on to become governors: Brevet Brigadier General William R. Marshall of the 7th Minnesota Infantry; Lucius F. Hubbard of the 5th Minnesota Infantry, who became a brevet brigadier general before mustering out; and Southern Sergeant Thomas Seay. Marshall, a Republican, became Minnesota's fifth governor, serving his state from November 7, 1865 to January 9, 1870. He died in 1896 at Pasadena, California. The city of Marshall, Minnesota, and Marshall County, Minnesota, are named after him.[10] Hubbard, a Republican, went on to serve as the ninth governor of Minnesota from January 10, 1882 to January 5, 1887. Later, President William McKinley appointed Hubbard a brigadier general in the Spanish-American War. On February 15, 1913, he passed away in Minneapolis, Minnesota. Hubbard County, Minnesota, is named after him.[11] Seay, who was an orderly sergeant for the 62nd Alabama, became the 27th governor of that same state. He served one term, from 1886 to 1890. Seay passed away in 1896 at the age of 49 in Greensboro, Alabama.[12]

At least seven officers (four Confederate, three Union) who participated in the Mobile campaign went on to represent their respective states in the U.S. Congress.

In 1875, Confederate General Francis M. Cockrell, also a Democrat, was elected to the U.S. Senate, where he served for 30 years. The Missourian earned respect from both parties as a powerful member of the Senate Appropriation and Military Affairs Committee. Speaker of the House Joseph Cannon said of him: "Cockrell is the best legislator in Congress. He has experience, judgment, and patriotism." He was often mentioned as a potential Presidential candidate by his peers.[13] When Cockrell left the Senate in 1905, newly elected President Theodore Roosevelt, a Republican, appointed him to the Interstate Commerce Commission. When his six-year term expired with the Interstate Commerce Commission, President Taft appointed him Commissioner for the United States to relocate the boundary line between Texas and the territory of New Mexico. At the age of 77, Cockrell camped out in the open New Mexico territory, supervising the 500-mile boundary line survey. In 1913, President Woodrow Wilson appointed him to be the civilian member of the Board of Ordnance and Fortifications, where he served until his death two years later.[14]

Confederate General Randall L. Gibson, a Democrat, served in the U.S. House of Representatives from 1874 to 1882. From 1882 until his death on December 15, 1892, he served Louisiana in the U.S. Senate. He played an instrumental role in coordinating, with wealthy New Orleans businessman Paul R. Tulane, the transition of his alma mater, the University of Louisiana, into the prestigious private Tulane University. Gibson served as president of Tulane's Board of Administration from 1884 until his death. Gibson Hall at Tulane is named in honor of this brave general.[15]

Colonel Thomas H. Herndon, 36th Regiment of Alabama Infantry, remained in Mobile and became a prominent lawyer of the city he once helped defend. Herndon, a Democrat, unsuccessfully ran for governor of Alabama in 1872. Later he represented Alabama's First District in the U.S. House of Representatives from 1879 until his death in 1883.[16]

Two Union officers went on to represent Illinois in Congress. Colonel John McNulta, 94th Illinois, served from March 4, 1873 to March 3, 1875, and General John I. Rinaker, 122nd Illinois, served from June 5, 1896, to March 3, 1897.[17]

Federal General William A. Pile, who commanded the 1st Brigade, 1st Division, U.S.C.T., in the siege of Fort Blakeley, was elected to the U.S. House of Representatives in 1866. After his stint in Congress, he served as territorial governor of New Mexico and was appointed ambassador to Venezuela by President Grant. He helped found and served as mayor of Monrovia, California. Pile died July 7, 1889, in Monrovia.[18]

Confederate Lieutenant Thomas B. Catron of the 3rd Missouri Battery went on to serve as one of New Mexico's first U.S. senators.[19]

Union General C. C. Andrews, the commander of the 2nd Division of the XIII Corps, was appointed an ambassador to Sweden and Norway from 1869 to 1877. Andrews also served as consul-general to Brazil from 1882 to 1885. Later, Andrews served as Minnesota state forestry commissioner and was a strong proponent of regulated forestry practices. The General C. C. Andrews State Forest in Pine County, Minnesota, was named in his honor.[20]

Confederate Colonel Elijah Gates, of the 1st/3rd Missouri Cavalry Battalion, was elected state treasurer for Missouri in 1873. Later President Cleveland appointed him U.S. marshal for the western district of Missouri. Gates died on March 4, 1915, at the age of 88.[21]

General James T. Holtzclaw of the Confederate States Army remained in Alabama following the surrender. He resumed his legal practice and served on the Alabama Railroad Commission until shortly before his death in 1893 in Montgomery, Alabama.[22]

Confederate General Dabney H. Maury was appointed ambassador to Colombia from 1887 to 1889 by President Grover Cleveland. Maury tried his hand at several ventures in the years before this appointment. He is most noted for founding the Southern Historical Society in 1868. This organization produced over 52 volumes of historical writings and was the dominant source of literature in defense of the "Lost Cause."[23]

Another non-governmental venture Maury engaged in was a turpentine distilling operation at St. Tammany Parish, Louisiana. The enterprise was doomed to failure due to events Maury was associated with during the war. In 1864, Maury ordered his cousin, Colonel Harry Maury, and the 15th Confederate Cavalry, to put down an anti-Confederate uprising in Jones County, Mississippi. The 2016 movie *Free State of Jones*, starring Matthew McConaughey, depicts the Jones County Rebellion. Although his role was omitted from the film, Colonel Maury carried out his work against the deserters of Jones County without mercy, causing the "Southern Yankees" of Jones County to vilify the surname Maury. Unfortunately, General Maury unwittingly set up a distilling operation in a location inhabited by some of the same people the 15th Confederate Cavalry had driven out of Jones County during the war. There, he was the subject of threats and never left his home unarmed. After his business suffered a considerable setback from an arson attack, Maury decided to relocate and pursue other less hazardous ventures.[24]

President Andrew Johnson appointed General Peter J. Osterhaus, Canby's chief of staff, as U.S. consul at Lyon, France in 1866. In 1868, Osterhaus was reappointed by President Grant until he resigned in 1877. Afterward, Osterhaus settled in Germany, where he died in 1915.[25]

Colonel Isaac W. Patton of the 22nd Louisiana Infantry returned to New Orleans, where he was elected mayor in 1878. Patton, the great uncle of the famous World War II General George S. Patton III, died at the age of 62 on February 9, 1890.[26]

Union General James R. Slack, who commanded the 1st Brigade, 1st Division of the XIII Corps, resumed his law practice in Huntington, Indiana. Later, he was appointed to the 28th Circuit Judicial Court. Slack unsuccessfully ran for U.S. Congress in 1881, the year of his death.[27]

Federal General A. J. Smith of the XVI Corps remained in the army until 1869. President Grant then appointed him postmaster of St. Louis, Missouri, where he lived until his death in 1897 at the age of 82.[28]

Union General Thomas K. Smith served as consul in Panama, during the administration of President Andrew Johnson. He spent most of the rest of his life in retirement at his residence in Jonesdale, Pennsylvania, suffering from diseases he incurred during the war. Smith died there at the age of 67 on December 14, 1887.[29]

During the first administration of Grover Cleveland, Colonel Phillip B. Spence of the 12th Mississippi Cavalry was appointed postmaster of Newport, Kentucky. During his tenure as postmaster, Spence was given the opportunity to name a small community in Kentucky. He chose the name Brent after his father and son. During Cleveland's second administration, he was appointed United States consul to Quebec, Canada. After a long period of illness, Spence, at the age of 78, passed away in Cincinnati in 1915.[30]

General Andrew B. Spurling, commander of the 2nd Maine Union Cavalry, was elected sheriff of Hancock County, Maine. Later, he was appointed post office inspector with headquarters at Chicago, where he died in 1906.[31]

Confederate General Bryan M. Thomas, whose reserve brigade defended the right side of the line at Fort Blakeley, was appointed by fellow ex-Confederate General James Longstreet as deputy U.S. marshal for Dalton, Georgia. He also served as the superintendent of the Dalton public schools. He passed away on July 16, 1905 at the age of 69.[32]

Career Soldiers and Good Americans

Union Generals Gordon Granger and Frederick F. Steele remained in the army until their deaths. On January 10, 1876, Granger died after a paralytic stroke at his military headquarters in Santa Fe, New Mexico.[33] Steele passed away in 1868 in California when an apoplectic fit caused him to fall from a buggy.[34]

General John P. Hawkins also remained in the U.S. Army, serving in many capacities, until retirement at the age of 64. He died on February 7, 1914, in Indianapolis, Indiana.[35]

U.S. Army Colonel Henry C. Merriam was one of 14 soldiers awarded the Congressional Medal of Honor for distinguished service in the attack of Fort Blakeley. He received the prestigious medal on June 28, 1894, "for voluntarily and successfully leading his regiment over the works in advance of orders, permission having been given at his own request."[36] He remained in the service until reaching retirement age in 1901. Achieving the rank of major general, he was also noted for designing the "Merriam Pack," a knapsack used by infantry personnel. He passed away on November 12, 1912, in Portland, Maine.[37]

Admiral Henry K. Thatcher remained in the navy and went on to command the North Pacific Squadron until he retired at the age of 62 in 1868. He passed away in 1880 at his home in Winchester, Massachusetts.[38]

Confederate Sergeant Benjamin H. Bounds of the 4th Mississippi Infantry went on to serve as an ordained minister in north Mississippi and northwest Texas. He died of pneumonia on November 8, 1911, in Greenville, Texas.[39]

Captain Albert C. Danner, 1st Missouri Infantry, was another Confederate officer who chose to make Mobile his home. Danner used the same energy and character he demonstrated throughout the conflict to become a highly regarded merchant. In the postwar years, Danner led various Mobile-based companies. He became a leading manufacturer, a pioneer in Alabama's coal industry, and a prominent exporter of lumber. His business ventures significantly contributed to the revitalization of Mobile's economy and infrastructure. Captain Danner also made generous philanthropic contributions to the community he once helped defend in the last siege. He passed away in 1921, leaving a legacy as one of the most prominent figures in the history of Mobile.[40]

Confederate Commodore Ebenezer Farrand also settled in Alabama, where he became an insurance representative in Montgomery. Later, he became a co-owner of the Railway Hotel in Attalla, Alabama, where he died on March 17, 1873.[41]

Colonel Samuel H. Lockett, Chief Engineer for the Department of Alabama, Mississippi and East Louisiana, went on to teach at LSU, where Lockett Hall is named after him. Later he served as an engineer in the Egyptian army and went on to work on the design of the foundation of the Statute of Liberty.[42]

Southern General Richard Taylor interceded with President Andrew Johnson on behalf of his former brother-in-law, Jefferson Davis, and proposed less punitive Reconstruction sanctions. He wrote a book on his Civil War experiences entitled *Destruction and Reconstruction; Personal Experiences of the Late War.* Taylor died penniless in New York City and was buried at the Metairie Cemetery in New Orleans in 1879.[43]

Union Adjutant Wales W. Wood returned to his law practice in Belvidere, Illinois, where he lived the remainder of his life. During his career, he served his community as city attorney and eventually county judge. Wood died on August 8, 1909, at the age of 72.[44]

U.S. Army Private William Wiley returned to Illinois, where he worked as a farmer. On November 12, 1902, he passed away in Monmouth, Illinois, at 64 years of age.[45]

Union Sergeant Charles O. Musser moved to Nebraska, where he too worked as a farmer. He died on March 10, 1938. He was believed to have lived longer than any other member of the 29th Iowa.[46]

Private Richard A. Spink of the U.S. Army became the city treasurer for Oshkosh, Wisconsin. He was 91 years old when he died on May 10, 1935.[47]

Federal army musician Andrew F. Sperry worked as a clerk in the registration division of the post office for 30 years. He passed away in Washington, DC, on March 15, 1911.[48]

Confederate Sergeant William P. Chambers resumed a career in teaching at Kinterbish, Alabama. He died on January 11, 1916, at the age of 77 in Forrest County, Mississippi.[49]

Corporal Edgar W. Jones of the Confederate States Army became a reverend and the editor of the *Jones Valley Times*, near Birmingham, Alabama.[50]

Confederate Private Philip Stephenson also became a reverend. As a Presbyterian minister, he served congregations in Tennessee, Missouri, Maryland, Pennsylvania, and Virginia. On March 12, 1916, Stephenson died in Richmond, Virginia.[51]

The *Lady Slocomb*

One of the more interesting stories that occurred in the postwar years involved the fate of the cannon *Lady Slocomb*. Named in honor of Washington Artillery Captain Cuthbert Slocomb's wife, the cast iron cannon was reportedly made at Tredegar, Virginia, in 1862. The 8-inch iron columbiad cannon weighed 8,566 pounds and was 10 feet long.[1] During the siege of Spanish Fort, the big gun was skillfully manned by the 5th Company of the Washington Artillery at Redoubt 3, also known as Battery Blair, where it fired 144 charges, 1,440 pounds of powder, and over 7,500 pounds of shot and shell.[2]

The Blue and Gray Veterans Union, a group of Union and Confederate veterans living near Mobile, Alabama, was organized on July 4, 1890, on the battlefield of Spanish Fort. To their amazement, the veterans group discovered the old gun on the ground where it was disabled 25 years earlier. On March 7, 1891, Augustus W. Sibley, owner of the land where the battle of Spanish Fort took place, sold the title to the cannon to the Blue and Gray Union for one dollar. The following week the *Lady Slocomb*, at a cost of $285.25, was transported to downtown Mobile where it became a peace monument commemorating the "Valor of American Soldiers and the Sweet Dawn of Peace." Before the cannon was sent to the city, there was a charge of canister discovered in the barrel and removed.[3]

Mobile residents Dr. Seymour Bullock and Thomas P. Brewer were instrumental in bringing the cannon to Mobile. Bullock, a 49-year-old former bluecoat, was president of the Blue and Gray Union. He served with the 24th Regiment of the New York Cavalry as quartermaster sergeant. After the war, he relocated to Mobile to practice medicine.[4] Brewer, an ex-Confederate, was vice president of the Blue and Gray Union and a lieutenant commander of the Admiral Semmes Camp of the United Confederate Veterans. He had served as a captain with Hood's Texas Brigade in Virginia, surrendered his company at Appomattox Court House, and was well known in the city and even ran for mayor.[5]

Although neither Bullock nor Brewer fought at Spanish Fort, they helped organize the Blue and Gray Union in Mobile, where they both resided.[6] The two became

The *Lady Slocomb* and members of the Blue-Gray Union at the Spanish Fort battlefield just before the cannon's removal to Mobile in March of 1891. (*Courtesy of* Fairhope Museum of History)

close friends through their association with the Union and even traveled together to Washington, DC, where they received confirmation that the Treasury Department had no claim to the title of the gun.[7] However, a falling-out in their friendship occurred, causing them to become mortal enemies. Bullock's wife claimed the two had an argument at a Blue and Gray Union meeting, the details of which were lost to history.[8] Their feud led to a tragedy at Navy Cove, 4 miles from Fort Morgan, where both men had summer cottages.[9]

Brewer attempted to avoid a confrontation after a family member warned that Bullock intended to shoot him. As he fished from the shore of Navy Cove on Thursday, October 15, 1891, Bullock approached in his boat and fired his shotgun at him, missing due to the rocking of the boat. Before Bullock could shoot again, Brewer returned fire with his shotgun and killed him. Following the shooting he surrendered himself to the sheriff. There were no witnesses; however, a subsequent investigation found both double barrel shotguns used had discharged only one round. Brewer never served time for the shooting as it was determined to be a case of self-defense. He went on to become prominent in local government and served as treasurer for the city of Mobile.[10]

The shotgun duel between Bullock and Brewer may have ultimately led to Mobile losing the cannon to New Orleans. It is believed that the tragedy at Navy Cove led the Blue and Gray Union to dissolve and allowed veterans of the Washington Artillery the opportunity to make a strong bid for the *Lady Slocomb*.[11]

Henry Badger, prominent Confederate veteran and citizen of Mobile, paid for the transportation of the *Lady Slocomb* from Spanish Fort to Mobile in 1891. When the Blue and Gray Union ceased to exist, ownership of the big gun was transferred to Badger since he had paid for it to be transported. After he passed away on May 28, 1896, newspaper reports indicated his estate proposed selling the *Lady Slocomb* to the highest bidder.[12]

Veterans of the 5th Company of the Washington Artillery, led by Lieutenant James A. Chalaron, had wanted the cannon in New Orleans ever since it came to Mobile. They had even petitioned the Secretary of the United States Treasury for the right to purchase it. On June 4, 1891, General Randall L. Gibson, who was then serving in the U.S. Senate, wrote to the Secretary of the Treasury on their behalf. He requested that the cannon be turned over to the survivors of Slocomb's Battery as a memorial to honor their brave captain but was denied. When Badger's estate offered the cannon to the highest bidder in 1896, they took full advantage of the opportunity to acquire it.[13]

After much deliberation, it was finally decided the cannon should be sold to the group of Washington Artillery veterans and brought back to their hometown of New Orleans. In March 1899, Chalaron and other veterans of the 5th Company of the Washington Artillery arrived in Mobile to complete the purchase of the cannon. Veterans of the Washington Artillery and the 14th Texas Dismounted Cavalry then shared the expense of having the big gun moved to New Orleans, where it was dedicated to the memory of Captain Cuthbert Slocomb and "the men who gave their lives for its defense."[14] Union Colonel Algernon S. Badger, no relation to Henry Badger, was a guest of honor at the unveiling ceremony there on September 19, 1899. Badger, a veteran of the Mobile campaign, had served in the Federal's 1st Louisiana Cavalry. "I appreciate deeply the invitation to sit here beside this gun to-day, for once upon a time I had the pleasure of being in front of it; I am glad to say a little to one side. That gun did awful work for a few days," said Badger at the ceremony.[15]

Today, the *Lady Slocomb* can be seen outside the Confederate Museum on Camp Street in New Orleans. Many citizens of Mobile resented the removal of the cannon. The topic remains a bitter subject with some residents of the city to this day.

APPENDIX 2

Historical Locations of the Mobile Campaign Today

The Mobile Bay area features a "Civil War Trail" available as a guide for enthusiasts interested in visiting the locations mentioned in this book. The website featuring this self-guided tour can be found at: http://www.battleofmobilebay.com/about-the-trail/default.aspx.

Located at the eastern end of Dauphin Island, Fort Gaines is a well-preserved historic site. The fort features the anchor of Admiral Farragut's flagship the USS *Hartford*, original cannons, a blacksmith shop, kitchens, a museum, gift shop, and tunnels. Guided tours are done in period uniform and include cannon-firing demonstrations and blacksmithing.[1]

Fort Morgan, located at the Mobile Point Peninsula, is operated by the Alabama Historical Commission. The coastal fort features a museum, nature areas, gift shops, and a boat launch.[2]

Fort Barrancas, the staging camp for Steele's Column, is located near Warrington, at northwest Florida's Naval Air Station. The National Park Service currently operates the fort.

The Spanish Fort battlefield was developed into a residential subdivision called Spanish Fort Estates from the 1960s through the early 2000s by the Fuller family through their company, Fuller Brothers. Historical markers are located throughout the neighborhood denoting then-extant locations of various regiments and fortifications from the period of the War for Southern Independence. A significant portion of two of the three elevated defensive positions of the Confederate earthworks have been destroyed—the original Spanish Fort (from colonial times) and Red Fort. The third elevated fortification, Fort McDermott—the most prominent position of the fort and highest promontory in Spanish Fort, Alabama—remains remarkably well preserved. In 2011, Mrs. George [Anne] Fuller, Jr., the granddaughter of Captain A. C. Danner, donated Fort McDermott to Raphael Semmes Camp 11 of the Sons of Confederate Veterans. The Semmes Camp cleared 150 years' growth of vegetation and dedicated the site as Fort McDermott Confederate Memorial Park on April 11, 2015. The Semmes Camp and donations entirely funded the reclamation thereof—no public

Fort McDermott (*Courtesy of* Pam Swan)

funds were utilized. Though a private park, it is open to the public and comprises a 3-acre site containing the lower parapet, moat, upper parapet, parade ground, and artillery emplacements of the original fortifications.[3]

Fort Blakeley, the site of the last major battlefield of the Civil War, is now a popular state park. In his 1867 book, General C. C. Andrews wrote, "Over the fields of Blakely [sic], the bushes are beginning to grow up, and in a few years another forest will no doubt cover the ground. But many of the trenches will remain. The storms of centuries will not wear them away."[4] Today, the 2,000-acre property boasts about being the home of some of the "richest history and greatest natural diversity in the state of Alabama." As Andrews predicted, another forest now covers most of the ground. The rifle pits, much of the Union breastworks, and the 3-mile-long Confederate earthen fortifications are still visible today. Fort Blakeley is a must-see for Civil War and camping enthusiasts.[5]

Batteries Huger and Tracy are accessible by boat on the Apalachee River. The remnants of the old water batteries are still vaguely discernible today.

Mobile's Magnolia Cemetery is the resting place of many soldiers, North and South, killed in the Mobile campaign. Private John Randall, the last soldier killed in the Mobile campaign, and Confederate General Braxton Bragg, among others, are buried there.

The location of the Whistler skirmish, near "Rebel Road" and the ruins of the Mobile & Ohio Machine Shop in present-day Prichard, Alabama, has no visible historical markers.

The McGhee Farm, location of the ceasefire agreement, closed to the public in 2014. It can still be seen from the road in Kushla, Alabama.

The Citronelle final surrender site is marked with historical placards and serves as a Boy Scout lodge.

Endnotes

Summary of Principal Events

1   United States War Department, *The War of Rebellion: Official Records of the Union and Confederate Armies [ORA]*, vol. 49, pts. 1 and 2 (Washington, DC: Government Printing Office, 1897); Michael D. Shipler, "The Mobile Campaigns March – April 1865," in *Military Order of Stars & Bars* (Mobile, AL, 2006), 62–63.

Preface

1   "Review of the Mobile Campaign," *Burlington (IA) Weekly Hawk-Eye,* April 29, 1865, 1.

2   Walter George Smith, *Life and Letters of Thomas Kilby Smith Brevet Major-General, United States Volunteers, 1820–1887* (New York: G. P. Putnam's Sons, 1898), 387; "Federals Move to Attack Forts of Mobile," *Washington (DC) Herald,* March 21, 1915, 23; *ORA,* Series 1, Vol. 45, pt. 2, 419–420.

3   "In Mobile Bay," *Osage City (KS) Free Press,* November 29, 1888, 2.

Prologue

1   Benjamin C. Truman, "The War in the Southwest," *New York Times,* February 28, 1865, 1.

2   C. B. Johnson, "In Camp and Field: A Medical Man's Memory of War-Time," *Arkansas City (KS) Weekly Republican Traveler,* October 7, 1887, 7; Stephen A. Cobb, "The Siege of Mobile," *Beloit College Archives Web Page,* accessed March 7, 2015, http://www.beloit.edu/archives/documents/ archival_collections/civil_war/reminiscence_cobb/; "The Fall of Mobile and Defenses," *Cincinnati (OH) Enquirer,* April 21, 1865, 2.

3   Michael Thomason and Henry M. McKiven, "Secession, War, and Reconstruction, 1850–1874," in *Mobile: The New History of Alabama's First City* (Tuscaloosa: University of Alabama Press, 2001), 105–107.

4   Mary E. Brooks, "War Memories," n.d., *Norman Nicholson Collection, Mobile Historic Preservation Society, Mobile, AL*; William Howard Russell, "Recollections of the Civil War," *North American Review* 166, no. 497 (April 1898): 49; David D. Porter, *The Naval History of the Civil War* (New York: Sherman Publishing Company, 1886), 565–600; Michael A. Sweetman, "Capture of Blakeley," *Washington (DC) National Tribune,* May 19, 1892, 1; "Cargo of Blockade Runner Denbigh Reveals Much About Civil War-era Mobile," AL.com, accessed January 29, 2017, http://blog.al.com/entertainment-press-register/2011/11/cargo_of_blockade_runner_denbi.html.

5   Smith, *Thomas Kilby Smith,* 388.

6   Joseph E. Johnston and Simon B. Bolivar were among the generals present at the ball. Augusta Evans Wilson was a noted Mobile author. Brooks, "War Memories."

7   Truman, "The War in the Southwest," 1; "Review of the Mobile Campaign," 1.

8 Located in downtown Mobile on Royal Street near the Mobile River, the Battle House was Mobile's most luxurious hotel in the city during the war. Destroyed by fire in 1905, the hotel was rebuilt in 1908 and remained open until 1974. In 2007, the Battle House reopened and is once again known as Mobile's finest hotel. William Miller Owen, *In Camp and Battle with the Washington Artillery of New Orleans: A Narrative of Events During the Late War from Bull Run to Appomattox and Spanish Fort* (Boston, MA: Ticknor, 1885), 203–205.

9 Jack Friend, *West Wind, Flood Tide: The Battle of Mobile Bay* (Annapolis, MD: Naval Institute Press, 2004), 224.

10 Ibid, 240; Truman, "The War in the Southwest," 1; "Review of the Mobile Campaign," 1.

11 C. C. Andrews, *History of the Campaign of Mobile* (New York: D. Van Nostrand, 1867), 10.

12 Charles J. Allen, "Some Account and Recollections of the Operations Against the City of Mobile and Its Defences, 1864 and 1865," *Glimpses of the Nation's Struggle* (St. Paul: St. Paul Book and Stationery Company, 1887), 55.

13 Ibid, 55.

14 United States War Department, *A Compilation of the Official Records of the Union and Confederate Navies in the War of the Rebellion [ORN]* (Washington, DC: Government Printing Office, 1894), Series 1, vol. 22, 41; "Grierson's Great Raid," *New Orleans (LA) Times Picayune*, January 20, 1865, 1; *ORA*, Series 1, vol. 45, 753.

15 "The Gulf," *New York Times*, March 7, 1865, 4.

16 "The Fall of Mobile and Defenses," 2.

17 "Interesting from Mobile," *The Philadelphia Inquirer*, March 31, 1865, 8; Allen, "Operations Against the City of Mobile," 55.

18 Chester G. Hearn, *Mobile Bay and the Mobile Campaign: The Last Great Battles of the Civil War* (Jefferson, NC; London: McFarland, 1993), 9–10; Andrews, *Campaign of Mobile*, 9.

19 Truman, "The War in the Southwest," 1.

20 Ulysses S. Grant, *The Civil War Memoirs of Ulysses S. Grant* (New York: Tom Doherty Associates, LLC, 2002), 431.

21 J. Thomas Scharf, *History of the Confederate States Navy* (New York: Rogers & Sherwood, 1887), 591–593.

22 ORA, Series 1, vol. 45, part 2, 734.

23 Ibid, 419–420.

24 Grant, *Memoirs*, 213.

25 Ibid, 431; *ORA*, Series 1, vol. 45, part 2, 419–420.

26 Grant, *Memoirs*, 431–432; *ORA*, Series 1, vol. 49, Part 1, 780–781, 875.

27 Max L. Heyman, *Prudent Soldier: A Biography of Major General E. R. S. Canby, 1817–1873: His Military Service in the Indian Campaigns, in the Mexican War, in California, New Mexico, Utah, and Oregon; in the Civil War in the Trans-Mississippi West, and As Military Governor in the Post-War South* (Glendale, California: Arthur H. Clark, 1959), 195, 201–202; "Edward R. S. Canby," National Park Service, accessed March 10, 2016, http://www.nps.gov/resources/person.htm? id=57.

28 John C. Palfrey, "The Capture of Mobile, 1865," in *The Mississippi Valley, Tennessee, Georgia, Alabama, 1861–1864* (Boston: The Military Historical Society of Massachusetts, 1910), 538.

29 "Edward R. S. Canby."

30 "Mobile," *Philadelphia (PA) Inquirer*, February 14, 1865, 2; "Yankee Accounts from Mobile," *Raleigh (NC) Daily Progress*, February 22, 1865, 2.

31 "Mobile," *Philadelphia (PA) Inquirer*, February 14, 1865, 2; "Yankee Accounts from Mobile," *Raleigh (NC) Daily Progress*, February 22, 1865, 2; "Fall of Mobile and Defenses," *Cincinnati (OH) Enquirer*, 2; "Department of the Gulf," *New York Times*, March 20, 1865, 8.

32 "The Defenses of Mobile," *Cincinnati (OH) Enquirer*, May 20, 1865, 1; "From Mobile," *Detroit (MI) Free Press*, February 14, 1865, 4.

33 "Souvenirs of the War," *New Orleans (LA) Daily Crescent,* March 19, 1866, 4.

34 "From the South," *Detroit (MI) Free Press,* October 17, 1864, 4.

35 "From Mobile," *Cleveland (OH) Daily Leader,* April 3, 1865; "Our New Orleans Correspondence," *New York Times,* March 20, 1865, 8.

36 Henry C. Merriam, "The Capture of Mobile," *War Papers, Read Before The Commandery of the State of Maine Military Order of the Loyal Legion of the United States* 3 (1908): 231; Benjamin C. Truman, "Campaign in Alabama," *New York Times,* 1; Jeffery N. Lash, "A Yankee in Gray: Danville Leadbetter and the Defenses of Mobile Bay, 1861–1863," *Civil War History: A Journal of the Middle Period* 36, no. 3 (1991): 209; Andrews, *Campaign of Mobile,* 10.

37 Pierre Gustave Toutant Beauregard was a noted Confederate general who commanded at Fort Sumter, the first battle of the Civil War. Beauregard served in various roles throughout the war, including commander of the Department of the West. "Review of the Mobile Campaign," *Burlington (IA) Weekly Hawk-Eye,* 1; "Telegraphic Dispatches," *Salem Weekly Oregon Statesman,* March 13, 1865, 1.

38 "Yankee Accounts from Mobile," *Raleigh (NC) Daily Progress,* 2.

39 T. Michael Parrish, *Richard Taylor: Soldier Prince of Dixie* (Chapel Hill: University of North Carolina Press, 1992), 405.

40 Ezra J. Warner, *Generals in Gray: Lives of the Confederate Commanders* (Baton Rouge: Louisiana State University Press, 1959), 299–300.

41 Warner, *Generals in Gray,* 215; Arthur W. Bergeron, *Confederate Mobile* (Jackson: University Press of Mississippi, 1991), 28.

42 Sidney A. Smith and C. Carter Smith, eds., *Mobile: 1861–1865* (Chicago, IL: Wyvern Press of S. F. E., 1964), 19.

43 Truman, "War in the Southwest," 1.

44 Philip Daingerfield Stephenson, *The Civil War Memoir of Philip Daingerfield Stephenson, D. D.: Private, Company K, 13th Arkansas Volunteer Infantry, and Loader, Piece No. 4, 5th Company, Washington Artillery, Army of Tennessee, CSA,* ed. Nathaniel Cheairs Hughes (Conway, AR: UCA Press, 1995), 358.

45 Palfrey, "The Capture of Mobile, 1865," 556.

46 *ORA,* Series 1, vol. 45, 734–735.

Chapter 1

1 Dabney H. Maury, "The Defence of Mobile in 1865," *Southern Historical Society Papers,* Richmond, VA (September 1877): 4.

2 Ned Stiles had been left for dead at Altoona. Federals found him and gave him kind attention and he was exchanged and came back South. Philip Daingerfield Stephenson and Nathaniel Cheairs Hughes, *The Civil War Memoir of Philip Daingerfield Stephenson, D. D.: Private, Company K, 13th Arkansas Volunteer Infantry, and Loader, Piece No. 4, 5th Company, Washington Artillery, Army of Tennessee, CSA* (Conway, AR: UCA Press, 1995), 355.

3 Johnson, "In Camp and Field," 7; Cobb, "The Siege of Mobile"; "Fall of Mobile and Defenses," *Cincinnati (OH) Enquirer,* 2.

4 Friend, *West Wind,* 224.

5 Ibid, 231, 232, 240; Andrews, *Campaign of Mobile,* 20; "Souvenirs of the War," *New Orleans (LA) Daily Crescent,* 4.

6 Palfrey, "The Capture of Mobile, 1865," 539.

7 Robert C. Conner, *General Gordon Granger: The Savior of Chickamauga and the Man Behind "Juneteenth"* (Havertown, PA: Casemate, 2013), 160–163; Grant, *Memoirs,* 107.

8 "General Gordon Granger," *Hillsboro (OH) Highland Weekly News,* February 10, 1876, 3.

9   Edward G. Miller and W. J. Lemke, editor, *Captain Edward Gee Miller of the 20th Wisconsin* (Fayetteville, AR: Washington County Historical Society, 1960).

10   *ORA*, Series 1, vol. 48, pt. I, 1001; *ORA*, Series 1, vol. 49, pt. I, 864, 907.

11   "More Seven Thirties to be Issued," *Richmond (IN) Weekly Palladium*, March 16, 1865, 2.

12   *ORN*, Series 1, vol. 21, 543.

13   J. Gordon Taylor, "From Knoxville to Mobile Bay," *Sketches of War History* 6 (1908): 60–61; Andrews, *Campaign of Mobile*, 20.

14   Bergeron, *Confederate Mobile*, 196.

15   Andrews, *Campaign of Mobile*, 20.

16   "Souvenirs of the War," *New Orleans (LA) Daily Crescent*, 4.

17   *ORN*, Series 1, vol. 21, 530.

18   Loyall Farragut, *The Life of David Glasgow Farragut, First Admiral of the United States Navy, Embodying His Journal and Letters* (New York: D. Appleton, 1879), 468–470; Sweetman, "Capture of Blakeley," 1; Allen, "Operations Against the City of Mobile," 68–69; Andrews, *Campaign of Mobile*, 20.

19   "More Seven Thirties," *Richmond (IN) Weekly Palladium*, 3; Johnson, "In Camp and Field," 7.

20   Richard Taylor, *Destruction and Reconstruction: Personal Experiences of the Late War* (New York: Longmans, Green, 1955), 218–219; Friend, *West Wind*, 240.

21   "Souvenirs of the War," *New Orleans (LA) Daily Crescent*, 4.

22   Warner, *Generals in Gray*, 187; St. John Richardson Liddell and Nathaniel Cheairs Hughes, *Liddell's Record* (Baton Rouge: Louisiana University Press, 1997), 8.

23   Liddell and Hughes, *Liddell's Record*, 8.

24   In December 1864, the Federals sent three expeditions: General Davidson's from Mississippi, Frederick Steele's from Pensacola, and one from Fort Morgan, under General Granger. Cobb, "Siege of Mobile."

25   Liddell and Hughes, *Liddell's Record*, 191.

26   Ibid, 191; "Affairs About Mobile," *Raleigh (NC) Daily Conservative*, January 3, 1865, 2.

27   Liddell and Hughes, *Liddell's Record*, 191; Dunbar Rowland, *The Official and Statistical Register of the State of Mississippi, 1908* (Nashville, TN: Brandon, 1908), 812; "Affairs About Mobile," *Raleigh (NC) Daily Conservative,* 2.

28   "To the Men and Boys of Middle and South Alabama," *Mobile Advertiser and Register*, December 12, 1864.

29   Conner, *Gordon Granger*, 158–159.

30   Charles Carlock and V. M. Owens, *History of the Tenth Texas Cavalry (Dismounted) Regiment, 1861–1865: "If We Ever Got Whipped, I Don't Recollect It"* (N. Richland Hills, TX: Smithfield, 2001), 225.

31   Robert Patrick, *Reluctant Rebel: The Secret Diary of Robert Patrick, 1861–1865*, ed. F. Jay Taylor (Baton Rouge: Louisiana State University Press, 1996), 250–251.

32   James Bradley, *The Confederate Mail Carrier, or, From Missouri to Arkansas Through Mississippi, Alabama, Georgia and Tennessee An Unwritten Leaf of the "Civil War"* (Mexico, MO: J. Bradley, 1894), 223.

33   Jane M. Johansson, "Gibson's Louisiana Brigade During the 1864 Tennessee Campaign," *Tennessee Historical Quarterly* 64, no. 3 (Fall 2005): 186–195; Stephenson, *Civil War Memoir*, 355.

34   Maury, "Defence of Mobile," 6.

35   Richard Taylor Papers, Manuscript Collection 40, Louisiana Research Collection, Tulane University, New Orleans, LA; "ADAH: Samuel Lockett," Alabama Department of Archives and History, accessed September 2, 2017, http://www.archives.state.al.us/marshall/S_Lockett.html; "Major Samuel H. Lockett," Official Site: The Battle of Champion Hill (May 16, 1863), accessed September 2, 2017, http://battleofchampionhill.org/lockett1.htm.

36　General William T. Sherman's army left a trail of destruction through Georgia. In January 1865, Sherman's army marched north to launch the Carolinas campaign. "North Carolina History Project: Carolinas Campaign (January 1865–April 1865)," accessed October 17, 2015, http://www.northcarolinahistory.org/encyclopedia/882/entry.

37　Taylor Papers, 10 (emphasis in original).

38　*ORA*, Series I, vol. 49, pt. 1, 1056; Taylor, *Destruction and Reconstruction,* 210.

39　"Mobile Items – A Letter from Mobile," *Richmond (VA) Dispatch*, October 18, 1864, 1.

40　Taylor Papers.

41　Maury, "Defense of Mobile," 6.

42　Parrish, *Richard Taylor*, 433.

43　Joseph Baumer, "Memories of the War," History Museum of Mobile, Mobile, AL, n.d.

44　Johansson, "Gibson's Louisiana Brigade," 186–195.

45　Owen, *In Camp and Battle*, 420.

46　Edgar W. Jones and David A. Pulcrano, *History of the Eighteenth Alabama Infantry Regiment* (Birmingham, AL: C. D. A. Pulcrano, 1994), 62.

47　Charles Boarman Cleveland, "With the Third Missouri Regiment. Reminiscences of Charles Boarman Cleveland," *Confederate Veteran* 31 (1923): 20.

48　William P. Chambers, *Blood & Sacrifice, The Civil War Journal of a Confederate Soldier,* ed. Richard A. Baumgartner (Huntington, WV: Blue Acorn, 1994), 201–202.

49　Ibid; Carlock and Owens, *History of the Tenth Texas*, 225–226; Laura Roberts Pillans, "Diary of Mrs. Laura Roberts Pillans, 11 July 1863 – 2 November 1865," History Museum of Mobile, Mobile, AL; *Janesville (WI) Weekly Gazette*, March 23, 1865, 3.

50　On August 9, the *Mobile (AL) Tribune* and later, on August 14, the *New Orleans (LA) Times Democrat* reported "Farrand succeeds Buchanan." "Summary of News," *New Orleans (LA) Times Democrat*, August 14, 1864, 4; "Ebenezer Farrand," CSN Foundation, 290, accessed September 21, 2016 https://sites.google.com/site/290foundation/290-standing-orders/ebenezer-farrand-csn.

51　Edward S. Cooper, *Traitors: The Secession Period, November 1860–July 1861* (Madison, NJ: Fairleigh Dickinson University Press, 2008), 70–72; George F. Pearce, *Pensacola During the Civil War: A Thorn in the Side of the Confederacy* (Gainesville: University Press of Florida, 2000), 21–23; Scharf, *History of the Confederate States Navy*, 601.

52　"Civil War Reference Web Page," accessed July 12, 2015, http://www.civilwarreference.com/people/index.php? peopleID=719.

53　*ORA*, Series 1, vol. 49, pt. 2, 934–935.

54　Ibid, *955*.

55　"From the South," *Detroit (MI) Free Press*, 4; George S. Waterman, "Afloat-Afield-Afloat. Notable Events of the Civil War," *Confederate Veteran* 12 (1899): 490.

56　Scharf, *History of the Confederate States Navy*, 592.

57　Taylor Papers.

58　*ORN*, Series 1, vol. 21, 902–903, 931; Clive Cussler, "Search for the C. S. S. Hunley, the U. S. S. Cumberland and the C. S. S. Florida," last modified July 1980, www.numa.net/expeditions/hunley-c-s-s/; "John P. Halligan," Find A Grave, accessed December 21, 2016, http://findagrave.com/cgi-bin/fg, cgi? page=gr&GRid=26753869.

59　*ORN*, Series 1, vol. 21, 748; John S. Sledge, *The Mobile River* (Columbia: University of South Carolina Press, 2015), 139.

60　*ORA,* Series 1, vol. 49, pt. 1, 934–935; *ORN*, Series 1, vol. 22, 267–269; R. Thomas Campbell, *Hunters of the Night: Confederate Torpedo Boats in the War Between the States* (Shippensburg, PA: Burd Street Press, 2000), 84–86; *ORA*, Series 1, vol. 2, 781; *ORA*, vol. 49, pt. 2, *13*; "Incident On Board the Octorara," *Harper's Weekly*, February 25, 1865.

61　*ORA*, Series 1, vol. 49, pt. 1, 930–931.

62 Ibid, 934–935; *ORN*, Series 1, vol. 22, 267–269; Campbell, *Hunters of the Night*, 84–86; *ORA*, Series 1, vol. 2, 781; *ORA*, Series 1, vol. 49, pt. 2, *13*; "Octorara," *Harper's Weekly*.

63 *ORA*, Series 1, vol. 49, pt. 1, 934–935; *ORN*, Series 1, vol. 22, 267–269; Campbell, *Hunters of the Night*, 84–86; *ORA*, Series 1, vol. 2, 781; *ORA*, Series 1, vol. 49, pt. 2, *13*; "Octorara," *Harper's Weekly*.

64 *ORA*, Series 1, vol. 49, pt. 2, 13, 934–935; Sidney H. Schell, "Submarine Weapons Tested at Mobile During the Civil War," *Alabama Review* 45 (July 1992): 178–179; "Octorara," *Harper's Weekly*.

65 *ORA*, Series 1, vol. 49, pt. 2, 13, 934–935; Sidney H. Schell, "Submarine Weapons Tested at Mobile During the Civil War," *Alabama Review* 45 (July 1992): 178–179; "Octorara," *Harper's Weekly*.

66 *ORA*, Series 1, vol. 49, 780–781.

67 "Souvenirs of the War," *New Orleans (LA) Daily Crescent*, 4.

Chapter 2

1 Stephenson, *Civil War Memoir*, 356–357.

2 James M. Williams, *From That Terrible Field: Civil War Letters of James M. Williams, Twenty-First Alabama Infantry Volunteers*, ed. John Kent Folmar (Tuscaloosa: University of Alabama Press, 1981), 150.

3 Carlock and Owens, *History of the Tenth Texas*, 225–226.

4 Chambers, *Blood & Sacrifice*, 203.

5 Carlock and Owens, *History of the Tenth Texas*, 225–226.

6 Ibid.

7 Stephenson, *Civil War Memoir*, 356–357.

8 Ibid; Pillans, "Diary"; *Janesville (WI) Weekly Gazette*, 3.

9 Chambers, *Blood & Sacrifice*, 203–204.

10 Williams, *From That Terrible Field*, 158.

11 "First Missouri Brigade," *Mobile (AL) Weekly Advertiser and Register*, March 4, 1865, 1; "The Hampton Roads Peace Conference: A Final Test of Lincoln's Presidential Leadership," MLibrary Digital Collections, accessed September 20, 2016, http://quod.lib.umich.edu/j/jala/2629860.0021.104/–hampton-roads-peace-conference-a-final-test-of-lincolns? rgn=main; view=fulltext.

12 Jones and Pulcrano, *History of the Eighteenth Alabama*, 63.

13 Chambers, *Blood & Sacrifice*, 202–203.

14 "First Missouri Brigade," *Mobile (AL) Weekly Advertiser and Register*, 1.

15 Taylor, *Destruction and Reconstruction*, 210; Parrish, *Richard Taylor*, 423.

16 *ORA*, Series 1, vol. 49, pt. 2, 1199.

17 *ORA*, Series 4, vol. 2, 941.

18 "Depredations of the Enemy at Fish River," *Mobile (AL) Evening Telegraph*, March 23, 1865).

19 Ibid, 191.

20 James M. McPherson, *For Cause and Comrades: Why Men Fought in the Civil War* (Oxford: Oxford University Press, 1997), 109–114.

21 Bruce C. Levine, *Confederate Emancipation: Southern Plans to Free and Arm Slaves During the Civil War* (Oxford: Oxford University Press, 2006), 113.

22 Carlock and Owens, *History of the Tenth Texas*, 226–227.

23 R. C. Beckett, "A Sketch of the Career of Company B, Armistead's Cavalry Regiment," in *Publications of the Mississippi Historical Society*, Vol. 8, ed. Franklin Lafayette Riley (Oxford, MS: Mississippi Historical Society, 1905), 42–43.

24 Chambers, *Blood & Sacrifice*, 202–203.

25   "First Missouri Brigade," *Mobile (AL) Weekly Advertiser and Register*, 1.

26   Chambers, *Blood & Sacrifice*, 202–203.

27   *ORA*, Series 1, vol. 49, pt. 1, 781.

28   Ibid, 1161–1162.

29   "Colored Troops in the Rebel Army," *New York Times*, March 5, 1865.

30   *ORA*, Series 1, vol. 49, pt. 1, 1161–1162.

31   Ibid, 318.

32   Kate Cumming, *Kate: The Journal of a Confederate Nurse*, ed. Richard Barksdale Harwell (Baton Rouge: Louisiana State University Press, 1959), 307.

33   Richard Taylor, *Manuscript Collection 40*, p. 8, Louisiana Research Collection, Tulane University, New Orleans, La..

34   Chambers, *Blood & Sacrifice*, 203–204.

35   "Gen. Jos. E. Johnston," *Mobile (AL) Evening News*, March 4, 1865, 1.

36   "From Mobile," *Cleveland (OH) Daily Leader*, 1.

37   Although Johnston did not receive the letter until 10 years after the war, it deeply moved him. Owen, *In Camp and Battle*, 420.

38   *ORA*, Series I, vol. 49, pt. 2, 694.

39   *ORA*, Series I, vol. 49, pt. 2, 951.

40   Ibid; Dabney H. Maury, "Defense of Spanish Fort," *Southern Historical Society Papers* 39 (1914): 133.

41   *Merriam Webster* defines "abatis" as a "defensive obstacle formed by felled trees with sharpened branches facing the enemy"; the *Free Dictionary* defines "chevaux-de-frise" as "a portable defensive obstacle, typically a beam from which rows of sharpened stakes protrude, used in field fortifications." *Merriam-Webster*, accessed December 9, 2016, https://www.merriam-webster.com/dictionary/abatis; TheFreeDictionary.com, accessed December 9, 2016, http://legal-dictionary.thefreedictionary.com/chevaux-de-frise; Jones and Pulcrano, *History of the Eighteenth Alabama*, 64–67; Allen, "Operations Against the City of Mobile," 73.

42   Thomas H. Herndon, "My Dear Wife," Thomas Hoard Herndon Papers, History Museum of Mobile, Mobile, AL.

43   Stephenson, *Civil War Memoir*, 360.

44   Ibid, 205.

45   Ibid, 358.

46   George Little and James Robert Maxwell, *A History of Lumsden's Battery, C. S. A* (Tuscaloosa, AL: The Echo Library, 1905), 43.

47   Ibid, 43.

48   Maury, "Defense of Mobile," 4.

49   James A. Chalaron, "Spanish Fort Fight Near Mobile Bay," *New Orleans (LA) Times Picayune*, September 24, 1899, 24.

Chapter 3

1   Taylor, *Destruction and Reconstruction*, 218; "The Capture of Mobile," *Harper's Weekly*, May 6, 1865, 275.

2   Conner, *Gordon Granger*, 160–163; Grant, *Memoirs*, 431; Lurton Dunham Ingersoll, *Iowa and the Rebellion: A History of the Troops Furnished by the State of Iowa to the Volunteer Armies of the Union, Which Conquered the Great Southern Rebellion of 1861–5* (Philadelphia, PA: J. B. Lippincott, 1866), 193.

3   "Andrew J. Smith," Civil War Trust: Saving America's Civil War Battlefields, accessed

October 11, 2015, http://www.civilwar.org/education/history/biographies/andrew-j-smith.html; Allen, "Operations Against the City of Mobile," 71; "The Gulf," *New York Times*, March 7, 1865, 4.

4   Palfrey, "The Capture of Mobile," 539.

5   "Andrew J. Smith," Civil War Trust: Saving America's Civil War Battlefields, accessed October 11, 2015, http://www.civilwar.org/education/history/biographies/andrew-j-smith.html; Allen, "Operations Against the City of Mobile," 71; "The Gulf," *New York Times*, March 7, 1865, 4.

6   "Gen. A. J. Smith," *Washington (DC) National Tribune*, September 20, 1906, 3.

7   Ibid; "Death of Gen. A. J. Smith," *New York Times*, January 31, 1897, 2; Leslie J. Perry, "A Gallant Soldier," *New York Sun*, February 21, 1897, 10; "Gen. A. J. Smith Dies of Paralysis At St. Louis," *Nashville (TN) Tennessean*, January 31, 1897, 9.

8   Spink, R. A., "The Capture of Spanish Fort," *Washington (DC) National Tribune*, October 29, 1908, 7; Allen, "Operations Against the City of Mobile," 70.

9   Merriam, "Capture of Mobile," 232.

10 A. F. Sperry, *History of the 33d Iowa Infantry Volunteer Regiment, 1863–6*, eds. Gregory J. W. Urwin and Cathy Kunzinger Urwin (Fayetteville: University of Arkansas Press, 1999), 122.

11 Charles O. Musser, *Soldier Boy: The Civil War Letters of Charles O. Musser, 29th Iowa*, ed. Barry Popchock (Iowa City: University of Iowa Press, 1995), 188; Ebenezer B. Mattocks, "Mobile Campaign," Museum Collections Up Close: Minnesota Historical Society, accessed November 7, 2016, last modified February 25, 2015, http://discussions.mnhs.org/collections/?s=mobile+campaign.

12 Musser, *Soldier Boy*, 188.

13 Johnson, "In Camp and Field," 1.

14 Musser, *Soldier Boy*, 188; Mattocks, "Mobile Campaign."

15 Thomas B. Marshall, *History of the Eighty-Third Ohio Volunteer Infantry* (Cincinnati, OH: The Eighty-Third Ohio Volunteer Infantry Association, 1912), 154.

16 On Friday, February 3, 1865, Slack's Brigade traveled on the overloaded steamers on a nearly 136-mile voyage that took them from the dock at Lakeside (New Orleans) across the southeastern corner of Lake Pontchartrain, through the narrow pass called the Rigolets, across Lake Borgne into the Mississippi Sound and on to Fort Gaines. James R. Slack, *Slack's War: Selected Civil War Letters of General James R. Slack, 47th Indiana Volunteer Infantry, to His Wife, Ann, 1862–1865*, ed. David Williamson (Jefferson, NC: McFarland, 2012), 265–272.

17 *ORA*, Series I, vol. 49, pt. 1, 92.

18 "Department of the Gulf," *New York Times*, 1.

19 Scharf, *History of the Confederate States Navy*, 593; William Wiley, *The Civil War Diary of a Common Soldier: William Wiley of the 77th Illinois Infantry* (Baton Rouge: Louisiana State University Press, 2001), 140–143.

20 Smith, *Thomas Kilby Smith*, 380.

21 Ibid, 382.

22 Sperry, *33rd Iowa*, 123–126.

23 Johnson, "In Camp and Field," 7.

24 Slack, *Slack's War*, 274.

25 Cobb was assigned to duty at Fort Morgan a few days after the battle of Mobile Bay. Cobb, "The Siege of Mobile."

26 Ibid.

27 Johnson, "In Camp and Field," 7.

28 Smith, *Thomas Kilby Smith*, 382.

29 Ibid.

30 Slack and Williamson, *Slack's War*, 271; "A Tale of Revenge," *Perrysburg Journal*, September 11, 1903, 6.

31   Musser, *Soldier Boy*, 188–191.

32   Smith, *Thomas Kilby Smith*, 380, 382.

33   In 1881 Hubbard became the governor of Minnesota. L. F. Hubbard, *L. F. Hubbard and the Fifth Minnesota Letters of a Union Volunteer,* ed. N. B. Martin (San Francisco, CA: San Francisco State College, 1956), Mobile Historic Preservation Society, Norman Nicholson Collection, Mobile, AL, 67.

34   Spink, "Capture of Spanish Fort," 7.

35   Slack and Williamson, *Slack's War*, 271.

36   "Diary of John Thomas, 1864–1865," Mrs. W. R. ArcherDolph Briscoe Center for American History, University of Texas, Austin, TX. Mrs. W. R. Archer, Austin, Tx. Eugene C. Barker History Center Archives, 1958)
     Provided to me by Mike Bunn, Director, Historic Blakeley State Park
     Mrs. W. R. Archer, Austin, Tx. Eugene C. Barker History Center Archives, 1958)
     Provided to me by Mike Bunn, Director, Historic Blakeley State Park
     Mrs. W. R. Archer, Austin, Tx. Eugene C. Barker History Center Archives, 1958

37   Ibid.

38   Sperry, *33rd Iowa*, 123–126.

39   Musser, *Soldier Boy*, 188–191.

40   John F. Lacey, "Major-General Frederick Steele," University of Iowa Research online, accessed October 15, 2016, http://ir.uiowa.edu/annals-of-iowa/vol3/iss5/8; Lacey, "Major-General Frederick Steele," in *Annals of Iowa* (Des Moines: Iowa Division of Historical Museum and Archives, 1897), 425, 433, 437; "The Battle at Vicksburg," *Philadelphia (PA) Inquirer*, January 16, 1863, 3.

41   John F. Lacey, "Major-General Frederick Steele," University of Iowa Research online, accessed October 15, 2016, http://ir.uiowa.edu/annals-of-iowa/vol3/iss5/8; Lacey, "Major-General Frederick Steele," in *Annals of Iowa* (Des Moines: Iowa Division of Historical Museum and Archives, 1897), 425, 433, 437; "The Battle at Vicksburg," *Philadelphia (PA) Inquirer*, January 16, 1863, 3; *ORA*, Series 1, vol. 45, pt. 2, 84.

42   Lacey, "Steele," 425, 433, 437.

43   Slack arrived on Fort Gaines and went into camp around February 10 and reported immediately to Gordon Granger, commanding the District of West Florida and South Alabama. Slack, *Slack's War*, 270–274.

44   Wiley, *Civil War Diary*, 140–143.

45   Sweetman, "Capture of Blakeley," 1.

46   Marshall, *Eighty-Third Ohio*, 154–159.

47   The 64-year-old Admiral Farragut was granted furlough on account of exhaustion and declining health. Farragut left the Gulf Coast for his home in New York on his flagship *Hartford* in late November 1864. Farragut, *David Glasgow Farragut*, 472–473; Porter, *Naval History of the Civil War*, 780; *ORN*, Series 1, vol. 22, 32, 47, 56.

48   *ORA*, Series 1, vol. 45, pt. 2, 614.

49   Lucius F. Hubbard, "Civil War Papers" [Read before the Minnesota Historical Society Executive Council] St. Paul, MN: Minnesota Historical Society, 1907, 620.

50   Porter, *Naval History of the Civil War,* 781; Musser, *Soldier Boy*, 191; Sperry, *33rd Iowa*, 126; "Department of the Gulf," *New York Times*, 8.

51   Porter, *Naval History of the Civil War,* 781; Musser, *Soldier Boy*, 191; Sperry, *33rd Iowa*, 126; "Department of the Gulf," *New York Times*, 8.

52   Porter, *Naval History of the Civil War,* 781; Musser, *Soldier Boy*, 191; Sperry, *33rd Iowa*, 126; "Department of the Gulf," *New York Times*, 8.

53   Wiley, *Civil War Diary*, 140.

54   Ibid.

55   *ORA*, Series 1, vol. 49, pt. 1, 875.

56 Hubbard, *Fifth Minnesota Letters,* 67.

57 *ORA*, Series 1, vol. 49, pt. 1, 884, 905.

58 Wiley, *Civil War Diary*, 143; Sperry, *33rd Iowa*, 128; Musser, *Soldier Boy*, 191; "Department of the Gulf," *New York Times*, 1.

59 Wiley, *Civil War Diary*, 143; Sperry, *33rd Iowa*, 128; "Department of the Gulf," *New York Times*, 1.

60 Wales W. Wood, *A History of the Ninety Fifth Regiment Illinois Infantry Volunteers: From Its Organization in the Fall of 1862, until its Final Discharge from the United States Service in 1865* (Chicago, IL: Tribune Book and Job Printing Office, 1865), 164.

61 Hubbard, *Fifth Minnesota Letters,* 67.

62 "Mobile," *Philadelphia (PA) Inquirer*, 2.

63 "A Woman from Mobile," *Cleveland (OH) Daily Leader*, March 21, 1865, 1; Hubbard, *Fifth Minnesota Letters*, 67.

Chapter 4

1 *ORN*, Series 1, vol. 21, 533–534.

2 Ibid; "Our New Orleans Correspondence," *New York Times*, 8.

3 *ORA*, vol. 49, pt. 1, 864–865, 906.

4 Hubbard, "Civil War Papers," 622.

5 Musser, *Soldier Boy*, 195–197; Sperry, *33rd Iowa*, 128–130.

6 "The Fall of Mobile and Defenses," *Cincinnati (OH) Enquirer*, 2; "The Mobile Campaign," *Washington (DC) National Tribune*, July 21, 1887, 6; "Federals Move To Attack Forts Guarding Mobile," *The Washington Herald*, 23.

7 "The Fall of Mobile and Defenses," *Cincinnati (OH) Enquirer*, 2; "The Mobile Campaign," *Washington (DC) National Tribune*, July 21, 1887, 6; "Federals Move To Attack Forts Guarding Mobile," *The Washington Herald*, 23.

8 Slack, *Slack's War*, 471; Ingersoll, *Iowa and the Rebellion*, 471.

9 Wiley, *Civil War Diary*, 143.

10 Musser, *Soldier Boy*, 195.

11 Ibid.

12 Ibid, 195; Sperry, *33rd Iowa*, 129.

13 Allen, "Operations Against the City of Mobile," 73; *ORA*, Series I, vol. 49, pt. 1, 230.

14 Wiley, *Civil War Diary*, 143.

15 Ibid; *ORA*, Series I, vol. 49, pt. 2, 169, 170, 179.

16 *ORA*, Series I, vol. 49, pt. 2, 174; Wiley, *Civil War Diary*, 143.

17 Sperry, *33rd Iowa*, 129.

18 Musser, *Soldier Boy*, 195.

19 Merriam, "Capture of Mobile," 234.

20 John W. Fry, "Capture of Mobile," *The National Tribune*, October 29, 1865, 1.

21 Musser, *Soldier Boy*, 195.

22 Wiley, *Civil War Diary*, 144; Allen, "Operations Against the City of Mobile," 74.

23 Sperry, *33rd Iowa*, 130.

24 Ibid.

25 Wiley, *Civil War Diary*, 143.

26 Musser, *Soldier Boy*, 196.

27 Ibid.

28 Ibid.

29 Wiley, *Civil War Diary*, 144.

30 Sperry, *33rd Iowa*, 132; Musser, *Soldier Boy*, 196.

31 *ORA*, Series I, vol. 49, pt. 1, 124-125, 127-131, 134.

32 Spink, "Capture of Spanish Fort," 7.

33 Ibid; Porter, *Naval History of the Civil War*, 781–782; Palfrey, "The Capture of Mobile, 1865," 556.

34 James K. Newton, "The Siege of Mobile," *Alabama Historical Quarterly* 20 (1958): 595–600.

35 Joseph Stockton, *War Diary of Brevet Brigadier General Joseph Stockton* (Chicago, IL: John T. Stockton, 1910), 29; Wiley, *Civil War Diary*, 144.

36 Stockton, *War Diary*, 29; Wiley, *Civil War Diary*, 144; *ORN*, Series 1, vol. 22, 65; Palfrey, "The Capture of Mobile, 1865," 540.

37 Stockton, *War Diary*, 29; Wiley, *Civil War Diary*, 144; *ORN*, Series 1, vol. 22, 65; "Canby," *Philadelphia (PA) Inquirer*, April 3, 1865, 2; *ORA*, Series I, vol. 49, pt. 1, 93.

38 "Canby," *Philadelphia (PA) Inquirer*, 2; Wood, *Ninety Fifth Regiment*, 164; *ORN*, Series 1, vol. 22, 65.

39 "Canby," *Philadelphia (PA) Inquirer*, 2; Wood, *Ninety Fifth Regiment*, 164; *ORN*, Series 1, vol. 22, 65.

40 "Canby," *Philadelphia (PA) Inquirer*, 2; Wood, *Ninety Fifth Regiment*, 164; *ORN*, Series 1, vol. 22, 65; Wood, *Ninety Fifth Regiment*, 164–166.

41 Edward O. Nye, "The Diary of Edward O. Nye," From the Collection of Charles H. Hooper of the John Pelham Historical Association, Mobile Historic Preservation Society, Norman Nicholson Collection, Mobile, AL.

42 Ibid.

43 Ibid.

44 Wood, *Ninety Fifth Regiment*, 164–166.

45 Nye, "Diary."

46 Jean R. Freedman, "Albert Cashier's Secret," Opinionator, last modified January 28, 2014, https://opinionator.blogs.nytimes.com/2014/01/28/albert-cashiers-secret/.

47 Ibid.

48 Ibid; "Canby," *Philadelphia (PA) Inquirer*, 2.

49 Nye, "Diary"; "Canby," *Philadelphia (PA) Inquirer*, 2.

50 Wood, *Ninety Fifth Regiment*, 167–169.

51 Ibid.

52 Chambers, *Blood & Sacrifice*, 208.

53 Warner, *Generals in Gray*, 104.

54 Nye, "Diary."

55 Stockton, *War Diary*, 29.

56 Ibid; Nye, "Diary."

57 Chambers, *Blood & Sacrifice*, 208.

58 Chambers, *Blood & Sacrifice*, 208.

59 Nye, "Diary."

60 Stockton, *War Diary*, 29; Wood, *Ninety Fifth Regiment*, 169; "From Below," *Mobile (AL) Evening Telegraph*, March 23, 1865, 1.

61 *ORA*, Series I, vol. 49, pt. 1, 1142; "Lady Slocomb," *New Orleans (LA) Times-Picayune*, September 9, 1899, 9.

62 Liddell and Hughes, *Liddell's Record*, 194.

63 Ibid.

64 Ibid.

65 "Depredations," *Mobile (AL) Evening Telegraph*, 1.

66 Williams, *From That Terrible Field*, 157.

67 Robert Tarleton, "The Civil War Letters of Robert Tarleton," *Alabama Historical Quarterly* 32 (Spring and Summer 1970): 78–79.

68 A redoubt is a small, supplementary fortification. *Cincinnati Daily Commercial*, March 21, 1865; "Canby," *Philadelphia (PA) Inquirer*, 2.

69 "Review of the Mobile Campaign," *Burlington (IA) Weekly Hawk-Eye*, 1.

70 Ibid.

71 "The Defense of Mobile," *Mobile (AL) Evening Telegraph*, March 23, 1865, 1.

72 Joe A. Mobley, "The Siege of Mobile, August 1864–April 1865," *Alabama Historical Quarterly* 38 (Winter 1976): 250–270.

73 "Mobile," *Philadelphia (PA) Inquirer*, 2; "Blown Up," *Mobile (AL) Advertiser and Register*, April 8, 1865, 1.

74 "Mobile," *Philadelphia (PA) Inquirer*, 2; "Blown Up," *Mobile (AL) Advertiser and Register*, April 8, 1865, 1.

75 Williams, *From That Terrible Field*, 157.

76 On March 31, 1865, at 6 p.m., Privates Elijah Wynn and Thomas Elam, both members of Company F, 21st Alabama Infantry, were executed by musketry for the crime of desertion at Fort Blakeley. Both men deserted at Point Clear on September 11, 1863. *Mobile (AL) Register and Advertiser*, April 2, 1865.

Chapter 5

1 "Lady Slocomb," *New Orleans (LA) Times-Picayune*, 9.

2 *ORA*, Series I, vol. 49, pt. 1, 314–315.

3 Bradley, *Confederate Mail Carrier*, 224.

4 Liddell and Hughes, *Liddell's Record*, 194.

5 *ORA*, Series I, vol. 49, pt. 1, 202.

6 Francis Marion Cockrell II, *The Senator from Missouri. The Life and Times of Francis Marion Cockrell* (New York: Exposition Press, 1962), 21, 520.

7 Stephenson, *Civil War Memoir*, 355–356.

8 Diplomaticus, "'Old Garden Sass': The Most Modest Man In The Senate," *Chicago (IL) Inter Ocean*, March 27, 1904, 30; Champ Clark, "Champ Clark Stories," *Ogden (UT) Standard*, September 2, 1901, 8.

9 Cockrell, *Senator from Missouri*, 520; "Elijah Gates Dies After Prolonged Illness," *Chillicothe (MO) Constitution-Tribune*, March 11, 1915, 3.

10 Chambers, *Blood & Sacrifice*, 209.

11 Maury, "Defense of Spanish Fort," 131; *ORA*, Series I, vol. 49, pt. 1, 318; Stephenson, *Civil War Memoir*, 359–360, 365–367.

12 *ORA*, Series I, vol. 49, pt. 2, 1148.

13 Beckett, "Company B," 32–50.

14 Philip B. Spence, "The Last Fight," *Louisville (KY) Courier-Journal*, March 31, 1892, 7; "Colonel Philip B. Spence," *Confederate Veterans Magazine* 23 (1915): 181; Fay Hempstead, *Historical Review of Arkansas: Its Commerce, Industry and Modern Affairs*, 3rd ed. (Chicago: Lewis, 1911), 1295.

15 Spence, "Last Fight," 7.

16 Ibid; *ORN*, Series 1, vol. 22, 66.

17 "From Mobile," *Wheeling (WV) Daily Intelligencer*, April 3, 1865, 3.

18 *ORA*, Series I, vol. 49, pt. 1, 170.

19 Originally printed in the *New Orleans (LA) Times* on March 27, 1865. "Yankee Accounts from Mobile," *Mobile (AL) Advertiser and Register*, April 8, 1865, 1.

20 Three Sibleys served in the 15th Confederate Cavalry: brothers Artemus and Walter, and Origen Jr., all members of the prominent Baldwin County family. Artemus and Walter were the sons of 76-year-old mill owner Cyrus Sibley. Artemus worked as an overseer prior to the war and lived next door to his father. Lt. Origen Sibley Jr., 25 years old, was the son of 66-year-old Origen Sibley. The relationship of Cyrus and Origen is unknown but their mills were 4 miles apart. David Williamson, *The 47th Indiana Volunteer Infantry: A Civil War History* (Jefferson, NC: McFarland, 2012), 268, 407.

21 *ORA*, Series I, vol. 49, pt. 2, 1149.

22 *ORA*, Series I, vol. 49, pt. 1, 141.

23 Otto E. Wolf, "OTTO E. WOLF. CIVIL WAR LETTERS," Fort Pickering, Tennessee - Madison County Historical Society, accessed March 19, 2018, http://madcohistory.org/wp-content/uploads/2017/11/OW_1865_final.pdf.

24 Musser, *Soldier Boy*, 196–197; Wales W. Wood, "Capture Forts About Mobile," *Belvidere (IL) Republican-Northwestern*, January 29, 1907, 8.

25 Allen, "Operations Against the City of Mobile," 87.

26 Wood, "Capture Forts," 8.

27 Sperry, *33rd Iowa*, 132–133.

28 Florence Dolive Scott, *Daphne: A History of Its People and Their Pursuits, As Some Saw It and Others Remember It* (Mobile, AL: Jordan, 1965), 204.

29 Stockton, *War Diary*, 29.

30 Wood, *Ninety Fifth Regiment*, 169; Spence, "Last Fight," 7; Allen, "Operations Against the City of Mobile," 74.

31 Johnson, "In Camp and Field," 7.

32 Spence, "Last Fight," 7; Charles S. Hill, "The Last Battle of the War – Recollections of the Mobile Campaign," *War Papers and Personal Reminiscences 1861–1865*, vol. 1 (St. Louis, MO: Becktold, 1892), 179.

33 "The Attack of Mobile," *New York Times*, April 9, 1865, 8.

34 Marshall became the fifth governor of Minnesota after the war. John Danielson, *History of Company G, of 7th Minnesota Volunteers, War of the Rebellion, August 12, 1862 – August 16, 1865*, Minnesota Historical Society, St. Paul, MN, 18; William R. Marshall, *Minnesota in the Civil War*, vol. 2, 624; Allen, "Operations Against the City of Mobile," 74.

35 Musser, *Soldier Boy*, 197; Wiley, *Civil War Diary*, 145.

36 Spence, "Last Fight," 7.

37 Stephenson, *Civil War Memoir*, 360.

38 *ORA*, Series I, vol. 49, pt. 1, 141, 224, 246; ORA, Series I, vol. 49, pt. 2, 1162–1163.

39 Stephenson, *Civil War Memoir*, 360.

40 *ORA*, Series I, vol. 49, pt. 1, 141, 224, 246; ORA, Series I, vol. 49, pt. 2, 1162–1163.

41 Stephenson, *Civil War Memoir*, 360.

42 "From Mobile," *Nashville (TN) Daily Union*, April 14, 1865, 1.

43 Eli Davis, "That Hard Siege at Spanish Fort," *Confederate Veteran* 12 (1904): 591.

44 Liddell and Hughes, *Liddell's Record*, 194; Bradley, *Confederate Mail Carrier*, 224; ORA, Series I, vol. 49, pt. 1, 158; Allen, "Operations Against the City of Mobile," 76; Musser, *Soldier Boy*, 197.

45 Maury, "Defense of Mobile," 7.

46 Maury, "Defense of Spanish Fort," 133.

47 Slack, *Slack's War*, 277–278.

48 "The Mobile Expedition," *New Orleans (LA) Times-Democrat*, April 8, 1865, 2.

49 Palfrey, "The Capture of Mobile, 1865," 556.

50 Maury, "Defense of Spanish Fort," 133; Stephenson, *Civil War Memoir*, 358–359.

51 Sperry, *33rd Iowa*, 139.

52 *ORA*, Series 1, vol. 45, 735.

53 *ORA*, Series I, vol. 49, pt. 1, 315.

54 Jones and Pulcrano, *History of the Eighteenth Alabama*, 64–67.

55 Marshall, *Eighty-Third Ohio*, 164–165.

56 *ORA*, Series I, vol. 49, pt. 2, 1186.

57 Ibid, 1187.

58 Ibid.

59 Sean Michael O'Brien, *Mobile, 1865: Last Stand of the Confederacy* (Westport, CT: Praeger, 2001), 151.

60 Andrews, *Campaign of Mobile*, 165–166.

61 "Gen. James T. Holtzclaw, Montgomery," *New Orleans (LA) Times-Democrat*, July 19, 1893, 1.

62 "Capture of Mobile," *Harper's Weekly*, 275.

63 Allen, "Operations Against the City of Mobile," 72.

64 Liddell and Hughes, *Liddell's Record*, 194.

65 Arthur Bergeron, "The Twenty-Second Louisiana Consolidated Infantry in the Defense of Mobile, 1864–1865," *Alabama Historical Quarterly* 38 (Fall 1976): 212.

66 "Department of the Gulf," *New York Times*, March 25, 1865, 1.

67 "The Distinguished Dead," *New Orleans (LA) Times Picayune*, February 10, 1890, 3; "General George S. Patton, Sr.: Civil War Veteran," Warfare History Network, accessed May 16, 2017, http://warfarehistorynetwork.com/daily/civil-war/general-george-s-patton-sr-civil-war-veteran/.

68 "NH 48925 Lieutenant Thomas B. Huger, CSN," Naval History and Heritage Command, accessed February 14, 2016, http://www.history.navy.mil/our-collections/photography/numerical-list-of-images/nhhc-series/nh-series/NH-48000/NH-48925.html.

69 *ORA*, Series I, vol. 49, pt. 1, 98.

70 "Edward Dorr Tracy (1833–1863): Find A Grave Memorial," Find A Grave, accessed February 14, 2016, http://www.findagrave.com/cgi-bin/fg.cgi? page=gr&GRid=9093.

71 Liddell and Hughes, *Liddell's Record*, 190; "From Mobile Bay," *New Orleans (LA) Times Picayune*, April 9, 1865, 1; Waterman, "Afloat-Afield-Afloat," 21–24; *ORA*, Series I, vol. 49, pt. 1, 98.

Chapter 6

1 *ORA*, Series I, vol.49, pt. 2, 1169, 1174; Musser, *Soldier Boy*, 197.

2 Marshall, *Eighty-Third Ohio*, 164–165.

3 Hubbard, *Fifth Minnesota Letters*, 68; *ORA*, Series 1, vol. 45, pt. 2, 614; "Woman from Mobile," *Cleveland (OH) Daily Leader*, 1.

4 "Attack of Mobile," *New York Times*, 8.

5 Alden McLellan, "Vivid Reminiscences of War Times," *Confederate Veteran* 14 (1906): 264–266.

6 T. G. Carter, "That Charge at Spanish Fort," *Confederate Veteran* 13 (1906): 226; Charles J. Allen, "Operations Against the City of Mobile," 76.

7 Hearn, *Mobile Bay and the Mobile Campaign*, 221.

8 Stockton, *War Diary*, 29.

9 Wood, *Ninety Fifth Regiment*, 171.

10 *ORA*, Series I, vol. 49, pt. 1, 229; Merriam-Webster defines a traverse as a protective projecting wall or bank of earth in a trench. *Merriam-Webster*, accessed September 11, 2016, http://www.merriam-webster.com/dictionary/traverse.

11 Hubbard, "Civil War Papers," 628.

12 "Mobile Expedition," *New Orleans (LA) Times-Democrat*, 2.

13 Sperry, *33rd Iowa*, 135.

14 *ORA*, Series 1, vol. 49, pt. 1, 154.

15 Musser, *Soldier Boy*, 198–199.

16 Sperry, *33rd Iowa*, 135.

17 *ORA*, Series 1, vol. 49, pt. 1, 154, 233; "Mobile Expedition," *New Orleans (LA) Times-Democrat*, 2.

18 Allen, "Operations Against the City of Mobile," 76; Benjamin C. Truman, "The Campaign in Alabama," *The New York Times*, April 24, 1865, 1..

19 Hill, "Last Battle," 188–189.

20 Smith, *Thomas Kilby Smith*, 384.

21 Dabney H. Maury, "How the Confederacy Changed Naval Warfare," *Southern Historical Papers* 22 (1894): 78.

22 "In Mobile Bay," *Osage City (KS) Free Press*, 3.

23 Smith, *Thomas Kilby Smith*, 383.

24 "Interesting from Mobile," *Philadelphia (PA) Inquirer*, 2.

25 John N. Chamberlin, *Captaining the Corps d'Afrique: The Civil War Letters of John Newton Chamberlin*, ed. Jim Bisbee (Jefferson, NC: McFarland, 2016), 109.

26 Jones and Pulcrano, *History of the Eighteenth Alabama*, 64.

27 Bergeron, "Twenty-Second Louisiana," 209.

28 Waterman, "Afloat-Afield-Afloat," 491; *ORN*, Series 1, vol. 22, 67–68; Stephenson, *Civil War Memoir*, 360.

29 Slack, *Slack's War*, 279.

30 "From Mobile," *Daily Milwaukee (WI) News*, April 22, 1865, 1.

31 Stephenson, *Civil War Memoir*, 360.

32 "From Mobile," *Detroit (MI) Free Press*, 3.

33 "Fall of Mobile and Defenses," *Cincinnati (OH) Enquirer*, 2; "An Iron Clad Fleet," *New Orleans (LA) Times-Democrat*, July 23, 1866, 7; *ORN*, Series 1, vol. 22, 72–74.

34 Milton F. Perry, *Infernal Machines: The Story of Confederate Submarine and Mine Warfare* (Baton Rouge: Louisiana State University Press, 1985), 186.

35 Musser, *Soldier Boy*, 199.

36 Waterman, "Afloat-Afield-Afloat," 491.

37 "Blown Up," *Mobile (AL) Advertiser and Register*, 1.

38 Smith, *Thomas Kilby Smith*, 386.

39 George P. Hunt, "Letter to Miss Eames," April 1, 1865, To Arms Antiques, Fairhope, AL.

40 "Attack of Mobile," *New York Times*, 8; *ORN*, Series 1, vol. 22, 74–75.

41 G. J. Rains, "Torpedoes," *Southern Historical Papers* 3 (1877): 260; Maury, "Naval Warfare," 78.

42 "Souvenirs of the War," *New Orleans (LA) Daily Crescent*, 4.

43 "Yankee Accounts from Mobile," *Mobile (AL) Advertiser and Register*.

44 Cobb, "The Siege of Mobile"; "Yankee Accounts from Mobile," *Mobile (AL) Advertiser and Register*.

45 "Capture of Mobile," *New Orleans (LA) Times-Democrat*, April 14, 1865, 1.

46 Davis, "That Hard Siege," 591.

47 The Lady Slocomb is prominently displayed outside the Confederate Museum in New Orleans, LA. Waterman, "Afloat-Afield-Afloat," 54.

48 "The Mobile Expedition," *New Orleans (LA) Times-Democrat*, 2.

49 "The Siege of Mobile," *New York Times*, April 21, 1865.

50 *ORA*, Series I, vol. 49, pt. 2, 1199; Andrews, *Campaign of Mobile*, 140; "The Last Shot," *Los Angeles (CA) Herald*, August 23, 1897, 8; "The Lady Slocumb," *Mobile (AL) Daily Register*, March 15, 1891; "Lady Slocomb: The Silent Witness," *New Orleans (LA) Times Picayune*, September 20, 1899, 9; Nathaniel Cheairs Hughes, *The Pride of the Confederate Artillery: The Washington Artillery in the Army of Tennessee* (Baton Rouge: Louisiana State University Press, 1997), 270.

51 Andrews, *Campaign of Mobile*, 134–135.

52 William S. McNeil, "Silence of Peace," *Philadelphia (PA) Times*, n.d.

53 H. P. Van Cleve, *Annual Report of the Adjutant General of the State of Minnesota for the Year Ending December 1, 1866, and of the Military Forces of the State from 1861 to 1866* (St. Paul, MN: Pioneer Print, 1866), 43.

54 Ibid, 236.

55 Stockton, *War Diary*, 29–30.

56 "Souvenirs of the War," *New Orleans (LA) Daily Crescent*, 4.

57 "Siege of Mobile," *New York Times*, April 21, 1865 (emphasis in original).

58 Allen, "Operations Against the City of Mobile," 79; "Our Special Account," *New York Times* online, accessed August 6, 2016, http://www.nytimes.com/1865/04/24/news/our-special-account-preparation-start-investment-spanish-fort-what-flert-did.html? pagewanted=all.

59 "Souvenirs of the War," *New Orleans (LA) Daily Crescent*, 4.

60 McNeil, "Silence of Peace"; "Field and Staff Officers, 1st Battalion, Alabama Artillery," Access Genealogy, accessed March 22, 2016, https://www.accessgenealogy.com/alabama/field-and-staff-officers-1st-battalion-alabama-artillery.htm; "Battle Unit Details – The Civil War," U.S. National Park Service, accessed March 22, 2016, http://www.nps.gov/civilwar/search-battle-units-detail. htm? battleUnitCode=CAL0001BA; Thomas Waverly Palmer, "Andrews, George William, and A. B.: 1900 Graduates with Titled Degrees," *A Register of the Officers and Students of the University of Alabama, 1831–1901* (Tuscaloosa, AL: University Press, n.d.), 57.

61 "Souvenirs of the War," *New Orleans (LA) Daily Crescent*, 4.

62 Maury, "Defense of Mobile," 9; N. T. Mconaughy, "Gallant Col. William E. Burnett," *Confederate Veteran*, August 1909, 66.

63 "Confederate States Staff Officers: G Surnames," Access Genealogy, accessed September 10, 2017, https://www.accessgenealogy.com/military/confederate-states-staff-officers-g-surnames.htm.

64 Harrison commanded the CSS *Morgan* during the battle of Mobile Bay. The vessel was relatively unscathed during the battle, which caused Harrison to be criticized for staying out of range of Farragut's guns and prematurely retiring from the engagement. After the battle, at 11 p.m. on the same day, he and his crew made a daring escape up the bay, while being hotly pursued by "two monitors and two double enders." Against the odds, he managed to guide the *Morgan* to the safety of Mobile at daybreak. Apparently, Harrison continued to command the *Morgan* during the early stages of the siege of Mobile. After this incident, Captain Joseph Fry replaced him. *ORN*, Series 1, vol. 22, 60, 98; *ORN*, Series 1, vol. 21, 575,577–578, 583–587; "The Fighting at Mobile," *Richmond (VA) Dispatch*, August 16, 1864, 1; Tarleton, "Civil War Letters,"51–81.

65 Allen, "Operations Against the City of Mobile," 76.

66 Danielson, *Company G*, 18; Newton, "Siege of Mobile," 596–597.

67 Sperry, *33rd Iowa*, 140.

68 Andrews, *Campaign of Mobile*, 237.

69 Ibid, 78; *ORA*, Series I, vol. 49, pt. 1, 150, 231; *ORA*, vol. 39, pt. 2, 815; Definition of "towser" by *Merriam-Webster Dictionary* online, accessed August 6, 2016, http://www.merriam-webster. com/dictionary/towser.

70 "Lady Slocomb: The Silent Witness," *New Orleans (LA) Times Picayune*, 9.

71 T. J. Hunt, *Observations of T. J. Hunt in the Civil War: Narrative of the Military Life of T. J. Hunt in the Sioux Indian and Civil Wars of 1862–1865*, 29.

72 "Lady Slocomb: The Silent Witness," *New Orleans (LA) Times Picayune*, 141.

73 Jones and Pulcrano, *History of the Eighteenth Alabama*, 64.

74 Chamberlin, *Corps d'Afrique*, 109.

75 Jones and Pulcrano, *History of the Eighteenth Alabama*, 65.

76 "Souvenirs of the War," *New Orleans (LA) Daily Crescent*, 4.

77   Maury, "Defense of Spanish Fort."

78   Herndon, "My Dear Wife."

79   Jones and Pulcrano, *History of the Eighteenth Alabama*, 65.

80   Hubbard, "Civil War Papers," 629.

81   "Mobile Expedition," *New Orleans (LA) Times-Democrat*, 2.

82   Allen, "Operations Against the City of Mobile," 77; *ORA*, Series I, vol. 49, pt. 1, 229; *Gum-tree Mortar Barrel*, Minnesota Historical Collections Database, 4225. H576, September 4, 2016, Minnesota Historical Society, St. Paul, MN.

83   "Fall of Mobile and Defenses," *Cincinnati (OH) Enquirer*, 2.

84   Smith, *Thomas Kilby Smith*, 383–384.

85   Musser, *Soldier Boy*, 199; "The Siege of Mobile," *Boston (MA) Liberator*, April 14, 1865, 3.

86   Andrews, *Campaign of Mobile*, 165–166.

87   Maury, "Defense of Spanish Fort," 132.

88   Hubbard, *Fifth Minnesota Letters*, 68.

89   Chamberlin, *Corps d' Afrique*, 109.

Chapter 7

1   Chamberlin, *Corps d'Afrique*, 116.

2   *ORA*, Series I, vol. 49, pt. 1, 790; Andrews, *Campaign of Mobile*, 112.

3   N. A. Williams and J. M. Whayne, *Arkansas Biography: A Collection of Notable Lives* (Fayetteville: University of Arkansas Press, 2000), 271.

4   Horace Greeley, *The American Conflict: A History of the Great Rebellion in the United States of America, 1860–'65* (Hartford, CT: O. D. Case, 1864), 555–556.

5   Lacey, "Steele," 432.

6   Chamberlin, *Corps d'Afrique*, 116.

7   Marshall, *Eighty-Third Ohio*, 157–159.

8   Sweetman, "Capture of Blakeley," 1; *ORA*, Series I, vol. 49, pt. 2, 119.

9   Marshall, *Eighty-Third Ohio*, 157–159.

10   James M. Dunn, *Diary of Private James M. Dunn, 97th Illinois Volunteer Infantry. Ca. March 31–August 9, 1865*, File # 1865-12, National Park Service, Gulf Islands National Seashore, Florida District Library, Fort Pickens, FL, 1.

11   Ibid; John W. Schlagle, "John W. Schlagle Diary, 1865," Collection No. SC1313, Indiana Historical Society, Indianapolis, IN.

12   *ORA*, Series I, vol. 10, pt. 2, 299.

13   Warner, *Generals in Gray*, 50–51.

14   *ORA*, Series I, vol. 23, pt. 2, Serial 042, 553-554.

15   *ORA*, Series I, vol. 23, pt. 2, Serial 042, 553-554; Schlagle, "Diary."

16   *ORA*, Series I, vol. 23, pt. 2, Serial 042, 553-554; Andrews, *Campaign of Mobile*, 109–110; *ORA*, Series I, vol. 49, pt. 1, 280.

17   *ORA*, Series I, vol. 23, pt. 2, Serial 042, 553-554; Andrews, *Campaign of Mobile*, 109–110; *ORA*, Series I, vol. 49, pt. 1, 280.

18   O'Brien, *Last Stand*, 64.

19   Ibid; *ORA*, Series I, vol. 49, pt. 1, 280.

20   *ORA*, Series I, vol. 49, pt. 1, 280, 313.

21   *ORA*, Series I, vol. 49, pt. 1, 281, 285; O'Brien, *Last Stand*, 64.

22   *ORA*, Series I, vol. 49, pt. 1, 135, 200; Andrews, *Campaign of Mobile*, 112.

23 *ORA*, Series I, vol. 49, pt. 1, 309–310, 781, 875.

24 *ORA*, Series I, vol. 49, pt. 1, 309–310; "Biographies of Butler County Alabama," Genealogy Trails History Group, accessed September 9, 2017, http://genealogytrails.com/ala/butler/bios_1.html#wattsthomas.

25 *ORA*, vol. 49, pt. 1, 309–310; "General Steele Flanking Mobile," *Washington (DC) National Tribune*, April 10, 1865, 2.

26 *ORA*, vol. 49, pt. 1, 309–310; "General Steele Flanking Mobile," *Washington (DC) National Tribune*, April 10, 1865, 2.

27 Merriam, "Capture of Mobile," 236.

28 Ibid.

29 Andrews, *Campaign of Mobile*, 116–117.

30 James M. Dunn, *Diary of Private James M. Dunn, 97th Illinois Volunteer Infantry* (Fort Pickens: File # 1865-12, National Park Service, Gulf Islands National Seashore, Florida District Library, 1865), 3.

31 Henry W. Hart, "Letters of Henry W. Hart, Second Connecticut Light Artillery, Second Division, XII Corps," Mobile Historic Preservation Society, Norman Nicholson Collection, Mobile, AL.

32 Lacey, "Steele,"435–436.

33 Dunn, *Diary*, 3.

34 Newton, "Siege of Mobile," 597.

35 Sweetman, "Capture of Blakeley," 1.

36 Taylor, *Destruction and Reconstruction*, 221; Waterman, "Afloat-Afield-Afloat," 21.

37 *ORA*, vol. 49, pt. 1, 136, 311; Chambers, *Blood & Sacrifice*, 227–230.

38 Dunn, *Diary*, 3.

39 Sperry, *33rd Iowa*, 150–151; Waterman, "Afloat-Afield-Afloat," 21.

40 Truman, "Campaign in Alabama," 1.

41 "Souvenirs of the War," *New Orleans (LA) Daily Crescent*, 4.

42 Sperry, *33rd Iowa*, 150–151; McLellan, "Vivid Reminiscences," 264.

43 Truman, "Campaign in Alabama," 1.

44 Taylor, *Destruction and Reconstruction*, 221; Waterman, "Afloat-Afield-Afloat," 21; Liddell and Hughes, *Liddell's Record*, 194.

45 Sperry, *33rd Iowa*, 150–151.

46 *Cheval de frise* is an anti-cavalry obstacle consisting of a wood frame with projecting wooden spikes. Wiley, *Civil War Diary*, 150.

47 Dunn, *Diary*, 3.

48 *ORA*, vol. 49, pt. 1, 283.

49 Ibid, 209.

50 Spence, "Last Fight," 7.

51 Andrews, *Campaign of Mobile*, 181.

52 Ibid, 183–184.

53 A. J. Hill, *History of Company E of the Sixth Minnesota Regiment of Volunteer Infantry*, contrib. Charles J. Stees (St. Paul, MN: Civil War Classic Library, 1869), 29–30.

54 Charles W. Johnson, "Narrative of the Sixth Minnesota," in *Minnesota in the Civil and Indian Wars, 1861–1865* (Salem, MA: Higginson Book Company, 1866), 327.

55 Hill, "Last Battle," 183.

56 Andrews, *Campaign of Mobile*, 172–173.

57 Spence, "Last Fight," 7.

58 Andrews, *Campaign of Mobile*, 183; "Mobile Expedition," *New Orleans (LA) Times-Democrat*, 2.

59 Lacey, "Steele," 8.

Chapter 8

1 Davis, "That Hard Siege," 591.
2 Andrews, *Campaign of Mobile*, 252–256.
3 Joseph Boyce, *Captain Joseph Boyce and the 1st Missouri Infantry, C. S. A.*, ed. William C. Winter (St. Louis: University of Missouri Press, 2011), 216–217.
4 Andrews, *Campaign of Mobile*, 252–256.
5 Mark Lyons, "Letters," 1865, Doy Leale McCall Rare Book and Manuscript Library, University of South Alabama, Mobile, AL, 146.
6 "Mobile Expedition," *New Orleans (LA) Times-Democrat*, 2.
7 Ibid, 242; Slack, *Slack's War*, 281–282.
8 Maury, "Defense of Spanish Fort," 132.
9 *ORA*, vol.49, pt. 2, 1176–1177.
10 Ibid, 1180.
11 *ORA*, Series I, vol. 49, pt. 1, 315.
12 Jones and Pulcrano, *History of the Eighteenth Alabama*, 64–67.
13 Ibid.
14 *ORA*, Series I, vol.49, pt. 1, 314.
15 *ORA*, Series I, vol. 49, pt. 2, 1192.
16 Maury, "Defense of Spanish Fort," 135.
17 Herndon, "My Dear Wife."
18 Waterman, "Afloat-Afield-Afloat," 23.
19 *ORA*, Series I, vol. 49, pt. 2, 1201.
20 Maury, "Defense of Spanish Fort," 136.
21 Stephenson, *Civil War Memoir*, 360.
22 *ORA*, Series I, vol. 49, pt. 2, 1201.
23 "Capture of Spanish Fort," *Bloomington (IL) Pantagraph*, May 3, 1865, 1.
24 *ORA*, Series I, vol. 49, pt. 2, 1201.
25 *ORA*, Series I, vol. 49, pt. 2, 1204.
26 Ibid, 1205.
27 Ibid, 1204–1205.
28 Gibson's mention of his officer's African-American servants being armed appears in his original hand-written report. This excerpt was mysteriously omitted from the published Official Records. Donald E. Dixon, "Randall Lee Gibson," (master's thesis, Louisiana State University, 1971); Randall L. Gibson, *Randall Lee Gibson Papers* (Baton Rouge, LA: Louisiana State University Archives, 1865); *ORA*, Series I, vol. 49, pt. 1, 314.
29 A sortie is a sudden attack coming from a fortified position. Slack, *Slack's War*, 277.
30 *ORA*, Series I, vol.49, pt. 1, 315–316.
31 Stockton, *War Diary*, 29.
32 Corporal Haydock in Sperry, *33rd Iowa*, 139.
33 Wiley, *Civil War Diary*, 147.
34 Carter, "That Charge," 226.
35 Ibid; Jones and Pulcrano, *History of the Eighteenth Alabama*, 70.
36 Bergeron, "Twenty-Second Louisiana," 210; Brigadier General Randall Lee Gibson to Brigadier General St. John R. Liddell, Randall Lee Gibson Papers, Manuscript Collection 316, Louisiana Research Collection, Tulane University, New Orleans, LA.
37 *ORA*, Series I, vol.4 9, pt. 1, 226.
38 Andrews, *Campaign of Mobile*, 84–87.

39 *ORA*, Series I, vol. 49, pt. 1, 226.

40 Dabney Maury, Clement Stanford Watson Papers, Manuscript Collection 711, Louisiana Research Collection, Tulane University, New Orleans, LA.

41 Herndon, "My Dear Wife."

42 Ibid.

43 Stephenson, *Civil War Memoir*, 358–359.

44 Baumer, "Memories of War."

45 Jones and Pulcrano, *History of the Eighteenth Alabama*, 64–67.

46 "Souvenirs of the War," *New Orleans (LA) Daily Crescent*, 4.

47 William L. Cameron, "The Battles Opposite Mobile," *Confederate Veteran* 23 (1915): 305; *ORA*, Series I, vol. 49, pt. 1, 317.

48 Raymond Schmandt and Josephine H. Schulte, eds., *A Civil War Diary: The Diary of Spring Hill College Between the Years 1860–1865* (Mobile, AL: Spring Hill College Press, 1892).

49 Andrew Cornette, *Father Cornette's Notes from the Annals of Spring Hill College*, 1872, Spring Hill College Archives, Mobile, AL, 182–184.

50 *ORA*, Series I, vol. 49, pt. 1, 319.

51 Charles J. Boyle, *Twice Remembered: Moments in the History of Spring Hill College* (Mobile, AL: The Friends of Spring Hill Library, 1993).

52 Cornette, *Annals*, 182–184.

53 Mrs. John Randolph Eggleston, "The Women of the Confederacy," *Southern Historical Society Papers* 34 (1906): 193.

54 "Souvenirs of the War," *New Orleans (LA) Daily Crescent*, 4.

55 *Mobile (AL) Advertiser and Register*, April 9, 1865.

56 Mary Douglass Waring-Harrison, *Miss Waring's Journal: 1863–1865*, ed. Thad Holt (Chicago, IL: Wyvern Press of S. F. E., 1964), 25.

57 James L. Ray, "Soldier Remembers Mobile," Austin, TX, January 17, 1929, Mobile Historic Preservation Society, Norman Nicholson Collection, Mobile, AL.

58 Ibid.

59 Johnson, "In Camp and Field," 7 (Letter originally appeared in a Mobile, AL paper).

60 Ray, "Soldier Remembers."

61 Cumming, *Kate*, 306–307; Ray, "Soldier Remembers."; Waring-Harrison, *Journal*, 13–14; Stephenson, *Civil War Memoir*, 360; "Lady Slocomb," 9.

62 "Souvenirs of the War," *New Orleans (LA) Daily Crescent*, 4.

Chapter 9

1 "Souvenirs of the War," *New Orleans (LA) Daily Crescent*, 4.

2 Maury, "Defense of Spanish Fort," 130.

3 "From the 95th Illinois," *Woodstock (IL) Sentinel*, May 10, 1865, 1.

4 Stephenson, *Civil War Memoir*, 363–364.

5 Jones and Pulcrano, *History of the Eighteenth Alabama*, 68.

6 Stephenson, *Civil War Memoir*, 363–364.

7 Thomas Jefferson Hunt, *Observations of T. J. Hunt in the Civil War: Narrative of the Military Life of T. J. Hunt in the Sioux Indian and Civil Wars of 1862–1865*, Transcript, n.d., 29.

8 Ibid, 29.

9 Hill, *Company E*, 30.

10 *ORA*, Series I, vol. 49, pt. 2, 1219.

11 Maury, "Defense of Spanish Fort," 132.

12 "Our Special Account," 1.

13 Andrews, *Campaign of Mobile*, 143; Robert L. Barry, "The Lookout Battery," *Confederate Veteran* (1922): 385; O'Brien, *Last Stand*, 107; The Civil War Diary of Charles Henry Snedeker, n. p.; *ORA*, Series I, vol. 49, pt. 1, 277.

14 Jones and Pulcrano, *History of the Eighteenth Alabama*, 64, 70; Andrews, *Campaign of Mobile*, 151.

15 Stephenson, *Civil War Memoir*, 364–365; *ORA*, Series I, vol. 49, pt. 1, 229.

16 In his book, *History of the Campaign of Mobile*, C. C. Andrews writes that the Lumsden battery was relieved by Perry's Chattanooga battery on April 6, 1865. This is a mistake; Captain T. J. Perry led the Marion Artillery from Florida. Captain Robert L. Barry led the Chattanooga "Lookout" battery. Andrews mistook Perry for Barry. Although there is an account in the official records listing Colonel David Coleman as commander of Ector's Brigade, General Gibson wrote in his official report that Colonel J. A. Andrews led the brigade at Spanish Fort; Andrews, Julius A., "The Handbook of Texas Online," Texas State Historical Association (TSHA), accessed January 8, 2018. https://tshaonline.org/handbook/online/articles/fan61; Andrews, *Campaign of Mobile*, 143; Robert L. Barry, "The Lookout Battery," *Confederate Veteran* (1922): 385; O'Brien, *Last Stand*, 107; Zella Armstrong, "Daring Deeds of Barry's Artillery," *The Sunny South*, August 25, 1901, np; ORA, Series I, vol. 49, pt. 1, 1046.

17 Andrews, *Campaign of Mobile*, 154; ORA, Series I, vol. 49, pt. 1, 96, 200, 275–278; Little and Maxwell, *A History of Lumsden's Battery, C. S. A*, 66.

18 *ORA*, Series I, vol. 49, pt. 1, 229, 267, 275; Andrews, *Campaign of Mobile*, 155.

19 Andrews, *Campaign of Mobile*, 153–154; "From the 95th Illinois," *Woodstock (IL) Sentinel*, 1.

20 The flags of the 9th and 14th Texas were not captured. Ship Island prisoner rolls reveal that the 32nd Texas had 30 men captured, while the 10th Texas only had four men captured. National Archives and Records Service, *Selected Records of the War Department Relating to Confederate Prisoners of War, 1861–65*, Roll 136, Vol. 406–408 (Washington: National Archives, National Archives and Records Service, General Services Administration, 1965). *ORA*, Series I, vol. 49, pt. 1, 232, 269, 313, 1046; "Flag," American Civil War Museum: Online Collections, accessed January 9, 2018, http://moconfederacy.pastperfectonline.com/webobject/8E6CAF5A-67A1-440 2-B250-284917542464; Madaus, Howard Michael. *The Battle Flags of the Confederate Army of Tennessee*. Milwaukee, WI: Milwaukee Public Museum, 1976, 80.

21 *ORA*, Series I, vol. 49, pt. 1, 275; Armstrong, "Daring Deeds," n.p.; United States War Department, Office of Commissary General of Prisoners, National Archives and Records Service, "Confederate Prisoners."

22 *ORA*, Series I, vol. 49, pt. 1, 275; Andrews, *Campaign of Mobile*, 153–154; Joseph Nixon, Clement Stanford Watson Papers, Manuscript Collection 711, Louisiana Research Collection, Tulane University, New Orleans, LA; W. Bailey, "The Star Company of Ector's Texas Brigade," *Confederate Veteran* 22 (1914): 405.

23 Cyrus B. Comstock, *The Diary of Cyrus B. Comstock*, ed. Marlin E. Sumner (Dayton, OH: Morningside House, 1987).

24 "From the 95th Illinois," *Woodstock (IL) Sentinel*, 1.

25 *ORA*, Series I, vol. 49, pt. 1, 318; W. Bailey, "The Star Company of Ector's Texas Brigade," *Confederate Veteran* 22 (1914): 405; "Fourteenth Texas Cavalry," The Handbook of Texas Online, Texas State Historical Association, accessed June 9, 2016, https://tshaonline.org/handbook/online/articles/qkf14; Allen, "Operations Against the City of Mobile," 80–81; "Our Special Account"; "Spanish Fort," *Washington (DC) National Tribune*, 4.

26 Some sources mistakenly list Clarke's rank as captain. However, Gibson's official report listed his rank as lieutenant. Allen, "Operations Against the City of Mobile," 80–81; "Our Special Account";

"Spanish Fort," *Washington (DC) National Tribune*, 4; Andrews, *Campaign of Mobile*, 156–157; *ORA*, Series I, vol. 49, pt. 1, 278, 317–318.

27 Andrews, *Campaign of Mobile*, 155–157; *ORA*, Series 1, vol. 49, pt. 2, 1219; *ORA*, Series I, vol. 49, pt. 1, 318.

28 *ORA*, Series I, vol. 49, pt. 1, 268, 317–318.

29 Andrews, *Campaign of Mobile*, 165.

30 "Souvenirs of the War," *New Orleans (LA) Daily Crescent*, 4.

31 Allen, "Operations Against the City of Mobile," 80–81; "Our Special Account"; *ORA*, Series I, vol. 49, pt. 1, 229; "Spanish Fort," *Washington (DC) National Tribune*, January 28, 1886, 3; Andrews, *Campaign of Mobile*, 151–157.

32 Palfrey, "The Capture of Mobile, 1865," 537.

33 Maury, "Defense of Spanish Fort," 132.

34 *ORA*, Series I, vol. 49, pt. 1, 318.

35 Ibid, 1219.

36 "The Lady Slocomb," *The Times Democrat*, September 20, 1899, 3; "Lady Slocomb: The Silent Witness," *New Orleans (LA) Times Picayune*, 3; ORA, Series I, vol. 49, pt. 1, 318; *ORA*, Series I, vol. 49, pt. 2, 1204, 1219.

37 Truman, "Campaign in Alabama," 1.

38 Allen, "Operations Against the City of Mobile," 80–81; "Our Special Account."

39 Allen, "Operations Against the City of Mobile," 80–81; "Our Special Account."; "From the 95th Illinois," *Woodstock (IL) Sentinel*, 1.

40 Andrews, *Campaign of Mobile*, 165; Maury, "Defense of Spanish Fort," 134.

41 "Souvenirs of the War," *New Orleans (LA) Daily Crescent*, 4.

42 Maury, "Defense of Spanish Fort," 131; *ORA*, Series I, vol. 49, pt. 1, 318; Stephenson, *Civil War Memoir*, 365–367.

43 Maury, "Defense of Spanish Fort," 131; *ORA*, Series I, vol. 49, pt. 1, 318; Stephenson, *Civil War Memoir*, 365–367.

44 T. L. Bayne, "Our Fallen Comrades," *South Historical Society Papers* 11 (1883): 329.

45 *Confederate Military History Extended Edition, Vol. 7: Alabama* (Wilmington, NC: Confederate, 1899), 616.

46 "Lady Slocomb: The Silent Witness," *New Orleans (LA) Times Picayune*, 7.

47 Ibid, 7; Stephenson, *Civil War Memoir*, 365–367.

48 Maury, "Spanish Fort," 131; Maury, "Defense of Mobile," 7.

49 "Lady Slocomb: The Silent Witness," *New Orleans (LA) Times Picayune*, 7; Stephenson, *Civil War Memoir*, 365–367.

50 Jones and Pulcrano, *History of the Eighteenth Alabama*, 70.

51 Cornette, *Annals*, 182–184.

52 Stephenson and Hughes, *Memoir*, 365–367.

53 Maury, "Defense of Spanish Fort," 131; *ORA*, Series I, vol. 49, pt. 1, 318.

54 Maury, "Defense of Mobile," 7.

55 Liddell and Hughes, *Liddell's Record*, 190–191.

56 Spink, "Capture of Spanish Fort," 7; "A Week of Victory," *Nashville (TN) Daily Union*, April 21, 1865; Maury, "Defense of Spanish Fort," 132; Truman, "Campaign in Alabama," 1.

57 *ORA*, Series I, vol. 49, pt. 1, 318; Truman, "Campaign in Alabama," 1.

58 Baumer, "Memories of War."

59 Milo Washington Scott, "Diary of Pvt. Milo Washington Scott," in *Confederate Reminiscences and Letters 1861–1865*, vol. 23 (Cartersville, GA: Georgia Division United Daughters of the Confederacy, 2007), 73.

60 Musser, *Soldier Boy*, 200–201.

61 Lauren Barker, "Amused at the Many Accounts," *Washington (DC) National Tribune*, August 25, 1910, 3.

62 Spink, "Capture of Spanish Fort," 7.

63 Sperry, *33rd Iowa*, 143–144.

64 A. Y. Barnard, "Says It was the Thirteenth," *Washington (DC) National Tribune*, August 25, 1910, 3.

65 "How Fort Blakely Was Taken," *Washington (DC) National Tribune*, August 25, 1865, 3.

66 Newton, "Siege of Mobile," 599.

67 Wood, "Capture Forts," 6.

68 Andrews, *Campaign of Mobile*, 236.

69 Chamberlin, *Corps d'Afrique*, 110.

70 "From the 95th Illinois," *Woodstock (IL) Sentinel*, 1.

71 Truman, "Campaign in Alabama," 1; "Capture of Mobile," *New Orleans (LA) Times Democrat*, 1.

72 "Capture of Mobile," *New Orleans (LA) Times Democrat*, 1; "From the 95th Illinois," *Woodstock (II.) Sentinel*, 1.

73 Truman, "Campaign in Alabama," 1.

74 Newton, "Siege of Mobile," 599.

75 Ibid, 147.

76 *ORA*, Series I, vol. 49, pt. 1, 319.

77 Ryland Todhunter, "Ector's Texas Brigade," *Confederate Veteran* 7 (1899): 312.

78 Truman, "Campaign in Alabama," 1.

79 Maury, "Defense of Spanish Fort," 136.

80 "Souvenirs of the War," *New Orleans (LA) Daily Crescent*, 4.

81 Andrews, *Campaign of Mobile*, 165–166.

82 Taylor, *Destruction and Reconstruction*, 221.

83 Maury, "Defense of Spanish Fort," 135.

84 Ibid, 135.

85 Ibid, 135.

Chapter 10

1 Andrews, *Campaign of Mobile*, 189.

2 *ORA*, Series I, vol. 49, pt. 2, 295.

3 Musser, *Soldier Boy*, 201.

4 "The Campaign in Alabama," *New York Times*, April 24, 1865, 1; "The Capture of Mobile," *Buffalo (NY) Commercial Advertiser*, April 24, 1865, 2.

5 Merriam, "The Capture of Mobile," 244.

6 Stephenson, *Civil War Memoir*, 365–367.

7 Boyce, *1st Missouri*, 219.

8 Andrews, *Campaign of Mobile*, 191.

9 *ORA*, Series I, vol. 49, pt. 2, 297.

10 *ORA*, Series I, vol. 49, pt. 1, 291.

11 *ORA*, Series I, vol. 49, pt. 2, 299.

12 Marshall, *Eighty-Third Ohio*, 162; *ORA*, Series I, vol. 49, pt. 2, 298.

13 Merriam, "Capture of Mobile," 244.

14 Andrews, *Campaign of Mobile*, 192.

15 "Robert E. Lee Surrenders – Apr 09, 1865," History.com, accessed December 11, 2015, http://www.history.com/this-day-in-history/robert-e-lee-surrenders.

16 *ORA*, Series I, vol. 49, pt. 2, 306; Andrews, *Campaign of Mobile*, 193.

17 Ben H. Bounds and Charles L. Bounds, *Ben H. Bounds, 1840–1911, Methodist Minister and Prominent Mason: Biography and Highlights from His Early Life and Civil War Memoirs* (Columbus, OH: J. O. Moore, 1962), 20; Andrews, *Campaign of Mobile*, 200–201.

18 Andrews, *Campaign of Mobile*, 217.

19 "A. J. Smith's Guerrillas," *Washington (DC) National Tribune*, April 28, 1887, 6.

20 Hill, *Company E*, 30.

21 "A. J. Smith's Guerrillas," *Washington (DC) National Tribune*, 6.

22 Lacey, "Steele," 434.

23 "A. J. Smith's Guerrillas," *Washington (DC) National Tribune*, 6.

24 *ORA*, Series I, vol. 49, pt. 1, 143.

25 "The Capture of Mobile," *Buffalo Commercial*, April 24, 1865, 2.

26 Hart, "Letters."

27 *ORA*, Series I, vol. 49, pt. 1, 291.

28 Ibid; Chester Barney, *Recollections of Field Service with the 20th Iowa Infantry Volunteers, or, What I Saw in the Army: Embracing Accounts of Marches, Battles, Sieges, and Skirmishes, in Missouri, Arkansas, Mississippi, Louisiana, Alabama, Florida, Texas, and Along the Northern Border of Mexico* (Davenport, IA: Gazette Job Rooms, 1865), 308–309.

29 Sweetman, "Capture of Blakeley," 1.

30 Colby received the Congressional Medal of Honor for gallantry at Vicksburg. Carlos W. Colby, "An Incident Occurring at Fort Blakeley," *Washington (DC) National* Tribune, November 21, 1901, 6; "Illinois Civil War Muster and Descriptive Rolls Database," Illinois State Archives, accessed November 28, 2016, http://www.ilsos.gov/isaveterans/civilMusterSearch.do? key=49031.

31 T. G. Capps – Company E, 122nd Illinois, "Fort Blakely," *Washington (DC) National Tribune*, September 22, 1887, 3; Barney, *Recollections*, 308–309.

32 "Fall of Mobile and Defenses," *Cincinnati (OH) Enquirer*, 2.

33 Otto Wolf, *Letter of Otto Wolf, 117th Illinois Infantry, Second Brigade Second Division, XVI Corps*, April 12, 1865 (From the collection of his grandson, Olin W. Kriege, Springfield, IL, April 1976).

34 Barney, *Recollections*, 308–309.

35 "A Moving Tale," *Washington (DC) National Tribune*, October 21, 1909, 3.

36 Marshall, *Eighty-Third Ohio*, 164–165.

37 "Souvenirs of the War," *New Orleans (LA) Daily Crescent*, 4.

38 Marshall, *Eighty-Third Ohio*, 164–165.

39 For this brave action, Sergeant Daniel B. Moore of Company B, 11th Wisconsin Infantry, was awarded the Congressional Medal of Honor in 1900, 35 years after the battle of Fort Blakeley. "After Many Years," *Phillipsburg (KS) Herald*, September 13, 1900.

40 *ORA*, Series I, vol. 49, pt. 1, 313; United States, *The Medal of Honor of the United States Army* (Washington [D. C.]: U. S. G. P. O., 1948), 202–203.

41 A moistened wool sponge staff was used to clean the artillery bores. Allen, "Operations Against the City of Mobile," 83.

42 Andrews, *Campaign of Mobile*, 200.

43 "How Fort Blakeley Was Taken," *Washington (DC) National Tribune*, 3.

44 Cleveland, "With the Third Missouri," 197.

45 *ORA*, Series I, vol. 49, pt. 1, 1188.

46 Boyce, *1st Missouri*, 219.

47 David Marshall Scott, letter to Thomas M. Owen, September 24, 1910, Alabama Department of Archives and History, 62nd Alabama Infantry File, 3–4.

48 Andrews, *Campaign of Mobile*, 217.

49   E. W. Tarrant, "After the Fall of Fort Blakely," *Confederate Veteran* 25 (1917): 152.

50   Boyce, *1st Missouri*, 221.

51   Bergeron, *Confederate Mobile*, 193; Robert N. Rosen, *The Jewish Confederates* (Columbia: University of South Carolina Press, 2000), 160.

52   Cameron, "Battles Opposite Mobile," 306.

53   *ORA*, Series I, vol. 49, pt. 1, 287, 289–290; Lieutenant Walter Chapman, "Dear Parents," April 11, 1865, Mobile Historic Preservation Society, Norman Nicholson Collection, Mobile, AL.

54   The controversial battle of Fort Pillow occurred almost a year before the assault of Fort Blakeley. Allegedly, an unusually high number of the Union garrison, about half of which were African-American soldiers, were killed after surrendering by troopers under General Nathan Bedford Forrest. Regardless of what really happened at Fort Pillow, the U.S.C.T. that assaulted Fort Blakeley sought to avenge the alleged atrocities. Wiley, *Civil War Diary*, 150–151; Stephenson, *Civil War Memoir*, 368.

55   E. W. Tarrant, "The Siege and Capture of Fort Blakely," *Confederate Veteran* 23 (1915): 457–458.

56   Hill, *Company E*, 30.

57   Marshall, *Eighty-Third Ohio*, 164–165.

58   "Fall of Mobile and Defenses," Cincinnati (OH) Enquirer, 2.

59   Marshall, *Eighty-Third Ohio*, 164–165; Samuel Ivins, "Fort Blakely," *Washington (DC) National Tribune*, March 14, 1865, 3; *ORA*, Series I, vol. 49, pt. 1, 289; William Macy, "The Civil War Diary of William Macy," *Indiana Magazine of History* 60, no. 2 (1934): 194.

60   "Mobile Expedition," *New Orleans (LA) Times-Democrat*, 6.

61   Merriam, "Capture of Mobile," 247.

Chapter 11

1   Sweetman, "Capture of Blakeley," 1.

2   Lyons, "Letters," 147; "Capture of Fort Blakeley," *Washington (DC) National Tribune,* September 2, 1892, 1; Andrews, *Campaign of Mobile,* 220; Liddell and Hughes, *Liddell's Record*, 196; O'Brien, *Last Stand*, 202.

3   Private Samuel P. Combs, "A Sharpshooter's Story," *Washington (DC) National Tribune*, December 15, 1887, 3.

4   *ORN*, Series 1, vol. 22, 101–102.

5   Cameron, "Battles Opposite Mobile," 305–306.

6   Bennett commanded the CSS *Gaines* during the battle of Mobile Bay on August 5, 1864. He and his crew escaped in small boats to Mobile, under the cover of darkness, the same day as the battle. *ORN*, Series 1, vol. 21, 588–590; *ORN*, Series 1, vol. 22, 101–102.

7   Stephenson, *Civil War Memoir*, 368.

8   Liddell and Hughes, *Liddell's Record*, 196.

9   Ibid, 197.

10   McLellan, "Vivid Reminiscences," 264.

11   R. S. Bevier, *History of the First and Second Missouri Confederate Brigades. 1861–1865. And, From Wakarusa to Appomattox, a Military Anagraph* (St. Louis, MO: Bryan, Brand, 1879), 266–267.

12   Ibid.

13   Andrews, *Campaign of Mobile*, 221.

14   *ORA*, Series I, vol. 49, pt. 2, 305.

15   Boyce, *1st Missouri*, 221.

16   "Mobile Expedition," *New Orleans (LA) Times-Democrat*, 6.

17 Joel K. Emmet went on to become a famous stage actor. Emmet gained the nickname "Our Fritz" from the famous role in the play *Fritz, Our Cousin German*. "Departed Stage Favorites," *The Illustrated American 7* (May 23, 1891): 401; "Mobile Expedition," *New Orleans (LA) Times-Democrat*, 6.

18 "Bounds and Bounds," *Methodist Minister*, 19.

19 *ORA*, Series I, vol. 49, pt. 1, 287, 289–290; Chapman, "Dear Parents."

20 Andrews, *Campaign of Mobile*, 201; O'Brien, *Last Stand*, 199.

21 Sperry, *33rd Iowa*, 152–153.

22 Ibid, 201.

23 "Beeves" is an archaic plural term referring to cattle. "Mobile Expedition," *New Orleans (LA) Times-Democrat*, 6.

24 Johnson, "In Camp and Field," 7.

25 "Fighting Them Over," *Washington (DC) National Tribune*, February 25, 1865, 3.

26 "Capture of Fort Blakeley," *Washington (DC) National Tribune*, 457–458; Musser, *Soldier Boy*, 201.

27 Hart, "Letters."

28 Chamberlin, *Corps d'Afrique*, 110.

29 Allen, "Operations Against the City of Mobile," 86; Smith, *Thomas Kilby Smith*, 383–384.

30 Ibid; *ORA*, Series I, vol. 49, pt. 1, 202.

31 "Fall of Mobile," *Canyon City (TX) News*, February 16, 1906, 1.

32 Hart, "Letters"; *ORA*, Series I, vol. 49, pt. 1, 202.

33 Hart, "Letters"; *ORA*, Series I, vol. 49, pt. 1, 202.

34 Boyce, *1st Missouri*, 219.

35 *ORA*, Series I, vol. 49, pt. 1, 202.

36 Wiley, *Civil War Diary*, 151; Marshall, *Eighty-Third Ohio*, 166; Hart, "Letters"; "Civil War Journal of James B. Lockney WIS. 28th Regiment, Co. G," James R. Shirey, accessed October 25, 2014, http://jshirey.brinkster.net/CivilWar/.

37 Dunn, *Diary*, 5.

38 *ORA*, Series I, vol. 49, pt. 2, 311.

39 Andrews, *Campaign of Mobile*, 220.

40 Dunn, *Diary*, 5.

41 "Souvenirs of the War," *New Orleans (LA) Daily Crescent*, 4.

42 Liddell and Hughes, *Liddell's Record*, 195–196.

43 Taylor, *Destruction and Reconstruction*, 221.

44 Andrews, *Campaign of Mobile*, 224.

45 Hill, "Last Battle," 190.

46 Andrews, *Campaign of Mobile*, 224; "Souvenirs of the War," *New Orleans (LA) Daily Crescent*, 4.

47 Maury, "Defense of Spanish Fort," 134.

48 Sweetman, "Capture of Blakeley," 1; Marshall, *Eighty-Third Ohio*, 166; Stephenson, *Civil War Memoir*, 368.

Chapter 12

1 Andrews, *Campaign of Mobile*, 223; "Souvenirs of the War," *New Orleans (LA) Daily Crescent*, 4; Michael Fitzgerald, "From Unionists to Scalawags: Elite Dissent in Civil War Mobile," *Alabama Review* 55, no. 2 (2002): 106.

2 Pillans, "Diary."

3 Jones and Pulcrano, *History of the Eighteenth Alabama*, 71; Dabney H. Maury, "My Dear General," History Museum of Mobile, Mobile, AL.

4 Andrews, *Campaign of Mobile*, 223; "Souvenirs of the War," *New Orleans (LA) Daily Crescent*, 4; Fitzgerald, "From Unionists to Scalawags," 106.

5 Andrews, *Campaign of Mobile*, 164; "Civil War Journal of James B. Lockney."

6 *ORA*, Series 1, vol. 49, pt. 2, 1226 (emphasis in the original).

7 William Cato and Judge R. C. Beckett, "A Sketch of the career of Company B Armistead's Cavalry Regiment," *The Mississippi Historical Society*, vol. 8, 32–50.

8 Ibid; Taylor, *Destruction and Reconstruction*, 222; Maury, "Defense of Spanish Fort," 136; Stephenson, *Civil War Memoir*, 371; Daniel Greary, "Diary," 1865, Doy Leale McCall Rare Book and Manuscript Library, University of South Alabama, Mobile, AL, 2; Spence, "Last Fight," 7; "Civil War Journal of James B. Lockney"; Beckett, "Company B," 32–50; Allen, "Operations Against the City of Mobile," 70.

9 Waring-Harrison, *Journal*, 13–14.

10 Brooks, "War Memories."

11 B. B. Cox, "Mobilian Tells of this City in Civil War Days," *Mobile (AL) Press Register*, November 1, 1914, 5A.

12 Napier Bartlett, *Military Record of Louisiana* (Baton Rouge: Louisiana State University Press, 1964), 28.

13 William Rix, *Incidents of Life in a Southern City During the War: A Series of Sketches Written for the Rutland Herald* (Rutland, VT: n.p., 1880), 19–21.

14 Ibid.

15 Ibid; *ORA,* Series 1, vol. 49, pt. 2, 1227, 1231, 1241; "Disgraceful," *Mobile (AL) Daily News*, April 13, 1865.

16 Spence, "Last Fight," 7.

17 *ORA*, Series 1, vol. 49, pt. 2, 1226–1227; Spence, "Last Fight," 7.

18 *ORA*, Series 1, vol. 49, pt. 2, 1226–1227 (emphasis in the original).

19 Maury, "Defense of Mobile," 3.

20 Wiley, *Civil War Diary*, 152; Still, *Iron Afloat*, 224–226; Scharf, *History of the Confederate States Navy*, 595; David Smithweck, *In Search of the CSS Huntsville and CSS Tuscaloosa* (Mobile, AL: David M. Smithweck, 2016), 60–61; Cameron, "Battles Opposite Mobile," 306.

21 Cameron, "Battles Opposite Mobile," 306.

22 Maury, "Defense of Mobile," 10; "Souvenirs of the War," *New Orleans (LA) Daily Crescent*, 4.

23 Liddell and Hughes, *Liddell's Record*, 195.

24 Andrews, *Campaign of Mobile*, 228.

25 Pillans, "Diary."

26 Andrews, *Campaign of Mobile*, 227, 229–230; Maury, "Defense of Spanish Fort," 131.

27 Maury, "Defense of Spanish Fort," 131.

28 Ibid.

29 *ORA*, Series 1, vol. 49, pt. 1, 98; *ORA*, Series 1, vol. 49, pt. 2, 334.

30 *ORA*, Series 1, vol. 49, pt. 1, 98; *ORA*, Series 1, vol. 49, pt. 2, 334.

31 *ORA*, Series 1, vol. 49, pt. 1, 98; *ORA*, Series 1, vol. 49, pt. 2, 334.

32 "Fighting Them Over," *Washington (DC) National Tribune*, 3.

33 Andrews, *Campaign of Mobile*, 230.

34 Maury, "Defense of Mobile," 7.

35 *ORA,* Series 1, vol. 49, pt. 2, 383.

36 Ann Quigley, "The Diary of Ann Quigley," *Gulf Coast Historical Review* 4, no. 2 (Spring 1989): 89–98.

37 Pillans, "Diary."

38 Little River Bridge, Eliska, nd Claiborne are near Monroeville, Alabama. *ORA*, Series 1, vol. 49, pt. 1, 98; *ORA*, Series 1, vol. 49, pt. 2, 364, 1250.

39   Lucas brought most of his command except the 31st Massachusetts Mounted Infantry. *ORA*, Series 1, vol. 49, pt. 1, 98.

40   *ORA*, Series 1, vol. 49, pt. 1, 98; *ORA*, Series 1, vol. 49, pt. 2, 364, 1250.

41   *ORA*, Series 1, vol. 49, pt. 2, 1226.

42   *ORA*, Series 1, vol. 49, pt. 1, 98; *ORA*, Series 1, vol. 49, pt. 2, 364, 1250.

43   *ORA*, Series 1, vol. 49, pt. 1, 98; *ORA*, Series 1, vol. 49, pt. 2, 364, 1250.

44   Bert Blackmon, "Captain T. C. English's Unusual Family Relationship," in *Military Order of Stars & Bars* (Mobile, AL, 2003), 37.

45   *ORA*, Series 1, vol. 49, pt. 1, 373–374.

46   "Survivor of Final Civil War Battles Tells of Heroism of Confederate Men," *Mobile Press Register*, January 27, 1913.

47   *ORA*, Series 1, vol. 49, pt. 1, 373–374.

48   *ORA*, Series 1, vol. 49, pt. 1, 307; Andrews, *Campaign of Mobile*, 239–240.

49   *ORA*, Series 1, vol. 49, pt. 1, 307; Andrews, *Campaign of Mobile*, 239–240.

50   Taylor, *Destruction and Reconstruction*, 222; Maury, "Defense of Spanish Fort," 136; Stephenson, *Civil War Memoir*, 371; Greary, "Diary," 2; Spence, "Last Fight," 7; "Civil War Journal of James B. Lockney"; Beckett, "Company B," 32–50; Allen, "Operations Against the City of Mobile," 70.

51   Rix, *Incidents of Life*, 22.

52   Pillans, "Diary"; William Fulton, Personal Letter, April 12, 1865, Mobile Historic Preservation Society, Norman Nicholson Collection, Mobile, AL.

53   Waring-Harrison, *Journal*, 29–30.

54   *ORA*, Series 1, vol. 49, pt. 2, 1226.

55   "Depredations," *Mobile (AL) Evening Telegraph*.

56   Schmandt and Schulte, *Diary of Spring Hill College*.

57   Spence, "Last Fight," 7; *ORA,* Series 1, vol. 49, pt. 1, 348–349; Fitzgerald, "From Unionists to Scalawags," 118.

58   Cox, "Mobilian Tells," 5A.

59   Waring-Harrison, *Journal*, 29–30; "Disgraceful," *Mobile (AL) Daily News*.

60   Rix, *Incidents of Life*, 22–23.

61   Waring-Harrison, *Journal*, 29–30; "Disgraceful," *Mobile (AL) Daily News*.

62   *ORA*, Series 1, vol. 49, pt. 1, 859, 1050, 1052.

63   William Rix, *Incidents of Life*, 19–21.

64   *ORA*, Series 1, vol. 49, pt. 2, 1226 (emphasis in the original).

65   *ORA,* Series 1, vol. 49, pt. 1, 907.

66   Rix, *Incidents of Life*, 20–21; Mobley, "Siege of Mobile," 259; Spence, "Last Fight," 7.

67   Maury, "My Dear General."

68   Richard Taylor, "The Last Confederate Surrender," *Southern Historical Society Papers* 3 (March 1877): 155–158.

69   Greary, "Diary," 2–3.

70   Taylor, "Last Confederate Surrender," 155–158.

71   Ibid.

72   James H. Hutchisson, "Letter to Sis," Above Bladen, AL, April 13, 1865, Mobile Historic Preservation Society, Norman Nicholson Collection, Mobile, AL.

73   Jones and Pulcrano, *History of the Eighteenth Alabama*, 72.

Chapter 13

1   *ORA*, Series 1, vol. 49, pt. 2, 314; "Important from Mobile Bay," *New Orleans (LA) Times-Picayune*, April 11, 1865, 1.

2 "Spanish Fort, Alabama," *Cincinnati (OH) Daily Commercial*, April 9, 1865; "Week of Victory," *Nashville (TN) Daily Union*, 1; *ORA*, Series 1, vol. 49, pt. 2, 314.

3 *ORA*, Series 1, vol. 49, pt. 2, 314.

4 Maury, "My Dear General."

5 Benedict, a Medal of Honor winner at Gettysburg, was appointed Military Historian for Vermont. He was not present at the Mobile campaign. George Grenville Benedict, *History of the 7th Regiment Vermont Volunteers* (Burlington, VT: Free Press Association, 1891), 72–73; *ORA*, Series 1, vol. 49, pt. 1, 98; Andrews, *Campaign of Mobile*, 223; Taylor, *Destruction and Reconstruction*, 222.

6 Sperry, *33rd Iowa*, 153.

7 Ibid.

8 *ORA*, Series 1, vol. 49, pt. 1, 228.

9 Starke's Landing was located in present-day Daphne, Alabama. *ORA*, Series 1, vol. 49, pt. 1, 98, 143, 171, 175, 179; Wiley, *Civil War Diary*, 151; Slack, *Slack's War*, 285.

10 William H. Bentley, *History of the 77th Illinois Volunteer Infantry, Sept. 2, 1862–July 10, 1865* (Peoria, IL: E. Hine, 1883), 344–345; Cobb, "The Siege of Mobile"; "Civil War Journal of James B. Lockney"; *ORA*, Series 1, vol. 49, pt. 2, 340.

11 Wiley, *Civil War Diary*, 152.

12 Slack, *Slack's War*, 285.

13 *Army and Navy Journal*, January 9, 1897, 318.

14 Sperry, *33rd Iowa*, 153–154.

15 The Magnolia race track for many years held nationally renowned racing events. The landing occurred below the location of the future Air Force, Brookley Field. Cox, "Mobilian Tells," 5A; Caldwell Delaney, *The Story of Mobile* (Mobile, AL: HB Publications, 1953), 142.

16 Slack, *Slack's War*, 285; Spence, "Last Fight," 7; *ORA*, Series 1, vol. 49, pt. 1, 143.

17 Slack, *Slack's War*, 285.

18 *ORA*, Series 1, vol. 49, pt. 1, 179; Wiley, *Civil War Diary*, 152.

19 Wiley, *Civil War Diary*, 152.

20 Fulton, Letter; *New York Herald*, April 30, 1865; *Mobile (AL) Morning News*, May 11, 1865; Fitzgerald, "From Unionists to Scalawags," 118; Slack, *Slack's War*, 285; Delaney, *Story of Mobile*, 142; Charles Robson, *Representative Men of the South* (Philadelphia, PA: C. Robson, 1880), 330; Peggy Johnson, "Fall of Mobile Viewed Through Eyes of Youth," *Mobile (AL) Press Register*, November 27, 1960, 13.

21 *ORA*, Series 1, vol. 49 pt. 2, 6, 349; *ORA*, Series 1, vol. 49, pt. 1, 174–175.

22 Bentley, *77th Illinois*, 344–345.

23 Wiley, *Civil War Diary*, 152; "Civil War Journal of James B. Lockney"; "Adjutant General's Report," *8th Infantry Regiment Three Years' Service. Report of the Adjutant General of the State of Illinois*, vol. 1, 1900, revised by Brigadier General J. N. Reese, 1900, accessed December 28, 2014, http://www.civilwarindex.com/armyil/rosters/8th_il_infantry_3years_roster.pdf.

24 Pillans, "Diary."

25 Cox, "Mobilian Tells," 5A.

26 Ambrose S. Wight, "The Flag first hoisted at Mobile," *The Century Illustrated Monthly Magazine* (November 1890): 156.

27 Porter, *Naval History of the Civil War*, 782; Truman, "Campaign in Alabama."

28 Fulton, Letter.

29 Cobb, "The Siege of Mobile"; "General Orders No. 1," *Mobile (AL) Daily News*, April 13, 1865, 1; George Leonard Andrews, Union Brigadier General, "Letter to My Dear Wife," April 14, 1865, Mobile Historic Preservation Society, Norman Nicholson Collection, Mobile, AL.

30 Cobb, "The Siege of Mobile."

31 "From New Orleans," *Cleveland (OH) Daily Leader*, April 24, 1865, 1.

32 *ORA*, Series 1, vol. 49, pt. 2, 340.

33 Rix, *Incidents of Life*, 23.

34 Cobb, "The Siege of Mobile."

35 Rix, *Incidents of Life*, 23.

36 "Mobile," *Philadelphia (PA) Inquirer*, 2.

37 Cumming, *Kate*, 285, 306–307.

38 Pillans, "Diary."

39 "Southern Girl in Mobile Describes 'Yankee' Entrance," *Mobile (AL) Daily News*, May 11, 1865.

40 Fulton, Letter (emphasis in the original).

41 *ORA*, Series 1, vol. 49, pt. 2, 340; Cobb, "Siege of Mobile."

42 Fulton, Letter.

43 Truman, "Campaign in Alabama," 1.

44 Ibid.

45 Smith, *Thomas Kilby Smith*, 389–390.

46 Benjamin C. Truman, "The South as It Is," *The New York Times*, November 2, 1865, 1.

47 "Department of the Gulf," 8.

48 Waring-Harrison, *Journal*, 30–31.

49 Pillans, "Diary."

50 Waring-Harrison, *Journal*, 29–30.

51 Ibid; Sperry, *33rd Iowa*, 155.

52 Slack, *Slack's War*, 285.

53 Riketta Schroeder, Mary Schroeder and H. A. Schroeder, "Letter from Riketta Schroeder to her son Gillist Schroeder," *Civil War Letters From 1861 to April 1865*, History Museum of Mobile, Mobile, AL, 54.

54 Cox, "Mobilian Tells," 5A.

55 Fulton, Letter.

56 "Disgraceful," *Mobile (AL) Daily News*, 1; Benedict, *7th Regiment Vermont*, 72–73; Cobb, "The Siege of Mobile."

57 Slack, *Slack's War*, 285.

58 "Disgraceful," *Mobile (AL) Daily News*; "From Mobile," *Cleveland (OH) Daily Leader*, 1; Truman, "Campaign in Alabama," 1.

59 "Disgraceful," *Mobile (AL) Daily News*, 1.

60 Rix, *Incidents of Life*, 24.

61 Beckett, "Company B," 48, 32–50.

62 Spence, "Last Fight," 7; *ORA*, Series 1, vol. 49, pt. 2, 174–175.

63 "In Arrest," *Mobile Daily News*, April 13, 1865, 1.

64 "General Orders," *Mobile (AL) Daily News*; Pillans, "Diary," 21.

65 *Mobile (AL) Daily News*, April 17, 1865.

66 H. K. Thatcher, "Fall of Mobile," *New Berne (NC) Times*, April 28, 1865.

67 "From Mobile," *New Orleans (LA) Times-Democrat*, May 7, 1865, 2.

68 *ORA*, Series 1, vol. 49, pt. 1, 340.

69 Ibid, 357, 367, 451.

70 Barney, *Recollections*, 311.

71 *Mobile Daily News*, April 13, 1865, 1.

72 *Mobile (AL) Daily News*, April 13, 1865, 1; Admiral H. R. Thatcher, "Afternoon Dispatches," *Lawrence Daily Kansas Tribune*, April 27, 1865, 6.

73 *ORA*, Series 1, vol. 49, pt. 2, 337.

74 Cobb, "The Siege of Mobile"; "George S. Smith Diary, 1862–1866," Civil War Diaries and Letters, 0017, DIYHistory | Transcribe, accessed July 22, 2016, https://diyhistory.lib.uiowa.edu/transcribe/222/21477.

75 Stockton, *War Diary*, 31; Hill, *Company E*, 31.

76 *ORA*, Series 1, vol. 49, pt. 2, 334.

77 Benjamin H. Grierson, *A Just and Righteous Cause: Benjamin H. Grierson's Civil War Memoir*, eds. Bruce J. Dinges and Shirley A. Leckie (Carbondale: Southern Illinois University Press, 2008), 330–331; *ORA*, Series 1, vol. 49, pt. 2, 334.

78 Sperry, *33rd Iowa*, 156; Andrews, *Campaign of Mobile*, 223; Ingersoll, *Iowa and the Rebellion*, 571.

79 Fry, "Capture of Mobile," 1 (emphasis in original).

80 Bentley, *77th Illinois*, 346–347.

81 Ibid.

82 "At Four Mile Creek," *Nashville (TN) Tennessean*, June 11, 1899, 11; Taylor, *Destruction and Reconstruction*, 222; Beckett, "Company B," 32–50; Fry, "Capture of Mobile," 1.

83 "At Four Mile Creek," 11; Taylor, *Destruction and Reconstruction*, 222; Beckett, "Company B," 32–50; Fry, "Capture of Mobile," 1.

84 Bentley, *77th Illinois*, 346–347; *ORA*, Series 1, vol. 49, pt. 1, 223–224.

85 Wiley, *Civil War Diary*, 153–154.

86 Benedict, *7th Regiment Vermont*, 73–74.

87 *ORA*, Series 1, vol. 49, pt. 1, 223–224; Wiley, *Civil War Diary*, 153–154.

88 "At Four Mile Creek," 11

89 Benedict, *7th Regiment Vermont*, 73–74; Spence, "Last Fight," 7.

90 *ORA*, Series 1, vol. 49, pt. 1, 223–224.

91 Bentley, *77th Illinois*, 346–347; *ORA*, Series 1, vol. 49, pt. 1, 223–224.

92 Spence, "Last Fight," 7.

93 Beckett, "Company B," 32–50.

94 Spence, "Last Fight," 7; *ORA*, Series 1, vol. 49, pt. 1, 223–224.

95 "Dash Above Mobile," *New Orleans (LA) Times Picayune*, April 18, 1865, 1.

96 Wiley, *Civil War Diary*, 153; *ORA*, Series 1, vol. 49, pt. 1, 223–224.

97 Wiley, *Civil War Diary*, 153; Spence, "Last Fight," 7; *ORA*, Series 1, vol. 49, pt. 1, 223–224.

Chapter 14

1 Liddell and Hughes, *Liddell's Record*, 197–198.

2 *ORA*, Series 1, vol. 49, pt. 2, 368; Wiley, *Civil War Diary*, 154.

3 Bentley, *77th Illinois*, 347.

4 Slack, *Slack's War*, 288.

5 "Civil War Journal of James B. Lockney."

6 Hill, *Company E*, 31.

7 Hubbard, *Fifth Minnesota Letters*, 70–71; Bradley, *Confederate Mail Carrier*, 226.

8 Stockton, *War Diary*, 30–31.

9 Tarleton, "Civil War Letters," 80; Chambers, *Blood & Sacrifice*," 220.

10 Tarleton, "Civil War Letters," 80.

11 Maury, Clement Stanford Watson Papers.

12 Jones and Pulcrano, *History of the Eighteenth Alabama*, 72.

13 Liddell and Hughes, *Liddell's Record*, 197–198; Cockrell, *Senator from Missouri*, 25; Tarrant, "Siege and Capture," 458; Boyce, *1st Missouri*, 231; Smith, *Thomas Kilby Smith*, 392; Terry G. Scriber and Theresa Arnold-Scriber, *Ship Island, Mississippi* (Jefferson, NC: McFarland, 2008), 68.

14 Liddell and Hughes, *Liddell's Record*, 197–198.

15 Tarrant, "After the Fall," 152.

16 Dallas Morton, "Private War Record of Dallas Morton," *Records of Confederate Veterans Alive 1924–26 Compiled by the Oneonta Chapter of the United Daughters of the Confederacy*, ed. Vallie W. Miles (Oneonta, AL: Oneonta Chapter of the United Daughters of the Confederacy, 1926).

17 Cleveland, "With the Third Missouri," 20; Boyce, *1st Missouri*, 229.

18 Boyce, *1st Missouri*, 229.

19 Ibid, 232.

20 Ibid, 229.

21 Morton, "Private War Record."

22 Boyce, *1st Missouri*, 229.

23 Ibid, 230–235.

24 Ibid.

25 Morton, *"Private War Record."*

26 Scriber and Arnold-Scriber, *Ship Island*, 68; James A. P. Braxley Narratives, Alabama Department of Archives and History, Montgomery, AL.

27 Scriber and Arnold-Scriber, *Ship Island*, 68–71; Braxley Narratives; William A. Gibson Narrative, Henry S. Halbert Papers, LPR147, Alabama Department of Archives and History, Montgomery, AL.

28 Zed H. Burns, *Ship Island and the Confederacy* (Hattiesburg: University and College Press of Mississippi, 1971), 31.

29 Boyce, *1st Missouri*, 230–235.

30 "Official," *Mobile (AL) Daily News*, April 15, 1865; "Rejoicing over the Surrender of Mobile and Lee," *New York Times*, April 21, 1865, 5; "The Department of the Gulf," *New York Times*; "Arrival of the Fung Shuey from New-Orleans. The News of Mr. Lincoln's Assassination. PAINFUL EXCITEMENT IN THE CITY. Interesting Items from Mobile. FROM MOBILE. MILITARY MATTERS. ORDER BY GEN. CANBY. THE OCCUPATION OF THE CITY," *New York Times*, April 30, 1865 (emphasis in original); Musser, *Soldier Boy*, 203.

31 Chambers, *Blood & Sacrifice*, 221–222.

32 Ibid.

33 *ORA*, Series 1, vol. 49, pt. 2, 455.

34 Taylor Papers; Jones and Pulcrano, *History of the Eighteenth Alabama*, 71.

35 Cameron, "Battles Opposite Mobile," 306.

36 *ORA*, Series 1, vol. 49, pt. 2, 1240.

37 *ORA*, Series 1, vol. 49, pt. 2, 1263–1264.

38 Slack, *Slack's War*, 292–294.

39 Hubbard, *Fifth Minnesota Letters*, 70–71.

40 *ORA*, Series 1, vol. 49, pt. 2, 410–411, 451; Wiley, *Civil War Diary*, 156; Schroeder, Schroeder and Schroeder, "Civil War Letters," 54–55.

41 Wiley, *Civil War Diary*, 156.

42 Musser, *Soldier Boy*, 203.

43 Slack, *Slack's War*, 292–294.

44 Hubbard, *Fifth Minnesota Letters*, 70–71.

45 Marshall, *Eighty-Third Ohio*, 167.

46 Musser, *Soldier Boy*, 203.

47 Taylor, *Destruction and Reconstruction*, 222–223.

48 Chambers, *Blood & Sacrifice*, 220.

49 *ORA*, Series 1, vol. 49, pt. 2, 531–532.

50 Slack, *Slack's War*, 292–294; Marshall, *Eighty-Third Ohio*, 167.

Chapter 15

1 J. E. Walmsley, "The Last Meeting of the Confederate Cabinet," *The Mississippi Valley Historical Review* 6, no. 3 (1919): 336–349.

2 *ORA*, Series 1, vol. 49, pt. 2, 322–323.

3 Ibid, 322–323.

4 Taylor, *Destruction and Reconstruction*, 220–223.

5 Chambers, *Blood & Sacrifice*, 222; Taylor Papers; *ORA*, Series 1, vol. 49, pt. 1, 1255; Dabney H. Maury, *Recollections of a Virginian in the Mexican, Indian, and Civil Wars* (New York: Charles Scribner's Sons, 1894), 61.

6 Maury, *Recollections*, 61.

7 Chambers, *Blood & Sacrifice*, 220–222.

8 "Important from Mobile," *New Orleans (LA) Times Picayune*, May 7, 1865, 3.

9 *ORA*, Series 1, vol. 49 pt. 2, 440.

10 Ibid, 448.

11 Ibid, 455.

12 Ibid, 481.

13 *ORA*, Series 1, vol. 49, pt. 2, 455; Porter, *Naval History of the Civil War*, 784.

14 *ORA*, Series 1, vol. 49, pt. 2, 455; Porter, *Naval History of the Civil War*, 784.

15 Taylor, *Destruction and Reconstruction*, 225.

16 *ORA*, Series 1, vol. 49, pt. 2, 1270.

17 Musser, *Soldier Boy*, 203.

18 "From the Mobile News," *New Berne (NC) Times*, May 5, 1865, 2.

19 *ORA*, Series 1, vol. 49, pt. 2, 576–577.

20 Ibid, 531–532, 558–559.

21 Ibid, 531–532, 1278–1279; Taylor, *Destruction and Reconstruction*, 225.

22 Taylor, "Last Confederate Surrender," 155–158.

23 *ORA*, vol. 49, pt. 2, 1275.

24 Ibid.

25 Ibid, 1278–1279.

26 Ibid.

27 Ibid.

28 Maury, *Recollections*, 61.

29 Taylor, "Last Confederate Surrender," 155–158.

30 Albert C. Danner, "*Albert Carey Danner Papers, 1843–1921*," Family Memorandum 1904, History Museum of Mobile, Mobile, AL, 23.

31 *ORA*, Series 1, vol. 49, pt. 2, 593–595.

32 "The Last Surrender," *Worthington (MN) Advance*, August 29, 1897, 3.

33 *Pittsburgh (PA) Post-Gazette*, March 17, 1915, 4; *ORA*, Series 1, vol. 49, pt. 2, 599; Delaney, *Story of Mobile*, 142.

34 "Details of the Surrender," *Janesville (WI) Daily Gazette*, May 15, 1865, 2.

35 "News From Gen. Canby," *New Orleans (LA) Times-Democrat*, May 5, 1865, 3.

36 "Important From Mobile," *New Orleans (LA) Times Picayune*, 3; "Last Surrender," *Worthington (MN) Advance*, 3.

37 "Last Surrender," *Worthington (MN) Advance*, 3.

38 Musser, *Soldier Boy*, 204–205.

39 "The Fall of Mobile and Defenses," 2.

40 "The Last Surrender," *Worthington (MN) Advance*, August 29, 1897, 3.

41 "The Final Capture of the Last Defenders of Mobile," *New Orleans (LA) Times-Picayune*, September 22, 1866; "The War Not Yet Ended," Winchester (TN) *Home Journal*, October 6, 1866, 2.

Chapter 16

1 "Dick Taylor's Order of Surrender—His Praise of Gen. Canby—His Advice to his Men," *Raleigh (NC) Daily Standard*, June 3, 1865, 2.

2 Taylor, *Destruction and Reconstruction*, 226, 228–229.

3 Taylor Papers (Terms of Capitulation, General Order, no. 54).

4 On April 13, General Canby himself arrived in Mobile, replacing General Maury. Ironically General Canby had taken General Maury's office before. He first took his place in New Mexico at the beginning of the war. Maury, *Recollections*, 37.

5 Taylor, "Last Confederate Surrender," 155–158.

6 "Dick Taylor's Order of Surrender," *Raleigh (NC) Daily Standard*, 2.

7 Bentley, *77th Illinois*, 349.

8 Jones and Pulcrano, *History of the Eighteenth Alabama*, 72–73.

9 *ORA*, Series 1, vol. 49, pt. 2, 643.

10 Jones and Pulcrano, *History of the Eighteenth Alabama*, 72–73.

11 Ibid.

12 Taylor, "Last Confederate Surrender," 155–158.

13 Porter, *Naval History of the Civil War*, 782; Cameron, "Battles Opposite Mobile," 305–308; Scharf, *History of the Confederate States Navy*, 596.

14 "Surrender of Rebel Naval Officers," *New Orleans (LA) Times-Democrat*, May 15, 1865, 6.

15 Cameron, "Battles Opposite Mobile," 305–308.

16 "Mobile Items," *New Orleans (LA) Times-Picayune*, May 13, 1865, 7.

17 *ORA*, Series 1, vol. 49, pt. 2, 659.

18 Jones and Pulcrano, *History of the Eighteenth Alabama*, 75.

19 *ORA*, Series 1, vol. 49, pt. 1, 319.

20 *ORA*, Series 1, vol. 49, pt. 2, 661.

21 Stephenson, *Civil War Memoir*, 371.

22 Chambers, *Blood & Sacrifice*, 224.

23 Stephenson, *Civil War Memoir*, 371.

24 Maury, *Recollections*, 64.

25 Chambers, *Blood and Sacrifice*, 222–223.

26 *ORA*, Series 1, vol. 49, pt. 2, 660; Musser, *Soldier Boy*, 207.

27 "Last Surrender," *Worthington (MN) Advance*, 3.

28 *ORA*, Series 1, vol. 49, pt. 2, 593, 610.

29 Cleveland, "With the Third Missouri," 20; Bradley, *Confederate Mail Carrier*, 226.

30 McLellan, "Vivid Reminiscences," 265.

31 Tarrant, "After the Fall," 152.

32 Bradley, *Confederate Mail Carrier*, 226.

33 "Return of Generals Canby and Osterhaus," *Cincinnati (OH) Enquirer*, May 19, 1865, 3.

34 Allen, "Operations Against the City of Mobile," 86.

35 Ibid; "Miscellaneous News," *Daily Milwaukee (WI) News*, May 28, 1865, 1; Musser, *Soldier Boy*, 206–207.

36 Slack, *Slack's War*, 296.

37 Smith, *Thomas Kilby Smith*, 392.

38 Ibid.

39 "Last Surrender," *Worthington (MN) Advance*, 3.

40 "At Four Mile Creek," *Nashville (TN) Tennessean*, 11.

41 Cobb, "The Siege of Mobile."

42 Author Unknown, "Dear Sister Julia," May 26, 1865, History Museum of Mobile, Mobile, AL.

43 Cobb, "The Siege of Mobile."

44 "The Mobile Explosion," *New Berne (NC) Times*, June 14, 1865, 2.

45 Smith, *Thomas Kilby Smith*, 403.

46 Johnson, "In Camp and Field," 7.

47 Slack, *Slack's War*, 301–302.

48 Cobb, "The Siege of Mobile."

49 *ORA*, Series 1, vol. 49, pt. 2, 907, 914; Slack, *Slack's War*, 301–302; "Mobile Explosion," *New Berne (NC) Times*, 2.

50 "Mobile Explosion," *New Berne (NC) Times*, 2.

51 Cobb, "The Siege of Mobile."

52 *ORA*, Series 1, vol. 49, pt. 2, 907, 914; Slack, *Slack's War*, 301–302; "Mobile Explosion," *New Berne (NC) Times*, 2.

53 Salmon P. Chase, "Journals 1829–1872," in *The Salmon P. Chase Papers*, vol. 1, ed. John Niven (Kent, OH: Kent State University Press, 1993), 562–563.

54 *ORA*, Series 1, vol. 49, pt. 2, 907, 914; Slack, *Slack's War*, 301–302; "Mobile Explosion," *New Berne (NC) Times*, 2.

Chapter 17

1   *The Cincinnati Enquirer*, "The Fall of Mobile and Defenses," April 21, 1865, 2.

2   "From Mobile," *Detroit (MI) Free Press*, 3; Andrews, *Campaign of Mobile*, 10.

3   Owen, *In Camp and Battle,* 413–415.

4   "Surrender of Rebel Naval Officers," *New Orleans (LA) Times-Democrat*, 6.

5   Albert C. Danner, "Albert Carey Danner, 1843–1921," Family Historical Memorandum, 1904, Mobile, AL.

6   "At Four Mile Creek," *Nashville (TN) Tennessean*, 11.

7   "The Fall of Mobile and Defenses," 2; Truman, "The South As It Is," 1; "Siege of Mobile," *New York Times*, 8.

8   *New York Times*, April 21, 1865, 8.

9   "Review of the Mobile Campaign," *Burlington (IA) Weekly Hawk-Eye,* 1.

10 *ORA*, Series 1, vol. 49, pt. 1, 104.

11 General Maury wrote an article offering his review of General C. C. Andrews's book *The Campaign for Mobile*. Maury, "Defense of Mobile," 6.

12 *ORN*, Series 1, vol. 21, 533–534; "Our New Orleans Correspondence," *New York Times*, 8.

13 "Review of the Mobile Campaign," *Burlington (IA) Weekly Hawk-Eye,* 1; "Telegraphic Dispatches," *Salem Weekly Oregon Statesman*, March 13, 1865, 1; "Yankee Accounts from Mobile," *Raleigh (NC) Daily Progress,* 2.

14 Hubbard, *Fifth Minnesota Letters*, 68.

15 *ORA*, Series 1, vol. 49, pt. 1, 309–310.

16 Comstock, *Diary*, 316.

17 Grant, *Memoirs*, 490.

18 Ibid, 492–493.

19 Walmsley, "The Last Meeting," 336–349; Taylor, *Destruction and Reconstruction*, 222.

20 Walter George Smith, *Life and Letters of Thomas Kilby Smith Brevet Major-General, United States Volunteers, 1820–1887* (New York: G. P. Putnam's Sons, 1898), 387; "Federals Move To Attack Forts Guarding Mobile," *The Washington Herald*, March 21, 1915, 23; United States War Department, *The War of Rebellion: A Compilation of the Official Records of the Union and Confederate Armies*, Series 1, vol. 45, pt. 2 (Washington, DC: Government Printing Office, 1897), 419–420.

Epilogue

1   Heyman, *Prudent Soldier*, 375–377, 382.

2   Ibid.

3 Taylor, *Destruction and Reconstruction*, 226, 228–229.

4 "Wreath for Canby after 58 years," *Woodville (MS) Republican*, June 2, 1923, 2.

5 Grant, *The Civil War Memoirs*, 492–493.

6 Wayne E. Scrivener, "Alabama Anniversaries," *Anniston (AL) Star*, April 13, 1935, 2.

7 Liddell and Hughes, *Liddell's Record*, 205.

8 "A Frightful Homicide," *Knoxville (TN) News Sentinel*, November 28, 1871, 1.

9 "Brutal Murder of Gen. Joseph Bailey," *New York Times*, April 5, 1867; "General Joseph Bailey—Hero of the Red River," accessed February 14, 2016, http://www.generaljosephbailey. com/josephbailey/.

10 "William Rainey Marshall," National Governors Association, accessed February 14, 2016, http://www.nga.org/cms/home/governors/past-governors-bios/page_minnesota/col2-content/ main-content-list/title_marshall_william.html.

11 "Hubbard, Lucius F. (1836–1913)," Minnesota Encyclopedia | MNopedia, accessed February 14, 2016, http://www.mnopedia.org/person/hubbard-lucius-f-1836-1913.

12 "Thomas Seay," 18th Century History—The Age of Reason and Change, accessed June 4, 2016, http://history1700s.com/index.php/articles/14-guest-authors/109-three-governors-from-greens-boro-alabama.html? showall=&start=3.

13 Diplomaticus, "'Old Garden Sass,'" 30.

14 Cockrell, *Senator from Missouri*, 24–25, 29, 84, 90–91.

15 Warner, *Generals in Gray*, 104–105.

16 McLellan, "Vivid Reminiscences," 25–26.

17 "Rinaker, John Irving: Biography," Biographical Directory of the United States Congress, accessed February 17, 2016, http://bioguide.congress.gov/scripts/biodisplay.pl? index=R000261; "McNulta, John: Biographical Information," Biographical Directory of the United States Congress, accessed February 21, 2016, http://bioguide.congress.gov/scripts/biodisplay.pl? index=M000587.

18 "A Former New Mexico Governor Served As Monrovia's Second Mayor," Monrovia, CA Patch, accessed February 17, 2016, http://patch.com/california/monrovia/a-former-new-mexico-governor-served-as-monrovias-second-mayor.

19 "Catron, Thomas Benton Biographical Information," accessed December 20, 2017, http://bioguide. congress.gov/scripts/biodisplay.pl? index=C000253.

20 Stephen J. Pyne, *Year of the Fires: The Story of the Great Fires of 1910* (New York: Viking, 2001), 228–235; "State Forests: General Andrews: Minnesota DNR," Minnesota Department of Natural Resources: Minnesota DNR, accessed February 28, 2016, http://www.dnr.state.mn.us/ state_forests/sft00020/index.html.

21 "Elijah Gates Dies," *Chillicothe (MO) Constitution-Tribune*, 3; "Former Missouri Man, Civil War Veteran, Dies," *Topeka (KS) Daily Capital*, March 8, 1915, 15.

22 Warner, *Generals in Gray*, 304–305.

23 Warner, *Generals in Gray*, 215.

24 Maury, *Recollections*, 243–244; Warner, *Generals in Gray*, 215–216.

25 Mary Bobbitt Townsend, *Yankee Warhorse: A Biography of Major General Peter Osterhaus* (Columbia: University of Missouri Press, 2010), 201–202, 212–213.

26 "Distinguished Dead," *New Orleans (LA) Times Picayune*, 3.

27 "Civil War Indiana Biographies: James Richard Slack," Civil War Indiana, accessed February 21, 2016, http://civilwarindiana.com/biographies/slack_james_richard.html.

28 "A. J. Smith," *The Annals of Iowa*, vol. 3 (1897), 76–77, Iowa Research Online | University of Iowa Research, accessed February 14, 2016, http://ir.uiowa.edu/cgi/viewcontent.cgi? article=2219&-context=annals-of-iowa; L. R. Hamersly, *Officers of the Army and Navy (Regular and Volunteer) Who Served in the Civil War* (Philadelphia, PA: L. R. Hamersly, 1894), 324.

29 Hamersly, *Officers*, 111.
30 "Colonel Philip Brent Spence," RootsWeb.com Home Page, accessed July 19, 2015, http://www. rootsweb.ancestry.com/~kycampbe/philipspence.htm; "Colonel Philip B. Spence," *Confederate Veterans Magazine*, 181; "Col. P. B. Spence," *Nashville (TN) Tennessean*, February 17, 1915, 7.
31 "Gen. Spurling Dies in Chicago," *Elgin (IL) Daily Courier*, August 27, 1906, 1.
32 "General Longstreet appointed General Bryan M. Thomas," *Six Mile (AL) Bibb Blade*, August 25, 1881, 2.
33 Conner, *Gordon Granger*, 216.
34 Lacey, "Steele," 438.
35 John H. Eicher and David J. Eicher, *Civil War High Commands* (Stanford, CA: Stanford University Press, 2001), 288.
36 Merriam, "Capture of Mobile," 247; *ORA*, Series 1, vol. 49, part 1, 313.
37 Jack S. Ballard, *Commander and Builder of Western Forts: The Life and Times of Major General Henry C. Merriam, 1862–1901* (College Station: Texas A & M University Press, 2012), 145–147.
38 Porter, *Naval History of the Civil War*, 780.
39 Bounds and Bounds, *Methodist Minister*, 23–25.
40 Boyce, *1st Missouri*, 224; Danner, "Papers"; Danner, *"Albert Carey Danner,"* 24.
41 Spencer C. Tucker, *The Civil War Naval Encyclopedia*, 1st ed. (Santa Barbara, CA: ABC-CLIO, 2010), 185–186; "Our South Atlantic Neighbors," *Charleston (SC) Daily News*, March 7, 1873, 1.
42 "Major Samuel H. Lockett"; "Samuel Lockett."
43 Warner, *Generals in Gray*, 300; R. A. Brock, "Confederate Generals," *Southern Historical Society Papers* 22 (1894): 65.
44 "Judge W. W. Wood Passes Away After Long Illness," *Belvidere (IL) Republican-Northwestern*, August 10, 1909, 1.
45 "Obituary," *Monmouth (IL) Daily Review*, November 12, 1902; "RootsWeb's WorldConnect Project: Pat Thomas Gedcom," WorldConnect Project – Connecting the World One GEDCOM at Time, accessed October 3, 2016, http://wc.rootsweb.ancestry.com/cgi-bin/igm. cgi? op=GET&db=tyrilla&id=I17917.
46 Musser, *Soldier Boy*, 6; Dean Podoll, "Charles O. Musser," Omaha.com, accessed August 1, 2016, http://dataomaha.com/civilwar/171/charles-o-musser.
47 "Robert Angelo Spink," Oshkosh Public Museum, accessed August 1, 2016, http://oshkosh. pastperfect-online.com/20004cgi/mweb.exe? request=field; fldseq=359109.
48 "Andrew Fuller Sperry (1839–1911)," Find A Grave, accessed August 1, 2016, http://www. findagrave.com/cgi-bin/fg.cgi? page=gr&GRid=31211891.
49 "M214 Chambers (William Pitt) Diary," University of Southern Mississippi Libraries, accessed August 1, 2016, http://lib.usm.edu/legacy/archives/m214.htm; Chambers, *Blood & Sacrifice*, 5.
50 Jones and Pulcrano, *History of the Eighteenth Alabama*.
51 Stephenson, *Civil War Memoir*, 390–394.

Appendix 1

1 Contemporary newspaper reports indicated that the Lady Slocomb was made at Selma. However, it was later determined that certain markings on the big gun prove it was built at the Tredegar Foundry in Virginia. "Lady Slocomb: The Silent Witness," *New Orleans (LA) Times Picayune*, 3; "Last Shot," *Los Angeles (CA) Herald*, 8; "The Lady Slocomb," *Mobile (AL) Daily Register*; Larry J. Daniel and Riley W. Gunter, *Confederate Cannon Foundries* (Union City, TN: Pioneer Press, 1977), 7.
2 "Last Shot," *Los Angeles (CA) Herald*, 8.
3 Donnie Barrett, "Lady Slocumb," *Spanish Fort Historical Society News Letter* 2, no. 2 (August 1996).

4   "A Shotgun Duel," *Mobile (AL) Daily Register*, October 16, 1891, 1.

5   "Capt. Thomas Brewer," *Confederate Veteran Magazine* (December 1914); "Deaths Here and Elsewhere," *Pittsburgh (PA) Dispatch*, October 23, 1891, 5.

6   "A Shotgun Duel," *Mobile (AL) Daily Register*, October 16, 1891, 1.

7   Department of Treasury Archives, "Letters Sent by the Miscellaneous Division ("EK" Series), 1887–1906," vol. 12, pp. 148, 170, 248, Record Group 56, National Archives at College Park, MD.

8   "A Shotgun Duel," *Mobile (AL) Daily Register,* 1.

9   "Dr. Seymour Bullock Slain," *Atlanta (GA) Constitution*, October 16, 1891, 1.

10 Ibid.

11 "Last Shot," *Los Angeles (CA) Herald,* 8; Barrett, "Lady Slocumb"; *Washington (DC) Evening Times*, 4; "Gleanings of General Interest from the Gulf City," *New Orleans (LA) Times-Picayune*, March 2, 1899.

12 *Washington (DC) Evening Times,* September 16, 1896, 4; "An Historic Cannon," *San Francisco (CA) Call*, November 26, 1896.

13 Department of Treasury, "Miscellaneous Division."

14 Charles Elihu Slocum, *A Short History of the Slocums, Slocumbs and Slocombs of America: Genealogical and Biographical: Embracing Eleven Generations of the First-Named Family, from 1637 to 1881: With Their Alliances and the Descendants in the Female Lines As Far As Ascertained* (Syracuse, NY: C. E. Slocum, 1882), 508–509; "Last Shot," *Los Angeles (CA) Herald,* 8; Barrett, "Lady Slocumb"; *Washington (DC) Evening Times*, 4; "Gleanings of General Interest from the Gulf City," *New Orleans (LA) Times-Picayune*, March 2, 1899.

15 "The Lady Slocomb," *Mobile (AL) Daily Register*, 3.

Appendix 2

1   "Dauphin Island Park and Beach Fort Gaines," Dauphin Island Park and Beach, accessed October 8, 2016, http://dauphinisland.org/fort-gaines/.

2   "Fort Morgan Alabama Historical Site Information," Fort Morgan Historic Site, accessed October 8, 2016, http://fort-morgan.org/.

3   Description of Fort McDermott courtesy of A. J. Dupree, Mobile, Alabama.

4   Andrews, *Campaign of Mobile*, 226.

5   *Welcome to Historic Blakeley State Park* (Spanish Fort, AL: Historic Blakeley State Park, n.d.).

Bibliography

Archives and Manuscript Collections

Abraham Lincoln Presidential Library, Springfield, IL. SC 1166, Manuscripts Dept.
Letter of Private William H. Peter, Company D, 122nd Illinois Infantry.
Alabama Department of Archives and History. Montgomery, AL.
James A. P. Braxley Narratives.
William A. Gibson Narrative, Henry S. Halbert Papers, LPR147.
Scott, David Marshall, Letter to Thomas M. Owen, September 24, 1910. 62nd Alabama Infantry File.
Auburn University Archives and Special Collections, Auburn, AL.
The Civil War Diary of Charles H. Snedeker, RG 844.
Danner, Albert C. "Albert Carey Danner, 1843–1921." Family Historical Memorandum, 1904, Mobile, AL.
Department of Treasury Archives. "Letters Sent by the Miscellaneous Division ("EK" Series), 1887–1906." Vol. 12, pp. 148, 170, 248. Record Group 56. National Archives at College Park, MD.
Depauw University Archives. Roy O. West Library, Greencastle, IN.
Elijah E. Edwards Civil War Journals. Vol. 3.
Dolph Briscoe Center for American History. University of Texas, Austin, TX.
"Diary of John Thomas, 1864–1865."
Doy Leale McCall Rare Book and Manuscript Library. University of South Alabama, Mobile, AL.
Greary, Daniel. Diary, 1865.
Lyons, Mark. "Letters," 1865.
History Museum of Mobile. Mobile, AL.
Baumer, Joseph. "Memories of War." (Date Unknown).
"Dear Sister Julia." (Author Unknown). May 26, 1865.
Hamilton, Thomas Alexander. "Statement of T. A. Hamilton." October 25, 1924, Mobile, AL.
Herndon, Thomas H. "My Dear Wife." Thomas Hoard Herndon Papers.
Maury, Dabney H. "My Dear General."
Pillans, Laura R. "Diary of Mrs. Laura Roberts Pillans, 11 July 1863–2 November 1865," Mobile, AL.
Schroeder, Riketta, Mary Schroeder and H. A. Schroeder. "Civil War Letters From 1861 to April 1865."
Indianapolis Historical Society, Indianapolis, IN.
John W. Schlagle Diary, 1865. Collection No. SC1313.
Louisiana Historical Association Collection. Manuscripts Collection 55, Louisiana Research Collection.
Howard-Tilton Memorial Library, Tulane University, New Orleans, LA.
Washington Artillery Papers.
Louisiana Research Collection. Tulane University, New Orleans, LA.
Brigadier General Randall Lee Gibson to Brigadier General St. John R. Liddell, Randall Lee

Gibson Papers, Manuscripts Collection 316.

Dabney Maury, Clement Stanford Watson Papers, Manuscript Collection 711.

Richard Taylor Papers. Manuscript Collection 40.

Minnesota Historical Society. St. Paul, MN.

Danielson, John. *History of Company G, of 7th Minnesota Volunteers, War of the Rebellion, August 12, 1862 – August 16, 1865.*

Gum-tree Mortar Barrel. Minnesota Historical Collections Database, 4225. H576, Accessed September 4, 2016.

John Nelson Papers, 1860–1865.

Mobile Historic Preservation Society. Norman Nicholson Collection. Mobile, AL.

Andrews, George Leonard, Union Brigadier General. "Letter to My Dear Wife." April 14, 1865, Mobile, AL.

Beverly, Frances. General E. R. S Canby in the "Frances Beverly Papers." Minnie Mitchell Archives.

Brooks, Mary E. "War Memories."

Chapman, Lieutenant Walter. "Dear Parents." April 11, 1865.

"Dearest Mary," Letter from officer aboard US Steamer *Sebago.* June 6, 1865.

Fulton, William. Personal letter. April 12, 1865.

Hart, Henry W. "Letters of Henry W. Hart, Second Connecticut Light Artillery, Second Division, XII Corps."

Hubbard, L. F. *L. F. Hubbard and the Fifth Minnesota Letters of a Union Volunteer.* Edited by N. B. Martin. San Francisco, CA: San Francisco State College, 1956.

Hutchisson, James H. "Letter to Sis." Above Bladen, AL. April 13, 1865.

Nye, Edward O. "The Diary of Edward O. Nye." From the Collection of Charles H. Hooper of the John Pelham Historical Association.

Ray, James L. "Soldier Remembers Mobile." Austin, TX, January 17, 1929.

Watson, James Thomas Washington. "Statement of My War Record."

National Park Service, Gulf Islands National Seashore. Florida District Library, Fort Pickens, FL.

Dunn, James M. *Diary of Private James M. Dunn, 97th Illinois Volunteer Infantry. Ca. March 31–August 9, 1865.* File # 1865-12.

Spring Hill College Archives. Mobile, AL.

Cornette, Andrew. *Father Cornette's Notes from the Annals of Spring Hill College.* 1872.

To Arms Antiques, Fairhope, AL.

Hunt, George P. "Letter to Miss Earnes." April 1, 1865.

Primary Sources: Books and Articles

Allen, Charles J. "Some Account and Recollections of the Operations Against the City of Mobile and Its Defences, 1864 and 1865." *Glimpses of the Nation's Struggle* (1887): 54–88.

Andrews, C. C. *History of the Campaign of Mobile.* New York: D. Van Nostrand, 1867.

Bailey, W. "The Star Company of Ector's Texas Brigade." *Confederate Veteran* 22 (1914): 404–405.

Baker, James H. (Tenth Minnesota Regiment). *Minnesota in the Civil and Indian Wars, 1861–1865. Vol. 1.* Whitefish, MT: Kessinger Legacy Reprints, 2012.

Barney, Chester. *Recollections of Field Service with the Twentieth Iowa Infantry Volunteers, or, What I Saw in the Army: Embracing Accounts of Marches, Battles, Sieges, and Skirmishes, in Missouri, Arkansas, Mississippi, Louisiana, Alabama, Florida, Texas, and Along the Northern Border of Mexico.* Davenport, IA: Printed for the author at the Gazette Job Rooms, 1865.

Barry, Robert L. "The Lookout Battery." *Confederate Veteran* 30 (1922): 385.

Bartlett, Napier. *Military Record of Louisiana.* Baton Rouge, LA: Louisiana State University Press, 1964.

Bartlett, Robert F. *Roster of the Ninety-Sixth, Ohio Volunteer Infantry: 1862 to 1865.* Columbus, OH: Hann & Adair, 1895.

Bayne, T. L. "Our Fallen Comrades." *Southern Historical Society Papers* 11 (1883): 328–330.

Beckett, R. C. (a.k.a. "T. C."). "A Sketch of the Career of Company B, Armistead's Cavalry Regiment." In *Publications of the Mississippi Historical Society*, Vol. 8, edited by Franklin Lafayette Riley. Oxford, MS: Mississippi Historical Society, 1905.

Benedict, George Grenville. *History of the 7th Regiment Vermont Volunteers.* Burlington, VT: Free Press Association, 1891.

Bentley, William H. *History of the 77th Illinois Volunteer Infantry, Sept. 2, 1862–July 10, 1865.* Peoria, IL: E. Hine, 1883.

Boyce, Joseph. *Captain Joseph Boyce and the 1st Missouri Infantry, C. S. A.* Edited by William C. Winter. St. Louis: University of Missouri Press, 2011.

Bradley, James. *The Confederate Mail Carrier, or, From Missouri to Arkansas Through Mississippi, Alabama, Georgia and Tennessee An Unwritten Leaf of the "Civil War."* Mexico, MO: J. Bradley, 1894.

Brock, R. A. "Confederate Generals." *Southern Historical Society Papers* 22 (1894): 65.

Cameron, William L. "The Battles Opposite Mobile." *Confederate Veteran* 23 (1915): 305.

Carlock, Chuck, and V. M. Owens. *History of the Tenth Texas Cavalry (Dismounted) Regiment, 1861–1865: "If We Ever Got Whipped, I Don't Recollect It."* N. Richland Hills, TX: Smithfield, 2001.

Carter, T. G. "That Charge at Spanish Fort." *Confederate Veteran* 13 (1906): 226.

Chamberlin, John N. *Captaining the Corps d'Afrique: The Civil War Letters of John Newton Chamberlin.* Edited by Jim Bisbee. Jefferson, NC: McFarland, 2016.

Chambers, William Pitt. *Blood & Sacrifice, The Civil War Journal of a Confederate Soldier.* Edited by Richard A. Baumgartner. Huntington, WV: Blue Acorn, 1994.

Chase, Salmon. "Journals 1829–1872." In *The Salmon P. Chase Papers*, Vol. 1. Edited by John Niven. Kent, OH: Kent State University Press, 1993.

Cleveland, Charles Boarman. "With the Third Missouri Regiment. Reminiscences of Charles Boarman Cleveland." *Confederate Veteran* 31 (1923): 18–20.

"Colonel Philip B. Spence." *Confederate Veterans Magazine* 23 (1915): 181.

Comstock, Cyrus B. *The Diary of Cyrus B. Comstock.* Edited by Marlin E. Sumner. Dayton, OH: Morningside House, 1987.

Cumming, Kate. *Kate: The Journal of a Confederate Nurse.* Edited by Richard Barksdale Harwell. Baton Rouge: Louisiana State University Press, 1959.

Davis, Eli. "That Hard Siege at Spanish Fort." *Confederate Veteran* 12 (1904): 591.

Davis, Jefferson. *The Rise and Fall of the Confederate Government*, Vol. 2. New York: T. Yoseloff, 1958.

Eggleston, Mrs. John Randolph. "The Women of the Confederacy." *Southern Historical Society Papers* 34 (1906): 191–193.

Evans, Augusta. "Augusta J. Evans on Secession." Edited by Marie Bankhead Owen. *Alabama Historical Quarterly* (Spring 1941): 65–66.

Gibson, Randall L. *Randall Lee Gibson Papers.* Baton Rouge, LA: Louisiana State University Archives, 1865.

Grant, Ulysses S. *The Civil War Memoirs of Ulysses S. Grant.* New York: Tom Doherty, 2002.

Green, Arthur E. *Mobile Confederates from Shiloh to Spanish Fort: The Story of the 21st Alabama Infantry Volunteers: 21st Alabama Infantry Volunteers CSA Abstracted Compiled Service Records.* Westminster, MD: Heritage Books, 2012.

Grierson, Benjamin H. *A Just and Righteous Cause: Benjamin H. Grierson's Civil War Memoir.* Edited by Bruce J. Dinges and Shirley A. Leckie. Carbondale: Southern Illinois University Press, 2008.

Hawley, Thomas S. *"This Terrible Struggle for Life": The Civil War Letters of a Union Regimental Surgeon.* Edited by Dennis W. Belcher. Jefferson, NC: McFarland, 2012.

Hill, A. J. *History of the Company E, of the Sixth Minnesota Regiment of Volunteer Infantry*. Contributed by Charles J. Stees. Bethesda, MD: University Publications of America, 1993.

Hill, Charles S. "The Last Battle of the War – Recollections of the Mobile Campaign." *War Papers and Personal Reminiscences 1861–1865*. [Read before the Commandery of the State of Missouri, Military Order of the Loyal Legion of the United States.] Vol. 1. St. Louis, MO: Becktold, 1892.

Hubbard, Lucius F. "Civil War Papers." [Read before the Minnesota Historical Society Executive Council] St. Paul, MN: Minnesota Historical Society, 1907.

Hunt, Thomas Jefferson. *Observations of T. J. Hunt in the Civil War: A Narrative of the Military Life of T. J. Hunt in the Sioux Indian and Civil Wars of 1862–1865*. [Transcript]. n.d.

Ingersoll, Lurton Dunham. *Iowa and the Rebellion: A History of the Troops Furnished by the State of Iowa to the Volunteer Armies of the Union, Which Conquered the Great Southern Rebellion of 1861–5*. Philadelphia, PA: J. B. Lippincott, 1867.

Johnson, Charles W. "Narrative of the Sixth Minnesota." In *Minnesota in the Civil and Indian Wars, 1861–1865*. Salem, MA: Higginson, 1866.

Jones, Edgar W., and C. David A. Pulcrano. *History of the Eighteenth Alabama Infantry Regiment*. Birmingham, AL: C. D. A. Pulcrano, 1994.

Lacey, John F. "Major-General Frederick Steele." In *Annals of Iowa*. Des Moines: Iowa Division of Historical Museum and Archives, 1897.

Liddell, St. John Richardson, and Nathaniel Cheairs Hughes. *Liddell's Record*. Baton Rouge: Louisiana State University Press, 1997.

Little, George, and James Robert Maxwell. *A History of Lumsden's Battery, C. S. A.* Tuscaloosa, AL: The Echo Library, 1905.

LittleJohn, E. G. "Company G, 10th Texas Cavalry." *Confederate Veteran* 12 (1893–1932): 490.

Macy, William. "The Civil War Diary of William Macy." *Indiana Magazine of History* 60, no. 2 (1934): 195.

Marshall, Thomas B. *History of the Eighty-Third Ohio Volunteer Infantry*. Cincinnati, OH: The Eighty-Third Ohio Volunteer Infantry Association, 1912.

Maury, Dabney H. "The Defense of Mobile in 1865." *Southern Historical Society Papers* (September 1877): 6.

——. "Defense of Spanish Fort." *Southern Historical Society Papers* 39 (1914): 130–136.

——. "How the Confederacy Changed Naval Warfare." *Southern Historical Papers* 22 (1894): 75–81.

——. *Recollections of a Virginian in the Mexican, Indian and Civil Wars*. New York: Charles Scribner's Sons, 1894.

McLellan, Alden. "Vivid Reminiscences of War Times." *Confederate Veteran* 14 (1906): 264–266.

Mconaughy, N. T. "Gallant Col. William E. Burnett." *Confederate Veteran* 17 (1909): 399.

Memorial Addresses on the Life and Character of Thomas H. Herndon (a Representative from Alabama): Delivered in the House of Representatives and in the Senate, 48th Congress, First Session. Washington, DC: Government Printing Office, 1884.

Merriam, Henry C. "The Capture of Mobile." *War Papers, Read Before the Commandery of the State of Maine Military Order of the Loyal Legion of the United States* 3 (1908): 230–250.

Miller, Edward G., and W. J. Lemke, editor. *Captain Edward Gee Miller of the 20th Wisconsin*. Fayetteville, AR: Washington County Historical Society, 1960.

Minnesota in the Civil and Indian Wars, 1861–1865. Salem, MA: Higginson Book Co., 1994.

Musser, Charles O. *Soldier Boy: The Civil War Letters of Charles O. Musser, 29th Iowa*. Edited by Barry Popchock. Iowa City: University of Iowa Press, 1995.

Newton, James K. "The Siege of Mobile." *Alabama Historical Quarterly* 20 (1958): 595–600.

Owen, William Miller. *In Camp and Battle with the Washington Artillery of New Orleans: A Narrative of Events During the Late War from Bull Run to Appomattox and Spanish Fort*. Boston: Ticknor, 1885.

Palfrey, John C. "The Capture of Mobile, 1865." In *The Mississippi Valley, Tennessee, Georgia, Alabama, 1861–1864*, 8th ed. Boston, MA: The Military Historical Society of Massachusetts, 1910.

Patrick, Robert. *Reluctant Rebel: The Secret Diary of Robert Patrick, 1861–1865.* Edited by F. Jay Taylor. Baton Rouge: Louisiana State University Press, 1996.

Quigley, Ann. "The Diary of Ann Quigley." *Gulf Coast Historical Review* 4, no. 2 (Spring 1989): 89–98.

Rains, G. J. "Torpedoes." *Southern Historical Papers* 3 (1877): 255–260.

Rix, William. *Incidents of Life in a Southern City During the War: A Series of Sketches Written for the Rutland Herald.* Rutland, VT: n.p., 1880.

Russell, William Howard. "Recollections of the Civil War." *North American Review* 166, no. 497 (April 1898), 491–502.

Schmandt, Raymond, and Josephine H. Schulte, eds. *A Civil War Diary: The Diary of Spring Hill College Between the Years 1860–1865.* Mobile, AL: Spring Hill College Press, 1892.

Scott, Milo Washington. "Diary of Pvt. Milo Washington Scott." In *Confederate Reminiscences and Letters 1861–1865.* Vol. 23. Cartersville, GA: Georgia Division United Daughters of the Confederacy, 2007.

Slack, James R. *Slack's War: Selected Civil War Letters of General James R. Slack, 47th Indiana Volunteer Infantry, to His Wife, Ann, 1862–1865.* Edited by David Williamson. Jefferson, NC: McFarland, 2012.

Smith, Sidney A., and C. Carter Smith Jr., eds. *Mobile: 1861–1865.* Chicago, IL: Wyvern Press of S. F. E., 1964.

Smith, Walter George. *Life and Letters of Thomas Kilby Smith Brevet Major-General, United States Volunteers, 1820–1887.* New York: G. P. Putnam's Sons, 1898.

Sperry, A. F. *History of the 33rd Iowa Infantry Volunteer Regiment.* Edited by Gregory J. W. Urwin and Cathy Kunzinger Urwin. Fayetteville: University of Arkansas Press, 1999.

Stephenson, Philip Daingerfield. *The Civil War Memoir of Philip Daingerfield Stephenson, D. D.: Private, Company K, 13th Arkansas Volunteer Infantry, and Loader, Piece No. 4, 5th Company, Washington Artillery, Army of Tennessee, CSA.* Edited by Nathaniel Cheairs Hughes. Conway, AR: UCA Press, 1995.

Stockton, Joseph. *War Diary of Brevet Brigadier General Joseph Stockton.* Chicago, IL: John T. Stockton, 1910.

Tarleton, Robert. "The Civil War Letters of Robert Tarleton." *Alabama Historical Quarterly* 32 (Spring-Summer 1970): 51–81.

Tarrant, E. W. "The Siege and Capture of Fort Blakely." *Confederate Veteran* 23 (1915): 457–458.

——. "After the Fall of Fort Blakely." *Confederate Veteran* 25 (1917): 152.

Taylor, J. Gordon. "From Knoxville to Mobile Bay." *Sketches of War History* 6 (1908): 47–62.

Taylor, Richard. *Destruction and Reconstruction: Personal Experiences of the Late War.* New York: Longmans, Green, 1955.

——. "The Last Confederate Surrender." *Southern Historical Society Papers* 3 (March 1877): 155–158.

Todhunter, Ryland. "Ector's Texas Brigade." *Confederate Veteran* 7 (1899): 312.

United States War Department. *A Compilation of the Official Records of the Union and Confederate Navies in the War of the Rebellion [ORN].* Washington, DC: Government Printing Office, 1894.

United States War Department. *The War of Rebellion: Official Records of the Union and Confederate Armies [ORA].* Washington, DC: Government Printing Office, 1897.

United States War Department. Office of Commissary General of Prisoners. *Selected Records of the War Department Relating to Confederate Prisoners of War, 1861–65.* Roll 136, Vol. 406–408, Washington: National Archives, National Archives and Records Service, General Services Administration, 1965.

Walker, T. J. "Reminiscences of the Civil War." In *Confederate Reminiscences and Letters 1861–1865.* Vol. 20. Cartersville, GA: Georgia Division United Daughters of the Confederacy, 2003.

Waring-Harrison, Mary Douglas. *Miss Waring's Journal: 1863–1865.* Edited by Thad Holt. Chicago, IL: Wyvern Press of S. F. E., 1964.

Waterman, George S. "Afloat-Afield-Afloat. Notable Events of the Civil War." *Confederate Veteran* 12 (1899): 490–492.

——. "Afloat-Afield-Afloat. Notable Events of the Civil War." *Confederate Veteran* 13 (1900): 21–24.

——. "Afloat-Afield-Afloat. Notable Events of the Civil War." *Confederate Veteran* 14 (1906): 264–266.

Welcome to Historic Blakeley State Park. Spanish Fort, AL: Historic Blakeley State Park, n.d.

Wight, Ambrose S. "The Flag first hoisted at Mobile." *The Century Illustrated Monthly Magazine* (November 1890): 156.

Wiley, William. *The Civil War Diary of a Common Soldier: William Wiley of the 77th Illinois Infantry.* Edited by Terrence J. Winschel. Baton Rouge: Louisiana State University Press, 2001.

Williams, James M. "Post Civil War Mobile: The Letters of James M. Williams, May–September, 1865." *The Alabama Historical Quarterly* 38 (Fall-Winter 1970): 186–198.

——. *From That Terrible Field: Civil War Letters of James M. Williams, Twenty-First Alabama Infantry Volunteers.* Edited by John Kent Folmar. University: University of Alabama Press, 1981.

Wolf, Otto. *Letter of Otto Wolf, 117th Illinois Infantry, Second Brigade Second Division, XVI Corps.* April 12, 1865. (From the collection of his grandson, Olin W. Kriege, Springfield, IL, April 1976.)

Wood, Wales W. *A History of the Ninety-Fifth Regiment, Illinois Infantry Volunteers: From Its Organization in the Fall of 1862, Until Its Final Discharge from the United States Service, in 1865.* Chicago, IL: Tribune Book and Job Print Office, 1865.

Secondary Sources: Books and Articles

Ballard, Jack S. *Commander and Builder of Western Forts: The Life and Times of Major General Henry C. Merriam, 1862–1901.* College Station: Texas A & M University Press, 2012.

Barrett, Donnie. "Lady Slocumb." *Spanish Fort Historical Society News Letter* 2, no. 2 (August 1996): n.p.

Bergeron, Arthur W. *Confederate Mobile.* Jackson: University Press of Mississippi, 1991.

——. "The Twenty-Second Louisiana Consolidated Infantry in the Defense of Mobile, 1864–1865." *Alabama Historical Quarterly* 38 (Fall 1976): 204–213.

Bevier, R. S. *History of the First and Second Missouri Confederate Brigades. 1861–1865. And, From Wakarusa to Appomattox, a Military Anagraph.* St. Louis, MO: Bryan, Brand, 1879.

Blackmon, Bert. "Captain T. C. English's Unusual Family Relationship." In *Military Order of Stars & Bars,* 37. Mobile, AL, 2003.

Bounds, Ben H. and Charles L. Bounds. *Ben H. Bounds, 1840–1911, Methodist Minister and Prominent Mason: Biography and Highlights from His Early Life and Civil War Memoirs.* Columbus, OH: J. O. Moore, 1962.

Boyle, Charles J. *Gleanings from the Spring Hill College Archives.* Mobile, AL: Friends of Spring Hill College Library, 2004.

——. *Twice Remembered: Moments in the History of Spring Hill College.* Mobile, AL: Friends of the Spring Hill College Library, 1993.

Burns, Zed H. *Ship Island and the Confederacy.* Hattiesburg: University and College Press of Mississippi, 1971.

Campbell, R. Thomas, *Hunters of the Night: Confederate Torpedo Boats in the War Between the States.* Shippensburg, PA: Burd Street Publishing, 2000.

"Capt. Thomas Brewer." *Confederate Veteran Magazine* (December 1914): n.p.

Cockrell, Francis Marion. *The Senator from Missouri. The Life and Times of Francis Marion Cockrell. New York:* Exposition Press, 1962.

Confederate Military History Extended Edition. Vol. 7–Alabama. Wilmington, NC: Confederate, 1899.

Conner, Robert C. *General Gordon Granger: The Savior of Chickamauga and the Man Behind "Juneteenth."* Philadelphia, PA: Casemate, 2013.

Cooper, Edward S. *Traitors: The Secession Period, November 1860–July 1861.* Madison, NJ: Fairleigh Dickinson University Press, 2008.

Cortright, Vincent. "Last-Ditch Defenders at Mobile." *America's Civil War* 9, no. 6 (January 1997): 58.

Coulter, E. Merton. *The South During Reconstruction, 1865–1877.* Baton Rouge: Louisiana State University Press, 1947.

Daniel, Larry J., and Riley W. Gunter. *Confederate Cannon Foundries.* Union City, TN: Pioneer Press, 1977.

Delaney, Caldwell. *Madame Octavia Walton LeVert: The South's Most Famous Belle.* Mobile, AL: Historic Preservation Society, 1961.

——. *The Story of Mobile.* Mobile, AL: HB Publications, 1953.

"Departed Stage Favorites." *The Illustrated American 7* (May 1891): 401–402.

Dixon, Donald E. "Randall Lee Gibson." Master's thesis, Louisiana State University, 1971.

Eicher, John H., and David J. Eicher. *Civil War High Commands.* Stanford, CA: Stanford University Press, 2001.

Evans, Clement A. *Confederate Military History: A Library of Confederate States History.* Atlanta, GA: Confederate, 1899.

Farragut, Loyal. *The Life of David Glasgow Farragut, First Admiral of the United States Navy, Embodying His Journal and Letters.* New York: D. Appleton, 1879.

Fitzgerald, Michael. "From Unionists to Scalawags: Elite Dissent in Civil War Mobile." *Alabama Review* 55, no. 2 (2002): 106–121.

Friend, Jack. *West Wind, Flood Tide: The Battle of Mobile Bay.* Annapolis, MD: Naval Institute Press, 2004.

Gottschalk, Phil. *In Deadly Earnest: The History of the First Missouri Brigade, CSA.* Columbia: Missouri River Press, 1991.

Greeley, Horace. *The American Conflict: A History of the Great Rebellion in the United States of America, 1860–'65.* Hartford, CT: O. D. Case, 1866.

Hamersly, L. R. *Officers of the Army and Navy (Regular and Volunteer) Who Served in the Civil War.* Philadelphia, PA: L. R. Hamersly, 1894.

Hearn, Chester G. *Mobile Bay and the Mobile Campaign: The Last Great Battles of the Civil War.* Jefferson, NC: McFarland, 1993.

Hempstead, Fay. *Historical Review of Arkansas: Its Commerce, Industry and Modern Affairs.* 3rd ed. Chicago: Lewis, 1911.

Heyman, Max L. *Prudent Soldier: A Biography of Major General E. R. S. Canby, 1817–1873: His Military Service in the Indian Campaigns, in the Mexican War, in California, New Mexico, Utah, and Oregon; in the Civil War in the Trans-Mississippi West, and As Military Governor in the Post-War South.* Glendale, CA: Arthur H. Clark, 1959.

Hughes, Nathaniel Cheairs. *The Pride of the Confederate Artillery: The Washington Artillery in the Army of Tennessee* (Baton Rouge: Louisiana State University Press, 1997).

Johansson, Jane M. "Gibson's Louisiana Brigade During the 1864 Tennessee Campaign." *Tennessee Historical Quarterly* 64, no. 3 (Fall 2005):186–195.

Lash, Jeffery N. "A Yankee in Gray: Danville Leadbetter and the Defenses of Mobile Bay, 1861–1863." *Civil War History: A Journal of the Middle Period* 36, no. 3 (1991): 209.

Levine, Bruce C. *Confederate Emancipation: Southern Plans to Free and Arm Slaves During the Civil War.* Oxford: Oxford University Press, 2006.

Madaus, Howard Michael. *The Battle Flags of the Confederate Army of Tennessee.* Milwaukee, WI: Milwaukee Public Museum, 1976.

McPherson, James M. *For Cause and Comrades: Why Men Fought in the Civil War.* Oxford: Oxford University Press, 1997.

Military History Instructors Course. Fort Leavenworth, KS: Combat Studies Institute Press, n.d.

Mobley, Joe A. "The Siege of Mobile, August 1864–April 1865." *Alabama Historical Quarterly* 38 (Winter 1976): 250–270.

Morton, Dallas. *"Private War Record of Dallas Morton." Records of Confederate Veterans Alive 1924–26 Compiled by the Oneonta Chapter of the United Daughters of the Confederacy.* Edited by Vallie W. Miles. Oneonta, AL: Oneonta Chapter of the United Daughters of the Confederacy, 1926.

O'Brien, Sean Michael. *Mobile, 1865: Last Stand of the Confederacy.* Westport, CT: Praeger, 2001.

Palmer, Thomas Waverly. "Andrews, George William, and A. B.: 1900 Graduates With Titled Degrees." *A Register of the Officers and Students of the University of Alabama, 1831–1901.* Tuscaloosa, AL: University Press, 1901.

Parrish, T. Michael. *Richard Taylor: Soldier Prince of Dixie.* Chapel Hill: University of North Carolina Press, 1992.

Pearce, George F. *Pensacola During the Civil War: A Thorn in the Side of the Confederacy.* Gainesville: University Press of Florida, 2000.

Perry, Milton F. *Infernal Machines: The Story of Confederate Submarine and Mine Warfare.* Baton Rouge: Louisiana State University Press, 1985.

Porter, Admiral David D. *The Naval History of the Civil War.* New York: Sherman, 1886.

Pyne, Stephen J. *Year of the Fires: The Story of the Great Fires of 1910.* New York: Viking, 2001.

Robson, Charles. *Representative Men of the South.* Philadelphia, PA: C. Robson, 1880.

Rosen, Robert N. *The Jewish Confederates.* Columbia: University of South Carolina Press, 2000.

Rowland, Dunbar. *The Official and Statistical Register of the State of Mississippi, 1908.* Nashville, TN: Brandon Print, 1908.

Scharf, J. Thomas. *History of the Confederate States Navy from Its Organization to the Surrender of Its Last Vessel. Its Stupendous Struggle with the Great Navy of the United States; the Engagements Fought in the Rivers and Harbors of the South, and Upon the High Seas; Blockade-Running, First Use of Iron-Clads and Torpedoes, and Privateer History.* New York: Rogers & Sherwood, 1887.

Schell, Sidney H. "Submarine Weapons Tested at Mobile During the Civil War." *Alabama Review* 45 (July 1992), 178–179.

Scott, Florence Dolive. *Daphne: A History of Its People and Their Pursuits, As Some Saw It and Others Remember It.* Mobile, AL: Jordan, 1965.

Scriber, Terry G., and Theresa Arnold-Scriber. *Ship Island, Mississippi.* Jefferson, NC: McFarland, 2008.

Shipler, Michael D. "The Mobile Campaigns March – April 1865." In *Military Order of Stars & Bars.* Mobile, AL: 2006, 45–55, 62–63.

Silverman, Jason H. "Stars, Bars and Foreigners: The Immigrant and the Making of the Confederacy." *Journal of Confederate History* 1, no. 2 (Fall 1988): 269.

Sledge, John S. *The Mobile River.* Columbia: University of South Carolina Press, 2015.

Slocum, Charles Elihu. *A Short History of the Slocums, Slocumbs and Slocombs of America: Genealogical and Biographical: Embracing Eleven Generations of the First-Named Family, from 1637 to 1881: With Their Alliances and the Descendants in the Female Lines As Far As Ascertained.* Syracuse, NY: C. E. Slocum, 1882.

Smithweck, David. *In Search of the CSS Huntsville and CSS Tuscaloosa.* Mobile, AL: David M. Smithweck, 2016.

Still, William N., Jr. *Iron Afloat: The Story of the Confederate Armorclads.* Nashville, TN: Vanderbilt University Press, 1971.

Thomason, Michael, and Henry M. McKiven. "Secession, War, and Reconstruction, 1850–1874." In *Mobile: The New History of Alabama's First City.* Tuscaloosa: University of Alabama Press, 2001, 95–125.

Townsend, Mary Bobbitt. *Yankee Warhorse: A Biography of Major General Peter Osterhaus.* Columbia: University of Missouri Press, 2010.

Tucker, Spencer C. *The Civil War Naval Encyclopedia,* 1st ed. Santa Barbara, CA: ABC-CLIO, 2010.

United States. *The Medal of Honor of the United States Army*. Washington, DC: U. S. G. P. O., 1948.

Van Cleve, H. P. *Annual Report of the Adjutant General of the State of Minnesota for the Year Ending December 1, 1866, and of the Military Forces of the State from 1861 to 1866*. St. Paul, MN: Pioneer Print, 1866.

Walmsley, J. E. "The Last Meeting of the Confederate Cabinet." *The Mississippi Valley Historical Review* 6, no. 3 (1919), 336–349.

Warner, Ezra J. *Generals in Gray: Lives of the Confederate Commanders*. Baton Rouge: Louisiana State University Press, 1959.

Williams, N. A., and J. M. Whayne. *Arkansas Biography: A Collection of Notable Lives*. Fayetteville: University of Arkansas Press, 2000.

Williamson, David. *The 47th Indiana Volunteer Infantry: A Civil War History*. Jefferson, NC: McFarland, 2012.

Wyeth, John A. *Life of General Nathan Bedford Forrest*. Edison, NJ: Blue & Grey Press, 1996.

Newspapers

Anniston (AL) Star. "Alabama Anniversaries." April 13, 1935.

Armstrong, Zella. "Daring Deeds of Barry's Artillery." *The Sunny South* (Atlanta, GA), August 25, 1901.

Army and Navy Journal. January 9, 1897.

Atlanta (GA) Constitution. "Dr. Seymour Bullock Slain." October 19, 1891.

Atlanta (GA) Constitution. "Old Venomous." June 8, 1873.

Barker, Lauren. "Amused at the Many Accounts." *Washington (DC) National Tribune*. August 25, 1910.

Barnard, A. Y. "Says It was the Thirteenth." *Washington (DC) National Tribune*. August 25, 1910.

Belvidere (IL) Republican-Northwestern. "Judge W. W. Wood Passes Away After Long Illness." August 10, 1909.

Bloomington (IL) Pantagraph. "Capture of Spanish Fort." May 3, 1865.

Boston (MA) Liberator. "The Siege of Mobile." April 2, 1865.

Buffalo (NY) Commercial Advertiser. "The Capture of Mobile." April 24, 1865.

Burlington (IA) Weekly Hawk-Eye. "Review of the Mobile Campaign." April 29, 1865.

Canyon City (TX) News. "The Fall of Mobile." February 16, 1906.

Capps, T. G. "Fort Blakely." *Washington (DC) National Tribune*. September 22, 1887.

Chalaron, James A. "Spanish Fort Fight Near Mobile Bay." *New Orleans (LA) Times Picayune*. September 24, 1899.

Charleston (SC) Daily News. "Our South Atlantic Neighbors." March 7, 1873.

Chillicothe (MO) Constitution-Tribune. "Elijah Gates Dies After Prolonged Illness." March 11, 1915.

Cincinnati (OH) Daily Commercial. March 21, 1865.

Cincinnati (OH) Daily Commercial. "Spanish Fort, Alabama." April 9, 1865.

Cincinnati (OH) Enquirer. "The Defenses of Mobile." May 20, 1865.

Cincinnati (OH) Enquirer. "The Fall of Mobile and Defenses." April 21, 1865.

Cincinnati (OH) Enquirer. "Return of Generals Canby and Osterhaus." May 19, 1865.

Clark, Champ. "Champ Clark Stories." *Ogden (UT) Standard*. September 2, 1901.

Cleveland (OH) Daily Leader. "From Mobile." April 3, 1865.

Cleveland (OH) Daily Leader. "From New Orleans." April 24, 1865.

Cleveland (OH) Daily Leader. "A Woman From Mobile." March 21, 1865.

Colby, Carlos W. "An Incident Occurring at Fort Blakeley." *Washington (DC) National Tribune*. November 21, 1901.

Combs, Private Samuel P. "A Sharpshooter's Story." *Washington (DC) National Tribune*. December 15, 1887.

Cox, B. B. "Mobilian Tells of this City in Civil War Days." *Mobile (AL) Press Register.* November 1, 1914.

Craighead, Erwin. "Dropped Stitches from Mobile's Past." *Mobile (AL) Press Register.* May 5, 1929.

Daily Milwaukee (WI) News. "From Mobile." April 22, 1865.

Daily Milwaukee (WI) News. "Miscellaneous News." March 28, 1865.

Detroit (MI) Free Press. "From Mobile." February 14, 1865.

Detroit (MI) Free Press. "From the South." October 17, 1864.

Diplomaticus. "'Old Garden Sass': The Most Modest Man In The Senate." *Chicago (IL) Inter Ocean.* March 27, 1904.

Elgin (IL) Daily Courier. "Gen. Spurling Dies in Chicago." August 27, 1906.

Fry, John W. "Capture of Mobile." *Washington (DC) National Tribune.* October 29, 1865.

Harper's Weekly. "The Capture of Mobile." May 6, 1865.

Harper's Weekly. "Incident On Board the Octorara." February 25, 1865.

Hillsboro (OH) Highland Weekly News. "General Gordon Granger." February 10, 1876.

Ivins, Samuel. "Fort Blakeley." *Washington (DC) National Tribune.* March 14, 1865.

Janesville (WI) Weekly Gazette. March 23, 1865.

Janesville (WI) Weekly Gazette. "Details of the Surrender." May 15, 1865.

Johnson, C. B. "In Camp and Field, A Medical Man's Memory of War-Time." *Arkansas City (KS) Weekly Republican-Traveler.* October 7, 1887.

Johnson, Peggy. "Fall of Mobile Viewed Through Eyes of Youth." *Mobile (AL) Press Register.* November 27, 1960.

Knoxville (TN) News Sentinel. "A Frightful Homicide." November 28, 1871.

Lawrence Daily Kansas Tribune. April 6, 1865.

Los Angeles (CA) Herald. "The Last Shot." August 23, 1897.

Louisville (KY) Courier-Journal. "The Last Fight." March 31, 1892.

McNeil, William S. "Silence of Peace." *Philadelphia (PA) Times*, n.d.

Mobile (AL) Advertiser and Register. April 9, 1865.

Mobile (AL) Advertiser and Register. "Blown Up." April 8, 1865.

Mobile (AL) Advertiser and Register. "To the Men and Boys of Middle and South Alabama." December 12, 1864.

Mobile (AL) Advertiser and Register. "Yankee Accounts from Mobile." April 8, 1865.

Mobile (AL) Daily News. April 17, 1865.

Mobile (AL) Daily News. "Disgraceful." April 13, 1865.

Mobile (AL) Daily News. "General Orders No. 1." April 13, 1865.

Mobile (AL) Daily News. "Official." April 15, 1865.

Mobile (AL) Daily News. "Southern Girl in Mobile Describes 'Yankee' Entrance." May 11, 1865.

Mobile (AL) Daily Register. "The Lady Slocumb." March 15, 1891.

Mobile (AL) Daily Register. "A Shotgun Duel." October 16, 1891.

Mobile (AL) Evening News. "Gen. Jos. E. Johnston." March 4, 1865.

Mobile (AL) Evening Telegraph. "The Defense of Mobile." March 23, 1865.

Mobile (AL) Evening Telegraph. "Depredations of the Enemy at Fish River." March 23, 1865.

Mobile (AL) Evening Telegraph. "From Below." March 23, 1865.

Mobile (AL) Morning News. May 11, 1865.

Mobile (AL) Press Register. "Madame LeVert: Her Ball." October 4, 1964.

Mobile (AL) Press Register. "Toastin' the Town." June 6, 1955.

Mobile (AL) Press Register. "Survivor of Final Civil War Battles Tells of Heroism of Confederate Men." January 27, 1913.

Mobile (AL) Register and Advisor. April 2, 1865.

Mobile (AL) Weekly Advertiser and Register. "First Missouri Brigade." March 4, 1865.

Monmouth (IL) Daily Review. "Obituary." November 12, 1902.

Nashville (TN) Daily Union. "From Mobile." April 14, 1865.

Nashville (TN) Daily Union. "A Week of Victory." April 21, 1865.

Nashville (TN) Tennessean. "At Four Mile Creek." June 11, 1899.

Nashville (TN) Tennessean. "Col. P. B. Spence." February 17, 1915.

Nashville (TN) Tennessean. "Gen. A. J. Smith Dies of Paralysis at St. Louis." January 31, 1897.

New Berne (NC) Times. "From the Mobile News." May 5, 1865.

New Berne (NC) Times. "The Latest News." April 21, 1865.

New Berne (NC) Times. "The Mobile Explosion." June 14, 1865.

New Orleans (LA) Daily Crescent. "Souvenirs of the War." March 19, 1866.

New Orleans (LA) Times-Democrat. "Capture of Mobile." April 14, 1865.

New Orleans (LA) Times-Democrat. "From Mobile." May 7, 1865.

New Orleans (LA) Times-Democrat. "Gen. James T. Holtzclaw, Montgomery." July 19, 1893.

New Orleans (LA) Times-Democrat. "An Iron Clad Fleet." July 23, 1866.

New Orleans (LA) Times-Democrat. "The Mobile Expedition." April 8, 1865.

New Orleans (LA) Times-Democrat. "News From Gen. Canby." May 5, 1865.

New Orleans (LA) Times-Democrat. "The Lady Slocomb." September 20, 1899.

New Orleans (LA) Times-Democrat. "Special to the Times-Democrat." October 16, 1891.

New Orleans (LA) Times- Democrat. "Summary of News." August 14, 1864.

New Orleans (LA) Times-Democrat. "Surrender of Rebel Naval Officers." May 15, 1865.

New Orleans (LA) Times Picayune. "Additional from Mobile." April 21, 1865.

New Orleans (LA) Times Picayune. "Dash Above Mobile." April 18, 1865.

New Orleans (LA) Times Picayune. "The Distinguished Dead." February 10, 1890.

New Orleans (LA) Times Picayune. "The Final Capture of the Last Defenders of Mobile." September 22, 1866.

New Orleans (LA) Times Picayune. "From Mobile Bay." April 9, 1865.

New Orleans (LA) Times Picayune. "Further from Mobile." April 5, 1865.

New Orleans (LA) Times Picayune. "General Forrest to his Soldiers." May 16, 1865.

New Orleans (LA) Times Picayune. "Gleanings of General Interest from the Gulf City." March 2, 1899.

New Orleans (LA) Times Picayune. "Grierson's Great Raid." January 20, 1865.

New Orleans (LA) Times Picayune. "Important From Mobile." May 7, 1865.

New Orleans (LA) Times Picayune. "Important From Mobile Bay." April 11, 1865.

New Orleans (LA) Times Picayune. "In Defense of M'me LeVert." April 22, 1877.

New Orleans (LA) Times Picayune. "Lady Slocomb." September 9, 1899.

New Orleans (LA) Times Picayune. "Lady Slocomb: The Silent Witness." September 20, 1899.

New Orleans (LA) Times Picayune. "Mobile Items." May 13, 1865.

New Orleans (LA) Times Picayune. "Prisoners Captured at Blakeley." April 22, 1865.

New Orleans (LA) Times Picayune. "Social Life in Mobile." May 11, 1865.

New York Herald. April 30, 1865.

New York Times. "Arrival of the Fung Shuey from New-Orleans. The News of Mr. Lincoln's Assassination. PAINFUL EXCITEMENT IN THE CITY. Interesting Items from Mobile. FROM MOBILE. MILITARY MATTERS. ORDER BY GEN. CANBY. THE OCCUPATION OF THE CITY." April 30, 1865.

New York Times. "The Attack of Mobile." April 9, 1865.

New York Times. "Brutal Murder of Gen. Joseph Bailey." April 5, 1867.

New York Times. "The Campaign in Alabama." April 24, 1865.

New York Times. "Colored Troops in the Rebel Army." March 5, 1865.

New York Times. "Death of Gen. A. J. Smith." January 31, 1897.

New York Times. "Department of the Gulf." March 20, 1865.

New York Times. "Department of the Gulf." March 25, 1865.

New York Times. "The Department of the Gulf." April 30, 1865.

New York Times. "The Gulf." March 7, 1865, 4.

New York Times. "Our New Orleans Correspondence." March 20, 1865.

New York Times. "Rejoicing over the Surrender of Mobile and Lee." April 21, 1865.

New York Times. "The Siege of Mobile." April 21, 1865.

Osage City (KS) Free Press. "In Mobile Bay." November 29, 1888.

Perry, Leslie J. "A Gallant Soldier." *New York Sun.* February 21, 1897.

Perrysburg (OH) Journal. "A Tale of Revenge." September 11, 1903.

Philadelphia (PA) Inquirer. "The Battle at Vicksburg." January 16, 1863.

Philadelphia (PA) Inquirer. "Canby." April 3, 1865.

Philadelphia (PA) Inquirer. "Interesting from Mobile." March 31, 1865.

Philadelphia (PA) Inquirer. "Mobile." February 14, 1865.

Phillipsburg (KS) Herald. "After Many Years." September 13, 1900.

Pittsburgh (PA) Daily Commercial. "From Mobile." April 3, 1865.

Pittsburgh (PA) Dispatch. "Deaths Here and Elsewhere." October 23, 1891.

Pittsburgh (PA) Post-Gazette. March 17, 1915.

Raleigh (NC) Daily Conservative. "Affairs from Mobile." January 3, 1865.

Raleigh (NC) Daily Progress. "Yankee Accounts from Mobile." February 22, 1865.

Raleigh (NC) Daily Standard. "Dick Taylor's Order of Surrender – His Praise of Gen. Canby – His Advice to his Men." June 3, 1865.

Raleigh (NC) Daily Standard. "The Latest News." May 17, 1865.

Richmond (VA) Dispatch. "The Fighting at Mobile." August 16, 1864.

Richmond (VA) Dispatch. "Mobile Items: A Letter from Mobile." October 18, 1864.

Richmond (IN) Weekly Paladium. "More Seven Thirties to be Issued." March 16, 1865.

Salem Weekly Oregon Statesman. "Telegraphic Dispatches." March 13, 1865.

San Francisco (CA) Call. "An Historic Cannon." November 26, 1896.

Scrivener, Wayne E. "Alabama Anniversaries." *Anniston (AL) Star.* April 13, 1935.

Six Mile (AL) Bibb Blade. "General Longstreet appointed General Bryan M. Thomas." August 25, 1881.

Spink, R. A. "The Capture of Spanish Fort." *Washington (DC) National Tribune.* October 29, 1908.

St. Paul (MN) Globe. "Killed a Comrade." October 16, 1891.

Sweetman, Michael A. "Capture of Blakeley." *Washington (DC) National Tribune.* May 19, 1892.

Thatcher, Admiral H. R. "Afternoon Dispatches." *Lawrence Daily Kansas Tribune,* April 27, 1865.

Thatcher, H. K. "Fall of Mobile." *New Berne (NC) Times.* April 28, 1865.

Topeka (KS) Daily Capital. "Former Missouri Man, Civil War Veteran, Dies." March 8, 1915.

Truman, Benjamin C. "The War in the Southwest." *New York Times,* February 26, 1865, 1.

——. "The Campaign in Alabama." *New York Times,* April 24, 1865.

——. "The South As It Is." *New York Times,* November 2, 1865.

Washington (DC) Evening Times. September 16, 1896.

Washington (DC) Herald. "Federals Move To Attack Forts Guarding Mobile." March 21, 1915.

Washington (DC) National Tribune. "A. J. Smith's Guerrillas." April 28, 1887.

Washington (DC) National Tribune. "Capture of Fort Blakeley." September 2, 1892.

Washington (DC) National Tribune. "Fighting Them Over." February 25, 1865.

Washington (DC) National Tribune. "Gen. A. J. Smith." September 20, 1906.

Washington (DC) National Tribune. "General Steele Flanking Mobile." April 10, 1865.

Washington (DC) National Tribune. "How Fort Blakely Was Taken." August 25, 1865.

Washington (DC) National Tribune. "In Mobile Bay." October 13, 1887.

Washington (DC) National Tribune. "The Mobile Campaign." July 21, 1887.

Washington (DC) National Tribune. "A Moving Tale." October 21, 1909.

Washington (DC) National Tribune. "Spanish Fort." January 28, 1886.

Washington (DC) National Tribune. "Spanish Fort." November 24, 1892.

Wheeling (WV) Daily Intelligencer. "From Mobile." April 3, 1865.

Winchester (TN) Home Journal. "The War Not Yet Ended" October 6, 1866.

Wood, Wales W. "Capture Forts About Mobile." *Belvidere (IL) Republican-Northwestern.* January 29, 1907.

——. "The Mobile Forts." *Washington (DC) National Tribune,* January 24, 1907.

Woodstock (IL) Sentinel. "From the 95th Illinois." May 10, 1865.

Woodville (MS) Republican. "Wreath for Canby after 58 years." June 2, 1923.

Worthington (MN) Advance. "The Last Surrender." August 29, 1897.

Websites

"Abatis." Definition of Abatis by Merriam-Webster online dictionary. Accessed December 9, 2016. https://www.merriam-webster.com/dictionary/abatis.

"ADAH: Samuel Lockett." Alabama Department of Archives and History. Accessed September 2, 2017. http://www.archives.state.al.us/marschall/S_Lockett.html.

"Adjutant General's Report." *8th Infantry Regiment Three Years' Service. Report of the Adjutant General of the State of Illinois.* Vol. 1, 1900. Revised by Brigadier General J. N. Reese. Accessed December 28, 2014. http://www.civilwarindex.com/armyil/rosters/8th_il_infantry_3years_roster.pdf.

"A. J. Smith." *The Annals of Iowa.* Vol. 3, 1897. Iowa Research Online | University of Iowa Research. Accessed February 14, 2016. http://ir.uiowa.edu/cgi/viewcontent.cgi? article=2219&context=annals-of-iowa.

"Andrews, Julius A." The Handbook of Texas Online. Texas State Historical Association, Accessed January 8, 2018. https://tshaonline.org/handbook/online/articles/fan61.

"Andrew Fuller Sperry (1839–1911)." Find A Grave. Accessed August 1, 2016. http://www.findagrave.com/cgi-bin/fg.cgi? page=gr&GRid=31211891.

"Andrew J. Smith." Civil War Trust: Saving America's Civil War Battlefields. Accessed October 11, 2015. http://www.civilwar.org/education/history/biographies/andrew-j-smith.html.

"The Battle of Palmito Ranch." The Handbook of Texas Online. Accessed May 8, 2016. https://tshaonline.org/handbook/online/articles/qfp01.

"Battle Unit Details – The Civil War." U.S. National Park Service. Accessed March 22, 2016. http://www.nps.gov/civilwar/search-battle-units- detail.htm? battleUnitCode=CAL0001BA.

"Biographies of Butler County Alabama." Genealogy Trails History Group. Accessed September 9, 2017. http://genealogytrails.com/ala/butler/bios_1.html#wattsthomas.

"Cargo of Blockade Runner Denbigh Reveals Much About Civil War-era Mobile." AL.com. Accessed January 29, 2017. http://blog.al.com/entertainment-press-register/2011/11/cargo_of_blockade_runner_denbi.hrml.

"Catron, Thomas Benton Biographical Information." Accessed December 20, 2017. http://bioguide.congress.gov/scripts/biodisplay.pl? index=C000253.

"Chevaux-de-frise Legal Definition of Chevaux-de-frise." TheFreeDictionary.com. Accessed December 9, 2016. http://legal-dictionary.thefreedictionary.com/chevaux-de-frise.

"Civil War Indiana Biographies: James Richard Slack." Civil War Indiana. Accessed February 21, 2016. http://civilwarindiana.com/biographies/slack_james_richard.html.

"Civil War Journal of James B. Lockney WIS. 28th Regiment, Co. G." James R. Shirey. Accessed October 25, 2014. http://jshirey.brinkster.net/CivilWar/.

"Civil War Reference Page." Accessed July 12, 2015. http://www.civilwarreference.com/people/index. php? peopleID=719.

Cleve, H. P. "Annual Report of the Adjutant General of the State of Minnesota." Minnesota Adjutant General's Office. Last modified December 15, 1866. Accessed November 28, 2016. http://www. archive.org/stream/annualreport01minn#page/334/mode/2up.

Cobb, Stephen A. "The Siege of Mobile." Beloit College Archives Web Page. Accessed March 7, 2015. http://www.beloit.edu/archives/documents/archival_collections/civil_war/reminiscence_cobb.

"Colby, Carlos W." Illinois State Archives. Accessed November 28, 2016. http://www.ilsos.gov/ isaveterans/civilMusterSearch.do? key=49031.

"Colonel Philip Brent Spence." RootsWeb.com Home Page. Accessed July 19, 2015. http://www. rootsweb.ancestry.com/~kycampbe/philipspence.htm.

"Confederate States Staff Officers - G Surnames – Access Genealogy." Access Genealogy. Accessed September 10, 2017. https://www.accessgenealogy.com/military/confederate-states-staff-officers-g-surnames.htm.

Cussler, Clive. "Search for the C. S. S. Hunley, the U. S. S. Cumberland and the C. S. S. Florida." Last modified July 1980. www.numa.net/expeditions/hunley-c-s-s.

"Dauphin Island Park and Beach Fort Gaines." Dauphin Island Park and Beach. Accessed October 8, 2016. http://dauphinisland.org/fort-gaines/.

"Ebenezer Farrand." CSN Foundation. Accessed September 21, 2016. https://sites.google.com/ site/290foundation/290-standing-orders/ebenezer-farrand-csn.

"Edward Dorr Tracy (1833–1863) - Find A Grave Memorial." Find A Grave. Accessed February 14, 2016. http://www.findagrave.com/cgi-in/fg.cgi? page=gr&GRid=9093.

"Edward R. S. Canby." National Park Service. Accessed March 10, 2016. http://www.nps.gov/resources/ person.htm? id=57.

"8th Illinois Infantry." Civil War Index – Primary Source Material on the Soldiers and the Battles. Accessed August 12, 2015. http://www.civilwarindex.com/armyil/rosters/8th_il_infantry_3years_roster.pdf.

"Field and Staff Officers, 1st Battalion, Alabama Artillery." Access Genealogy. Accessed March 22, 2016. https://www.accessgenealogy.com/alabama/field-and-staff-officers-1st-battalion-alabama-artillery.htm.

"Flag." American Civil War Museum: Online Collections. Accessed January 9, 2018. http:// moconfederacy.pastperfectonline.com/webobject/8E6CAF5A-67A1-4402-B250-284917542464.

"A Former New Mexico Governor Served As Monrovia's Second Mayor." Monrovia, CA Patch. Accessed February 17, 2016. http://patch.com/california/monrovia/a-former-new-mexico-governor-served-as-monrovias-second-mayor.

"Fort Morgan Alabama Historical Site Information." Fort Morgan Historic Site. Accessed October 8, 2016. http://fort-morgan.org/.

"Fourteenth Texas Cavalry." The Handbook of Texas Online. Texas State Historical Association. Accessed June 9, 2016. https://tshaonline.org/handbook/online/articles/qkf14.

"General Joseph Bailey – Hero of the Red River." Accessed February 14, 2016. http://www. generaljosephbailey.com/josephbailey/.

"George S. Smith Diary, 1862–1866." Civil War Diaries and Letters, 0017. DIYHistory | Transcribe. Accessed July 22, 2016. https://diyhistory.lib.uiowa.edu/transcribe/222/21477.

"The Hampton Roads Peace Conference: A Final Test of Lincoln's Presidential Leadership." MLibrary Digital Collections. Accessed September 20, 2016. http://quod.lib.umich.edu/j/ jala/2629860.0021.104/–hampton-roads-peace-conference-a-final-test-of-lincolns? rgn=main; view=fulltext.

"History of 91st Illinois Infantry History." The Illinois Civil War Project. Accessed November 1, 2014. http://civilwar.illinoisgenweb.org/history/091.html.

"History of Spring Hill College." Spring Hill College. Accessed December 1, 2015. http://www.shc. edu/page/history-spring-hill-college.

"Hubbard, Lucius F. (1836–1913)." Minnesota Encyclopedia | MNopedia. Accessed February 16, 2016. http://www.mnopedia.org/person/hubbard-lucius-f-1836-1913.

"Illinois Civil War Muster and Descriptive Rolls Database." Illinois State Archives. Accessed November 28, 2016. http://www.ilsos.gov/isaveterans/civilMusterSearch.do? key=49031.

"John P. Halligan." Find A Grave. Accessed December 21, 2016. http://findagrave.com/cgi-bin/fg, cgi? page=gr&GRid=26753869.

Jean R. Freedman. "Albert Cashier's Secret." Opinionator. Last modified January 28, 2014. https:// opinionator.blogs.nytimes.com/2014/01/28/albert-cashiers-secret/.

Lacey, John F. "Major-General Frederick Steele." Iowa Research Online | University of Iowa Research. Accessed October 15, 2016. http://ir.uiowa.edu/annals-of-iowa/vol3/iss5/8.

"Legal Definition of Chevaux-de-frise." TheFreeDictionary.com. Accessed December 9, 2016. http:// legal-dictionary.thefreedictionary.com/chevaux-de-frise.

"M214 Chambers (William Pitt) Diary." University of Southern Mississippi Libraries. Accessed August 1, 2016. http://lib.usm.edu/legacy/archives/m214.htm.

"Major Samuel H. Lockett." Official Site: The Battle of Champion Hill (May 16, 1863). Accessed September 2, 2017. http://battleofchampionhill.org/lockett1.htm.

Mattocks, Ebenezer B. "Mobile Campaign." Museum Collections Up Close. Minnesota Historical Society. Accessed February 25, 2015. http://discussions.mnhs.org/collections/? s=mobile+campaign.

"McNulta, John: Biographical Information." Biographical Directory of the United States Congress. Accessed February 21, 2016. http://bioguide.congress.gov/scripts/biodisplay.pl? index=M000587.

"NH 48925 Lieutenant Thomas B. Huger, CSN." Naval History and Heritage Command. Accessed February 14, 2016. http://www.history.navy.mil/our-collections/photography/numerical-list-of-images/nhhc-series/nh-series/NH-48000/NH-48925.html.

"North Carolina History Project: Carolinas Campaign (January 1865–April 1865)." Accessed October 17, 2015. http://www.northcarolinahistory.org/encyclopedia/882/entry.

Wolf, Otto E. "OTTO E. WOLF. CIVIL WAR LETTERS." Fort Pickering, Tennessee - Madison County Historical Society. Accessed March 19, 2018. http://madcohistory.org/wp-content/uploads/2017/11/OW_1865_final.pdf.

"Our Special Account." NYTimes.com. Accessed October 15, 2016. http://www.nytimes.com/1865/04/24/news/our-special-account-preparation-start-investment-spanish-fort-what-flert-did.html? pagewanted=all.

Podoll, Dean. "Charles O. Musser." Omaha.com. Accessed August 1, 2016. http://dataomaha.com/civilwar/171/charles-o-musser.

"Rinaker, John Irving: Biography." Biographical Directory of the United States Congress. Accessed February 17, 2016. http://bioguide.congress.gov/scripts/biodisplay.pl? index=R000261.

"Robert Angelo Spink." Oshkosh Public Museum. Accessed August 1, 2016. http://oshkosh.pastperfect-online.com/20004cgi/mweb.exe? request=field; fldseq=359109.

"Robert E. Lee Surrenders – Apr 09, 1865." History.com. Accessed December 11, 2015. http://www.history.com/this-day-in-history/robert-e-lee-surrenders.

"RootsWeb's WorldConnect Project: Pat Thomas Gedcom." WorldConnect Project – Connecting the World One GEDCOM at a Time. Accessed October 3, 2016. http://wc.rootsweb.ancestry.com/cgi-bin/igm.cgi? op=GET&db=tyrilla&id=I17917.

"The Siege of Mobile." NYTimes.com. Accessed December 2, 2016. http://www.nytimes.com/1865/04/20/news/siege-mobile-detail-operations-preceding-capture-city-siege-spanish-fort.html.

"Sixteenth Confederate Cavalry Aka The Twelfth Mississippi Cavalry." Accessed August 12, 2015. http://www.16thconfederatecavalry.com/index.html.

"State Forests: General Andrews: Minnesota DNR." Minnesota Department of Natural Resources: Minnesota DNR. Accessed October 15, 2016. http://www.dnr.state.mn.us/state_forests/sft00020/index.html.

"Tenth Texas Cavalry." Texas State Historical Association. Accessed December 14, 2014. http://www.tshaonline.org/handbook/online/articles/qkt13.

"Thomas Seay." 18th Century History – The Age of Reason and Change. Accessed October 15, 2016. http://history1700s.com/index.php/articles/14-guest-authors/109-three-governors-from-greensboro-alabama.html? showall=&start=3.

"Towser." Definition of Towser by Merriam-Webster online dictionary. Accessed October 15, 2016. http://www.merriam-webster.com/dictionary/towser.

"Traverse." Definition of Traverse by Merriam-Webster online dictionary. Accessed September 11, 2016. http://www.merriam-webster.com/dictionary/traverse.

"Warfare History Network » General George S. Patton, Sr.: Civil War Veteran." Warfare History Network. Accessed May 16, 2017. http://warfarehistorynetwork.com/daily/civil-war/general-george-s-patton-sr-civil-war-veteran/.

"William Rainey Marshall." National Governors Association. Accessed October 15, 2016. http://www.nga.org/cms/home/governors/past-governors-bios/page_minnesota/col2-content/main-content-list/title_marshall_william.html.

Maps

United States Army. Corps of Engineers. *Map of the defences of the city of Mobile. 1862–64*. Philadelphia, PA: Bowen, lith, 1866. Map. Library of Congress. Accessed March 15, 2016. https://www.loc.gov/item/99447254.

United States Army. Corps of Engineers. *Rebel defences, Mobile, Alabama, occupied by Union forces under Maj. Gen. E. R. S. Canby comdg*. Philadelphia, PA: Bowen, lith, 1866. Map. Library of Congress. Accessed October 10, 2017. https://www.loc.gov/item/99447255/.

United States Army. Corps of Engineers. *Rebel line of Works at Blakely*. Philadelphia, PA: Bowen, lith, 1866. Map. Library of Congress. Accessed September 9, 2017. https://www.loc.gov/item/2008628285/.

Shipler, Michael D. *Siege Operations at Spanish Fort, Mobile Bay*. Bay Minette, AL: 2017.

Stoots, Kevin. *Feint to Fowl River*. Mobile, AL: 2017.

Stoots, Kevin. *Approaches to Confederate Forts in Baldwin County*. Mobile, AL: 2017.

Index